DETAILED 2025 DAILY HOROSCOPES

Your Complete Guide to Astrology for Every Day of the Year

By
ASTROLOOM PUBLISHING

Table of Content

Yearly Trends for 2025   11

Important Astrological Events
in 2025   14

Annual Overview by Zodiac
Sign for 2025   18

Daily Horoscope for 365
Days   23

January 1, 2025   24

January 2, 2025   25

January 3, 2025   26

January 4, 2025   27

January 5, 2025   28

January 6, 2025   29

January 7, 2025   30

January 8, 2025   31

January 9, 2025   32

January 10, 2025   33

January 11, 2025   34

January 12, 2025   35

January 13, 2025   36

January 14, 2025   37

January 15, 2025   38

January 16, 2025   39

January 17, 2025   40

January 18, 2025   41

January 19, 2025   42

January 20, 2025   43

January 21, 2025   44

January 22, 2025   45

January 23, 2025   46

January 24, 2025   47

January 25, 2025   48

January 26, 2025   49

January 27, 2025   50

January 28, 2025   51

January 29, 2025   52

January 30, 2025   53

January 31, 2025   54

February 1, 2025   55

February 2, 2025   56

February 3, 2025   57

February 4, 2025   58

February 5, 2025   59

February 6, 2025   60

February 7, 2025   61

February 8, 2025   62

February 9, 2025   63

February 10, 2025	64	March 8, 2025	90
February 11, 2025	65	March 9, 2025	91
February 12, 2025	66	March 10, 2025	92
February 13, 2025	67	March 11, 2025	93
February 14, 2025	68	March 12, 2025	94
February 15, 2025	69	March 13, 2025	95
February 16, 2025	70	March 14, 2025	96
February 17, 2025	71	March 15, 2025	97
February 18, 2025	72	March 16, 2025	99
February 19, 2025	73	March 17, 2025	100
February 20, 2025	74	March 18, 2025	101
February 21, 2025	75	March 19, 2025	102
February 22, 2025	76	March 20, 2025	103
February 23, 2025	77	March 21, 2025	105
February 24, 2025	78	March 22, 2025	107
February 25, 2025	79	March 23, 2025	108
February 26, 2025	80	March 24, 2025	109
February 27, 2025	81	March 25, 2025	110
February 28, 2025	82	March 26, 2025	111
March 1, 2025	83	March 27, 2025	112
March 2, 2025	84	March 28, 2025	113
March 3, 2025	85	March 29, 2025	114
March 4, 2025	86	March 30, 2025	115
March 5, 2025	87	March 31, 2025	116
March 6, 2025	88	April 1, 2025	117
March 7, 2025	89	April 2, 2025	118

April 3, 2025	119	April 29, 2025	157
April 4, 2025	120	April 30, 2025	158
April 5, 2025	121	May 1, 2025	160
April 6, 2025	122	May 2, 2025	162
April 7, 2025	124	May 3, 2025	163
April 8, 2025	125	May 4, 2025	164
April 9, 2025	126	May 5, 2025	165
April 10, 2025	128	May 6, 2025	166
April 11, 2025	129	May 7, 2025	167
April 12, 2025	130	May 8, 2025	169
April 13, 2025	132	May 9, 2025	170
April 14, 2025	134	May 10, 2025	172
April 15, 2025	135	May 11, 2025	174
April 16, 2025	137	May 12, 2025	176
April 17, 2025	139	May 13, 2025	178
April 18, 2025	141	May 14, 2025	179
April 19, 2025	142	May 15, 2025	181
April 20, 2025	144	May 16, 2025	182
April 21, 2025	146	May 17, 2025	184
April 22, 2025	148	May 18, 2025	185
April 23, 2025	149	May 19, 2025	187
April 24, 2025	150	May 20, 2025	189
April 25, 2025	151	May 21, 2025	191
April 26, 2025	153	May 22, 2025	193
April 27, 2025	155	May 23, 2025	195
April 28, 2025	156	May 24, 2025	196

May 25, 2025	198	June 20, 2025	242
May 26, 2025	200	June 21, 2025	244
May 27, 2025	201	June 22, 2025	245
May 28, 2025	202	June 23, 2025	246
May 29, 2025	203	June 24, 2025	247
May 30, 2025	205	June 25, 2025	249
May 31, 2025	207	June 26, 2025	251
June 1, 2025	209	June 27, 2025	253
June 2, 2025	211	June 28, 2025	255
June 3, 2025	213	June 29, 2025	257
June 4, 2025	215	June 30, 2025	258
June 5, 2025	216	July 1, 2025	260
June 6, 2025	218	July 2, 2025	261
June 7, 2025	220	July 3, 2025	262
June 8, 2025	222	July 4, 2025	264
June 9, 2025	223	July 5, 2025	266
June 10, 2025	225	July 6, 2025	267
June 11, 2025	227	July 7, 2025	269
June 12, 2025	229	July 8, 2025	271
June 13, 2025	230	July 9, 2025	273
June 14, 2025	232	July 10, 2025	274
June 15, 2025	234	July 11, 2025	276
June 16, 2025	236	July 12, 2025	278
June 17, 2025	238	July 13, 2025	280
June 18, 2025	239	July 14, 2025	281
June 19, 2025	240	July 15, 2025	282

July 16, 2025	283	August 11, 2025	322
July 17, 2025	284	August 12, 2025	323
July 18, 2025	286	August 13, 2025	324
July 19, 2025	287	August 14, 2025	325
July 20, 2025	288	August 15, 2025	327
July 21, 2025	289	August 16, 2025	328
July 22, 2025	291	August 17, 2025	329
July 23, 2025	293	August 18, 2025	330
July 24, 2025	295	August 19, 2025	332
July 25, 2025	296	August 20, 2025	334
July 26, 2025	297	August 21, 2025	336
July 27, 2025	299	August 22, 2025	338
July 28, 2025	301	August 23, 2025	339
July 29, 2025	302	August 24, 2025	340
July 30, 2025	304	August 25, 2025	342
July 31, 2025	306	August 26, 2025	344
August 1, 2025	307	August 27, 2025	345
August 2, 2025	309	August 28, 2025	347
August 3, 2025	311	August 29, 2025	349
August 4, 2025	312	August 30, 2025	351
August 5, 2025	314	August 31, 2025	353
August 6, 2025	315	September 1, 2025	354
August 7, 2025	316	September 2, 2025	356
August 8, 2025	318	September 3, 2025	357
August 9, 2025	319	September 4, 2025	358
August 10, 2025	321	September 5, 2025	359

September 6, 2025	360	October 2, 2025	400
September 7, 2025	362	October 3, 2025	402
September 8, 2025	363	October 4, 2025	403
September 9, 2025	364	October 5, 2025	404
September 10, 2025	366	October 6, 2025	406
September 11, 2025	368	October 7, 2025	408
September 12, 2025	370	October 8, 2025	409
September 13, 2025	371	October 9, 2025	410
September 14, 2025	372	October 10, 2025	411
September 15, 2025	374	October 11, 2025	413
September 16, 2025	376	October 12, 2025	415
September 17, 2025	378	October 13, 2025	417
September 18, 2025	380	October 14, 2025	418
September 19, 2025	381	October 15, 2025	419
September 20, 2025	382	October 16, 2025	421
September 21, 2025	384	October 17, 2025	423
September 22, 2025	386	October 18, 2025	424
September 23, 2025	387	October 19, 2025	426
September 24, 2025	389	October 20, 2025	428
September 25, 2025	391	October 21, 2025	430
September 26, 2025	393	October 22, 2025	432
September 27, 2025	395	October 23, 2025	433
September 28, 2025	396	October 24, 2025	434
September 29, 2025	397	October 25, 2025	435
September 30, 2025	398	October 26, 2025	436
October 1, 2025	399	October 27, 2025	437

October 28, 2025	439	November 23, 2025	480
October 29, 2025	440	November 24, 2025	482
October 30, 2025	442	November 25, 2025	483
October 31, 2025	444	November 26, 2025	485
November 1, 2025	446	November 27, 2025	487
November 2, 2025	448	November 28, 2025	488
November 3, 2025	449	November 29, 2025	489
November 4, 2025	450	November 30, 2025	491
November 5, 2025	452	December 1, 2025	493
November 6, 2025	454	December 2, 2025	495
November 7, 2025	456	December 3, 2025	496
November 8, 2025	458	December 4, 2025	498
November 9, 2025	459	December 5, 2025	500
November 10, 2025	461	December 6, 2025	502
November 11, 2025	463	December 7, 2025	504
November 12, 2025	464	December 8, 2025	506
November 13, 2025	466	December 9, 2025	508
November 14, 2025	468	December 10, 2025	510
November 15, 2025	470	December 11, 2025	511
November 16, 2025	472	December 12, 2025	512
November 17, 2025	473	December 13, 2025	513
November 18, 2025	474	December 14, 2025	514
November 19, 2025	475	December 15, 2025	515
November 20, 2025	476	December 16, 2025	517
November 21, 2025	477	December 17, 2025	518
November 22, 2025	479	December 18, 2025	520

December 19, 2025	521	December 26, 2025	534
December 20, 2025	523	December 27, 2025	535
December 21, 2025	525	December 28, 2025	537
December 22, 2025	527	December 29, 2025	539
December 23, 2025	528	December 30, 2025	540
December 24, 2025	530	December 31, 2025	542
December 25, 2025	532	Conclusion	544

Yearly Trends for 2025

As we step into 2025, the celestial landscape offers a year rich with opportunities for growth, transformation, and self-discovery. The energy of the year is dynamic, pushing individuals to break free from old patterns and embrace the changes necessary for personal evolution. This year, the planets align in ways that encourage both collective and personal reflection, offering moments of introspection, as well as outward action.

One of the defining energetic themes of 2025 is **transformation through adaptation**. With several key planetary shifts occurring, it will be important to stay flexible and open to change. Those who embrace fluidity will find themselves better positioned to take advantage of the opportunities presented. Saturn, known for its influence on structure, discipline, and long-term growth, continues its transit through Pisces, encouraging us to dissolve rigid boundaries and think creatively about our personal goals and the world around us. It's a time to let go of what no longer serves us, making space for new possibilities.

Jupiter, the planet of expansion and abundance, spends the majority of the year in Taurus, bringing a grounded yet prosperous energy. Under this influence, we are encouraged to cultivate stability and security, particularly in our financial lives. It's a year where steady progress is rewarded, and patience becomes a valuable asset. Jupiter in Taurus favors practical growth—be it in career, relationships, or personal ambitions. It's a great time for setting solid foundations that can lead to lasting success. However, because Taurus can also represent stubbornness, there will be moments when letting go of old habits becomes necessary in order to grow.

Retrogrades are always significant markers of reflection and review, and in 2025, **Mercury** retrogrades in earth signs will further emphasize the importance of grounding and practicality. These periods may slow down communication or travel, but they offer an opportunity to reassess our goals and ensure we are moving in the right direction. Patience and flexibility during these times will be key.

Venus, the planet of love and relationships, brings a softer touch to the year as it makes its transit through Leo and Virgo. This dynamic invites us to examine our relationships more deeply—are they aligned with our true desires and values? Venus in Leo will add a passionate, creative flair to relationships, making it an excellent time for romance and personal expression. As Venus moves into Virgo later in the year, attention to detail and care in nurturing connections will be rewarded, promoting a more grounded and thoughtful approach to love.

A powerful influence to watch this year is the presence of **Pluto** as it transitions between Capricorn and Aquarius. Pluto, the planet of transformation and rebirth, brings deep shifts in societal structures and personal power dynamics. While in Capricorn, Pluto continues to dismantle outdated systems and power structures, encouraging each of us to reconsider how we approach authority in our lives. As it briefly enters Aquarius, the energy shifts toward innovation and collective reform, offering a glimpse into the future of community and global consciousness.

Eclipses in 2025 will be particularly potent, bringing themes of closure and new beginnings. The **solar and lunar eclipses** will touch the Taurus-Scorpio and Aries-Libra axes, creating powerful moments for releasing what no longer serves us and stepping into new phases of life. Eclipses are always moments of heightened energy, where the cosmos pushes us to make bold changes. Pay attention to these cosmic events, as they may bring clarity, revelation, and a push toward long-overdue transformation.

In summary, 2025 is a year for **embracing change with intention**, laying solid foundations for the future, and aligning ourselves with the natural rhythms of life. While the planetary movements may challenge us to reconsider our approach to stability, love, and personal growth, the rewards will be worth the effort. By staying adaptable and grounded, we can navigate the year's energetic shifts with grace, emerging stronger, wiser, and more in tune with our true selves.

Important Astrological Events in 2025

In 2025, the stars align to bring us a series of powerful astrological events that will shape the year's energetic landscape. These celestial occurrences—retrogrades, eclipses, and conjunctions—serve as cosmic markers, guiding us through moments of reflection, transformation, and forward momentum. Let's explore the most significant astrological events of the year and how they will influence our daily lives.

Mercury Retrogrades

As always, Mercury's retrogrades are highly anticipated astrological events, known for their impact on communication, technology, and travel. In 2025, Mercury retrogrades occur in **earth signs**, emphasizing the importance of grounding, patience, and practicality. During these retrograde periods, we are encouraged to slow down, review our plans, and avoid rushing into decisions. Mercury retrograde can create temporary disruptions, but these are opportunities for reevaluation and growth.

Key Mercury Retrograde Dates:

- **January 1 – January 25** (in Capricorn): The year begins with Mercury retrograde in Capricorn, urging us to reexamine our long-term goals and career plans. This is a time to focus on practical details, clear miscommunications, and make sure we're on a solid path before moving forward.

- **May 18 – June 11** (in Taurus): Mercury retrograde in Taurus calls for financial reassessment. This period highlights the need to reflect on how we manage resources, encouraging us to slow down and prioritize stability over risk-taking.

- **September 18 – October 9** (in Virgo): The final retrograde in Virgo brings attention to health, routines, and organization. It's a good time to review our daily habits, ensuring that they support our well-being and long-term goals.

While Mercury retrograde is often viewed with apprehension, it is important to remember that these periods are opportunities for reflection and improvement. Use them to revisit old projects, repair what's broken, and refine your approach to communication.

Venus Retrograde

In addition to Mercury's retrogrades, **Venus retrograde** will take place from **July 24 to September 6** in **Leo**. Venus retrograde is a time to reassess our relationships, values, and self-worth. In the passionate sign of Leo, this retrograde will encourage us to reflect on how we express love and creativity. It's a period where we may question the authenticity of our relationships and whether they align with our true desires. Romantic relationships could experience challenges during this time, but it's an opportunity to strengthen bonds by addressing underlying issues.

Venus retrograde is also a time to be cautious about financial decisions, especially when it comes to luxury purchases or investments. Reflect on what truly brings you joy and avoid impulsive spending. The energy of Leo, while bold and extravagant, asks us to look inward and ensure that our external pursuits match our inner values.

Eclipses

Eclipses are known for their ability to catalyze change, often marking pivotal moments in our lives. In 2025, we will experience several eclipses that touch on the **Taurus-Scorpio** and **Aries-Libra** axes. These eclipses will bring themes of closure, transformation, and new beginnings, making them powerful moments to release what no longer serves us and to embrace new paths.

Key Eclipse Dates:

- **April 14, 2025**: **Total Solar Eclipse in Aries** – This solar eclipse brings the energy of new beginnings, encouraging bold action and leadership. Aries, a sign of courage and independence, invites us to take decisive steps toward personal growth and to embrace our inner warrior. This is a time to plant seeds for future success and focus on individual empowerment.

- **April 29, 2025**: **Lunar Eclipse in Scorpio** – The Scorpio lunar eclipse brings intense emotional transformation. Scorpio is known for its depth and intensity, and this eclipse will push us to confront our deepest fears and desires. It's a powerful time for emotional healing, releasing toxic patterns, and embracing transformation.

- **October 2, 2025**: **Solar Eclipse in Libra** – The Libra solar eclipse emphasizes balance, harmony, and relationships. It's a time to reset partnerships, seek justice, and restore equilibrium in all areas of life. This eclipse invites us to create harmony between our personal needs and the needs of those around us, fostering cooperation and unity.

- **October 17, 2025**: **Lunar Eclipse in Taurus** – The lunar eclipse in Taurus brings the energy of grounding and stability. Taurus is focused on security, material comfort, and sensuality. This eclipse may bring to light issues related to finances, values, and self-worth, prompting us to reevaluate our relationship with the material world. It's a time to release attachments to what no longer brings value to our lives.

Eclipses often bring sudden changes or revelations, making these dates significant for personal transformation. Pay attention to what arises during these periods, as they are powerful cosmic events that can set you on a new trajectory.

Pluto Transits

One of the most important astrological events of 2025 is **Pluto's transition** between **Capricorn and Aquarius**. Pluto, the planet of transformation, power, and rebirth, will briefly dip into Aquarius, giving us a glimpse of what's to come in the years ahead. Pluto in Capricorn continues its work of dismantling outdated structures, both personally and collectively. As it enters Aquarius, we'll see the beginnings of societal shifts toward innovation, technology, and collective empowerment.

This Pluto transit asks us to think about how we engage with authority and power in our lives, and how we can harness transformative energy for the greater good. Aquarius, as a forward-thinking sign, encourages us to embrace change and think about the future of humanity. It's a powerful time for revolutionizing outdated systems and creating more equitable communities.

In summary, 2025's most important astrological events offer both challenges and opportunities for growth. Mercury and Venus retrogrades will invite us to slow down and reflect, while eclipses will push us toward change and transformation. With Pluto's influence, we are reminded that transformation is inevitable, and embracing it can lead to profound personal and collective evolution. Keep these key dates in mind as you navigate the year ahead, using the wisdom of the stars to guide your journey.

Annual Overview by Zodiac Sign for 2025

Each zodiac sign will experience unique energies in 2025, shaped by planetary movements and cosmic influences. This overview provides a glimpse into what each sign can expect in terms of **health, work, love, and relationships**, along with the most **critical** and **luckiest dates** to watch for. Whether you're looking to navigate challenges or seize opportunities, this guide will help you align with the stars for a fulfilling year ahead.

Aries (March 21 – April 19)

2025 will be a transformative year for Aries, bringing exciting opportunities for growth. **In health**, you'll feel energized, especially during the first half of the year. However, Mars' influence may lead to moments of burnout, so remember to balance work and rest. **At work**, you'll be driven to take on leadership roles, and new career opportunities may present themselves. In **love**, your relationships will deepen, especially during Venus's retrograde in Leo, which will prompt you to reflect on your romantic needs.

- **Luckiest Dates:** April 14 (Solar Eclipse in Aries), June 24, October 3
- **Critical Dates:** May 18 – June 11 (Mercury Retrograde in Taurus), October 2 (Solar Eclipse in Libra)

Taurus (April 20 – May 20)

With Jupiter in your sign for much of 2025, Taurus can expect a year of **abundance and stability**. **Your health** will improve as you focus on grounding practices, such as yoga or nature walks. Financial growth is likely, and **your career** will see steady progress, particularly during the second half of the year. **Relationships** will flourish, especially with Jupiter's influence encouraging long-term commitment and security. However, be cautious during Mercury retrograde in Taurus, which may cause delays or miscommunication.

- **Luckiest Dates:** May 25, July 15, December 1
- **Critical Dates:** April 29 (Lunar Eclipse in Scorpio), September 18 – October 9 (Mercury Retrograde in Virgo)

Gemini (May 21 – June 20)

2025 will be a year of intellectual expansion for Gemini. You'll thrive in **social and work environments,** particularly in projects that allow for communication and creativity. **Health** may require extra attention, especially during Mercury's retrograde phases, when stress and burnout could impact your well-being. **Love and relationships** will bring moments of joy, but also require honest communication to avoid misunderstandings.

- **Luckiest Dates:** June 10, August 3, November 15
- **Critical Dates:** May 18 – June 11 (Mercury Retrograde in Taurus), October 17 (Lunar Eclipse in Taurus)

Cancer (June 21 – July 22)

2025 brings a focus on **emotional growth** and personal transformation for Cancer. **In health**, you'll need to prioritize self-care and emotional balance. Professionally, you'll make steady progress, but the key will be finding a work-life balance. **Relationships** will be deepened, especially during the Moon's transit through water signs, providing you with opportunities to strengthen family and romantic bonds.

- **Luckiest Dates:** July 10, September 7, December 24
- **Critical Dates:** January 1 – January 25 (Mercury Retrograde in Capricorn), October 17 (Lunar Eclipse in Taurus)

Leo (July 23 – August 22)

With **Venus retrograde** in Leo this year, your **love life** will be under the spotlight. You may find yourself reflecting on your relationships and reconsidering what you truly want in both romance and friendships. **In health**, you'll feel strong, but the second half of the year might bring moments of over-exertion, so balance is crucial. **Career** opportunities will abound, especially when you embrace your natural leadership qualities.

- **Luckiest Dates:** July 25, August 10, December 15
- **Critical Dates:** July 24 – September 6 (Venus Retrograde in Leo), October 2 (Solar Eclipse in Libra)

Virgo (August 23 – September 22)

2025 will be a year of **practical progress** for Virgo. **Health** routines will be emphasized, and you'll benefit from reassessing your habits during Mercury retrograde in Virgo. **Work** will bring new opportunities, particularly in projects that require attention to detail and organization. **Love** will require patience, especially during retrogrades, but relationships that are built on trust and stability will thrive.

- **Luckiest Dates:** March 18, August 25, October 30
- **Critical Dates:** September 18 – October 9 (Mercury Retrograde in Virgo), April 14 (Solar Eclipse in Aries)

Libra (September 23 – October 22)

2025 will emphasize **balance** for Libra. **Health** will improve as you focus on harmony in both physical and emotional realms. Professionally, you'll have opportunities to work on creative projects that align with your personal values. In **relationships**, expect growth, but also moments of reflection during the solar eclipse in Libra.

- **Luckiest Dates:** October 2 (Solar Eclipse in Libra), November 11, December 20
- **Critical Dates:** April 29 (Lunar Eclipse in Scorpio), July 24 – September 6 (Venus Retrograde in Leo)

Scorpio (October 23 – November 21)

2025 will be a transformative year for Scorpio, with a strong focus on **emotional and personal growth**. **Health** will be closely tied to your emotional well-being, so practicing mindfulness and self-care will be essential. Professionally, you'll experience powerful changes, particularly during the eclipses in Scorpio. **Love** will deepen, with opportunities for transformative relationships.

- **Luckiest Dates:** April 29 (Lunar Eclipse in Scorpio), September 23, November 8
- **Critical Dates:** October 2 (Solar Eclipse in Libra), January 1 – January 25 (Mercury Retrograde in Capricorn)

Sagittarius (November 22 – December 21)

2025 will be a year of **exploration** for Sagittarius. **In health**, maintaining balance between activity and rest will be crucial. **Career** opportunities will be abundant, especially in areas that allow you to expand your knowledge and skills. **Love** will be adventurous, with opportunities for new experiences in relationships.

- **Luckiest Dates:** May 5, November 22, December 9
- **Critical Dates:** May 18 – June 11 (Mercury Retrograde in Taurus), October 17 (Lunar Eclipse in Taurus)

Capricorn (December 22 – January 19)

Capricorns will find 2025 to be a year of **steady progress** and growth. **Health** will benefit from consistent routines, and **work** will offer new challenges that align with your long-term goals. **Relationships** will require attention, particularly during Mercury retrograde in Capricorn, but clear communication will help you overcome any obstacles.

- **Luckiest Dates:** January 8, July 3, October 19
- **Critical Dates:** January 1 – January 25 (Mercury Retrograde in Capricorn), April 29 (Lunar Eclipse in Scorpio)

Aquarius (January 20 – February 18)

2025 will bring **innovation** and **creativity** to Aquarius. **Health** will benefit from holistic approaches, and **work** will open up exciting opportunities for collaboration and innovation. **Love** will require reflection, especially during Venus retrograde, but strong relationships will deepen.

- **Luckiest Dates:** February 2, June 14, December 23
- **Critical Dates:** July 24 – September 6 (Venus Retrograde in Leo), September 18 – October 9 (Mercury Retrograde in Virgo)

Pisces (February 19 – March 20)

For Pisces, 2025 will be a year of **spiritual growth** and emotional healing. **In health**, focus on mindfulness and emotional well-being. **Work** will bring steady progress, especially in creative fields. **Relationships** will flourish, with opportunities for deep emotional connections, particularly during the Pisces moon phases.

- **Luckiest Dates:** March 20, July 16, November 29
- **Critical Dates:** April 14 (Solar Eclipse in Aries), October 2 (Solar Eclipse in Libra)

Daily Horoscope for 365 Days

January 1, 2025

Daily Insights: On January 1, 2025, the Moon is in Pisces, highlighting emotions, intuition, and introspection. Venus in Capricorn brings a grounded approach to relationships and finances. This is a good day for reflecting on personal goals and emotional well-being.

Aries: You may feel drawn to solitude today, which could help you recharge. Trust your gut instincts when it comes to future plans.

Taurus: It's a good time to focus on your finances. You may receive valuable advice from someone close to you regarding future investments.

Gemini: Social interactions are important today. Conversations with friends may spark new ideas, so be open to different perspectives.

Cancer: You're highly intuitive today, and it's a perfect moment to focus on self-care and family connections. Home feels like a sanctuary.

Leo: Your energy may be centered on your social circle. Planning future gatherings or trips will lift your spirits.

Virgo: Career matters take priority today. Use your logical thinking to plan ahead, but don't neglect emotional needs.

Libra: Harmony in relationships will come easily today. This is a good time to reflect on how you can maintain balance in your connections.

Scorpio: Emotional intensity may surface. It's a good day for self-reflection and discussing any lingering feelings with a trusted friend.

Sagittarius: Relationships with loved ones may require extra attention. Clear communication can help resolve any misunderstandings.

Capricorn: Stability is the theme today. You're feeling confident and ready to set your long-term goals into motion, particularly in work and love.

Aquarius: Inspiration will come from unexpected places today. Embrace your creative side and share your ideas with others.

Pisces: With the Moon in your sign, you'll feel especially intuitive and emotionally connected. It's a great day for relaxation and reflection.

For those born on January 1: People born on this day possess Capricorn's ambition combined with Pisces' emotional depth, making them both determined and empathetic. 2025 will offer opportunities for growth in both personal and professional life, but they must balance their drive for success with the need for emotional fulfillment.

Daily Insights: The Moon remains in Pisces, amplifying intuition and creativity. Today is perfect for finishing up unfinished emotional business or engaging in artistic pursuits. Mars in Sagittarius adds a bit of energy to inspire action.

Aries: Your dreams and subconscious thoughts could hold valuable insights today. Use this to guide your decisions.

Taurus: Trust your instincts when dealing with close friends or family. You may need to offer support, but balance it with your own needs.

Gemini: New ideas flow freely today. Channel them into your projects, and be open to collaborating with others for the best results.

Cancer: It's a day for deep emotional reflection. Nurture yourself and spend time with loved ones who bring you comfort.

Leo: Creative energy is at its peak. Let yourself indulge in artistic projects or hobbies that inspire you and bring joy.

Virgo: Pay attention to any hidden details in conversations or documents today. Your analytical mind will serve you well in identifying important nuances.

Libra: Harmony in relationships continues to be a focus. Seek out beauty and balance in your interactions, especially in romantic settings.

Scorpio: Emotions may run deep today. It's a good time for private reflection, but don't hesitate to confide in someone you trust if needed.

Sagittarius: Your adventurous side is awake today, but remember to balance it with practical responsibilities. Plan something exciting for the near future.

Capricorn: Today, you're focused on practical matters. It's an ideal day to set short-term goals that align with your larger plans.

Aquarius: Innovative ideas may come to you suddenly. Be ready to jot them down and consider how they might fit into your long-term vision.

Pisces: Emotions are heightened today, making it a good time to engage in creative expression or spiritual reflection.

For those born on January 2: Those born today share Capricorn's ambition with an intuitive edge, influenced by the Moon in Pisces. 2025 will be a year for building strong foundations while balancing emotional and spiritual growth. Focus on long-term stability while remaining open to creative insights.

Daily Insights: The Moon moves into Aries today, bringing a burst of energy and motivation. This is a great time to start new projects or take initiative. The influence of Mars in Sagittarius encourages boldness and optimism.

Aries: You're feeling energized and ready to tackle new challenges. Trust your instincts and move forward with confidence.

Taurus: Although the energy around you is fast-paced, stay grounded. Focus on what you can control and don't let others rush you.

Gemini: New ideas come to you easily today. It's a great time to brainstorm or collaborate with like-minded individuals.

Cancer: Emotions may feel more intense than usual. Allow yourself time to process your feelings before making any big decisions.

Leo: Your natural leadership skills are highlighted today. Take charge of situations that require direction, but stay mindful of others' opinions.

Virgo: It's a good day to organize your thoughts and take action on any lingering tasks. Focus on productivity without overanalyzing.

Libra: Social interactions may be fast-paced today. Keep things light and avoid overcommitting to too many plans at once.

Scorpio: You may feel driven to push through emotional barriers. Today is perfect for confronting challenges and emerging stronger.

Sagittarius: Your adventurous spirit is alive and well. Use this energy to explore new opportunities or start something exciting.

Capricorn: It's a day for strategic planning. Focus on long-term goals and don't be afraid to take bold steps toward achieving them.

Aquarius: Creativity is high today. You'll find inspiration in unexpected places, so stay open to new experiences.

Pisces: You may feel more assertive than usual, which can help you stand up for yourself in situations where you've been holding back.

For those born on January 3: People born on this day combine Capricorn's discipline with Aries' pioneering spirit, giving them the drive to achieve great things. In 2025, they'll find success by staying focused on their goals while embracing opportunities for growth. This year is ideal for pushing boundaries and stepping into leadership roles.

Daily Insights: The Moon continues its journey through Aries, fueling a sense of drive and urgency. Mercury aligns with Jupiter, enhancing communication and optimism. It's a good day to express your ideas or take bold steps toward your goals.

Aries: Your confidence is high today. Trust your instincts and don't hesitate to act on your ideas.

Taurus: Stay focused on your long-term goals. Avoid distractions and keep a steady pace toward what you want to achieve.

Gemini: Your communication skills shine today. It's a great time to share your thoughts with others or work on a creative project.

Cancer: You may feel the need to balance personal and professional responsibilities. Prioritize self-care to avoid feeling overwhelmed.

Leo: Leadership opportunities may arise today. Take charge of situations that require guidance, but be mindful of others' input.

Virgo: Organization is key today. Make a plan and stick to it, as this will help you feel more in control of your tasks.

Libra: Social interactions bring positive energy today. You may find yourself networking or reconnecting with friends.

Scorpio: Your determination is strong, making it a good day for tackling complex challenges. Trust in your resilience.

Sagittarius: Adventure is calling! Whether it's exploring new ideas or planning a future trip, today is a great time for expansion.

Capricorn: Practicality meets optimism today. Use this energy to make progress on your goals while staying open to new possibilities.

Aquarius: Inspiration strikes when you least expect it. Be ready to embrace creative solutions and new perspectives.

Pisces: Emotions may run high, but you'll find strength in self-reflection. Take time to center yourself before making important decisions.

For those born on January 4: Individuals born on this day possess Capricorn's ambition coupled with Aries' fiery drive. 2025 will be a year of significant growth for them, especially in their professional life. They'll find success by staying disciplined while embracing bold opportunities. It's a year to step out of their comfort zone and chase big goals.

January 5, 2025

Daily Insights: The Moon remains in Aries for most of the day, keeping energy levels high, but later transitions into Taurus, encouraging a shift toward practicality and comfort. The day is perfect for completing tasks and then relaxing.

Aries: Your energy remains high, but as the day progresses, you'll feel the need to slow down and enjoy some well-deserved rest.

Taurus: You'll feel more grounded as the Moon enters your sign. Focus on practical matters and enjoy the small pleasures in life.

Gemini: Early in the day, you're driven to complete tasks quickly. By evening, you'll crave comfort and relaxation.

Cancer: You'll feel a shift from action to reflection. Use the later part of the day for self-care and emotional balance.

Leo: Keep up the momentum in the morning, but allow yourself to unwind as the day winds down. A quiet evening will recharge you.

Virgo: It's a productive day, especially as the Moon enters Taurus. Tackle practical tasks and make time for relaxation.

Libra: Social interactions may feel fast-paced early in the day. By evening, enjoy a calm night with loved ones.

Scorpio: You're driven to complete challenging tasks early on. As the day progresses, focus on grounding yourself and enjoying life's comforts.

Sagittarius: Adventure and excitement dominate the first part of your day. Later, a quiet and comfortable evening brings balance.

Capricorn: Productivity is key today. You'll find success by focusing on long-term goals while enjoying simple pleasures by day's end.

Aquarius: Creativity and innovation flow easily today. By evening, take a step back and appreciate the progress you've made.

Pisces: You may feel a strong drive to act early in the day. Later, turn inward and focus on creating a peaceful environment for yourself.

For those born on January 5: People born on this day are practical yet driven, with the grounded nature of Taurus complementing Capricorn's ambition. 2025 will be a year of careful planning and steady progress. Their ability to remain patient and focused will help them achieve significant milestones.

Daily Insights: The Moon in Taurus brings stability and a focus on comfort. It's an excellent day for managing practical matters, enjoying life's pleasures, and finding emotional security. Venus in Capricorn also encourages commitment in relationships.

Aries: Slow down and enjoy the day. Focus on tasks that bring you long-term benefits and give yourself time to relax.

Taurus: Today is all about you. You're feeling grounded and ready to handle anything that comes your way with ease.

Gemini: You might feel a little restless today, but grounding activities like organizing or spending time with loved ones will help.

Cancer: Today brings a sense of emotional stability. It's a good day to connect with family and focus on creating a peaceful home environment.

Leo: Practical tasks take priority today. Stay focused on your responsibilities, and treat yourself to something luxurious by the end of the day.

Virgo: Productivity is high today, and you'll feel great satisfaction in completing your tasks. Reward yourself with some relaxation afterward.

Libra: Balance is your theme today. Focus on work in the morning, but make sure to enjoy the beauty and comfort around you later in the day.

Scorpio: You'll find comfort in routine tasks today. It's a great day for planning ahead and making sure everything is in order.

Sagittarius: You may feel the need to slow down and focus on practical matters today. Take time to enjoy the small things in life.

Capricorn: You're feeling more secure and grounded today. Use this energy to solidify your plans and enjoy some downtime.

Aquarius: The day brings a desire for stability and comfort. Take a break from fast-paced activities and appreciate the moment.

Pisces: Today is a great day for emotional grounding. Focus on creating a peaceful environment around you and enjoying simple pleasures.

For those born on January 6: Born under the influence of the Moon in Taurus, these individuals are grounded, practical, and persistent. In 2025, they'll find success by remaining patient and focusing on long-term goals. It's a year for solidifying foundations and making steady progress.

January 7, 2025

Daily Insights: With the Moon still in Taurus, the focus remains on stability, comfort, and practical matters. This is a great day for focusing on personal finances, work projects, or home life. Mars in Sagittarius adds a touch of optimism and adventure to the day.

Aries: Keep a steady pace today. Focus on practical matters and avoid rushing. The rewards will come with patience.

Taurus: You're in your element today. Focus on tasks that bring you a sense of satisfaction and comfort.

Gemini: Practical concerns may slow you down, but try to focus on small, achievable goals for the day.

Cancer: Emotional stability is key today. Focus on nurturing yourself and those around you, creating a sense of peace.

Leo: You may feel the need to handle practical matters first. Once those are out of the way, enjoy a moment of luxury.

Virgo: Today is a perfect day to get organized. Your practical nature will shine as you tackle tasks and make progress.

Libra: Seek balance between work and relaxation today. Practical tasks will give you a sense of accomplishment.

Scorpio: You're driven to handle personal matters today. Focus on grounding yourself and ensuring things are in order.

Sagittarius: The day may feel slower than usual, but it's a good time to focus on practicalities and prepare for future adventures.

Capricorn: You'll feel productive and ready to tackle practical matters. Use this energy to solidify your plans.

Aquarius: Slow down and focus on grounding yourself. Take time for relaxation and simple pleasures.

Pisces: It's a great day for emotional reflection. Focus on creating a peaceful environment and taking care of your needs.

For those born on January 7: With the Moon in Taurus influencing their birth, these individuals are practical and grounded. 2025 will be a year of steady progress, where patience and persistence will pay off. It's a year to focus on building strong foundations for the future.

January 8, 2025

Daily Insights: The Moon moves into Gemini, shifting the energy toward communication, curiosity, and social interactions. This is a great day for connecting with others, learning new things, and sharing ideas.

Aries: You'll feel mentally stimulated today. Engage in conversations that challenge your thinking and broaden your perspective.

Taurus: The energy picks up as the Moon moves into Gemini. Focus on communication and sharing your thoughts with others.

Gemini: With the Moon in your sign, you're feeling energized and ready to explore new ideas. It's a great day for learning and socializing.

Cancer: Emotional balance is key today. Conversations with friends or loved ones can help you feel more centered.

Leo: You're in the mood for socializing. Engage with others, share ideas, and enjoy the intellectual stimulation.

Virgo: Stay open to new information today. Your analytical mind will help you sort through details and find what's most useful.

Libra: Social interactions are lively today. Enjoy engaging with others and sharing your thoughts.

Scorpio: Mental stimulation is key today. Focus on learning new things and expanding your horizons.

Sagittarius: Your adventurous spirit thrives today. It's a great time to explore new topics or engage in exciting conversations.

Capricorn: Use today's energy to brainstorm and share ideas. You may find practical solutions to ongoing challenges.

Aquarius: Your mind is buzzing with ideas. Take time to jot them down and explore new perspectives.

Pisces: Conversations with others can help you find emotional clarity. Stay open to new insights and perspectives.

For those born on January 8: Those born with the Moon in Gemini are naturally curious and communicative. In 2025, they'll find success by embracing new ideas and expanding their knowledge. It's a year for learning, connecting with others, and broadening horizons.

Daily Insights: The Moon continues its transit through Gemini, amplifying curiosity and the desire for mental stimulation. Mercury in Capricorn encourages practical thinking, making it a good day for combining creativity with structure.

Aries: Stay curious and open to new ideas today. Conversations with others can provide valuable insights.

Taurus: Communication is key today. Focus on expressing your thoughts clearly and being open to feedback.

Gemini: Your mental energy is high, and it's a great day for learning, sharing ideas, and connecting with others.

Cancer: Balance emotional and mental energy today. Talking through your thoughts with a trusted friend will bring clarity.

Leo: Your social energy is strong, and you'll enjoy engaging with others. Take time to share ideas and learn from those around you.

Virgo: Stay focused on the details today. Your analytical skills will help you find practical solutions to ongoing tasks.

Libra: Conversations flow easily today. It's a good day to engage in lively discussions and share your perspective.

Scorpio: Curiosity leads the way today. Explore new topics or ideas that pique your interest.

Sagittarius: You're eager to learn and explore. Engage in conversations that expand your horizons and challenge your views.

Capricorn: It's a good day to brainstorm and think practically about how to achieve your goals. Balance creativity with structure.

Aquarius: Mental stimulation is key today. Seek out new ideas and share your thoughts with others.

Pisces: Conversations can bring emotional clarity today. Be open to listening and learning from others' perspectives.

For those born on January 9: Those born on this day are intellectual and curious, influenced by the Moon in Gemini. 2025 will be a year of mental expansion and learning. Success will come through communication, collaboration, and staying open to new ideas.

Daily Insights: The Moon remains in Gemini, fueling curiosity, communication, and mental agility. As Mercury aligns with Uranus, unexpected ideas or revelations may emerge, making today exciting and full of potential.

Aries: New insights may come from unexpected conversations. Stay open to change and embrace spontaneity today.

Taurus: Communication brings clarity to a long-standing issue. Stay flexible and be ready to adapt to new ideas.

Gemini: With the Moon in your sign, your energy and communication skills are at their peak. It's a great day to network and share your ideas.

Cancer: Mental clarity and emotional insight combine today. Don't be afraid to express how you truly feel in a calm, clear manner.

Leo: Today is full of engaging conversations. Be prepared for some unexpected but exciting news or ideas.

Virgo: Your analytical mind will help you navigate today's surprises. Use your logic to approach unexpected challenges.

Libra: Social interactions are stimulating and could lead to exciting new possibilities. Stay open to innovative ideas.

Scorpio: Insights from deep conversations may lead to breakthroughs. Today is great for exploring new perspectives.

Sagittarius: Curiosity drives you today. Seek out new ideas and embrace conversations that challenge your viewpoints.

Capricorn: It's a great day for brainstorming and finding practical solutions. Be open to unconventional ideas.

Aquarius: Innovative thoughts are flowing today. Let your creativity shine and share your unique ideas with the world.

Pisces: Conversations with friends or colleagues may bring emotional clarity. Stay open to their insights and feedback.

For those born on January 10: Those born today are curious and inventive, influenced by the Moon in Gemini. 2025 will be a year of exciting discoveries and mental growth. Success will come through open communication, embracing innovation, and staying adaptable to change.

Daily Insights: The Moon transitions into Cancer, bringing a focus on home, family, and emotional well-being. This is a great day to connect with loved ones, nurture relationships, and focus on self-care.

Aries: You may feel more sensitive today. Focus on nurturing your emotional needs and spend time with loved ones.

Taurus: A good day to retreat and recharge. Focus on creating a peaceful environment at home.

Gemini: You're feeling introspective today. Spend time in quiet reflection or with close family members.

Cancer: The Moon is in your sign, bringing emotional clarity. It's a great day for self-care and tending to your personal needs.

Leo: Family and home life take center stage today. Focus on creating harmony in your surroundings.

Virgo: Practical tasks at home will bring you a sense of comfort and stability. Organize your space to create peace.

Libra: You may feel the need for emotional balance today. Spend time with those who make you feel supported.

Scorpio: Deep emotional conversations can lead to healing today. Open up to someone you trust.

Sagittarius: While you usually seek adventure, today you'll feel more inclined to stay close to home and focus on emotional connections.

Capricorn: It's a good day to focus on family matters. Nurturing relationships will bring you emotional fulfillment.

Aquarius: You may feel more sensitive than usual today. Take time to reflect and recharge emotionally.

Pisces: Your intuition is strong today, making it a great time for emotional reflection and self-care.

For those born on January 11: Born under the influence of the Moon in Cancer, these individuals are deeply emotional and nurturing. 2025 will be a year of personal growth and healing. Focus on emotional well-being, family connections, and creating a harmonious home life.

Daily Insights: The Moon in Cancer continues to emphasize emotions, home, and family. With Venus in Capricorn, there's also a focus on building strong, committed relationships, whether personal or professional.

Aries: Today's energy encourages you to focus on your emotional well-being. Spend time in quiet reflection.

Taurus: Home life takes priority today. Focus on creating a warm and comforting environment for yourself and loved ones.

Gemini: You may feel the need to nurture your close relationships. Spend quality time with those who matter most.

Cancer: The Moon remains in your sign, making this an ideal day for self-care and strengthening family bonds.

Leo: Pay attention to your emotional needs today. Take a break from the spotlight and focus on personal fulfillment.

Virgo: Organize your home and surroundings to bring emotional balance. Practical tasks can have a calming effect.

Libra: Focus on nurturing your relationships today. Emotional connections bring comfort and stability.

Scorpio: It's a good day to open up emotionally. Sharing your feelings with a trusted person will bring relief.

Sagittarius: Today is perfect for emotional grounding. Focus on personal connections and nurturing your inner world.

Capricorn: Commitment and stability are the themes of the day. Strengthen your bonds with loved ones through honest communication.

Aquarius: Emotional balance is key today. Take a break from your usual routine to focus on self-care.

Pisces: Your intuition is heightened. Use this to guide your emotional decisions and connect with your inner self.

For those born on January 12: Those born on this day are deeply connected to family and home, influenced by the nurturing energy of Cancer. In 2025, they'll find fulfillment through strengthening personal relationships and creating a solid foundation in their emotional life.

Daily Insights: The Moon remains in Cancer, urging you to focus on emotional connections and home matters. Mars in Sagittarius continues to bring optimism and action, making it a day of balancing emotional needs with productive energy.

Aries: Embrace your emotions today but also channel your energy into productive tasks that bring you peace of mind.

Taurus: You'll feel the urge to retreat into your comfort zone. Nurture yourself and focus on personal well-being.

Gemini: Emotional conversations with family or friends will bring clarity. Be open and honest about your feelings.

Cancer: The Moon in your sign keeps emotions high. Focus on what brings you comfort and security.

Leo: Balance your emotional needs with practical tasks today. Focus on what makes you feel grounded.

Virgo: Emotional clarity will help you tackle tasks at home. Stay organized and centered.

Libra: Family matters take precedence. Focus on nurturing relationships and finding emotional balance.

Scorpio: Today is a great day for deep reflection. Emotional insights will help guide your decisions moving forward.

Sagittarius: Balance your adventurous spirit with emotional grounding today. Focus on personal connections.

Capricorn: Stability is important to you today. Strengthen your emotional bonds with loved ones and find comfort in routine.

Aquarius: You may feel more introspective than usual. Take time to reflect on your emotional needs.

Pisces: Emotional sensitivity is heightened, making it a good day for self-care and introspection.

For those born on January 13: Those born on this day are sensitive, intuitive, and deeply connected to their emotions, thanks to the influence of Cancer. In 2025, they'll find emotional growth by focusing on their inner world and nurturing close relationships.

Daily Insights: The Moon transitions into Leo, bringing a shift from introspection to self-expression and creativity. This is a great day for taking the spotlight, sharing your talents, and focusing on your passions.

Aries: The energy shifts in your favor today. You're feeling confident and ready to take charge of a situation.

Taurus: Creativity flows today, but don't forget to balance it with your practical responsibilities.

Gemini: It's a great day for socializing and sharing your ideas. You'll feel energized by positive interactions.

Cancer: Embrace the shift in energy and allow yourself to shine. Focus on what makes you feel confident.

Leo: The Moon in your sign amplifies your natural leadership and creativity. Take charge and express yourself boldly.

Virgo: Your attention to detail will help you stand out today. Focus on using your practical skills creatively.

Libra: It's a good day to focus on your personal relationships and find joy in connecting with others.

Scorpio: The shift in energy encourages you to express your inner passions. Don't be afraid to let your creative side shine.

Sagittarius: Adventure and creativity combine today. Use this energy to explore new ways of expressing yourself.

Capricorn: It's a great day for creative problem-solving. Use your disciplined approach to achieve something unique.

Aquarius: Your innovative ideas will shine today. Share them with others and take the spotlight.

Pisces: Creativity and self-expression come naturally today. Focus on artistic projects or anything that allows you to express yourself.

For those born on January 14: Born under the influence of the Moon in Leo, these individuals are confident, creative, and charismatic. In 2025, they'll find success by embracing their leadership qualities and expressing their unique talents.

January 15, 2025

Daily Insights: The Moon continues its transit through Leo, boosting self-confidence and creativity. This is a day for self-expression, leadership, and pursuing passions. Use this fiery energy to make progress on personal projects.

Aries: Your leadership skills are in the spotlight today. Don't hesitate to take charge and inspire others.

Taurus: You're feeling more outgoing and creative than usual. Use this energy to focus on a passion project.

Gemini: Social interactions are lively today. Engage in conversations that allow you to share your ideas and creativity.

Cancer: Step outside your comfort zone and let yourself shine today. You may surprise yourself with what you can achieve.

Leo: With the Moon in your sign, confidence is at an all-time high. Use this energy to take bold steps toward your goals.

Virgo: Tap into your creativity today. Focus on tasks that allow you to use your practical skills in a new way.

Libra: Relationships take center stage today. Spend time connecting with loved ones and expressing your appreciation.

Scorpio: You're feeling passionate and motivated. Use this energy to push forward with personal projects or goals.

Sagittarius: Adventure and excitement are calling. Embrace new opportunities to express yourself and have fun.

Capricorn: Your focus shifts to creative problem-solving today. Use this energy to find new approaches to ongoing challenges.

Aquarius: Innovation comes naturally today. Share your ideas and step into the spotlight with confidence.

Pisces: Creativity flows easily today. Channel your energy into artistic or imaginative projects that bring you joy.

For those born on January 15: Individuals born on this day are naturally confident and creative, with the Moon in Leo boosting their leadership abilities. In 2025, they'll thrive by expressing their unique talents and embracing opportunities to take the lead in personal and professional pursuits.

Daily Insights: The Moon in Leo continues to encourage creativity and self-expression, but by evening, it transitions into Virgo, shifting the focus toward practicality, organization, and attention to detail. It's a good day to balance passion with structure.

Aries: Lead with confidence in the morning, but shift your focus to practical matters as the day progresses.

Taurus: Use the creative energy early in the day to focus on personal projects, then switch to practical tasks in the evening.

Gemini: Engage in lively conversations and express yourself in the morning. Later, focus on getting organized and planning ahead.

Cancer: Balance creativity and productivity today. Embrace the energy of self-expression early on, then shift to self-care and order.

Leo: The Moon in your sign still fuels your confidence. By evening, focus on organizing your thoughts and planning your next steps.

Virgo: As the Moon enters your sign, you'll feel a surge of motivation to organize and tackle tasks with precision.

Libra: Early in the day, express yourself freely. In the evening, shift to tasks that require attention to detail and structure.

Scorpio: Passion and motivation are strong in the morning, but as the day progresses, focus on bringing order to your plans.

Sagittarius: Enjoy the excitement of the day, but later, focus on practicalities and preparing for what's ahead.

Capricorn: Creativity leads the way in the morning, but by evening, switch gears and concentrate on productivity.

Aquarius: Take advantage of the creative energy early in the day. Later, focus on refining your plans and organizing your thoughts.

Pisces: You'll feel more creative and expressive in the morning. As the day progresses, focus on practical steps toward your goals.

For those born on January 16: These individuals have a unique blend of creativity and practicality, influenced by the transition from Leo to Virgo. In 2025, they'll excel by balancing their artistic talents with a structured approach to achieving their goals.

Daily Insights: The Moon in Virgo brings a focus on organization, productivity, and attention to detail. It's an ideal day for tackling tasks, improving routines, and focusing on health and well-being.

Aries: Today's energy is perfect for getting organized. Focus on creating order in your environment and routines.

Taurus: You'll feel grounded and productive today. Tackle practical tasks that require attention to detail.

Gemini: It's a great day for planning and organizing. Use your mental energy to sort through ideas and prioritize tasks.

Cancer: Focus on health and wellness today. Organizing your space and daily routine will bring you a sense of calm.

Leo: While the creative energy of the past days has been fun, today calls for a more practical approach. Focus on what needs to get done.

Virgo: The Moon in your sign enhances your natural organizational skills. Tackle any lingering tasks and enjoy the satisfaction of being productive.

Libra: You'll feel the need for balance today. Focus on organizing your thoughts and finding harmony in your environment.

Scorpio: Today is perfect for focusing on self-improvement. Use the practical energy to refine your plans and habits.

Sagittarius: You may feel the urge to organize and declutter today. Focus on practical matters and fine-tune your daily routine.

Capricorn: Productivity is key today. Take advantage of the Virgo Moon's energy to focus on details and finish important tasks.

Aquarius: It's a good day for refining ideas and organizing your thoughts. Focus on practical steps that will lead to future success.

Pisces: You'll feel more focused and grounded today. Tackle tasks that require precision and attention to detail.

For those born on January 17: These individuals are practical and detail-oriented, with a strong desire for order and organization. In 2025, they'll find success by focusing on refining their routines, improving efficiency, and paying attention to the details that matter.

Daily Insights: The Moon remains in Virgo, continuing to enhance productivity and focus on details. With Mercury in Capricorn, today is perfect for logical thinking, problem-solving, and making steady progress toward your goals.

Aries: Focus on practical tasks that require your attention. Today's energy supports productivity and precision.

Taurus: You're feeling grounded and motivated. Tackle tasks that require patience and attention to detail.

Gemini: It's a great day for organizing your thoughts and planning ahead. Use your mental energy to focus on practical solutions.

Cancer: Your focus is on improving your daily routine and organizing your environment. Small changes can make a big difference.

Leo: Stay grounded and focused on practical matters today. It's a good time to finish any tasks you've been putting off.

Virgo: The Moon continues to highlight your strengths in organization and productivity. Use this energy to make progress on your goals.

Libra: You'll feel the need for balance today. Focus on organizing both your physical space and your emotional well-being.

Scorpio: Practical tasks take priority today. Focus on completing what needs to be done before moving on to new projects.

Sagittarius: You may feel more detail-oriented than usual. Use this energy to refine your plans and improve your routines.

Capricorn: Your logical thinking is sharp today. Focus on problem-solving and making steady progress toward your goals.

Aquarius: Organizing your thoughts and ideas will bring clarity today. It's a great time to refine your plans and set clear intentions.

Pisces: You'll feel more grounded and focused today. Use this energy to tackle tasks that require attention to detail.

For those born on January 18: Those born on this day are detail-oriented and logical, with the influence of the Moon in Virgo sharpening their focus on productivity. In 2025, they'll find success by refining their goals, improving their routines, and staying dedicated to their tasks.

Daily Insights: The Moon enters Libra, bringing a focus on balance, relationships, and harmony. It's a day to connect with others, seek peace in your surroundings, and focus on creating equilibrium in all areas of life.

Aries: Focus on finding balance in your relationships today. Open communication will help you achieve harmony.

Taurus: Today is about seeking peace and stability. Focus on creating harmony in your environment and relationships.

Gemini: Social interactions are key today. Engage with others and work toward creating balanced, harmonious connections.

Cancer: Balance is the theme of the day. Focus on finding harmony between your personal and professional life.

Leo: Relationships take center stage today. Focus on creating balance and peace in your interactions with others.

Virgo: It's a good day to seek balance in your routine. Focus on harmonizing your personal and work life.

Libra: With the Moon in your sign, you'll feel a strong desire for harmony and balance. Focus on your relationships and personal well-being.

Scorpio: Today is about finding emotional balance. Reflect on your feelings and seek peace in your relationships.

Sagittarius: Socializing is favored today. Focus on creating harmonious connections with others and enjoying the company of loved ones.

Capricorn: Balance is key today. Focus on creating equilibrium between your responsibilities and personal desires.

Aquarius: Harmony in your social circles is important today. Engage in conversations that promote peace and understanding.

Pisces: Focus on finding emotional balance today. Seek harmony in your personal relationships and daily routine.

For those born on January 19: These individuals are naturally focused on balance and harmony, with the influence of the Moon in Libra enhancing their desire for peace. In 2025, they'll find fulfillment by focusing on creating equilibrium in their relationships and personal life.

Daily Insights: The Moon continues its journey through Libra, emphasizing harmony, relationships, and balance. With Mars in Sagittarius, there's also a drive for adventure and excitement, making it a great day for balancing action with peace.

Aries: Seek balance between your drive for action and the need for harmony in your relationships.

Taurus: Focus on balancing your responsibilities with personal desires. Find peace in routine tasks today.

Gemini: It's a great day for socializing and engaging in balanced, harmonious conversations with others.

Cancer: Balance your emotional needs with your professional responsibilities. Seek harmony in both areas.

Leo: Relationships are the focus today. Work toward creating balance and peace in your interactions with loved ones.

Virgo: Find equilibrium in your daily routine. Focus on harmonizing work and relaxation for a productive yet peaceful day.

Libra: The Moon in your sign enhances your desire for harmony. Focus on personal relationships and creating balance in your life.

Scorpio: Seek emotional balance today. Reflect on your feelings and work toward creating inner peace.

Sagittarius: It's a good day to balance adventure with stability. Seek out new experiences while maintaining harmony in your relationships.

Capricorn: Balance is key today. Focus on harmonizing your personal desires with your professional responsibilities.

Aquarius: Relationships are highlighted today. Work toward creating peace and balance in your social circles.

Pisces: Focus on emotional balance today. Reflect on your inner world and seek harmony in your surroundings.

For those born on January 20: Those born on this day have a natural desire for balance and harmony, with the Moon in Libra emphasizing their need for peace in all areas of life. In 2025, they'll find success by focusing on creating equilibrium in their personal and professional pursuits.

January 21, 2025

Daily Insights: The Moon moves into Scorpio, bringing depth, intensity, and a focus on transformation. This is a day for deep reflection, emotional insight, and seeking truth in all matters. Use this energy to confront hidden issues and embrace change.

Aries: It's a day for deep reflection. Focus on emotional growth and confronting any lingering issues.

Taurus: The energy shifts toward intensity today. Focus on personal transformation and addressing emotional matters.

Gemini: Dive deep into your thoughts and emotions. It's a good day for introspection and personal insight.

Cancer: You'll feel emotionally intense today. Use this energy to work through any unresolved feelings or issues.

Leo: Today calls for emotional depth. Focus on personal transformation and embracing change.

Virgo: Introspection is key today. Reflect on your feelings and work toward emotional healing and growth.

Libra: It's a day for deep emotional work. Focus on transforming any lingering issues in your relationships.

Scorpio: With the Moon in your sign, you'll feel emotionally powerful. Use this energy to focus on personal growth and transformation.

Sagittarius: Embrace the intensity of the day and focus on personal transformation. It's a great time for self-reflection.

Capricorn: Emotional growth is important today. Take time to confront any unresolved issues and focus on healing.

Aquarius: The energy of the day encourages deep reflection. Use this time for personal insight and emotional transformation.

Pisces: Emotional intensity is high today. Focus on personal growth and transformation by addressing hidden feelings.

For those born on January 21: Those born on this day are deeply emotional and intuitive, influenced by the transformative energy of Scorpio. In 2025, they'll experience personal growth through emotional introspection and embracing change. It's a year for transformation and deep insight.

Daily Insights: The Moon continues its transit through Scorpio, encouraging deep emotional reflection and transformation. This is a powerful day for facing hidden truths, embracing change, and focusing on personal growth. Use this intense energy wisely.

Aries: Embrace the transformative energy of today. Focus on letting go of old habits that no longer serve you.

Taurus: Emotional intensity is high today. Take time to reflect on personal growth and address any hidden feelings.

Gemini: Dive into your emotions and explore the depths of your inner self. Today is a great day for personal insight and transformation.

Cancer: Use the deep emotional energy to nurture yourself and reflect on your past experiences. Emotional healing is key today.

Leo: Transformation is on the horizon. Embrace the changes and focus on personal growth, even if it feels uncomfortable at first.

Virgo: Introspection will help you resolve lingering emotional issues. Take time to reflect and allow yourself to grow.

Libra: It's a powerful day for emotional growth. Focus on finding balance in your relationships and addressing unresolved feelings.

Scorpio: With the Moon in your sign, today brings an opportunity for deep personal transformation. Embrace this energy and focus on emotional growth.

Sagittarius: Reflect on your emotional journey and embrace changes that will lead to personal development. Transformation is on the way.

Capricorn: Today calls for emotional introspection. Address unresolved feelings and focus on healing and moving forward.

Aquarius: The emotional intensity of the day will help you see things clearly. Use this insight to transform your approach to relationships and personal growth.

Pisces: Your intuition is strong today. Use this to guide you through emotional transformation and personal reflection.

For those born on January 22: People born on this day are deeply emotional and transformative, influenced by the intense energy of Scorpio. In 2025, they'll experience significant personal growth through deep emotional reflection and embracing change. This is a year of transformation and emotional empowerment.

Daily Insights: The Moon transitions into Sagittarius, shifting the energy toward optimism, adventure, and exploration. It's a great day for pursuing new ideas, expanding your horizons, and seeking out new experiences. Embrace a sense of freedom and adventure.

Aries: Adventure calls today! Take a break from routine and explore something new, whether it's a place, idea, or activity.

Taurus: You may feel a bit restless today. Seek out new experiences or ideas that challenge your usual routine.

Gemini: Your curiosity is piqued today. It's a great day for learning, exploring new topics, or connecting with interesting people.

Cancer: Step outside your comfort zone today. Embrace the adventurous energy and try something new.

Leo: You're feeling bold and ready for adventure. Take a leap of faith and explore opportunities for personal growth.

Virgo: It's a day for broadening your horizons. Focus on learning something new or exploring fresh perspectives.

Libra: The adventurous energy encourages you to seek balance between work and play. Don't be afraid to embrace spontaneity.

Scorpio: After days of emotional intensity, today brings a lighter, more adventurous energy. Explore new ideas and have fun.

Sagittarius: The Moon in your sign boosts your adventurous spirit. Embrace new experiences and expand your horizons.

Capricorn: Today's energy encourages you to break free from routine. Try something new, whether it's a hobby or a fresh perspective on work.

Aquarius: You're feeling curious and eager to explore new possibilities. Use this energy to connect with others and share innovative ideas.

Pisces: Your sense of adventure is heightened today. Embrace new experiences that allow you to express your creativity.

For those born on January 23: Born under the adventurous energy of Sagittarius, these individuals are optimistic, curious, and open to new experiences. In 2025, they'll find success by embracing opportunities for growth and adventure. It's a year for expanding horizons and seeking out fresh perspectives.

Daily Insights: The Moon remains in Sagittarius, fueling a desire for freedom, exploration, and learning. With Jupiter's influence, today is a great day to think big, set ambitious goals, and take bold steps toward your dreams.

Aries: You're feeling adventurous and ready for new experiences. Take bold steps toward achieving your goals today.

Taurus: Use today's expansive energy to think big and plan for the future. Don't be afraid to aim higher than usual.

Gemini: Your curiosity is heightened. It's a great day for exploring new ideas or starting a learning project that excites you.

Cancer: Step outside your comfort zone today and embrace the possibilities of something new. Personal growth comes from pushing boundaries.

Leo: Adventure and excitement fill your day. Use this energy to explore new opportunities, whether in your personal or professional life.

Virgo: The expansive energy encourages you to explore new ways of thinking. Be open to changing your perspective on an issue.

Libra: Balance your adventurous spirit with practicality today. It's a great time to set new goals and work toward them with optimism.

Scorpio: Today brings an opportunity for exploration. Whether it's traveling, learning something new, or trying a fresh approach, embrace the adventure.

Sagittarius: With the Moon still in your sign, your energy is high. Take bold steps toward your dreams and enjoy the journey along the way.

Capricorn: Use today's optimistic energy to set ambitious goals. It's a great day for planning and taking action toward your long-term vision.

Aquarius: You're feeling inspired and ready to explore new possibilities. Use this energy to connect with others and share innovative ideas.

Pisces: Adventure is calling today. Whether it's through travel, learning, or creative expression, embrace the new opportunities coming your way.

For those born on January 24: These individuals are adventurous, optimistic, and visionary, influenced by the Moon in Sagittarius. In 2025, they'll thrive by embracing opportunities for exploration and setting ambitious goals. It's a year for thinking big and taking bold steps toward their dreams.

Daily Insights: The Moon in Sagittarius brings an optimistic and adventurous energy. It's a great day to focus on expanding your horizons, whether through travel, learning, or new experiences. The Sun's alignment with Jupiter encourages positivity and growth.

Aries: You'll feel inspired to take on new challenges. Embrace adventure and stay open to learning something new.

Taurus: Today encourages you to step out of your comfort zone. Exploring new opportunities will bring growth.

Gemini: You're craving excitement and new experiences. Engage in something that broadens your perspective.

Cancer: Adventure awaits, but balance your need for excitement with personal responsibilities. Focus on what inspires you.

Leo: It's a day for exploration and creativity. Share your ideas with others and embrace new experiences.

Virgo: Use today's energy to expand your knowledge. Learning something new will bring satisfaction and growth.

Libra: Social interactions are lively today. Engage in conversations that challenge your views and offer fresh perspectives.

Scorpio: Emotional growth is highlighted today. Focus on expanding your understanding of yourself and others.

Sagittarius: The Moon in your sign amplifies your adventurous spirit. It's a great day to pursue new opportunities.

Capricorn: Focus on expanding your career goals. Take advantage of today's optimistic energy to plan for future success.

Aquarius: You're feeling inspired to explore new ideas. Embrace innovation and stay open to creative solutions.

Pisces: It's a day for emotional expansion. Engage in activities that bring you emotional fulfillment and growth.

For those born on January 25: People born on this day are naturally adventurous and optimistic, with a desire to explore new horizons. In 2025, they'll find success by embracing opportunities for growth, both personally and professionally.

Daily Insights: The Moon remains in Sagittarius, continuing the focus on optimism, adventure, and learning. It's a good day to pursue new experiences and think big. With Mars in Capricorn, there's also a push for discipline and focus on long-term goals.

Aries: Your adventurous spirit is high, but remember to stay disciplined. Focus on balancing exploration with responsibility.

Taurus: It's a good day for learning something new. Stay open to expanding your knowledge, but remain focused on practical matters.

Gemini: You're in the mood for excitement. Pursue new experiences, but keep an eye on long-term plans.

Cancer: Emotional expansion continues to be a theme. Focus on growth and healing while maintaining stability at home.

Leo: Today is perfect for pursuing creative projects. Let your imagination soar, but stay grounded in your responsibilities.

Virgo: Balance your desire for adventure with your need for structure. Focus on practical goals while exploring new ideas.

Libra: Social interactions are stimulating today. Engage with others in ways that promote growth and learning.

Scorpio: You're feeling adventurous, but remember to stay grounded. Use this energy to explore your inner world and emotional needs.

Sagittarius: The Moon in your sign keeps the energy high. Take advantage of today's optimism to pursue new opportunities.

Capricorn: Discipline and adventure go hand in hand today. Focus on expanding your horizons while staying committed to your goals.

Aquarius: Your innovative ideas are flowing. Stay open to new ways of thinking while maintaining focus on the bigger picture.

Pisces: Emotional growth is key today. Engage in activities that promote healing and emotional expansion.

For those born on January 26: Born with the Moon in Sagittarius, these individuals are naturally curious and adventurous. In 2025, they'll find fulfillment by embracing opportunities for growth and staying disciplined in their pursuit of success.

Daily Insights: The Moon transitions into Capricorn, bringing a shift from adventure to discipline and focus. It's a day for setting goals, making plans, and working toward long-term success. With Venus in Capricorn, relationships may also take on a more serious and committed tone.

Aries: It's a good day for focusing on your long-term goals. Discipline and hard work will bring you closer to success.

Taurus: Practical matters take priority today. Focus on your responsibilities and make steady progress toward your goals.

Gemini: After a period of excitement, it's time to focus on structure and discipline. Set clear goals and work toward them.

Cancer: Family and home life take precedence today. Focus on creating stability and long-term security for your loved ones.

Leo: Today is perfect for setting career goals. Focus on your long-term ambitions and take practical steps toward achieving them.

Virgo: Organization is key today. Focus on creating structure in your daily routine and making progress on important tasks.

Libra: Relationships take on a more serious tone today. Focus on building long-term stability and commitment in your connections.

Scorpio: It's a day for focusing on your career and long-term goals. Stay disciplined and make steady progress.

Sagittarius: After a period of excitement, today calls for practicality. Focus on organizing your thoughts and setting realistic goals.

Capricorn: The Moon in your sign amplifies your focus on discipline and long-term success. It's a great day to make progress on your goals.

Aquarius: Practicality takes precedence today. Focus on organizing your thoughts and setting realistic expectations for the future.

Pisces: Emotional discipline is important today. Focus on creating stability in your emotional life and setting healthy boundaries.

For those born on January 27: Born under the influence of the Moon in Capricorn, these individuals are disciplined, focused, and committed to long-term success. In 2025, they'll find success by staying organized, setting clear goals, and working diligently toward achieving them.

Daily Insights: The Moon continues its journey through Capricorn, emphasizing discipline, responsibility, and long-term planning. It's a good day for focusing on practical matters, making progress toward your goals, and building a strong foundation for the future.

Aries: Focus on your long-term goals today. Discipline and hard work will help you make significant progress.

Taurus: Practical matters take center stage. Focus on your responsibilities and take steady steps toward success.

Gemini: It's a day for focusing on structure and discipline. Set clear goals and work toward them with determination.

Cancer: Stability in your home life is important today. Focus on creating a secure and supportive environment for your loved ones.

Leo: Career goals take priority today. Stay focused on your long-term ambitions and make practical progress.

Virgo: Organization is key. Use today's energy to organize your space and your thoughts, setting the stage for future success.

Libra: Relationships may take on a more serious tone. Focus on building stability and commitment in your connections.

Scorpio: It's a great day for focusing on your career and long-term goals. Discipline and hard work will bring rewards.

Sagittarius: Practicality is important today. Focus on organizing your thoughts and setting realistic expectations for the future.

Capricorn: The Moon in your sign encourages you to stay disciplined and focused on your long-term goals. Make steady progress today.

Aquarius: Practicality takes precedence. Focus on organizing your thoughts and setting realistic expectations for the future.

Pisces: Emotional discipline is key today. Focus on creating stability in your emotional life and setting healthy boundaries.

For those born on January 28: Those born under the Moon in Capricorn are disciplined, practical, and focused on long-term success. In 2025, they'll thrive by staying organized and committed to their goals, building a strong foundation for the future.

Daily Insights: The Moon remains in Capricorn, continuing to emphasize discipline, structure, and practicality. However, as the day progresses, the Moon transitions into Aquarius, bringing a shift toward innovation, creativity, and social connections.

Aries: Focus on your long-term goals in the morning. As the day progresses, embrace new ideas and creative solutions.

Taurus: Practical matters take priority early in the day. Later, focus on expanding your social connections and exploring new ideas.

Gemini: The morning is great for discipline and structure. By evening, you'll feel more inclined to engage with others and explore innovative ideas.

Cancer: Focus on creating stability in your personal life. As the day progresses, embrace the energy of new ideas and social connections.

Leo: The day starts with a focus on your career. Later, shift your attention to creative pursuits and social interactions.

Virgo: Organization and discipline dominate the morning. By evening, allow yourself to explore new ways of thinking and engage with others.

Libra: Relationships take on a more serious tone early in the day. As the day progresses, embrace the energy of creativity and social connections.

Scorpio: It's a day for focusing on long-term goals in the morning. Later, allow yourself to explore new ideas and social opportunities.

Sagittarius: The day begins with practicality, but by evening, you'll feel inspired to explore new possibilities and engage with others.

Capricorn: The Moon in your sign encourages discipline and focus early in the day. As the energy shifts, embrace creative solutions and innovative ideas.

Aquarius: As the Moon moves into your sign later in the day, you'll feel more energized and inspired to embrace new ideas and social connections.

Pisces: Emotional discipline is key early in the day. Later, focus on creativity and expanding your horizons through social interactions.

For those born on January 29: Those born on this day have a natural balance between discipline and creativity, influenced by the transition from Capricorn to Aquarius. In 2025, they'll find success by staying committed to their goals while embracing innovation and social connections.

Daily Insights: The Moon in Aquarius brings a focus on innovation, creativity, and social connections. It's a great day to explore new ideas, engage with others, and embrace your individuality. With Venus in Aquarius, relationships may take on a more unconventional tone.

Aries: It's a great day for exploring new ideas and embracing your unique perspective. Social interactions bring excitement.

Taurus: Focus on expanding your horizons today. Engage with others and explore new ways of thinking.

Gemini: Creativity flows easily today. Engage with others and share your ideas in social settings.

Cancer: Today encourages you to step outside of your comfort zone and explore new ways of connecting with others.

Leo: Your creative energy is high today. Focus on pursuing your passions and engaging with others who inspire you.

Virgo: Innovation and creativity are key today. Embrace new ways of thinking and explore unique solutions.

Libra: Relationships take on a creative and unconventional tone today. Focus on engaging with others in new and exciting ways.

Scorpio: Your desire for personal growth is strong today. Embrace new ideas and be open to unconventional ways of thinking.

Sagittarius: It's a great day for exploring new perspectives. Social interactions and creative pursuits bring excitement.

Capricorn: Step outside of your usual routine and embrace innovation. Focus on finding new solutions to old problems.

Aquarius: With the Moon in your sign, you're feeling energized and inspired. Embrace your individuality and share your ideas with others.

Pisces: Today is perfect for creative and social pursuits. Engage with others and explore new ways of expressing yourself.

For those born on January 30: Born under the influence of the Moon in Aquarius, these individuals are creative, innovative, and socially connected. In 2025, they'll find success by embracing their individuality and exploring new ideas and opportunities.

Daily Insights: The Moon continues its journey through Aquarius, amplifying creativity, individuality, and social connections. It's a day for embracing innovation, sharing ideas, and thinking outside the box. With Mars in Capricorn, there's also a focus on balancing creativity with discipline.

Aries: You're feeling creative and energized today. Focus on new ideas while maintaining discipline in your goals.

Taurus: Engage with others and explore new ideas. Today's energy encourages innovation and collaboration.

Gemini: Your creative energy is high. Use today's momentum to explore new projects and share your ideas with others.

Cancer: Step outside your comfort zone and engage with new perspectives. Social interactions bring inspiration.

Leo: Creativity and innovation are at the forefront today. Focus on expressing yourself and collaborating with others.

Virgo: Use today's energy to think outside the box. Focus on creative solutions to practical problems.

Libra: Relationships take on an exciting tone today. Engage with others in unconventional ways and embrace new perspectives.

Scorpio: Your desire for personal growth is strong today. Use your creativity to explore new possibilities.

Sagittarius: Social interactions and creative pursuits bring excitement today. Focus on engaging with others and exploring new ideas.

Capricorn: Innovation meets discipline today. Focus on balancing creativity with your long-term goals.

Aquarius: The Moon in your sign amplifies your creativity and individuality. Embrace your unique perspective and share your ideas with others.

Pisces: It's a day for exploring creativity and connecting with others. Use your imagination to find new ways to express yourself.

For those born on January 31: Those born on this day are creative, innovative, and independent, influenced by the Moon in Aquarius. In 2025, they'll thrive by embracing their individuality and pursuing unique ideas and opportunities.

Daily Insights: The Moon remains in Aquarius, encouraging individuality, creativity, and a focus on social connections. It's a great day to embrace new ideas, connect with others, and explore innovative solutions to challenges.

Aries: You're feeling inspired to think outside the box. Today's energy is perfect for pursuing creative ideas and sharing them with others.

Taurus: Engage in conversations that challenge your usual way of thinking. Embrace new perspectives and be open to change.

Gemini: Social interactions bring excitement today. It's a great time to collaborate with others and explore creative projects.

Cancer: You may feel the urge to break away from routine today. Focus on connecting with like-minded individuals and exploring new ideas.

Leo: Creativity and innovation are at the forefront today. Take the lead in a new project or share your unique vision with others.

Virgo: It's a great day for problem-solving and finding innovative solutions to practical issues. Think outside the box.

Libra: Relationships take on a more unconventional tone today. Embrace new ways of connecting with loved ones and friends.

Scorpio: You're feeling introspective but also open to new ideas. Use this energy to explore personal growth through creative expression.

Sagittarius: Adventure and creativity are calling you today. Embrace the unexpected and seek out exciting opportunities.

Capricorn: While you're focused on your goals, today's energy encourages you to explore new approaches and innovative ideas.

Aquarius: With the Moon in your sign, you're feeling energized and ready to embrace your individuality. Share your unique ideas with the world.

Pisces: It's a good day for exploring your imagination and connecting with others on a creative level. Use your intuition to guide you.

For those born on February 1: Those born under the Moon in Aquarius are independent, creative, and forward-thinking. In 2025, they'll thrive by embracing their individuality and pursuing innovative ideas. It's a year for breaking away from tradition and exploring new paths.

Daily Insights: The Moon transitions into Pisces, bringing a shift toward emotional depth, intuition, and creativity. Today is ideal for reflection, artistic expression, and connecting with your inner self. The Sun in Aquarius encourages a balance between individuality and emotional awareness.

Aries: Your intuition is strong today. Trust your gut instincts and take time for reflection and self-care.

Taurus: You may feel more introspective than usual. Use this energy to explore your inner world and connect with your emotions.

Gemini: Creativity and imagination are heightened today. Focus on artistic projects or activities that allow you to express yourself.

Cancer: Emotional connections are important today. Reach out to loved ones and spend time nurturing your relationships.

Leo: You may feel the need to slow down and focus on your emotional well-being. Take time for quiet reflection and creative expression.

Virgo: Today is perfect for exploring your intuition. Use your analytical skills to dive deep into your emotions and gain clarity.

Libra: Relationships take on a deeper, more emotional tone today. Focus on connecting with others on a meaningful level.

Scorpio: Your emotional intensity is heightened today. Use this energy for self-reflection and exploring your inner feelings.

Sagittarius: You're feeling more introspective than usual. Focus on emotional growth and nurturing your creative side.

Capricorn: It's a good day for quiet reflection. Focus on your emotional well-being and explore creative outlets that bring you peace.

Aquarius: While you're usually focused on innovation, today encourages you to connect with your emotions and explore your inner world.

Pisces: With the Moon in your sign, your intuition and creativity are heightened. It's a great day for self-reflection and artistic expression.

For those born on February 2: Born with the Moon in Pisces, these individuals are intuitive, emotional, and creative. In 2025, they'll thrive by embracing their imagination and exploring their inner world. It's a year for personal growth through emotional and artistic expression.

Daily Insights: The Moon in Pisces continues to encourage emotional reflection, intuition, and creativity. It's a good day for self-care, meditation, and connecting with your deeper feelings. Venus in Aquarius adds a touch of unconventionality to relationships and creativity.

Aries: Today is a good day for introspection. Focus on your emotional well-being and listen to your intuition.

Taurus: You may feel more sensitive than usual. Use this energy to connect with loved ones and nurture your emotional bonds.

Gemini: Creativity flows easily today. Engage in activities that allow you to express your imagination and inner feelings.

Cancer: Your emotions are heightened today. Spend time reflecting on your personal needs and nurturing your relationships.

Leo: It's a good day to focus on your emotional well-being. Engage in creative activities that help you relax and recharge.

Virgo: Introspection is key today. Focus on your inner world and use your analytical skills to gain emotional clarity.

Libra: Relationships take on a deeper tone today. Focus on emotional connections and nurturing your bonds with loved ones.

Scorpio: Your emotional intensity is high today. Use this energy for self-reflection and exploring your inner world.

Sagittarius: You may feel more introspective than usual. Focus on emotional growth and connecting with your intuition.

Capricorn: Today is ideal for self-care and reflection. Take a break from your usual routine and focus on your emotional well-being.

Aquarius: While you're usually focused on the future, today encourages you to connect with your emotions and reflect on your inner world.

Pisces: With the Moon in your sign, your creativity and intuition are at their peak. Use this energy for artistic expression and emotional growth.

For those born on February 3: Those born under the Moon in Pisces are intuitive, creative, and deeply emotional. In 2025, they'll thrive by embracing their artistic talents and exploring their inner world. It's a year for emotional growth and self-discovery.

Daily Insights: The Moon remains in Pisces, encouraging introspection, creativity, and emotional connection. Today is perfect for focusing on self-care, artistic expression, and spending time with loved ones. Mars in Capricorn adds a touch of discipline, helping you balance creativity with responsibility.

Aries: Your emotions are strong today. Take time for self-reflection and focus on balancing your emotional and practical needs.

Taurus: It's a good day for nurturing relationships. Focus on emotional connections and creating a sense of harmony in your environment.

Gemini: Creativity and imagination are heightened. Engage in artistic activities or anything that allows you to express your emotions.

Cancer: Your intuition is strong today. Focus on emotional well-being and connect with loved ones on a deeper level.

Leo: Today is perfect for quiet reflection and creative expression. Take time for self-care and emotional growth.

Virgo: Emotional clarity comes from introspection. Use today's energy to gain insight into your feelings and inner world.

Libra: Relationships take on a more emotional tone. Focus on connecting with others in a meaningful and supportive way.

Scorpio: Your emotional intensity is high today. Use this energy for deep self-reflection and personal growth.

Sagittarius: You're feeling more introspective than usual. Focus on emotional healing and creative expression.

Capricorn: While you're focused on your goals, today encourages you to balance discipline with emotional well-being.

Aquarius: It's a good day to explore your emotions and engage in creative pursuits. Take time for self-reflection.

Pisces: The Moon in your sign amplifies your creativity and intuition. Use this energy to express yourself artistically and connect with your inner world.

For those born on February 4: People born on this day are deeply emotional, intuitive, and creative, influenced by the Moon in Pisces. In 2025, they'll find fulfillment by embracing their artistic talents and focusing on emotional growth. It's a year for self-discovery and personal reflection.

Daily Insights: The Moon moves into Aries, bringing a burst of energy, motivation, and confidence. Today is ideal for starting new projects, taking action, and pursuing your goals with enthusiasm. The Sun in Aquarius continues to encourage individuality and innovation.

Aries: You're feeling energized and ready to take on new challenges. Use today's motivation to pursue your goals with confidence.

Taurus: It's a good day for taking action. Focus on practical steps toward your goals while maintaining your usual steady pace.

Gemini: You're feeling inspired and motivated. Use this energy to pursue creative projects or engage in exciting new ventures.

Cancer: Your confidence is high today. Focus on taking action in areas of your life that need attention or growth.

Leo: Today is perfect for pursuing your passions. Take the lead in a project or activity that excites you.

Virgo: Use today's energy to tackle tasks that require focus and determination. Stay organized and take action.

Libra: You're feeling motivated to take action in your relationships. Focus on creating balance and harmony through proactive steps.

Scorpio: Today's energy encourages you to take bold action. Focus on pursuing your goals with determination and focus.

Sagittarius: Adventure is calling! Use today's energy to explore new opportunities and embrace exciting challenges.

Capricorn: You're feeling driven and focused today. Use this energy to make progress toward your long-term goals.

Aquarius: Today is perfect for pursuing innovative ideas. Take action on projects that align with your unique vision.

Pisces: After a period of introspection, you're ready to take action. Focus on pursuing your goals with confidence and determination.

For those born on February 5: Born with the Moon in Aries, these individuals are confident, motivated, and action-oriented. In 2025, they'll thrive by pursuing their goals with enthusiasm and taking bold steps toward success. It's a year for embracing challenges and seizing opportunities.

Daily Insights: The Moon remains in Aries, continuing to fuel energy, confidence, and a desire for action. It's a great day to tackle challenges head-on, initiate new projects, and focus on personal goals. With Venus in Aquarius, relationships may take on an exciting, unconventional tone.

Aries: You're feeling bold and ready to take action. Use today's energy to push forward with your personal goals.

Taurus: It's a day for focusing on progress. Take steady, determined steps toward achieving what you've set out to do.

Gemini: Your energy is high today. Use it to engage in activities that excite you, and don't shy away from new experiences.

Cancer: You may feel more confident than usual. Use this to tackle personal challenges and assert yourself where needed.

Leo: Leadership opportunities arise today. Step into your role with confidence and inspire others to follow your lead.

Virgo: Focus on taking practical action toward your goals. Today's energy supports productivity and achievement.

Libra: Relationships may feel invigorating today. Use this energy to explore new dynamics or engage in exciting activities with loved ones.

Scorpio: Your determination is strong today. Focus on pursuing your goals with intensity and passion.

Sagittarius: Adventure and excitement are on the horizon. Take action on something you've been wanting to explore or experience.

Capricorn: Discipline and action come easily today. Use this energy to focus on long-term goals and make concrete progress.

Aquarius: You're feeling inspired to take action on innovative ideas. Don't hesitate to pursue what excites you most.

Pisces: After a period of reflection, you're ready to take action. Use today's energy to pursue your dreams with confidence.

For those born on February 6: Those born under the Moon in Aries are energetic, confident, and action-oriented. In 2025, they'll find success by embracing challenges and taking decisive steps toward their goals. It's a year for bold moves and personal growth.

Daily Insights: The Moon shifts into Taurus, bringing a sense of stability, patience, and practicality. It's a day to focus on steady progress, long-term goals, and enjoying life's simple pleasures. With Mars in Capricorn, discipline and hard work are emphasized.

Aries: Today is about slowing down and focusing on practical matters. Take your time and work steadily toward your goals.

Taurus: The Moon in your sign enhances your sense of stability. It's a great day for grounding yourself and making practical progress.

Gemini: You may feel a shift toward a more grounded energy today. Focus on practical tasks and taking steady steps forward.

Cancer: It's a good day for focusing on comfort and security. Spend time nurturing yourself and those around you.

Leo: Focus on long-term goals today. Practical steps and steady progress will bring you closer to achieving what you desire.

Virgo: Use today's energy to get organized and focus on details. It's a productive day for planning and making steady progress.

Libra: Relationships feel stable and secure today. Focus on creating harmony and enjoying the simple pleasures of connection.

Scorpio: Your determination is strong today, but remember to pace yourself. Focus on steady, practical steps toward your goals.

Sagittarius: It's a good day to focus on grounding yourself. Take time to reflect on your long-term goals and how you can achieve them.

Capricorn: Discipline and focus are your strengths today. Use this energy to make concrete progress on your long-term goals.

Aquarius: You may feel a need to slow down today. Focus on practical matters and enjoy the process of steady progress.

Pisces: Today encourages you to find stability in your emotional life. Take time for self-care and focus on grounding your emotions.

For those born on February 7: Born under the influence of the Moon in Taurus, these individuals are grounded, patient, and practical. In 2025, they'll find success by focusing on long-term goals and enjoying the simple pleasures of life. It's a year for steady progress and personal fulfillment.

February 8, 2025

Daily Insights: The Moon continues its journey through Taurus, emphasizing stability, practicality, and comfort. Today is perfect for working on long-term goals, focusing on financial matters, and enjoying life's material pleasures. The Sun in Aquarius encourages balance between practicality and innovation.

Aries: Focus on steady progress toward your goals. It's a day for patience and practical actions.

Taurus: You're feeling grounded and stable today. Focus on personal growth and making steady progress in all areas of life.

Gemini: Practical matters take center stage today. Focus on organizing your thoughts and working on long-term plans.

Cancer: It's a great day to focus on home and family. Nurture your loved ones and create a sense of security in your environment.

Leo: Focus on practical tasks today. Your ability to balance creativity with discipline will lead to success.

Virgo: Today is all about productivity and practicality. Stay organized and work steadily toward your goals.

Libra: Relationships feel stable and secure today. Focus on building long-term harmony and enjoying meaningful connections.

Scorpio: You're feeling determined and focused. Use today's energy to make steady progress toward your long-term goals.

Sagittarius: It's a good day for grounding yourself. Focus on practical matters and enjoying the simple pleasures of life.

Capricorn: Discipline and practicality come naturally today. Focus on making steady progress in your career and personal goals.

Aquarius: Balance practicality with creativity today. Focus on finding innovative solutions to practical problems.

Pisces: It's a good day for grounding your emotions. Take time for self-care and focus on creating emotional stability.

For those born on February 8: Those born under the Moon in Taurus are practical, grounded, and patient. In 2025, they'll thrive by focusing on long-term goals and building a stable foundation for the future. It's a year for steady progress and enjoying life's material comforts.

Daily Insights: The Moon in Taurus continues to encourage stability, but as it transitions into Gemini later in the day, the energy shifts toward communication, curiosity, and mental stimulation. It's a great day to balance practical matters with social interactions and learning.

Aries: Focus on practical tasks early in the day, but later, embrace social interactions and conversations that stimulate your mind.

Taurus: The day starts with a focus on stability, but as the energy shifts, you'll feel more inclined to engage in lively conversations.

Gemini: The Moon enters your sign later today, bringing mental clarity and energy. It's a great time for socializing and sharing ideas.

Cancer: The morning is perfect for focusing on practical matters, while the evening encourages you to engage in stimulating conversations.

Leo: Balance your need for stability with social interactions today. Focus on practical tasks in the morning, and embrace creative ideas later.

Virgo: It's a productive day, but later on, you'll feel more social and curious. Engage in conversations that broaden your perspective.

Libra: Relationships feel grounded early in the day. Later, you'll feel more inclined to engage in lively conversations and social activities.

Scorpio: Focus on long-term goals in the morning, but be open to new ideas and stimulating conversations later in the day.

Sagittarius: It's a day for balancing stability with excitement. Focus on practical matters early, then embrace your curiosity in the evening.

Capricorn: Your disciplined nature will help you tackle practical tasks, but later in the day, allow yourself to engage in stimulating conversations.

Aquarius: The day starts with a focus on practicality, but as the energy shifts, you'll feel inspired to share your ideas and socialize.

Pisces: It's a good day for grounding your emotions early on. In the evening, you'll feel more inclined to engage in lively conversations.

For those born on February 9: Born with the Moon transitioning from Taurus to Gemini, these individuals are both practical and intellectually curious. In 2025, they'll thrive by balancing their need for stability with their desire for social interaction and learning. It's a year for practical achievements and mental growth.

Daily Insights: The Moon in Gemini brings a focus on communication, curiosity, and social interactions. Today is perfect for learning new things, engaging in conversations, and sharing ideas. With Mercury in Capricorn, there's also a focus on practical thinking and problem-solving.

Aries: Your mind is sharp today, and it's a great time to engage in conversations that challenge your thinking.

Taurus: You may feel more social than usual. Focus on connecting with others and sharing your ideas in a productive way.

Gemini: The Moon in your sign enhances your communication skills. It's a great day for learning, networking, and exchanging ideas.

Cancer: Engage in conversations that stimulate your mind today. It's a good time to learn something new or share your thoughts with others.

Leo: Focus on creative problem-solving today. Conversations with others may bring fresh insights and new perspectives.

Virgo: It's a good day for organizing your thoughts and communicating clearly. Use this energy to tackle any outstanding tasks.

Libra: Social interactions are lively today. Engage with others in conversations that bring new ideas and perspectives.

Scorpio: Your curiosity is heightened today. Use this energy to explore new topics and engage in deep conversations.

Sagittarius: It's a day for learning and expanding your horizons. Engage in stimulating conversations and embrace new ideas.

Capricorn: Practical thinking is enhanced today. Focus on problem-solving and making steady progress toward your goals.

Aquarius: Your innovative ideas shine today. Engage in conversations that allow you to explore new perspectives and share your unique insights.

Pisces: Your imagination is strong today. Use this energy to engage in creative conversations and explore new ideas.

For those born on February 10: People born under the Moon in Gemini are curious, communicative, and intellectually driven. In 2025, they'll thrive by engaging in learning opportunities, expanding their social circles, and exploring new ideas. It's a year for mental stimulation and personal growth.

Daily Insights: The Moon continues its journey through Gemini, keeping the focus on communication, curiosity, and learning. It's a great day for sharing ideas, socializing, and engaging in mental stimulation. With Venus in Aquarius, relationships take on a unique, unconventional tone.

Aries: You're feeling mentally sharp today. Engage in conversations that challenge your thinking and broaden your perspective.

Taurus: Social interactions are lively today. Focus on connecting with people who inspire new ideas and spark your curiosity.

Gemini: The Moon in your sign enhances your communication skills. Use this energy to express yourself and connect with others on a deeper level.

Cancer: It's a great day to learn something new or dive into a subject that interests you. Conversations with friends may provide valuable insights.

Leo: Creativity flows easily today. Share your ideas and collaborate with others to bring new projects to life.

Virgo: Mental clarity is strong today. Focus on organizing your thoughts and planning ahead for future tasks.

Libra: Socializing is key today. Engage with others in meaningful conversations and share your thoughts openly.

Scorpio: You're feeling curious and introspective. Use this energy to explore new ideas and uncover hidden truths through conversation.

Sagittarius: Adventure and learning are calling you. Use today's energy to explore new topics or engage in stimulating conversations.

Capricorn: Practical thinking comes easily today. Focus on solving problems and making progress toward your long-term goals.

Aquarius: Innovation is the theme of the day. Share your unique ideas and engage in conversations that push boundaries.

Pisces: Your imagination is heightened today. Focus on creative projects and engage with others in ways that inspire your inner world.

For those born on February 11: Born under the Moon in Gemini, these individuals are curious, communicative, and mentally agile. In 2025, they'll find success by embracing opportunities for learning and social engagement. It's a year for exploring new ideas and broadening their horizons.

February 12, 2025

Daily Insights: The Moon transitions into Cancer, shifting the focus toward home, family, and emotional well-being. Today is ideal for nurturing relationships, self-care, and focusing on your personal life. The Sun in Aquarius continues to encourage individuality and innovation.

Aries: You may feel more emotionally connected to your family today. Take time to nurture your relationships and focus on your personal life.

Taurus: Home and family take priority today. Focus on creating a sense of comfort and stability in your environment.

Gemini: After a period of mental stimulation, it's time to focus on your emotional well-being. Spend time with loved ones and reflect on your personal needs.

Cancer: With the Moon in your sign, you're feeling emotionally intuitive. It's a good day for self-care and nurturing your relationships.

Leo: Emotional balance is key today. Focus on creating harmony in your home life and tending to your personal needs.

Virgo: It's a day for reflection and emotional growth. Use this time to focus on your inner world and nurture your emotional well-being.

Libra: Relationships take on a deeper tone today. Focus on emotional connections and creating a sense of harmony with those around you.

Scorpio: You're feeling emotionally intense today. Use this energy to explore your feelings and connect with loved ones on a deeper level.

Sagittarius: While adventure is important to you, today calls for reflection and emotional balance. Focus on your personal life and relationships.

Capricorn: Your focus shifts to home and family today. Use this energy to create stability in your personal life and nurture your loved ones.

Aquarius: It's a good day to reflect on your emotional needs. Balance your desire for individuality with the importance of emotional connections.

Pisces: Your intuition is strong today. Focus on self-care and nurturing your emotional well-being.

For those born on February 12: Born under the Moon in Cancer, these individuals are emotionally intuitive, nurturing, and deeply connected to home and family. In 2025, they'll thrive by focusing on personal growth and strengthening their emotional connections. It's a year for self-care and emotional fulfillment.

Daily Insights: The Moon in Cancer continues to emphasize emotional well-being, home life, and nurturing relationships. It's a great day for self-reflection, connecting with loved ones, and creating a sense of comfort in your surroundings.

Aries: Focus on nurturing your emotional needs today. Spend time with family and create a sense of harmony in your personal life.

Taurus: It's a good day to focus on your home environment. Make changes that bring comfort and stability to your living space.

Gemini: You may feel more introspective today. Take time for self-care and focus on your emotional well-being.

Cancer: The Moon in your sign continues to heighten your intuition. Use this energy to nurture your relationships and focus on personal growth.

Leo: Emotional balance is key today. Take a step back from your usual activities and focus on creating harmony in your home life.

Virgo: Today encourages reflection and emotional clarity. Use this time to focus on your inner world and nurture your personal needs.

Libra: Relationships take center stage today. Focus on creating emotional connections and fostering harmony with loved ones.

Scorpio: You're feeling emotionally intense today. Use this energy to explore your feelings and connect with others on a deeper level.

Sagittarius: It's a day for reflection and emotional balance. Focus on your personal life and creating a sense of peace in your surroundings.

Capricorn: Home and family are your focus today. Use this time to nurture your relationships and create stability in your personal life.

Aquarius: Emotional reflection is important today. Take time to connect with your inner self and focus on emotional growth.

Pisces: Your intuition is strong today. Use this energy to explore your emotions and nurture your personal relationships.

For those born on February 13: Those born under the Moon in Cancer are emotionally intuitive, nurturing, and deeply connected to their personal life. In 2025, they'll find fulfillment by focusing on emotional growth, strengthening relationships, and creating a sense of stability at home.

Daily Insights: The Moon moves into Leo, shifting the focus from introspection to self-expression, creativity, and confidence. It's a day for stepping into the spotlight, sharing your talents, and focusing on your passions. With Venus in Aquarius, relationships take on an exciting, unconventional tone.

Aries: You're feeling confident and ready to take on new challenges. Use today's energy to focus on your passions and express yourself boldly.

Taurus: Creativity flows easily today. Focus on personal projects that bring you joy and allow you to showcase your talents.

Gemini: It's a great day for socializing and sharing your ideas with others. Use your communication skills to inspire those around you.

Cancer: After a period of emotional reflection, you're ready to step into the spotlight. Focus on expressing yourself and pursuing your passions.

Leo: With the Moon in your sign, your confidence is high. It's a perfect day for pursuing creative projects and embracing leadership opportunities.

Virgo: Focus on creative problem-solving today. Use your practical skills to bring your ideas to life in unique ways.

Libra: Relationships feel exciting and dynamic today. Embrace new ways of connecting with loved ones and explore creative possibilities.

Scorpio: Your passion is heightened today. Use this energy to pursue personal projects and express your unique talents.

Sagittarius: Adventure and excitement are calling you today. Use your creativity to explore new possibilities and embrace new challenges.

Capricorn: It's a great day for creative thinking and leadership. Focus on personal projects that allow you to express your talents.

Aquarius: Your innovative ideas shine today. Use this energy to engage in creative projects and share your unique perspective with others.

Pisces: After a period of introspection, you're ready to express yourself creatively. Use today's energy to focus on personal growth and self-expression.

For those born on February 14: Born under the Moon in Leo, these individuals are confident, creative, and charismatic. In 2025, they'll find success by embracing leadership opportunities and expressing their unique talents. It's a year for stepping into the spotlight and pursuing personal passions.

February 15, 2025

Daily Insights: The Moon in Leo continues to amplify creativity, confidence, and self-expression. Today is perfect for focusing on personal projects, embracing leadership roles, and sharing your unique talents with the world. With Mars in Capricorn, there's also a focus on discipline and long-term goals.

Aries: You're feeling bold and ready to take action. Use today's energy to pursue personal projects and showcase your talents.

Taurus: Creativity is your strength today. Focus on personal projects that allow you to express your unique talents.

Gemini: Social interactions are lively today. Use your communication skills to inspire and engage with others in creative ways.

Cancer: It's a day for self-expression and personal growth. Focus on pursuing your passions and sharing your ideas with others.

Leo: The Moon in your sign continues to enhance your confidence and creativity. Step into a leadership role and pursue your goals with enthusiasm.

Virgo: Focus on creative problem-solving today. Use your practical skills to bring your ideas to life in unique ways.

Libra: Relationships feel dynamic and exciting today. Embrace new ways of connecting with loved ones and explore creative possibilities.

Scorpio: Your passion is heightened today. Use this energy to pursue personal projects and express your unique talents.

Sagittarius: Adventure and excitement are calling you today. Use your creativity to explore new possibilities and embrace new challenges.

Capricorn: Discipline and creativity come together today. Focus on long-term goals while allowing yourself to think outside the box.

Aquarius: Your innovative ideas shine today. Use this energy to engage in creative projects and share your unique perspective with others.

Pisces: After a period of introspection, you're ready to express yourself creatively. Use today's energy to focus on personal growth and self-expression.

For those born on February 15: Born with the Moon in Leo, these individuals are confident, creative, and charismatic. In 2025, they'll find fulfillment by embracing leadership opportunities and expressing their unique talents. It's a year for pursuing passions and stepping into the spotlight.

Daily Insights: The Moon in Leo continues to amplify confidence and creativity, but as it transitions into Virgo later in the day, the focus shifts toward practicality, organization, and attention to detail. It's a great day to balance your passions with productive tasks.

Aries: Use the creative energy early in the day to express yourself, but later, focus on organizing your plans and taking practical steps forward.

Taurus: The morning brings a burst of creativity, while the evening is perfect for focusing on long-term goals and practical matters.

Gemini: Social interactions are vibrant today, but by the evening, you'll want to focus on tasks that require your attention to detail.

Cancer: Your confidence is high today, but as the energy shifts, focus on personal well-being and organizing your thoughts.

Leo: The Moon in your sign gives you a boost of energy, but as the day progresses, focus on grounding yourself and getting organized.

Virgo: As the Moon moves into your sign later today, you'll feel more motivated to tackle practical tasks and improve your routine.

Libra: Relationships are in the spotlight today, but by evening, focus on balancing your social life with personal responsibilities.

Scorpio: Early in the day, your passion shines, but later, use the energy to focus on productivity and self-improvement.

Sagittarius: The day starts with creative energy, and by evening, you'll feel the need to focus on practical matters and organizing your life.

Capricorn: Early in the day, embrace creativity and self-expression. As the day progresses, focus on long-term goals and practical actions.

Aquarius: Your innovative ideas shine today. Later, shift your focus to refining your plans and getting organized.

Pisces: It's a day for balancing creativity and practicality. Use the evening to focus on tasks that require attention to detail.

For those born on February 16: Born under the transition from Leo to Virgo, these individuals possess a balance of creativity and practicality. In 2025, they'll thrive by expressing their talents while staying focused on achieving their goals. It's a year for personal growth through a combination of passion and discipline.

February 17, 2025

Daily Insights: The Moon in Virgo brings a focus on organization, productivity, and attention to detail. Today is perfect for tackling practical tasks, refining your plans, and focusing on health and well-being. With Mercury in Capricorn, clear communication and disciplined thinking are key.

Aries: Focus on getting organized today. It's a great day for tackling tasks that require discipline and attention to detail.

Taurus: Practicality is your strength today. Use this energy to make progress on long-term goals and take care of your health.

Gemini: Your analytical mind is sharp today. Use this energy to organize your thoughts and communicate clearly with others.

Cancer: It's a good day for focusing on your well-being. Pay attention to your health and daily routine, and make necessary improvements.

Leo: Today's energy encourages you to focus on practical matters. Get organized and make steady progress on your goals.

Virgo: The Moon in your sign enhances your natural strengths in organization and productivity. Use this energy to tackle important tasks.

Libra: It's a day for finding balance between work and relaxation. Focus on practical matters, but don't forget to take care of yourself.

Scorpio: Your attention to detail is heightened today. Use this energy to focus on long-term goals and refine your plans.

Sagittarius: It's a good day for grounding yourself and focusing on practical matters. Take care of your responsibilities and get organized.

Capricorn: Discipline comes naturally today. Focus on making steady progress toward your long-term goals and improving your routine.

Aquarius: While you're usually focused on big ideas, today's energy encourages you to focus on the details and refine your plans.

Pisces: Today is perfect for focusing on your well-being. Take time to reflect on your health and make improvements where necessary.

For those born on February 17: Born under the influence of the Moon in Virgo, these individuals are practical, organized, and detail-oriented. In 2025, they'll find success by focusing on productivity, health, and self-improvement. It's a year for refining their plans and making steady progress toward their goals.

February 18, 2025

Daily Insights: The Moon in Virgo continues to emphasize productivity and organization, but as it transitions into Libra later in the day, the focus shifts toward balance, relationships, and harmony. It's a good day for finding equilibrium between work and personal life.

Aries: The day starts with a focus on productivity, but by evening, you'll want to focus on creating balance in your relationships.

Taurus: It's a day for getting organized, but as the evening approaches, focus on finding harmony in your personal life.

Gemini: You're productive early in the day, but later, you'll feel the need to engage in social interactions and create balance in your life.

Cancer: Focus on practical matters during the day, but as the evening progresses, shift your focus to nurturing your relationships.

Leo: It's a great day for tackling practical tasks, but by evening, focus on bringing harmony to your personal and social life.

Virgo: The Moon in your sign helps you stay productive, but as it moves into Libra, focus on creating balance in all areas of your life.

Libra: The day starts with a focus on productivity, but as the Moon enters your sign later, you'll feel a need to bring balance and harmony into your relationships.

Scorpio: Productivity is your strength today, but later, focus on finding equilibrium between your responsibilities and personal life.

Sagittarius: It's a day for focusing on practical matters, but as the energy shifts, you'll feel more inclined to engage in social interactions.

Capricorn: Discipline and productivity are key today, but by evening, focus on balancing your work and personal life.

Aquarius: Early in the day, focus on refining your plans, but later, shift your attention to relationships and creating harmony.

Pisces: It's a good day for focusing on health and well-being. As the day progresses, focus on creating balance in your relationships.

For those born on February 18: Born under the transition from Virgo to Libra, these individuals are practical and detail-oriented but also seek balance and harmony in life. In 2025, they'll find success by focusing on their personal growth and creating equilibrium in their relationships.

Daily Insights: The Moon in Libra brings a focus on relationships, harmony, and balance. Today is ideal for social interactions, resolving conflicts, and finding equilibrium in your personal and professional life. With Venus in Aquarius, there's also an emphasis on creativity and innovation in relationships.

Aries: Focus on creating balance in your relationships today. It's a great day for resolving conflicts and nurturing connections.

Taurus: Harmony is the theme of the day. Focus on finding balance in your personal life and creating a peaceful environment.

Gemini: Social interactions are lively today. Engage with others in meaningful conversations and work toward creating harmony in your relationships.

Cancer: Balance is key today. Focus on finding equilibrium between your personal and professional responsibilities.

Leo: It's a day for creating harmony in your life. Focus on relationships and finding balance between work and play.

Virgo: Today encourages you to focus on your relationships. Work on resolving any conflicts and creating harmony with loved ones.

Libra: With the Moon in your sign, you're feeling the need for balance and harmony. Focus on nurturing your relationships and personal well-being.

Scorpio: It's a good day for resolving conflicts and finding balance in your personal life. Focus on creating harmony in your relationships.

Sagittarius: Social interactions bring joy today. Engage with others and work toward creating balance in your relationships.

Capricorn: Balance is the theme of the day. Focus on finding equilibrium between your work and personal life.

Aquarius: Relationships take center stage today. Focus on bringing creativity and innovation into your connections with others.

Pisces: It's a day for focusing on emotional balance. Take time to nurture your relationships and create harmony in your life.

For those born on February 19: Born under the Moon in Libra, these individuals are focused on balance, harmony, and relationships. In 2025, they'll thrive by creating equilibrium in their personal and professional lives, while nurturing their social connections and resolving conflicts.

Daily Insights: The Moon in Libra continues to encourage balance and harmony, but as it transitions into Scorpio later in the day, the energy shifts toward emotional intensity, transformation, and deeper connections. It's a good day for focusing on emotional growth and personal transformation.

Aries: The day starts with a focus on relationships, but by evening, you'll feel the need for emotional reflection and deeper connections.

Taurus: Focus on creating balance early in the day, but as the energy shifts, explore your emotions and seek personal transformation.

Gemini: The morning is great for socializing, but later, you'll want to focus on introspection and emotional growth.

Cancer: Relationships are the focus in the morning, but by evening, dive deep into your emotional world and seek personal growth.

Leo: Balance your personal and social life early in the day, but later, focus on exploring your inner self and emotional transformation.

Virgo: The day starts with harmony in relationships, but by evening, you'll feel drawn to deeper emotional connections and reflection.

Libra: The Moon in your sign encourages balance, but as it moves into Scorpio, focus on exploring your emotional depths and personal growth.

Scorpio: Emotional intensity rises as the day progresses. Use this energy to explore your feelings and focus on personal transformation.

Sagittarius: Social interactions are lively in the morning, but by evening, you'll feel more introspective and focused on emotional growth.

Capricorn: The day begins with a focus on balance, but later, shift your attention to personal transformation and emotional healing.

Aquarius: Focus on creating harmony in your relationships early in the day, but later, explore your emotional world and seek personal growth.

Pisces: Emotional reflection is key today. Take time to explore your feelings and focus on personal transformation by evening.

For those born on February 20: Born under the transition from Libra to Scorpio, these individuals are focused on balance and harmony but also possess emotional depth and intensity. In 2025, they'll thrive by balancing their relationships with personal transformation and emotional growth.

Daily Insights: The Moon in Scorpio brings emotional intensity, depth, and a focus on transformation. Today is perfect for introspection, diving deep into personal matters, and focusing on emotional healing. With Mars in Capricorn, there's also an emphasis on discipline and long-term goals.

Aries: Today's energy encourages emotional reflection. Use this time to explore your deeper feelings and focus on personal growth.

Taurus: You may feel more introspective than usual. Focus on emotional healing and addressing unresolved issues.

Gemini: It's a good day for introspection. Dive into your emotions and seek clarity in areas that have been weighing on you.

Cancer: Emotional intensity is heightened today. Use this energy to focus on healing and transforming your emotional world.

Leo: The energy of the day encourages you to explore your emotions. Focus on personal transformation and emotional growth.

Virgo: It's a day for deep reflection. Use this time to examine your feelings and work on emotional healing.

Libra: Today's energy encourages you to focus on emotional connections. Dive deeper into your relationships and explore what truly matters.

Scorpio: With the Moon in your sign, you're feeling emotionally powerful. Use this energy for personal transformation and deep emotional work.

Sagittarius: Emotional reflection is key today. Take time to explore your inner world and focus on personal growth.

Capricorn: It's a day for diving deep into your emotions. Use this time for reflection and personal transformation, especially in areas that need healing.

Aquarius: While you're often focused on innovation, today encourages you to reflect on your emotional needs and focus on healing.

Pisces: Your intuition is strong today. Use this energy to explore your emotions and focus on personal transformation.

For those born on February 21: Born under the Moon in Scorpio, these individuals are emotionally intense, intuitive, and transformative. In 2025, they'll find success by embracing emotional growth and focusing on deep personal transformation. It's a year for self-reflection and emotional healing.

Daily Insights: The Moon in Scorpio continues to bring emotional intensity and a focus on transformation, but with the Sun in Pisces, there's a heightened sense of intuition and creativity. It's a great day for diving deep into your emotions while exploring your creative and spiritual side.

Aries: Your emotions run deep today. Focus on self-reflection and personal transformation while staying in tune with your intuition.

Taurus: Emotional intensity continues to be a theme. Take time to reflect on your feelings and focus on creative ways to express yourself.

Gemini: It's a great day for exploring your inner world. Use your heightened intuition to guide your emotions and decisions.

Cancer: Your intuition is strong today. Focus on emotional healing and allow yourself to dive deep into personal matters.

Leo: Emotions are intense, but use this energy for creative expression. It's a good day for transforming your feelings into art or action.

Virgo: Today's energy encourages deep emotional work. Use this time to focus on healing and transforming areas of your life that need attention.

Libra: Relationships take on a deeper tone today. Focus on emotional connections and work on strengthening your bonds.

Scorpio: The Moon in your sign continues to amplify your emotional intensity. Use this energy for self-reflection and personal transformation.

Sagittarius: Introspection is key today. Use your intuition to explore your emotions and seek clarity in personal matters.

Capricorn: It's a good day for focusing on emotional transformation. Use this energy to reflect on your feelings and focus on growth.

Aquarius: Today encourages emotional and spiritual growth. Use your intuition to guide you in personal matters and focus on healing.

Pisces: Your creativity and intuition are heightened today. Use this energy for self-reflection and creative expression.

For those born on February 22: Born under the influence of the Moon in Scorpio and the Sun in Pisces, these individuals are deeply intuitive, emotional, and creative. In 2025, they'll thrive by embracing their emotional depth and focusing on personal transformation through creativity and spirituality.

Daily Insights: The Moon transitions into Sagittarius, bringing a sense of optimism, adventure, and a desire for expansion. It's a great day for exploring new opportunities, learning, and pursuing personal growth. The Sun in Pisces encourages balancing adventure with intuition and emotional awareness.

Aries: You're feeling energized and ready for adventure. Use today's optimism to explore new opportunities and expand your horizons.

Taurus: After a period of introspection, you're ready to step out of your comfort zone. Embrace new experiences and opportunities for growth.

Gemini: Your curiosity is piqued today. Use this energy to explore new topics or engage in conversations that broaden your perspective.

Cancer: Emotional balance is key today. Focus on balancing your personal growth with your need for adventure and exploration.

Leo: It's a day for stepping into new opportunities. Embrace your adventurous spirit and take bold steps toward personal growth.

Virgo: Adventure and learning are calling you today. Use this energy to explore new ideas and expand your knowledge.

Libra: It's a good day for social interactions and learning. Engage in conversations that challenge your views and inspire growth.

Scorpio: After a period of emotional intensity, you're ready for adventure. Use today's energy to focus on personal growth and expansion.

Sagittarius: The Moon in your sign brings a burst of energy and optimism. It's a great day to pursue new experiences and embrace adventure.

Capricorn: Today encourages you to explore new opportunities. Use your practical mindset to take advantage of personal growth possibilities.

Aquarius: You're feeling adventurous and ready for new experiences. Use this energy to explore ideas that push boundaries.

Pisces: Your intuition is strong today, and you're ready to explore new horizons. Use this energy to pursue personal growth and creative expression.

For those born on February 23: Born under the Moon in Sagittarius, these individuals are adventurous, optimistic, and eager for personal growth. In 2025, they'll thrive by embracing new opportunities, expanding their horizons, and focusing on learning and self-discovery.

February 24, 2025

Daily Insights: The Moon in Sagittarius continues to amplify optimism, adventure, and a desire for exploration. It's a day for embracing new experiences, learning something new, and broadening your perspective. With Venus in Aquarius, relationships may take on an unconventional, exciting tone.

Aries: Adventure is calling you today. Use your energy to explore new opportunities and expand your knowledge.

Taurus: You're feeling more open to new experiences today. Embrace the unknown and allow yourself to step out of your comfort zone.

Gemini: It's a great day for learning and exploring. Engage in conversations that inspire new ideas and perspectives.

Cancer: Balance your emotional needs with your desire for adventure today. Focus on personal growth while maintaining your emotional stability.

Leo: Your adventurous spirit is strong today. Use this energy to explore new opportunities and take bold steps toward your goals.

Virgo: The energy of the day encourages you to step out of your usual routine. Embrace new experiences and focus on learning.

Libra: Relationships feel exciting and dynamic today. Focus on connecting with others in meaningful, unconventional ways.

Scorpio: Your passion for personal growth is strong today. Use this energy to explore new experiences and broaden your perspective.

Sagittarius: With the Moon in your sign, your energy is high. Embrace adventure, pursue new opportunities, and enjoy the excitement of the day.

Capricorn: Today encourages you to explore new opportunities for personal growth. Use your practical mindset to take advantage of these experiences.

Aquarius: Your innovative ideas shine today. Use this energy to explore new ways of thinking and connect with others in exciting ways.

Pisces: Your intuition is strong today. Use this energy to explore new horizons and focus on personal growth through creative expression.

For those born on February 24: Born under the Moon in Sagittarius, these individuals are optimistic, adventurous, and eager for new experiences. In 2025, they'll find success by embracing opportunities for personal growth, learning, and expanding their horizons.

February 25, 2025

Daily Insights: The Moon remains in Sagittarius, continuing the focus on exploration, adventure, and personal growth. However, as it transitions into Capricorn later in the day, the energy shifts toward discipline, practicality, and long-term planning. It's a day for balancing adventure with responsibility.

Aries: Adventure and growth are key today, but as the day progresses, focus on your long-term goals and practical responsibilities.

Taurus: Start your day with an open mind and a sense of adventure, but later, shift your focus to stability and long-term planning.

Gemini: It's a great day for learning and exploring, but by evening, focus on organizing your thoughts and setting practical goals.

Cancer: The morning is perfect for embracing new experiences, but later, you'll want to focus on creating stability in your personal life.

Leo: Your adventurous spirit is strong early in the day, but as the energy shifts, focus on your responsibilities and long-term goals.

Virgo: Balance your desire for adventure with your need for structure today. Use the morning for exploration and the evening for planning.

Libra: Social interactions are exciting early in the day, but later, focus on creating balance and harmony in your personal life.

Scorpio: It's a day for adventure and learning, but as the energy shifts, focus on long-term goals and emotional growth.

Sagittarius: The Moon in your sign encourages adventure and optimism, but as the day progresses, focus on practical matters and future planning.

Capricorn: Early in the day, embrace adventure and new experiences, but later, the focus shifts to discipline and long-term success.

Aquarius: Today encourages adventure and learning, but as the energy shifts, focus on refining your ideas and setting clear goals.

Pisces: Adventure and intuition are heightened today, but as the evening approaches, focus on grounding yourself and planning for the future.

For those born on February 25: Born under the transition from Sagittarius to Capricorn, these individuals are adventurous but also disciplined and practical. In 2025, they'll find success by balancing their desire for exploration with their long-term goals and responsibilities.

Daily Insights: The Moon in Capricorn brings a focus on discipline, practicality, and long-term planning. It's a great day for setting goals, working hard, and making progress in your career or personal projects. With Mars in Capricorn, there's also a boost in determination and focus.

Aries: Focus on your long-term goals today. Discipline and hard work will help you make steady progress toward your ambitions.

Taurus: It's a good day for practical matters. Use your determination to tackle tasks that require attention and patience.

Gemini: Discipline is key today. Focus on organizing your ideas and making practical decisions for the future.

Cancer: It's a great day for focusing on home and personal responsibilities. Use today's energy to create stability in your environment.

Leo: Your leadership skills are enhanced today. Focus on taking practical steps toward your goals and inspiring others to follow your lead.

Virgo: Productivity is high today. Use this energy to focus on details and complete tasks that require careful planning.

Libra: It's a good day for balancing your responsibilities and personal relationships. Focus on creating harmony through practical actions.

Scorpio: You're feeling determined and focused today. Use this energy to pursue your goals with discipline and persistence.

Sagittarius: Adventure takes a backseat today as you focus on long-term planning and practical goals. Stay disciplined and grounded.

Capricorn: The Moon in your sign enhances your natural discipline and determination. It's a great day for making progress on your goals.

Aquarius: Use today's energy to focus on practical matters and set clear, achievable goals for the future.

Pisces: You're feeling grounded and focused today. Use this energy to work on long-term plans and set practical goals for your future.

For those born on February 26: Born under the Moon in Capricorn, these individuals are disciplined, hardworking, and focused on long-term success. In 2025, they'll thrive by setting clear goals and working steadily toward achieving them. It's a year for practical achievements and personal growth.

Daily Insights: The Moon in Capricorn continues to emphasize discipline, hard work, and practicality. It's a great day for focusing on your career, setting long-term goals, and making progress toward personal success. With Venus in Aquarius, relationships may take on a more unconventional tone, encouraging individuality and freedom.

Aries: Continue to focus on your long-term goals today. Your determination will help you make significant progress.

Taurus: It's a day for practicality and hard work. Focus on tasks that require patience and determination.

Gemini: Your practical mindset is strong today. Use this energy to plan for the future and focus on realistic goals.

Cancer: Focus on creating stability in your personal life today. Practical actions will bring a sense of security and comfort.

Leo: Leadership and discipline are key today. Focus on taking practical steps toward your long-term ambitions.

Virgo: Productivity continues to be high today. Focus on tasks that require attention to detail and careful planning.

Libra: Balance your personal relationships with your responsibilities today. Practical actions will help create harmony.

Scorpio: Your determination is strong, making it a great day for tackling long-term goals and staying focused on your ambitions.

Sagittarius: Adventure takes a backseat as you focus on practical matters. Stay grounded and work steadily toward your goals.

Capricorn: The Moon in your sign continues to enhance your discipline and focus. Use this energy to make progress on personal and professional goals.

Aquarius: Focus on practical matters today. Use your innovative thinking to find solutions that will benefit you in the long run.

Pisces: You're feeling grounded and focused on practical goals. Use today's energy to work on projects that require discipline and patience.

For those born on February 27: Born under the Moon in Capricorn, these individuals are disciplined, focused, and determined to achieve long-term success. In 2025, they'll thrive by setting realistic goals and working steadily toward their ambitions. It's a year for practical achievements and career growth.

Daily Insights: The Moon remains in Capricorn for most of the day, keeping the focus on discipline and long-term planning. However, as it transitions into Aquarius in the evening, the energy shifts toward innovation, creativity, and social connections. It's a good day to balance hard work with creativity and social interaction.

Aries: The day starts with a focus on your goals, but by evening, you'll feel inspired to explore new ideas and connect with others.

Taurus: Continue to focus on practical matters during the day, but later, embrace creativity and explore unconventional approaches to your goals.

Gemini: The day is perfect for disciplined work, but as the evening approaches, you'll feel energized to engage in social activities and innovative projects.

Cancer: Focus on long-term goals in the morning, and as the day progresses, shift your attention to creative solutions and social interactions.

Leo: Leadership and discipline are your strengths today, but by evening, embrace new ideas and collaborate with others on exciting projects.

Virgo: The day starts with productivity, but as the energy shifts, you'll feel more inclined to engage in creative problem-solving.

Libra: Balance your responsibilities early in the day with the opportunity for creativity and social interaction in the evening.

Scorpio: It's a day for practical achievements, but by evening, allow yourself to explore new perspectives and embrace innovation.

Sagittarius: Practicality takes precedence early in the day, but as the energy shifts, you'll feel inspired to explore new ideas and social connections.

Capricorn: The Moon in your sign continues to emphasize discipline, but as the energy shifts, focus on creative solutions and innovative thinking.

Aquarius: The evening brings a burst of creative energy. Use this time to explore innovative ideas and connect with others in meaningful ways.

Pisces: The day starts with a focus on practical matters, but by evening, your creativity and intuition will be heightened. Use this energy to explore new ideas.

For those born on February 28: Born under the transition from Capricorn to Aquarius, these individuals are disciplined and focused but also creative and innovative. In 2025, they'll find success by balancing their practical mindset with their unique, forward-thinking ideas. It's a year for combining discipline with creativity.

Daily Insights: The Moon in Aquarius brings a focus on creativity, innovation, and social interactions. Today is perfect for exploring new ideas, connecting with others, and embracing your individuality. The Sun in Pisces continues to encourage intuition and emotional awareness, creating a balance between logic and intuition.

Aries: Your creativity shines today. Use this energy to explore new ideas and engage in meaningful social interactions.

Taurus: Innovation is key today. Focus on finding creative solutions to challenges, and don't be afraid to think outside the box.

Gemini: It's a great day for socializing and sharing your ideas. Use your communication skills to inspire and connect with others.

Cancer: Balance your emotional sensitivity with creativity today. Focus on expressing yourself through artistic or innovative projects.

Leo: Leadership and creativity are your strengths today. Take charge of a project that allows you to showcase your unique ideas.

Virgo: Your analytical skills are complemented by a burst of creativity today. Use this energy to solve problems in innovative ways.

Libra: Relationships take on an exciting, unconventional tone today. Embrace new ways of connecting with loved ones.

Scorpio: Your desire for personal growth is strong today. Use this energy to explore new ideas and engage in meaningful conversations.

Sagittarius: It's a great day for exploring new perspectives and embracing adventure. Focus on expanding your horizons through learning.

Capricorn: While discipline is important, today encourages you to explore new ideas and embrace a more creative approach to your goals.

Aquarius: With the Moon in your sign, your creativity and individuality are amplified. Use this energy to share your unique vision with the world.

Pisces: Your intuition is strong today. Use this energy to explore creative projects and connect with others in meaningful ways.

For those born on March 1: Born under the Moon in Aquarius, these individuals are creative, innovative, and socially connected. In 2025, they'll thrive by embracing their individuality and exploring new ideas. It's a year for creativity, social interactions, and personal growth.

Daily Insights: The Moon in Aquarius continues to amplify creativity, innovation, and social connections. However, as it transitions into Pisces later in the day, the focus shifts toward emotional reflection, intuition, and creativity. It's a day for balancing social engagement with introspection.

Aries: Use the morning for social interactions and creative projects. As the day progresses, focus on self-reflection and emotional well-being.

Taurus: The day begins with innovation and creativity, but later, you'll feel more inclined to focus on your inner world and emotional needs.

Gemini: Social interactions are stimulating early in the day, but by evening, you'll want to focus on self-care and emotional balance.

Cancer: Your intuition is heightened as the Moon moves into Pisces. Use this energy to focus on your emotional well-being and personal growth.

Leo: The day starts with creative energy, but later, you'll feel more introspective. Focus on nurturing your emotional health.

Virgo: Early in the day, focus on creative problem-solving, but as the evening approaches, shift your attention to self-reflection and emotional clarity.

Libra: Relationships are exciting early in the day, but later, focus on creating emotional balance and connecting with loved ones on a deeper level.

Scorpio: The energy of the day encourages you to explore new ideas, but by evening, you'll feel more introspective and focused on emotional healing.

Sagittarius: Adventure and learning dominate the morning, but by evening, focus on connecting with your inner self and exploring your emotions.

Capricorn: Use the day for creative thinking and innovation, but as the energy shifts, focus on grounding yourself emotionally.

Aquarius: The Moon in your sign continues to amplify your creativity, but by evening, focus on emotional reflection and self-care.

Pisces: As the Moon enters your sign, your intuition and emotional sensitivity are heightened. Use this energy to focus on personal growth and creativity.

For those born on March 2: Born under the transition from Aquarius to Pisces, these individuals are creative and innovative but also deeply intuitive and emotional. In 2025, they'll find fulfillment by balancing their unique ideas with emotional reflection and personal growth. It's a year for creativity and introspection.

Daily Insights: The Moon in Pisces encourages emotional reflection, creativity, and intuition. It's a great day for focusing on your inner world, engaging in creative projects, and nurturing your emotional well-being. With Venus in Aquarius, relationships take on a unique, unconventional tone.

Aries: Your intuition is strong today. Use this energy to focus on your emotional health and engage in creative projects.

Taurus: It's a good day for introspection. Focus on emotional well-being and creative expression to find balance in your life.

Gemini: Creativity and imagination are heightened today. Use this energy to express yourself artistically and connect with your inner world.

Cancer: Your emotions are deep today. Focus on self-care and nurturing your relationships, as well as your personal growth.

Leo: Today is perfect for self-reflection. Focus on your emotional needs and engage in creative projects that bring you joy.

Virgo: Your intuition is heightened, and it's a good day for emotional clarity. Focus on organizing your thoughts and emotions.

Libra: Relationships take on a deeper, more emotional tone today. Focus on nurturing your connections with loved ones.

Scorpio: Your emotional intensity is heightened today. Use this energy for personal reflection and creative exploration.

Sagittarius: After a period of adventure, it's time for emotional reflection. Focus on your inner world and personal growth.

Capricorn: Today encourages emotional introspection. Use this energy to explore your feelings and engage in creative projects.

Aquarius: While you're usually focused on innovation, today encourages emotional reflection. Focus on your inner self and explore creative outlets.

Pisces: With the Moon in your sign, your intuition and creativity are at their peak. Use this energy for self-reflection and emotional growth.

For those born on March 3: Born under the Moon in Pisces, these individuals are intuitive, creative, and deeply emotional. In 2025, they'll thrive by embracing their artistic talents and focusing on personal growth through emotional reflection. It's a year for self-discovery and creativity.

March 4, 2025

Daily Insights: The Moon in Pisces continues to amplify intuition, creativity, and emotional reflection. It's a day for focusing on your inner world, nurturing your relationships, and exploring artistic or spiritual pursuits. With Mars in Capricorn, there's also a push for balancing emotional reflection with disciplined action.

Aries: Your emotions are strong today. Use this energy to focus on self-reflection and balance it with practical steps toward your goals.

Taurus: It's a day for emotional introspection and creativity. Focus on your inner world and use your imagination to explore new ideas.

Gemini: Your creativity is heightened today. Use this energy to engage in artistic projects or reflect on your emotional needs.

Cancer: Your intuition is strong today. Focus on emotional healing and nurturing your relationships through deep, meaningful conversations.

Leo: It's a good day for self-reflection. Use your creative energy to explore your emotions and express yourself artistically.

Virgo: Emotional clarity comes through reflection today. Focus on organizing your thoughts and balancing emotional needs with practical actions.

Libra: Relationships take on a deeper, more emotional tone today. Use this energy to nurture your connections and focus on personal growth.

Scorpio: Your emotional depth is amplified today. Use this energy to reflect on personal matters and engage in creative or spiritual pursuits.

Sagittarius: Today encourages emotional exploration. Use this energy to reflect on your personal needs and focus on inner growth.

Capricorn: Balance your emotional reflection with disciplined action today. Focus on achieving your goals while staying in tune with your emotional needs.

Aquarius: While you're usually focused on innovation, today encourages emotional reflection and creativity. Focus on self-care and personal growth.

Pisces: With the Moon in your sign, your intuition and creativity are strong. Use this energy for self-reflection and artistic expression.

For those born on March 4: Those born under the Moon in Pisces are highly intuitive, emotional, and creative. In 2025, they'll thrive by focusing on emotional reflection and artistic pursuits. It's a year for personal growth and exploring their inner world through creativity.

Daily Insights: The Moon in Pisces continues to bring a focus on creativity, intuition, and emotional awareness. However, as the Moon transitions into Aries later in the day, the energy shifts toward action, motivation, and confidence. It's a day for balancing emotional reflection with decisive action.

Aries: The day starts with introspection, but as the Moon enters your sign, you'll feel a surge of energy and motivation to take action.

Taurus: It's a day for balancing emotional reflection with practical steps. As the energy shifts, focus on moving forward with confidence.

Gemini: The morning is perfect for creative reflection, but by evening, you'll feel energized to pursue new ideas and take action.

Cancer: Emotional reflection is important early in the day, but as the energy shifts, focus on taking bold steps toward personal goals.

Leo: The day begins with introspection, but by evening, your confidence will rise, making it a great time to take action on your passions.

Virgo: Use the morning for emotional clarity and reflection. As the day progresses, you'll feel ready to take practical action.

Libra: The energy starts off introspective, but later in the day, focus on moving forward with confidence and embracing new opportunities.

Scorpio: Emotional reflection is key early in the day, but as the energy shifts, focus on taking action and pursuing your goals with determination.

Sagittarius: The morning is ideal for emotional introspection, but by evening, you'll feel energized to embrace new adventures and opportunities.

Capricorn: Balance introspection with action today. As the energy shifts, focus on making progress toward your goals with renewed motivation.

Aquarius: The day starts with creativity and reflection, but by evening, you'll feel ready to take bold steps toward your unique vision.

Pisces: With the Moon in your sign early on, focus on emotional reflection, but as the energy shifts, embrace the opportunity for decisive action.

For those born on March 5: Born under the transition from Pisces to Aries, these individuals are both intuitive and action-oriented. In 2025, they'll thrive by balancing emotional reflection with decisive action, embracing both their creative side and their determination to achieve their goals.

Daily Insights: The Moon in Aries brings energy, motivation, and a strong desire for action. It's a day to take charge, pursue your goals with confidence, and focus on new beginnings. With Mars in Capricorn, there's also a sense of discipline, making it a great day for combining ambition with practicality.

Aries: You're feeling energized and ready to take action. Use today's motivation to pursue your goals with confidence and determination.

Taurus: It's a great day for taking practical steps toward your goals. Focus on making steady progress while embracing new opportunities.

Gemini: Your energy is high today. Use this to engage in exciting projects and take bold steps toward your personal growth.

Cancer: It's a day for taking charge. Don't hesitate to act on your ambitions and focus on achieving your goals.

Leo: You're feeling confident and ready to lead. Use this energy to inspire others and take bold steps toward your goals.

Virgo: Your disciplined nature will serve you well today. Focus on practical tasks and take action toward your long-term ambitions.

Libra: It's a good day for taking decisive action in your relationships. Focus on creating balance while pursuing your personal goals.

Scorpio: Your determination is strong today. Use this energy to focus on your goals and take bold steps toward achieving them.

Sagittarius: Adventure and excitement are calling you today. Embrace new opportunities and take action on your dreams.

Capricorn: Discipline and ambition are your strengths today. Use this energy to make significant progress toward your goals.

Aquarius: Innovation and action come together today. Focus on pushing your ideas forward with confidence and determination.

Pisces: You're feeling motivated to take action. Use today's energy to focus on your goals and make decisive progress.

For those born on March 6: Born under the Moon in Aries, these individuals are confident, action-oriented, and ambitious. In 2025, they'll thrive by taking bold steps toward their goals and embracing new opportunities with enthusiasm and determination.

Daily Insights: The Moon in Aries continues to fuel motivation, confidence, and a desire for action. It's a day for pursuing new opportunities, taking charge, and focusing on personal goals. With Venus in Aquarius, relationships may feel exciting and unconventional, encouraging you to embrace new ways of connecting.

Aries: Your confidence is high today. Use this energy to take bold steps toward achieving your personal goals.

Taurus: Today is all about taking action. Focus on practical steps that will bring you closer to your ambitions.

Gemini: It's a great day for engaging in exciting projects and exploring new opportunities. Use your energy to take action on your ideas.

Cancer: Your determination is strong today. Use this to focus on your goals and make significant progress toward achieving them.

Leo: You're feeling confident and ready to lead. Step into your role as a leader and inspire others to follow your vision.

Virgo: Your disciplined approach will help you make steady progress today. Focus on practical tasks and take action toward your long-term goals.

Libra: It's a day for balancing your relationships with your personal ambitions. Take action to create harmony while pursuing your goals.

Scorpio: Your determination and focus are your strengths today. Use this energy to push forward with your goals and ambitions.

Sagittarius: Adventure and action go hand in hand today. Embrace new opportunities and take bold steps toward your dreams.

Capricorn: Your disciplined nature will help you stay focused on your goals today. Use this energy to make significant progress.

Aquarius: Innovation and creativity are strong today. Use this energy to take action on your unique ideas and projects.

Pisces: You're feeling motivated to take charge of your personal goals. Use today's energy to make decisive progress toward your ambitions.

For those born on March 7: Born under the Moon in Aries, these individuals are action-oriented, confident, and ambitious. In 2025, they'll find success by pursuing new opportunities and taking decisive steps toward their goals. It's a year for bold moves and personal growth.

Daily Insights: The Moon moves into Taurus, bringing a shift from action to stability and practicality. It's a day for focusing on long-term goals, enjoying life's comforts, and grounding yourself in practical matters. With Mars in Capricorn, there's a strong sense of discipline and determination.

Aries: After a period of action, today's energy encourages you to slow down and focus on practical, long-term goals.

Taurus: The Moon in your sign enhances your sense of stability and groundedness. Use this energy to focus on personal growth and long-term plans.

Gemini: Today is about balancing your energy with practicality. Focus on organizing your ideas and taking steady steps toward your goals.

Cancer: It's a great day for focusing on home and family matters. Use the energy of the day to create stability and security in your personal life.

Leo: Your focus shifts to practical matters today. Take time to plan for the future and focus on long-term stability.

Virgo: Productivity and organization are key today. Use this energy to tackle tasks that require discipline and attention to detail.

Libra: Relationships feel stable and secure today. Focus on creating harmony and balance while enjoying the comforts of life.

Scorpio: Your determination is steady today. Focus on long-term goals and take practical steps to achieve them.

Sagittarius: It's a good day for grounding yourself. Focus on practical matters and enjoy the simple pleasures of life.

Capricorn: Your disciplined approach continues to serve you well. Focus on long-term goals and make steady progress today.

Aquarius: While you're often focused on innovation, today encourages you to focus on practical matters and personal stability.

Pisces: It's a good day for grounding your emotions and focusing on practical goals. Take time to reflect on your long-term plans.

For those born on March 8: Born under the Moon in Taurus, these individuals are grounded, practical, and focused on long-term success. In 2025, they'll thrive by focusing on stability, personal growth, and enjoying life's simple pleasures. It's a year for practical achievements and personal fulfillment.

Daily Insights: The Moon in Taurus continues to emphasize stability, patience, and practicality. It's a great day for focusing on long-term goals, managing finances, and enjoying life's comforts. The Sun in Pisces encourages a balance between practicality and emotional well-being.

Aries: Focus on long-term stability today. Use your practical mindset to make steady progress on your goals.

Taurus: The Moon in your sign enhances your natural strengths. Focus on personal growth, long-term goals, and enjoying life's comforts.

Gemini: Today is perfect for focusing on practical matters. Organize your thoughts and take steady steps toward your long-term plans.

Cancer: Emotional stability is important today. Focus on nurturing your relationships and creating a sense of security at home.

Leo: It's a day for balancing your ambition with practicality. Focus on long-term goals and ensure you're building a solid foundation.

Virgo: Productivity and attention to detail are your strengths today. Use this energy to focus on tasks that require discipline and organization.

Libra: Relationships feel stable and secure today. Focus on creating harmony in your connections while enjoying life's simple pleasures.

Scorpio: Your determination is strong today. Use this energy to focus on long-term goals and make steady progress.

Sagittarius: It's a day for grounding yourself and focusing on practical matters. Take time to reflect on your long-term plans.

Capricorn: Your disciplined nature continues to serve you well. Focus on long-term stability and make practical decisions for your future.

Aquarius: Today encourages you to balance your creativity with practicality. Focus on building a solid foundation for your ideas.

Pisces: Emotional reflection is key today. Use the energy to focus on your long-term goals and create stability in your personal life.

For those born on March 9: Born under the Moon in Taurus, these individuals are practical, patient, and focused on stability. In 2025, they'll thrive by setting long-term goals and working steadily toward them. It's a year for personal growth and enjoying life's simple pleasures.

Daily Insights: The Moon in Taurus continues to bring a focus on stability, long-term goals, and practical matters. However, as it transitions into Gemini later in the day, the energy shifts toward curiosity, communication, and learning. It's a great day to balance practical tasks with mental stimulation.

Aries: Focus on practical matters early in the day, but later, embrace new ideas and engage in stimulating conversations.

Taurus: The day starts with a focus on stability, but by evening, you'll feel more curious and open to learning new things.

Gemini: The Moon enters your sign later in the day, bringing a burst of mental energy. It's a great time to share ideas and explore new topics.

Cancer: The day begins with a focus on emotional stability, but as the energy shifts, engage in social interactions and explore new perspectives.

Leo: It's a day for balancing practical matters with curiosity. Focus on long-term goals in the morning, but later, embrace new ideas.

Virgo: Productivity is high early in the day, but by evening, you'll feel more inclined to engage in social interactions and learning.

Libra: Relationships feel stable early in the day, but as the energy shifts, focus on communication and exploring new ideas with loved ones.

Scorpio: Your determination is strong in the morning, but later, you'll feel more curious and open to new perspectives.

Sagittarius: The day starts with a focus on practical matters, but by evening, you'll feel energized to explore new ideas and engage with others.

Capricorn: Discipline and focus are key early in the day, but as the energy shifts, you'll feel more inclined to explore new ways of thinking.

Aquarius: Practicality dominates the morning, but by evening, you'll feel more curious and eager to engage in conversations and learning.

Pisces: Emotional reflection is important early in the day, but later, focus on exploring new ideas and connecting with others in meaningful ways.

For those born on March 10: Born under the transition from Taurus to Gemini, these individuals are both practical and curious, balancing stability with a desire for learning. In 2025, they'll find success by embracing new ideas while staying grounded in their long-term goals.

Daily Insights: The Moon in Gemini brings a focus on communication, curiosity, and learning. Today is perfect for engaging in stimulating conversations, exploring new ideas, and connecting with others. The Sun in Pisces continues to emphasize intuition and emotional awareness, making it a day for balancing logic with feelings.

Aries: Your mind is sharp today. Use this energy to explore new ideas and engage in meaningful conversations.

Taurus: Curiosity drives you today. Focus on learning something new or engaging in discussions that challenge your usual way of thinking.

Gemini: The Moon in your sign enhances your communication skills. It's a great day to express yourself and connect with others.

Cancer: Balance your emotions with logic today. Engage in conversations that help you gain new perspectives while staying true to your feelings.

Leo: Your leadership skills are amplified through communication today. Focus on sharing your ideas and inspiring those around you.

Virgo: It's a great day for problem-solving. Use your analytical skills to explore new solutions and refine your plans.

Libra: Relationships take on a dynamic tone today. Engage in conversations that allow you to share your thoughts and strengthen your connections.

Scorpio: You're feeling curious and introspective today. Use this energy to explore new ideas and reflect on your personal growth.

Sagittarius: Adventure and learning go hand in hand today. Focus on expanding your knowledge and engaging in stimulating discussions.

Capricorn: It's a day for communication and planning. Use your practical mindset to organize your thoughts and take action on your ideas.

Aquarius: Your innovative ideas shine today. Use this energy to engage with others, share your thoughts, and explore new possibilities.

Pisces: While your intuition is strong, today encourages you to use logic to solve problems and engage in meaningful conversations.

For those born on March 11: Born under the Moon in Gemini, these individuals are curious, communicative, and intellectually driven. In 2025, they'll thrive by exploring new ideas, engaging in learning opportunities, and using their communication skills to connect with others.

Daily Insights: The Moon in Gemini continues to emphasize communication, learning, and curiosity. It's a day for sharing ideas, engaging in conversations, and expanding your mental horizons. With Mercury in Pisces, there's a balance between logic and intuition, making it a day for creative thinking and problem-solving.

Aries: Your curiosity is strong today. Use this energy to explore new ideas and engage in conversations that broaden your perspective.

Taurus: It's a good day for learning and communication. Focus on practical matters while staying open to new insights and ideas.

Gemini: The Moon in your sign keeps your energy high. Use this time to connect with others and share your unique ideas.

Cancer: Balance your emotions with logic today. Focus on communicating clearly and using your intuition to guide your decisions.

Leo: It's a great day for sharing your thoughts and leading conversations. Your ideas will inspire others, so don't hesitate to speak up.

Virgo: Problem-solving comes easily today. Use your analytical skills to tackle challenges and come up with creative solutions.

Libra: Social interactions are lively today. Engage in meaningful conversations and focus on strengthening your connections.

Scorpio: Your mind is sharp today. Use this energy to reflect on your personal growth and explore new ideas.

Sagittarius: It's a day for expanding your knowledge. Use your curiosity to explore new subjects and engage with others who inspire you.

Capricorn: Practical thinking is your strength today. Use this energy to organize your ideas and make progress on your goals.

Aquarius: Your innovative ideas shine today. Use this energy to share your thoughts and collaborate with others on exciting projects.

Pisces: Your intuition is heightened today. Use this energy to balance logic with creativity and engage in thoughtful discussions.

For those born on March 12: Born under the Moon in Gemini, these individuals are intellectually curious, communicative, and adaptable. In 2025, they'll find fulfillment by exploring new ideas, learning from others, and using their sharp minds to solve problems and engage with the world.

Daily Insights: The Moon moves into Cancer, shifting the focus toward emotional well-being, home life, and nurturing relationships. It's a day for self-care, connecting with loved ones, and focusing on creating emotional security. The Sun in Pisces continues to amplify intuition, making it a great day for emotional reflection and growth.

Aries: You may feel more sensitive than usual today. Focus on nurturing your emotional well-being and connecting with loved ones.

Taurus: It's a day for focusing on home and family. Use this energy to create a sense of stability and comfort in your personal life.

Gemini: After a period of mental stimulation, today encourages you to focus on your emotional needs and personal relationships.

Cancer: With the Moon in your sign, your emotional intuition is heightened. It's a good day for self-care and nurturing your close relationships.

Leo: Emotional balance is key today. Focus on creating harmony in your home life and nurturing your personal relationships.

Virgo: It's a day for reflection and emotional clarity. Use this energy to connect with your inner self and focus on personal growth.

Libra: Relationships take on a deeper, more emotional tone today. Focus on nurturing your connections and creating harmony in your personal life.

Scorpio: Your emotional intensity is heightened today. Use this energy for self-reflection and deepening your connections with others.

Sagittarius: It's a day for focusing on your personal life. Use this energy to nurture your home environment and create emotional stability.

Capricorn: Emotional reflection is key today. Take time to focus on your well-being and strengthen your relationships with loved ones.

Aquarius: While you're often focused on innovation, today encourages you to reflect on your emotional needs and focus on personal growth.

Pisces: Your intuition is strong today. Use this energy to focus on emotional healing, self-care, and nurturing your relationships.

For those born on March 13: Born under the Moon in Cancer, these individuals are nurturing, emotionally intuitive, and deeply connected to their home and family. In 2025, they'll find fulfillment by focusing on their emotional well-being, strengthening relationships, and creating stability in their personal life.

Daily Insights: The Moon in Cancer continues to emphasize emotional well-being, nurturing relationships, and focusing on home life. Today is ideal for self-care, spending time with loved ones, and creating a sense of security in your environment. The Sun in Pisces encourages deep emotional reflection and creativity.

Aries: You may feel emotionally sensitive today. Focus on nurturing your emotional well-being and connecting with family and friends.

Taurus: It's a day for focusing on home and family. Use this energy to create a sense of comfort and stability in your personal life.

Gemini: After a period of mental activity, today is a good day for emotional reflection and nurturing your close relationships.

Cancer: The Moon in your sign continues to heighten your emotional intuition. Focus on self-care and strengthening your bonds with loved ones.

Leo: Balance is key today. Focus on creating harmony in your personal life and nurturing the relationships that matter most.

Virgo: It's a day for emotional clarity and reflection. Use this energy to connect with your inner self and focus on personal growth.

Libra: Relationships take on a deeper, more emotional tone today. Focus on nurturing your connections and creating harmony in your personal life.

Scorpio: Your emotional depth is heightened today. Use this energy for self-reflection and deepening your relationships with those you care about.

Sagittarius: Today encourages emotional balance. Focus on your home environment and nurture your relationships to create stability.

Capricorn: It's a day for focusing on emotional well-being. Take time to nurture your personal relationships and create a sense of harmony.

Aquarius: Emotional reflection is key today. Use this energy to connect with your inner self and focus on nurturing your relationships.

Pisces: Your intuition is strong today. Use this energy for self-reflection and emotional healing, and focus on nurturing your loved ones.

For those born on March 14: Born under the Moon in Cancer, these individuals are emotionally intuitive, nurturing, and deeply connected to their home and family. In 2025, they'll thrive by focusing on emotional well-being, personal growth, and strengthening their relationships with loved ones.

Daily Insights: The Moon in Cancer continues to bring a focus on emotional well-being, home life, and nurturing relationships. However, as it transitions into Leo later in the day, the energy shifts toward self-expression, creativity, and confidence. It's a day for balancing emotional reflection with personal empowerment.

Aries: Focus on your emotional well-being in the morning, but as the day progresses, embrace your confidence and take action on personal goals.

Taurus: It's a day for balancing emotional reflection with creativity. Use the morning to focus on home and family, and later, express yourself through creative pursuits.

Gemini: The day starts with emotional reflection, but as the energy shifts, you'll feel more inclined to engage in social activities and share your ideas.

Cancer: The Moon in your sign encourages emotional self-care, but later in the day, you'll feel energized to focus on personal growth and creativity.

Leo: Your emotional intuition is strong in the morning, but as the Moon enters your sign later in the day, your confidence will rise. It's a great day for self-expression and pursuing your passions.

Virgo: Focus on emotional clarity in the morning, but later, you'll feel more inclined to engage in creative problem-solving and personal projects.

Libra: The morning is perfect for nurturing relationships, but by evening, focus on expressing yourself and embracing your individuality.

Scorpio: Emotional reflection is key in the morning, but as the day progresses, you'll feel more energized to pursue your goals with confidence.

Sagittarius: The day starts with a focus on personal well-being, but later, embrace your adventurous side and pursue new opportunities with enthusiasm.

Capricorn: Balance emotional reflection with personal growth today. Use the morning to focus on nurturing your relationships, and later, pursue your goals with confidence.

Aquarius: Emotional reflection is important in the morning, but by evening, you'll feel more inclined to express your creativity and connect with others.

Pisces: Your intuition is heightened in the morning, but as the energy shifts, focus on expressing yourself creatively and embracing your personal power.

For those born on March 15: Born under the transition from Cancer to Leo, these individuals are nurturing and emotionally intuitive, but also confident and creative. In 2025, they'll thrive by balancing their emotional well-being with personal empowerment and self-expression.

Daily Insights: The Moon in Leo brings a focus on self-expression, creativity, and confidence. It's a day to shine, embrace leadership, and pursue your passions. With Mars in Capricorn, there's also a sense of discipline and determination, making it a great day for combining ambition with creativity.

Aries: Your confidence is high today. Use this energy to take bold steps toward your goals and embrace leadership opportunities.

Taurus: Creativity flows easily today. Use this energy to focus on personal projects and express yourself through your work or hobbies.

Gemini: It's a great day for social interactions and sharing your ideas. Use your communication skills to inspire and connect with others.

Cancer: Your emotions are strong today, but focus on expressing yourself confidently and pursuing what you're passionate about.

Leo: The Moon in your sign amplifies your natural charisma and creativity. It's a perfect day to step into the spotlight and lead with confidence.

Virgo: Balance creativity with practicality today. Use your disciplined nature to focus on long-term goals while expressing your unique talents.

Libra: Relationships take on an exciting tone today. Focus on creative ways to connect with loved ones and embrace your individuality.

Scorpio: Your passion is strong today. Use this energy to pursue your personal goals with intensity and determination.

Sagittarius: Adventure and creativity are calling you today. Use this energy to explore new possibilities and express your ideas freely.

Capricorn: Leadership and discipline come naturally today. Use this energy to focus on personal projects and inspire those around you.

Aquarius: Your creativity shines today. Use this energy to pursue innovative ideas and share your unique perspective with others.

Pisces: It's a day for self-expression and personal growth. Use your creativity to focus on your goals and embrace new opportunities.

For those born on March 16: Born under the Moon in Leo, these individuals are confident, creative, and charismatic. In 2025, they'll thrive by stepping into leadership roles, embracing their talents, and pursuing their passions with determination and enthusiasm.

Daily Insights: The Moon in Leo continues to emphasize creativity, confidence, and leadership. It's a day for pursuing personal goals, expressing yourself, and embracing your talents. With Venus in Aquarius, relationships may take on an exciting, unconventional tone, encouraging you to connect with others in unique ways.

Aries: You're feeling bold and ready to take action. Use today's energy to focus on personal goals and embrace leadership opportunities.

Taurus: Your creativity is strong today. Focus on personal projects that allow you to express yourself and showcase your talents.

Gemini: It's a day for sharing your ideas and engaging in social interactions. Use your communication skills to inspire those around you.

Cancer: Your confidence is high today. Use this energy to pursue your passions and express your emotions in creative ways.

Leo: The Moon in your sign continues to amplify your charisma and creativity. It's a great day for taking charge and pursuing your dreams.

Virgo: Balance your disciplined nature with creativity today. Focus on long-term goals while expressing your unique talents.

Libra: Relationships feel dynamic and exciting today. Use this energy to connect with others in creative and unconventional ways.

Scorpio: Your determination is strong today. Use this energy to focus on your personal goals and pursue them with passion.

Sagittarius: It's a great day for exploring new ideas and expressing your creativity. Use this energy to embrace new opportunities.

Capricorn: Leadership and determination come easily today. Use this energy to focus on personal projects and inspire those around you.

Aquarius: Your innovative ideas shine today. Use this energy to pursue creative projects and connect with others in meaningful ways.

Pisces: It's a day for self-expression and creativity. Use your talents to focus on personal growth and pursue your goals with confidence.

For those born on March 17: Born under the Moon in Leo, these individuals are creative, confident, and natural leaders. In 2025, they'll thrive by embracing their talents, pursuing their passions, and stepping into leadership roles with enthusiasm.

Daily Insights: The Moon transitions into Virgo, shifting the focus from creativity and self-expression to practicality, organization, and attention to detail. It's a day for focusing on productivity, refining your plans, and tackling tasks that require discipline. With Mercury in Pisces, there's a balance between logic and intuition.

Aries: It's a day for focusing on practical matters. Use your energy to tackle tasks that require discipline and attention to detail.

Taurus: Your productivity is high today. Use this energy to focus on long-term goals and organize your thoughts and plans.

Gemini: After a period of creativity, today encourages you to focus on practical tasks. Use your analytical skills to refine your ideas.

Cancer: It's a good day for focusing on your personal well-being and organizing your home environment. Use this energy to create stability in your life.

Leo: After a burst of creative energy, today encourages you to focus on practical matters. Use your discipline to work toward your long-term goals.

Virgo: The Moon in your sign enhances your natural strengths. Use this energy to organize your tasks and focus on productivity.

Libra: It's a day for balancing relationships with practical responsibilities. Focus on creating harmony while tackling necessary tasks.

Scorpio: Your determination is strong today. Use this energy to focus on refining your plans and making steady progress toward your goals.

Sagittarius: Practical matters take precedence today. Use this energy to focus on your responsibilities and organize your thoughts.

Capricorn: Discipline and focus come naturally today. Use this energy to tackle long-term projects and make steady progress.

Aquarius: While you're often focused on innovation, today encourages you to focus on practical tasks and refine your plans.

Pisces: Your intuition is strong, but today's energy encourages you to balance creativity with practical thinking. Use this time to organize your thoughts and plans.

For those born on March 18: Born under the Moon in Virgo, these individuals are practical, organized, and detail-oriented. In 2025, they'll find success by focusing on productivity, refining their plans, and making steady progress toward their goals.

Daily Insights: The Moon in Virgo continues to emphasize productivity, organization, and attention to detail. It's a day for focusing on practical tasks, refining your routines, and making progress on long-term goals. With the Sun in Pisces, there's a balance between logic and creativity, making it a great day for problem-solving.

Aries: It's a day for focusing on productivity. Use your discipline to tackle tasks that require attention to detail and organization.

Taurus: Your practical mindset is strong today. Use this energy to focus on long-term goals and refine your plans for the future.

Gemini: Today encourages you to focus on practical tasks and organization. Use your analytical skills to solve problems and make progress.

Cancer: It's a good day for focusing on your personal well-being and creating structure in your life. Use this energy to organize your thoughts and environment.

Leo: Practicality is key today. Use your discipline to focus on long-term goals and ensure that your plans are well-organized.

Virgo: The Moon in your sign enhances your productivity. Use this energy to focus on your goals and tackle tasks that require precision.

Libra: Balance is important today. Focus on practical matters while ensuring that your relationships are harmonious and supportive.

Scorpio: Your determination is strong today. Use this energy to refine your plans and make steady progress toward achieving your goals.

Sagittarius: Practical matters take priority today. Use this energy to focus on your responsibilities and ensure that your plans are well-organized.

Capricorn: Discipline and focus are your strengths today. Use this energy to make significant progress on your long-term projects.

Aquarius: While you're often focused on big ideas, today encourages you to focus on the details and ensure that your plans are practical.

Pisces: Your intuition is heightened, but today encourages you to balance creativity with practicality. Use this energy to organize your thoughts and focus on your goals.

For those born on March 19: Born under the Moon in Virgo, these individuals are practical, disciplined, and detail-oriented. In 2025, they'll thrive by focusing on productivity, refining their routines, and making steady progress toward their long-term goals.

Daily Insights: The Moon in Virgo continues to bring a focus on productivity and organization, but as the Moon transitions into Libra later in the day, the energy shifts toward balance, relationships, and harmony. It's a day for balancing practical tasks with social interactions and personal connections.

Aries: Focus on productivity in the morning, but as the day progresses, shift your attention to relationships and finding balance in your life.

Taurus: The day begins with a focus on practical matters, but later, you'll feel more inclined to engage in social interactions and nurture your relationships.

Gemini: Your productivity is high early in the day, but by evening, focus on connecting with others and creating harmony in your personal life.

Cancer: It's a day for balancing work and relationships. Start by focusing on your responsibilities, but later, shift your attention to your personal connections.

Leo: Practical matters dominate the morning, but as the energy shifts, focus on finding balance between your goals and your relationships.

Virgo: The Moon in your sign enhances your productivity, but by evening, you'll feel more inclined to focus on social interactions and harmony.

Libra: The day starts with a focus on productivity, but as the Moon moves into your sign, you'll feel energized to focus on relationships and balance.

Scorpio: Focus on practical tasks early in the day, but later, you'll feel more inclined to engage in meaningful connections with others.

Sagittarius: It's a day for balancing responsibilities with social interactions. Start by tackling tasks, and later, focus on your relationships.

Capricorn: Discipline and productivity are your strengths today. Use the morning to make progress on your goals, but by evening, shift your focus to creating balance in your personal life.

Aquarius: While you're focused on practical matters in the morning, the evening encourages you to focus on your relationships and finding harmony.

Pisces: Your creativity is balanced with practicality today. Use the morning for organization, but by evening, focus on social interactions and personal growth.

For those born on March 20: Born under the transition from Virgo to Libra, these individuals are practical and organized but also focused on balance and harmony in their relationships. In 2025, they'll thrive by balancing their personal goals with their social connections, ensuring that both are nurtured.

Daily Insights: The Moon in Libra brings a focus on balance, relationships, and harmony. It's a great day for social interactions, resolving conflicts, and creating equilibrium in your personal and professional life. With the Sun entering Aries, there's also a sense of renewed energy and enthusiasm for taking action and pursuing goals.

Aries: The Sun enters your sign today, bringing a burst of energy and motivation. Use this time to focus on your goals while maintaining balance in your relationships.

Taurus: It's a day for creating harmony in your personal life. Focus on balancing your responsibilities with self-care and nurturing your relationships.

Gemini: Social interactions are lively today. Engage in conversations that help you connect with others and find common ground.

Cancer: Focus on balancing your home life and professional responsibilities. It's a good day for resolving any conflicts and creating harmony in your environment.

Leo: Relationships take center stage today. Use your natural charisma to connect with others and create a sense of balance in your interactions.

Virgo: It's a day for balancing work and personal life. Focus on creating harmony in your daily routine and nurturing your relationships.

Libra: With the Moon in your sign, you're feeling the need for balance and harmony. Focus on your relationships and personal well-being.

Scorpio: Today encourages you to find balance in your emotional life. Reflect on your relationships and work toward creating harmony.

Sagittarius: Social interactions are key today. Focus on connecting with friends and loved ones while maintaining balance in your responsibilities.

Capricorn: Balance is the theme of the day. Focus on creating harmony between your career and personal life, ensuring that both are nurtured.

Aquarius: It's a day for exploring new ideas and connecting with others. Use your innovative thinking to find balance in your personal and professional life.

Pisces: Emotional balance is important today. Focus on self-care and nurturing your relationships to create harmony in your life.

For those born on March 21: Born under the transition from Pisces to Aries, these individuals are both intuitive and action-oriented. In 2025, they'll thrive by balancing their emotional sensitivity with the drive to take action on their goals. It's a year for personal growth and finding harmony in their relationships.

March 22, 2025

Daily Insights: The Moon in Libra continues to emphasize balance, relationships, and harmony, but with the Sun now fully in Aries, there's also a strong sense of motivation and action. Today is ideal for focusing on your personal goals while maintaining balance in your relationships and social interactions.

Aries: You're feeling energized and ready to take action on your goals. Just be sure to balance your personal ambitions with your relationships.

Taurus: It's a day for focusing on harmony in your home and personal life. Use your practical nature to create balance between your responsibilities and self-care.

Gemini: Social interactions are highlighted today. Engage with others in meaningful ways while also focusing on your personal goals.

Cancer: Balance is key today. Focus on creating harmony between your professional life and your personal relationships.

Leo: Your leadership skills are in the spotlight today. Use your confidence to inspire others while maintaining balance in your personal life.

Virgo: It's a day for balancing your work and personal life. Focus on creating harmony in your daily routine and nurturing your relationships.

Libra: The Moon in your sign continues to enhance your need for balance and harmony. Focus on your relationships and personal well-being.

Scorpio: Emotional balance is important today. Reflect on your relationships and work toward resolving any conflicts in a harmonious way.

Sagittarius: Socializing is favored today, but make sure to balance your responsibilities with time for friends and loved ones.

Capricorn: Focus on balancing your career and personal life. Use today's energy to create harmony in both areas and ensure you're giving attention to your relationships.

Aquarius: It's a great day for exploring new ideas and connecting with others. Use your innovative thinking to create balance in your personal and professional life.

Pisces: Emotional reflection is important today. Focus on nurturing your relationships and creating harmony in your life.

For those born on March 22: Born under the Moon in Libra, these individuals are focused on balance, harmony, and relationships. In 2025, they'll thrive by creating equilibrium in their personal and professional lives while pursuing their goals with enthusiasm and determination.

Daily Insights: The Moon transitions into Scorpio, bringing a focus on emotional intensity, transformation, and deep connections. It's a day for introspection, exploring your inner world, and focusing on personal transformation. With Mars in Capricorn, there's also an emphasis on discipline and long-term goals.

Aries: Your emotions are deep today. Use this energy for self-reflection and focus on personal transformation while staying disciplined in your goals.

Taurus: Emotional intensity is high today. Focus on nurturing your close relationships and exploring your inner world.

Gemini: It's a day for deep conversations and emotional reflection. Use your communication skills to connect with others on a deeper level.

Cancer: Your intuition is strong today. Focus on personal transformation and emotional healing while staying disciplined in your responsibilities.

Leo: Emotional depth is heightened today. Use this energy to explore your personal growth and strengthen your emotional connections.

Virgo: It's a day for introspection and self-reflection. Use your analytical skills to explore your inner world and focus on emotional growth.

Libra: Relationships take on a deeper tone today. Focus on emotional connections and work toward creating stronger, more meaningful bonds.

Scorpio: With the Moon in your sign, you're feeling emotionally intense. Use this energy for personal transformation and emotional healing.

Sagittarius: It's a day for focusing on your inner world. Use this energy to explore your emotions and focus on personal growth.

Capricorn: Your determination is strong today. Use this energy to focus on long-term goals while also exploring your emotional needs.

Aquarius: Emotional reflection is key today. Use your innovative thinking to explore your feelings and focus on personal transformation.

Pisces: Your intuition is heightened, making it a good day for self-reflection. Use this energy to focus on emotional healing and growth.

For those born on March 23: Born under the Moon in Scorpio, these individuals are deeply emotional, intuitive, and transformative. In 2025, they'll thrive by focusing on personal transformation, emotional healing, and deepening their connections with others. It's a year for self-reflection and inner growth.

Daily Insights: The Moon in Scorpio continues to bring emotional intensity, depth, and a focus on transformation. It's a great day for self-reflection, exploring personal growth, and diving deep into your emotions. With the Sun in Aries, there's also a sense of drive and motivation to pursue your goals.

Aries: Your emotional depth is strong today. Use this energy to reflect on your personal goals and explore areas of emotional growth.

Taurus: It's a day for focusing on your close relationships. Use your emotional intuition to strengthen your connections and foster deeper bonds.

Gemini: Deep conversations are favored today. Use your communication skills to explore emotional topics and connect with others on a deeper level.

Cancer: Your emotions are intense today. Use this energy for self-reflection and emotional healing while staying focused on your personal goals.

Leo: It's a day for personal transformation. Use your confidence to explore your emotional needs and work on personal growth.

Virgo: Focus on introspection and emotional clarity today. Use your analytical skills to explore your inner world and work toward personal transformation.

Libra: Relationships take on a deeper tone today. Focus on creating emotional connections and working through any unresolved issues.

Scorpio: The Moon in your sign continues to amplify your emotional intensity. Use this energy for self-reflection and personal growth.

Sagittarius: Emotional reflection is key today. Use this time to explore your inner world and focus on personal transformation.

Capricorn: Your discipline is strong today. Use this energy to focus on long-term goals while also exploring your emotional needs.

Aquarius: It's a day for emotional introspection. Use your innovative thinking to explore your feelings and work toward emotional growth.

Pisces: Your intuition is heightened today. Use this energy for emotional healing and personal transformation.

For those born on March 24: Born under the Moon in Scorpio, these individuals are emotionally intense, intuitive, and focused on personal transformation. In 2025, they'll find success by embracing their emotional depth and focusing on self-reflection and growth. It's a year for inner healing and strengthening relationships.

Daily Insights: The Moon transitions into Sagittarius, bringing a shift from emotional introspection to adventure, optimism, and exploration. It's a day for pursuing new opportunities, expanding your horizons, and focusing on personal growth. With the Sun in Aries, there's a strong sense of motivation and drive to take action.

Aries: Your adventurous spirit is strong today. Use this energy to pursue new opportunities and take bold steps toward your goals.

Taurus: After a period of emotional introspection, today encourages you to explore new experiences and expand your horizons.

Gemini: It's a day for learning and exploration. Use your curiosity to engage with new ideas and connect with others in exciting ways.

Cancer: Adventure and optimism are calling you today. Use this energy to explore new possibilities and embrace personal growth.

Leo: Your confidence is high today. Use this energy to pursue new opportunities and take bold steps toward achieving your goals.

Virgo: It's a day for expanding your horizons. Use your practical mindset to explore new ideas and focus on personal growth.

Libra: Social interactions are lively today. Use this energy to connect with others, share your ideas, and explore new perspectives.

Scorpio: After a period of emotional intensity, today encourages you to focus on new opportunities and embrace adventure.

Sagittarius: The Moon in your sign amplifies your sense of adventure and optimism. It's a great day to explore new possibilities and pursue your passions.

Capricorn: While discipline is important, today encourages you to explore new ideas and take action on opportunities that excite you.

Aquarius: Your innovative ideas shine today. Use this energy to explore new possibilities and share your unique perspective with others.

Pisces: It's a day for adventure and personal growth. Use your intuition to guide you as you explore new opportunities and embrace change.

For those born on March 25: Born under the Moon in Sagittarius, these individuals are adventurous, optimistic, and eager to explore new possibilities. In 2025, they'll thrive by embracing opportunities for personal growth, learning, and expanding their horizons. It's a year for adventure and exploration.

Daily Insights: The Moon in Sagittarius continues to inspire adventure, optimism, and personal growth. It's a great day to explore new ideas, expand your horizons, and embrace opportunities for learning and self-discovery. With the Sun in Aries, there's an added boost of energy and motivation to take action on your goals.

Aries: Your adventurous spirit is high today. Use this energy to pursue new opportunities and take bold steps toward personal growth.

Taurus: It's a day for stepping out of your comfort zone. Explore new possibilities and embrace change with optimism.

Gemini: Curiosity drives you today. Use this energy to engage in stimulating conversations and explore new ideas.

Cancer: Adventure and personal growth are calling you today. Focus on expanding your horizons and embracing new experiences.

Leo: Your confidence is amplified today. Use this energy to lead with enthusiasm and explore new opportunities for growth.

Virgo: It's a great day for learning and personal development. Use your practical mindset to explore new topics and ideas.

Libra: Social interactions are exciting today. Engage in conversations that inspire new perspectives and broaden your worldview.

Scorpio: Adventure and optimism are your guides today. Embrace the unknown and focus on personal growth and self-discovery.

Sagittarius: The Moon in your sign enhances your natural adventurous spirit. It's a perfect day for pursuing your passions and exploring new possibilities.

Capricorn: It's a day for stepping away from your usual routine and exploring new opportunities. Use this energy to grow personally and professionally.

Aquarius: Your innovative thinking shines today. Use this energy to explore new possibilities and share your unique perspective with others.

Pisces: Personal growth is highlighted today. Use your intuition to guide you as you explore new experiences and embrace change.

For those born on March 26: Born under the Moon in Sagittarius, these individuals are adventurous, optimistic, and eager for personal growth. In 2025, they'll thrive by embracing new opportunities, learning, and expanding their horizons. It's a year for exploration and self-discovery.

Daily Insights: The Moon in Sagittarius continues to bring a sense of optimism, adventure, and curiosity. However, as the day progresses, the Moon transitions into Capricorn, shifting the focus toward discipline, practicality, and long-term goals. It's a day for balancing adventure with responsibility.

Aries: Start the day with adventure and optimism, but as the energy shifts, focus on setting practical goals and taking action to achieve them.

Taurus: The morning encourages you to explore new ideas, but by evening, you'll feel more inclined to focus on discipline and long-term planning.

Gemini: Use the morning for social interactions and learning, but later, shift your attention to practical tasks and organizing your goals.

Cancer: Adventure and optimism dominate the early part of the day, but as the Moon moves into Capricorn, focus on creating stability in your life.

Leo: The day begins with excitement and exploration, but as the energy shifts, focus on practical steps toward your long-term goals.

Virgo: Use the morning for exploration and personal growth, but by evening, shift your focus to organization and productivity.

Libra: Socializing is exciting early in the day, but as the energy shifts, focus on finding balance between your responsibilities and relationships.

Scorpio: It's a day for balancing optimism with discipline. Start with exploration, but later, focus on your long-term plans and goals.

Sagittarius: The Moon in your sign gives you a burst of energy, but as it transitions into Capricorn, focus on grounding yourself and setting practical goals.

Capricorn: Your adventurous spirit shines in the morning, but as the Moon enters your sign, discipline and focus on long-term goals take over.

Aquarius: Use the early part of the day for exploration, but later, focus on practical steps toward achieving your goals and staying disciplined.

Pisces: The day begins with exploration and optimism, but as the energy shifts, focus on grounding yourself and setting clear, achievable goals.

For those born on March 27: Born under the transition from Sagittarius to Capricorn, these individuals are both adventurous and disciplined. In 2025, they'll thrive by balancing their desire for exploration with their need for stability and long-term success. It's a year for growth through both adventure and responsibility.

March 28, 2025

Daily Insights: The Moon in Capricorn emphasizes discipline, practicality, and long-term planning. It's a great day for setting clear goals, focusing on productivity, and making progress in your personal and professional life. With Mars in Capricorn, there's an added boost of determination and focus.

Aries: Focus on your long-term goals today. Use your energy to make steady progress toward achieving your ambitions.

Taurus: It's a day for discipline and productivity. Focus on practical matters and take steps toward your long-term success.

Gemini: Your practical mindset is strong today. Use this energy to organize your thoughts and work on long-term plans.

Cancer: Emotional stability is important today. Focus on creating structure in your personal life and making progress on your goals.

Leo: Leadership and discipline are your strengths today. Use this energy to focus on long-term ambitions and inspire others to follow your lead.

Virgo: Productivity is high today. Use this energy to focus on tasks that require attention to detail and long-term planning.

Libra: It's a day for finding balance between your personal life and responsibilities. Focus on creating harmony while staying productive.

Scorpio: Your determination is strong today. Use this energy to focus on your long-term goals and make steady progress.

Sagittarius: While adventure is important, today encourages you to focus on grounding yourself and working toward practical goals.

Capricorn: The Moon in your sign enhances your natural discipline and determination. Use this energy to make significant progress on your long-term goals.

Aquarius: Focus on practical matters today. Use your innovative thinking to find solutions that will benefit you in the long run.

Pisces: It's a good day for grounding your emotions and focusing on practical goals. Use today's energy to work on projects that require discipline.

For those born on March 28: Born under the Moon in Capricorn, these individuals are disciplined, practical, and focused on long-term success. In 2025, they'll thrive by setting clear goals and working steadily toward achieving them. It's a year for personal growth through discipline and determination.

Daily Insights: The Moon in Capricorn continues to emphasize discipline, productivity, and long-term planning. However, as the Moon transitions into Aquarius later in the day, the energy shifts toward creativity, innovation, and social connections. It's a day for balancing practicality with creativity.

Aries: Use the morning for disciplined work and focus on your goals, but as the day progresses, embrace new ideas and social connections.

Taurus: The day starts with a focus on practical matters, but by evening, you'll feel more inclined to explore creative and innovative ideas.

Gemini: Productivity is high early in the day, but later, shift your focus to engaging in conversations that stimulate your mind and inspire new ideas.

Cancer: Focus on creating stability in the morning, but as the energy shifts, explore new ways to express your creativity and connect with others.

Leo: Leadership and discipline are key early in the day, but as the energy shifts, focus on social interactions and exploring new possibilities.

Virgo: It's a productive day for organizing your life, but later, embrace creativity and explore new ways to approach your tasks.

Libra: The day starts with a focus on productivity, but by evening, you'll feel more inclined to engage in social activities and explore innovative ideas.

Scorpio: Determination and discipline guide you early in the day, but as the energy shifts, focus on creative solutions and expanding your horizons.

Sagittarius: While productivity is important, today encourages you to embrace new ideas and engage with others in meaningful conversations.

Capricorn: The Moon in your sign continues to enhance your discipline, but by evening, focus on social connections and innovative thinking.

Aquarius: The evening brings a burst of creative energy. Use this time to explore innovative ideas and connect with others in meaningful ways.

Pisces: The day begins with practical tasks, but as the energy shifts, focus on your creative side and explore new ways to express yourself.

For those born on March 29: Born under the transition from Capricorn to Aquarius, these individuals are both disciplined and creative. In 2025, they'll find success by balancing their practical mindset with their innovative ideas. It's a year for combining discipline with creativity and social connections.

Daily Insights: The Moon in Aquarius brings a focus on creativity, innovation, and social interactions. It's a great day for exploring new ideas, connecting with others, and embracing your individuality. With Venus in Aries, relationships may take on an exciting and passionate tone.

Aries: Your creativity shines today. Use this energy to pursue new ideas and engage in exciting social interactions.

Taurus: It's a day for stepping out of your comfort zone. Embrace innovative ideas and explore new ways to connect with others.

Gemini: Your communication skills are highlighted today. Use this energy to engage in stimulating conversations and share your ideas with others.

Cancer: Creativity and innovation are calling you today. Use this energy to explore new ways of expressing yourself and connecting with others.

Leo: Leadership and creativity go hand in hand today. Focus on inspiring others and embracing new ideas that push boundaries.

Virgo: It's a great day for exploring creative solutions. Use your analytical skills to approach challenges in innovative ways.

Libra: Relationships are dynamic and exciting today. Focus on connecting with others in unconventional ways and embracing new perspectives.

Scorpio: Your passion for personal growth is strong today. Use this energy to explore new ideas and engage in meaningful conversations.

Sagittarius: Adventure and creativity are calling you today. Focus on expanding your horizons and embracing new opportunities.

Capricorn: While discipline is important, today encourages you to explore new ideas and engage in creative thinking.

Aquarius: With the Moon in your sign, your creativity and individuality are amplified. Use this energy to pursue innovative ideas and connect with others.

Pisces: Your intuition is strong today. Use this energy to explore creative projects and connect with others in meaningful ways.

For those born on March 30: Born under the Moon in Aquarius, these individuals are creative, innovative, and socially connected. In 2025, they'll thrive by embracing their individuality and exploring new ideas. It's a year for creativity, social interactions, and personal growth.

Daily Insights: The Moon in Aquarius continues to bring a focus on creativity, innovation, and social connections. It's a day for embracing new ideas, thinking outside the box, and engaging with others in meaningful ways. With Mars in Capricorn, there's also a drive for discipline and achieving long-term goals.

Aries: Your creativity and innovation are highlighted today. Use this energy to push forward with new ideas and collaborate with others.

Taurus: It's a day for stepping out of your comfort zone. Embrace unconventional ideas and explore new possibilities in your work and relationships.

Gemini: Social interactions are stimulating today. Engage in conversations that challenge your thinking and broaden your horizons.

Cancer: Creativity flows easily today. Use this energy to explore new ways of expressing yourself and connecting with others.

Leo: Leadership and creativity are your strengths today. Use this energy to inspire others and bring innovative ideas to life.

Virgo: It's a day for balancing your analytical skills with creativity. Use your practical mindset to bring innovative solutions to any challenges.

Libra: Relationships take on a dynamic tone today. Embrace new ways of connecting with loved ones and focus on shared goals.

Scorpio: Your determination is strong today, but don't be afraid to explore new ideas and embrace creative solutions.

Sagittarius: Adventure and learning are highlighted today. Use this energy to explore new opportunities and engage with others who inspire you.

Capricorn: While discipline is important, today encourages you to think outside the box and explore innovative ways to achieve your goals.

Aquarius: With the Moon in your sign, your creativity and individuality are amplified. Use this energy to focus on personal growth and explore new ideas.

Pisces: Your intuition is strong today. Use this energy to focus on creative projects and connect with others in unique and meaningful ways.

For those born on March 31: Born under the Moon in Aquarius, these individuals are innovative, creative, and socially connected. In 2025, they'll thrive by embracing their unique ideas and focusing on personal growth through social connections and creative expression.

Daily Insights: The Moon transitions into Pisces, bringing a shift toward emotional reflection, intuition, and creativity. It's a great day for focusing on your inner world, engaging in creative projects, and connecting with others on a deeper emotional level. With the Sun in Aries, there's still a strong push for action and achieving personal goals.

Aries: Your intuition is strong today. Use this energy to reflect on your personal goals and engage in creative projects that resonate with your emotions.

Taurus: It's a good day for emotional reflection. Focus on nurturing your relationships and exploring creative ways to express yourself.

Gemini: Creativity and intuition are heightened today. Use this energy to engage in artistic projects and connect with others on an emotional level.

Cancer: Your emotional sensitivity is amplified today. Focus on self-care and nurturing your close relationships, while also embracing your creativity.

Leo: While you're often focused on leadership, today encourages you to focus on emotional growth and creative self-expression.

Virgo: It's a day for introspection and emotional clarity. Use your analytical skills to explore your feelings and focus on personal growth.

Libra: Relationships take on a more emotional tone today. Focus on nurturing your connections and expressing your feelings in creative ways.

Scorpio: Your emotional intensity is heightened today. Use this energy for self-reflection and exploring your inner world.

Sagittarius: It's a day for focusing on your emotional well-being. Use your intuition to guide you in exploring creative projects and personal growth.

Capricorn: Emotional reflection is important today. Use this energy to balance your discipline with creativity and focus on your personal goals.

Aquarius: After a period of innovation, today encourages you to focus on your emotional needs and engage in creative projects that inspire you.

Pisces: With the Moon in your sign, your intuition and creativity are at their peak. Use this energy to focus on personal growth and emotional healing.

For those born on April 1: Born under the Moon in Pisces, these individuals are intuitive, creative, and emotionally sensitive. In 2025, they'll thrive by embracing their artistic talents and focusing on personal growth through emotional reflection and creative expression.

April 2, 2025

Daily Insights: The Moon in Pisces continues to encourage emotional reflection, intuition, and creativity. It's a great day for focusing on artistic projects, connecting with others on a deeper level, and exploring your inner world. With Venus in Aries, relationships may feel exciting and passionate, adding a sense of urgency to emotional connections.

Aries: Your intuition is strong today. Use this energy to focus on creative projects and deepen your emotional connections with loved ones.

Taurus: It's a day for introspection and emotional clarity. Focus on your personal growth and use your creativity to express your feelings.

Gemini: Creativity and imagination are heightened today. Use this energy to engage in artistic pursuits and explore your emotional world.

Cancer: Emotional reflection is important today. Focus on nurturing your relationships and using your intuition to guide your personal growth.

Leo: It's a day for self-expression and emotional connection. Use your creativity to explore your feelings and connect with others on a deeper level.

Virgo: Your intuition is strong today. Use this energy to balance your practical side with creative projects and emotional reflection.

Libra: Relationships take on a deeper, more emotional tone today. Focus on nurturing your connections and expressing your feelings openly.

Scorpio: Your emotional intensity is amplified today. Use this energy for personal reflection and focus on deepening your relationships.

Sagittarius: It's a day for emotional exploration. Use your intuition to guide you in creative projects and personal growth.

Capricorn: Emotional reflection is key today. Use this energy to explore your inner world and focus on balancing your emotional needs with your goals.

Aquarius: After a period of creativity and innovation, today encourages you to focus on emotional growth and deepening your connections with others.

Pisces: The Moon in your sign continues to amplify your intuition and creativity. Use this energy to focus on personal growth and emotional healing.

For those born on April 2: Born under the Moon in Pisces, these individuals are deeply intuitive, creative, and emotionally sensitive. In 2025, they'll thrive by embracing their artistic talents and focusing on personal growth through emotional reflection and creative expression.

Daily Insights: The Moon in Pisces continues to emphasize intuition, creativity, and emotional connection, but as it transitions into Aries later in the day, the energy shifts toward action, motivation, and confidence. It's a day for balancing emotional reflection with decisive action and goal setting.

Aries: Start the day with emotional reflection, but as the Moon enters your sign, you'll feel energized and ready to take action on your goals.

Taurus: The day begins with introspection, but later, you'll feel more motivated to focus on practical matters and personal goals.

Gemini: Use the morning for creative reflection, but by evening, shift your focus to taking bold steps toward your ambitions.

Cancer: Emotional reflection is important early in the day, but as the energy shifts, focus on taking action to achieve your personal goals.

Leo: The day starts with self-reflection, but later, you'll feel more energized to pursue your passions and take bold action.

Virgo: It's a day for balancing emotional clarity with practical action. Use the morning for introspection, but by evening, focus on your goals.

Libra: Relationships take on a deeper tone early in the day, but as the energy shifts, focus on taking bold steps toward achieving harmony in your life.

Scorpio: Emotional reflection is key early in the day, but later, you'll feel more determined to take action and pursue your goals.

Sagittarius: The day starts with introspection, but by evening, you'll feel energized to explore new opportunities and take action on your dreams.

Capricorn: Use the morning for emotional reflection, but as the Moon enters Aries, focus on taking practical steps toward your long-term goals.

Aquarius: The day begins with emotional reflection, but later, focus on pursuing your innovative ideas and taking action to achieve your goals.

Pisces: The Moon in your sign amplifies your intuition, but as the energy shifts, you'll feel more motivated to take action on your personal goals.

For those born on April 3: Born under the transition from Pisces to Aries, these individuals are both intuitive and action-oriented. In 2025, they'll thrive by balancing emotional reflection with taking bold steps toward their personal goals. It's a year for personal growth through both introspection and decisive action.

Daily Insights: The Moon in Aries brings a surge of energy, motivation, and confidence. It's a day for taking bold action, pursuing your goals, and embracing new opportunities. With Mars in Capricorn, there's also a sense of discipline, making it a perfect day for combining ambition with practical steps.

Aries: The Moon in your sign gives you a burst of energy and confidence. Use this to pursue your personal goals and take decisive action.

Taurus: It's a day for taking practical steps toward your long-term goals. Use your determination to make steady progress.

Gemini: Your energy is high today. Use this to explore new ideas and take action on projects that excite you.

Cancer: It's a day for stepping out of your comfort zone and taking bold action. Focus on pursuing your passions with confidence.

Leo: Your leadership skills are highlighted today. Use your energy to inspire others and take bold steps toward your goals.

Virgo: Discipline and focus are your strengths today. Use this energy to tackle practical tasks and work toward your long-term ambitions.

Libra: Relationships take on a dynamic tone today. Focus on balancing your personal goals with nurturing your connections.

Scorpio: Your determination is strong today. Use this energy to focus on your goals and take action with confidence.

Sagittarius: Adventure and excitement are calling you today. Use this energy to explore new possibilities and take bold steps toward your dreams.

Capricorn: Your disciplined approach will help you make steady progress today. Focus on your long-term goals and take practical steps toward achieving them.

Aquarius: Your innovative thinking shines today. Use this energy to pursue creative projects and share your ideas with confidence.

Pisces: It's a day for taking action on your personal goals. Use your intuition to guide you as you embrace new opportunities with confidence.

For those born on April 4: Born under the Moon in Aries, these individuals are confident, action-oriented, and ambitious. In 2025, they'll thrive by taking bold steps toward their goals and embracing new opportunities with enthusiasm and determination.

Daily Insights: The Moon in Aries continues to bring energy, confidence, and motivation. It's a day for taking bold action, pursuing new opportunities, and focusing on personal goals. With Venus in Aries, relationships may feel exciting and passionate, adding a dynamic element to personal interactions.

Aries: Your confidence is high today. Use this energy to pursue your goals and take decisive action in both your personal and professional life.

Taurus: It's a day for stepping out of your comfort zone and embracing new opportunities. Be bold in your actions and decisions.

Gemini: Your energy is high today. Use this momentum to explore new ideas and take action on projects you've been considering.

Cancer: Your intuition is strong today, but focus on taking practical steps to move forward with your goals and ambitions.

Leo: Leadership comes naturally to you today. Use your charisma and confidence to take charge and inspire those around you.

Virgo: It's a great day for practical actions. Use your focus and determination to make steady progress on your long-term goals.

Libra: Relationships are exciting today. Focus on balancing your personal ambitions with nurturing your connections to others.

Scorpio: Your determination is strong today. Use this energy to take bold action and move forward with your personal goals.

Sagittarius: Adventure is calling you today. Embrace new opportunities and take action on something you've been dreaming about.

Capricorn: Discipline and motivation are your strengths today. Use this energy to make significant progress on your long-term plans.

Aquarius: Your creativity shines today. Use this energy to pursue innovative ideas and take action on your personal goals.

Pisces: Your intuition is heightened, but today's energy encourages action. Use your instincts to guide you in taking bold steps toward your ambitions.

For those born on April 5: Born under the Moon in Aries, these individuals are bold, confident, and action-oriented. In 2025, they'll thrive by taking decisive steps toward their goals and embracing new opportunities with passion and determination.

April 6, 2025

Daily Insights: The Moon in Aries continues to bring a sense of motivation and drive, but as the day progresses, the Moon transitions into Taurus, shifting the focus toward stability, practicality, and long-term planning. It's a day for balancing bold actions with steady progress.

Aries: The day starts with energy and motivation, but as the Moon enters Taurus, focus on grounding yourself and taking practical steps toward your goals.

Taurus: The Moon enters your sign later today, bringing a sense of stability and comfort. Use this energy to focus on long-term goals and personal growth.

Gemini: Use the early part of the day for bold action, but later, focus on steady progress and grounding your ideas in practical steps.

Cancer: Start the day by taking action on your goals, but as the energy shifts, focus on nurturing stability in your personal life and relationships.

Leo: Your confidence is strong today, but as the day progresses, shift your focus to long-term planning and creating stability in your life.

Virgo: Use the morning to focus on bold decisions, but by evening, focus on practical actions and refining your plans for the future.

Libra: Relationships feel dynamic early in the day, but as the Moon moves into Taurus, focus on creating stability and balance in your personal connections.

Scorpio: Your energy is strong today. Start by taking bold steps, but later, shift your attention to grounding yourself and focusing on long-term goals.

Sagittarius: Adventure and excitement are calling early in the day, but later, focus on creating stability and making practical plans for the future.

Capricorn: Discipline and focus guide you throughout the day. Start with bold actions, but by evening, shift to focusing on practical matters and long-term stability.

Aquarius: Creativity and boldness are your strengths today. Use the morning for innovation, but as the day progresses, focus on practical solutions and steady progress.

Pisces: Your intuition is heightened early in the day, but later, focus on grounding your emotions and creating stability in your personal life.

For those born on April 6: Born under the transition from Aries to Taurus, these individuals are both bold and grounded. In 2025, they'll thrive by balancing their desire for action with the need for stability and long-term planning. It's a year for taking decisive steps while ensuring personal growth and security.

April 7, 2025

Daily Insights: The Moon in Taurus emphasizes stability, practicality, and a focus on long-term goals. It's a great day for working on projects that require patience and determination. With Mars in Capricorn, there's also a boost of discipline and focus, making it an ideal day for making steady progress.

Aries: Today's energy encourages you to slow down and focus on practical matters. Take steady steps toward your long-term goals.

Taurus: The Moon in your sign enhances your sense of stability and comfort. Use this energy to focus on personal growth and long-term planning.

Gemini: It's a day for grounding your ideas in practical actions. Focus on organizing your thoughts and making steady progress.

Cancer: Emotional stability is important today. Use this energy to nurture your personal life and create security in your relationships.

Leo: It's a great day for focusing on practical matters. Use your natural leadership skills to take charge of projects that require patience and perseverance.

Virgo: Productivity is high today. Use this energy to focus on tasks that require attention to detail and long-term planning.

Libra: Relationships feel grounded and stable today. Focus on creating harmony and nurturing your connections with loved ones.

Scorpio: Your determination is strong today. Use this energy to focus on your long-term goals and make steady progress.

Sagittarius: While adventure is important, today encourages you to focus on creating stability and working toward practical goals.

Capricorn: The disciplined energy of the day aligns with your natural strengths. Use this time to make significant progress on your long-term goals.

Aquarius: While innovation is important, today encourages you to focus on practical solutions and creating stability in your life.

Pisces: Emotional reflection is key today. Use this energy to ground yourself and focus on creating stability in your personal life.

For those born on April 7: Born under the Moon in Taurus, these individuals are practical, patient, and focused on stability. In 2025, they'll thrive by setting long-term goals and working steadily toward achieving them. It's a year for personal growth through discipline and determination.

Daily Insights: The Moon in Taurus continues to emphasize practicality, stability, and long-term planning. It's a day for focusing on projects that require patience and persistence. With Venus in Aries, there's also a dynamic energy in relationships, encouraging passion and excitement while maintaining balance.

Aries: It's a day for balancing bold actions with practical steps. Focus on steady progress while nurturing your personal relationships.

Taurus: The Moon in your sign continues to enhance your sense of stability. Use this energy to focus on personal goals and long-term success.

Gemini: While your mind is active, today's energy encourages you to focus on grounding your ideas and taking practical steps toward your goals.

Cancer: Emotional stability is key today. Focus on nurturing your home and relationships, creating a sense of security and comfort.

Leo: Leadership and practicality go hand in hand today. Use your confidence to guide you in making long-term decisions and steady progress.

Virgo: It's a productive day for focusing on your responsibilities. Use your disciplined nature to complete tasks that require attention to detail.

Libra: Relationships feel stable and secure today. Focus on creating harmony while balancing your personal goals with your connections to others.

Scorpio: Your determination is strong today. Use this energy to focus on your long-term goals and make steady progress toward achieving them.

Sagittarius: Adventure takes a backseat today as you focus on creating stability and taking practical steps toward your future.

Capricorn: The disciplined energy of the day helps you make steady progress. Use this time to work toward your long-term ambitions and goals.

Aquarius: While you're often focused on new ideas, today encourages you to focus on practical solutions and creating stability in your personal life.

Pisces: Emotional reflection is important today. Use this energy to ground yourself and focus on creating long-term security in your relationships.

For those born on April 8: Born under the Moon in Taurus, these individuals are patient, practical, and focused on long-term success. In 2025, they'll thrive by setting clear goals and making steady progress toward achieving them. It's a year for personal growth through persistence and stability.

Daily Insights: The Moon remains in Taurus, continuing to highlight practicality and stability. However, as it transitions into Gemini later in the day, the energy shifts toward curiosity, communication, and learning. It's a day for balancing practical tasks with engaging in stimulating conversations and exploring new ideas.

Aries: Start the day with practical actions, but as the Moon moves into Gemini, you'll feel more inclined to explore new ideas and engage in social interactions.

Taurus: The day begins with stability and focus on long-term goals, but later, shift your attention to learning and socializing.

Gemini: The Moon enters your sign later in the day, bringing a burst of mental energy. It's a great time for engaging in conversations and exploring new ideas.

Cancer: The day starts with a focus on creating stability in your personal life, but later, you'll feel more inclined to connect with others and share your thoughts.

Leo: It's a day for balancing your practical goals with engaging in stimulating social interactions. Use the evening for creative thinking and collaboration.

Virgo: Productivity is high early in the day, but as the energy shifts, you'll feel more inclined to engage in discussions and share your ideas.

Libra: Relationships feel stable early in the day, but by evening, focus on communicating openly and exploring new perspectives with loved ones.

Scorpio: Use the morning for disciplined work and practical goals, but later, shift your focus to exploring new ideas and engaging in meaningful conversations.

Sagittarius: The day begins with a focus on creating stability, but as the Moon enters Gemini, you'll feel more energized to explore new opportunities.

Capricorn: Discipline and practicality are key early in the day, but later, focus on engaging with others and exploring innovative solutions to your goals.

Aquarius: The day starts with practical matters, but by evening, shift your attention to creative thinking and socializing with those who inspire you.

Pisces: Emotional reflection is important early in the day, but as the energy shifts, focus on engaging with others and sharing your thoughts and ideas.

For those born on April 9: Born under the transition from Taurus to Gemini, these individuals are both practical and curious, balancing stability with a desire for learning and exploration. In 2025, they'll thrive by setting long-term goals while staying open to new ideas and opportunities for growth.

Daily Insights: The Moon in Gemini brings a focus on communication, curiosity, and learning. It's a day for engaging in stimulating conversations, exploring new ideas, and connecting with others. The Sun in Aries continues to provide energy and motivation, making it a great time for pursuing personal goals with enthusiasm.

Aries: Your energy is high today, and your curiosity is piqued. Use this to explore new ideas, engage in conversations, and pursue your goals with confidence.

Taurus: It's a day for balancing practicality with curiosity. Focus on learning something new or engaging in stimulating discussions.

Gemini: The Moon in your sign enhances your communication skills. It's a great day to express yourself and connect with others through conversations.

Cancer: Balance your emotional sensitivity with intellectual exploration today. Engage in discussions that allow you to gain new perspectives.

Leo: Creativity and curiosity are your strengths today. Use this energy to explore new ideas and collaborate with others on exciting projects.

Virgo: It's a day for balancing your analytical mind with curiosity. Engage in problem-solving and focus on expanding your knowledge.

Libra: Relationships take on a dynamic tone today. Focus on communication and engaging with loved ones in meaningful conversations.

Scorpio: Your mind is sharp today. Use this energy to explore new ideas and reflect on your personal growth through intellectual exploration.

Sagittarius: Adventure and learning go hand in hand today. Use your curiosity to explore new topics and engage in stimulating discussions.

Capricorn: While discipline is important, today encourages you to explore new ways of thinking and engage in social interactions.

Aquarius: Your innovative ideas shine today. Use this energy to explore creative solutions and share your thoughts with others.

Pisces: Your intuition is strong, but today encourages intellectual exploration. Use this energy to engage in conversations and expand your horizons.

For those born on April 10: Born under the Moon in Gemini, these individuals are curious, communicative, and eager to learn. In 2025, they'll thrive by exploring new ideas, engaging in meaningful conversations, and using their sharp minds to solve problems and connect with others.

Daily Insights: The Moon in Gemini continues to highlight curiosity, communication, and learning. It's a day for exploring new ideas, connecting with others through conversations, and sharing your thoughts. With Mercury in Aries, there's also a sense of directness in communication, making it a great time for clear and honest discussions.

Aries: Your communication skills are strong today. Use this energy to express yourself clearly and engage in stimulating conversations.

Taurus: It's a day for exploring new ideas and sharing your thoughts. Don't be afraid to engage in discussions that challenge your perspective.

Gemini: The Moon in your sign keeps your energy high. Use this time to connect with others, share your ideas, and explore new possibilities.

Cancer: Balance your emotions with logic today. Engage in conversations that help you gain new insights and broaden your perspective.

Leo: It's a great day for creative expression. Use your communication skills to share your ideas and collaborate with others.

Virgo: Your analytical mind is sharp today. Use this energy to focus on problem-solving and engage in thoughtful discussions.

Libra: Relationships are highlighted today. Focus on open and honest communication to strengthen your connections with loved ones.

Scorpio: It's a day for intellectual exploration. Use your curiosity to delve into new ideas and engage in conversations that inspire growth.

Sagittarius: Your adventurous spirit is strong today. Use this energy to explore new topics and engage in discussions that challenge your thinking.

Capricorn: It's a great day for balancing your practical mindset with intellectual curiosity. Engage in conversations that help you expand your knowledge.

Aquarius: Your innovative ideas are front and center today. Use this energy to explore creative solutions and share your unique perspective with others.

Pisces: While your intuition is strong, today encourages intellectual exploration. Engage in conversations that help you learn and grow.

For those born on April 11: Born under the Moon in Gemini, these individuals are curious, communicative, and intellectually driven. In 2025, they'll thrive by exploring new ideas, engaging in meaningful discussions, and using their sharp minds to connect with others and solve problems.

Daily Insights: The Moon in Gemini continues to emphasize communication, curiosity, and learning, but as it transitions into Cancer later in the day, the focus shifts toward emotional well-being, home life, and nurturing relationships. It's a day for balancing intellectual exploration with emotional reflection.

Aries: Use the morning for intellectual exploration, but as the Moon moves into Cancer, focus on nurturing your emotional well-being and relationships.

Taurus: The day starts with curiosity and communication, but later, shift your attention to creating stability in your home and personal life.

Gemini: The Moon in your sign keeps your mind active early in the day, but as it transitions into Cancer, focus on emotional reflection and self-care.

Cancer: As the Moon enters your sign, your emotional intuition is heightened. It's a great day for focusing on self-care and nurturing your relationships.

Leo: Start the day by engaging in social interactions, but as the energy shifts, focus on creating emotional balance and connecting with loved ones.

Virgo: Your analytical mind is sharp in the morning, but later, focus on emotional clarity and nurturing your personal relationships.

Libra: Relationships take on a deeper tone as the day progresses. Focus on balancing intellectual conversations with emotional connections.

Scorpio: It's a day for balancing intellectual exploration with emotional depth. Use the morning for learning, but later, focus on emotional healing.

Sagittarius: Adventure and learning are key in the morning, but as the Moon moves into Cancer, focus on creating emotional balance and stability in your life.

Capricorn: Discipline and focus guide you early in the day, but later, shift your attention to nurturing your emotional well-being and personal relationships.

Aquarius: The day begins with creativity and exploration, but as the energy shifts, focus on emotional reflection and connecting with others on a deeper level.

Pisces: Your intuition is heightened as the Moon enters Cancer. Use this energy to focus on emotional healing and nurturing your relationships.

For those born on April 12: Born under the transition from Gemini to Cancer, these individuals are both intellectually curious and emotionally intuitive. In 2025, they'll thrive by balancing their sharp minds with their emotional sensitivity, focusing on both learning and nurturing their relationships.

Daily Insights: The Moon in Cancer brings a focus on emotional well-being, home life, and nurturing relationships. It's a day for self-care, connecting with loved ones, and focusing on creating stability in your personal life. The Sun in Aries continues to provide energy and motivation, encouraging you to take action on your goals while maintaining emotional balance.

Aries: Your emotional intuition is strong today. Use this energy to focus on your personal well-being and nurturing your close relationships.

Taurus: It's a day for focusing on home and family. Use this energy to create stability in your personal life and nurture your loved ones.

Gemini: After a period of mental activity, today encourages you to focus on emotional reflection and nurturing your personal relationships.

Cancer: The Moon in your sign heightens your emotional sensitivity. It's a good day for self-care and focusing on your emotional well-being.

Leo: Balance is key today. Focus on creating harmony in your home life and nurturing your personal relationships while pursuing your goals.

Virgo: Emotional clarity comes through reflection today. Use this energy to connect with your inner self and focus on personal growth.

Libra: Relationships take on a deeper tone today. Focus on nurturing your connections and creating emotional harmony with loved ones.

Scorpio: Your emotional intensity is heightened today. Use this energy for self-reflection and emotional healing, focusing on deepening your connections.

Sagittarius: It's a day for focusing on emotional well-being. Use this energy to nurture your personal relationships and create a sense of stability.

Capricorn: Emotional reflection is key today. Take time to focus on your well-being and strengthen your relationships with loved ones.

Aquarius: While you're often focused on innovation, today encourages emotional reflection. Use this energy to connect with your inner self and nurture your relationships.

Pisces: Your intuition is strong today. Use this energy for emotional healing and focusing on your personal relationships and well-being.

For those born on April 13: Born under the Moon in Cancer, these individuals are emotionally intuitive, nurturing, and deeply connected to their home and family. In 2025, they'll thrive by focusing on their emotional well-being, nurturing their relationships, and creating stability in their personal lives.

Daily Insights: The Moon in Cancer continues to emphasize emotional well-being, nurturing relationships, and focusing on home life. It's a great day for self-care, spending time with loved ones, and creating a sense of stability in your environment. With Venus in Aries, relationships may also feel exciting and dynamic, adding a spark to personal connections.

Aries: Your emotional well-being is important today. Focus on nurturing your relationships and creating a sense of harmony in your personal life.

Taurus: It's a day for focusing on home and family. Use this energy to create a sense of stability and comfort in your surroundings.

Gemini: Emotional reflection is key today. Take time to nurture your personal relationships and focus on your emotional well-being.

Cancer: The Moon in your sign heightens your emotional intuition. It's a great day for self-care and strengthening your relationships with loved ones.

Leo: Balance your emotional needs with your personal goals today. Focus on creating harmony in your home life while pursuing your ambitions.

Virgo: Emotional clarity is important today. Use this energy to connect with your inner self and focus on personal growth and healing.

Libra: Relationships take on a deeper, more emotional tone today. Focus on nurturing your connections and creating harmony with loved ones.

Scorpio: Your emotional intensity is strong today. Use this energy for self-reflection and emotional healing, focusing on deepening your relationships.

Sagittarius: It's a day for focusing on emotional well-being. Use this energy to nurture your relationships and create a sense of stability in your life.

Capricorn: Emotional reflection is key today. Take time to focus on your personal relationships and strengthen the bonds with those you care about.

Aquarius: Emotional reflection is important today. Use this energy to connect with your inner self and nurture your relationships.

Pisces: Your intuition is heightened today. Use this energy for emotional healing and focus on nurturing your relationships and personal well-being.

For those born on April 14: Born under the Moon in Cancer, these individuals are emotionally intuitive, nurturing, and deeply connected to their home and family. In 2025, they'll thrive by focusing on their emotional well-being, nurturing their relationships, and creating stability in their personal lives.

April 15, 2025

Daily Insights: The Moon in Cancer continues to emphasize emotional reflection, nurturing, and focusing on home life. However, as the Moon transitions into Leo later in the day, the energy shifts toward self-expression, confidence, and creativity. It's a day for balancing emotional well-being with personal empowerment.

Aries: Start the day focusing on your emotional well-being, but as the Moon moves into Leo, you'll feel more confident and ready to take bold actions.

Taurus: The morning is ideal for nurturing your personal relationships, but later in the day, focus on expressing your creativity and stepping into the spotlight.

Gemini: The day starts with emotional reflection, but as the energy shifts, you'll feel more inclined to engage in social activities and express yourself.

Cancer: The Moon in your sign encourages emotional self-care, but as it enters Leo, your confidence will rise, making it a great time to focus on personal growth.

Leo: The Moon enters your sign later today, boosting your confidence and creativity. Use this energy to pursue your passions and take the lead in your projects.

Virgo: Emotional clarity is important early in the day, but as the energy shifts, focus on creative problem-solving and expressing your unique talents.

Libra: Relationships feel emotionally deep in the morning, but as the day progresses, focus on expressing yourself and embracing your individuality.

Scorpio: It's a day for balancing emotional reflection with personal empowerment. Start with self-care, but later, take bold steps toward your goals.

Sagittarius: The morning is perfect for focusing on emotional well-being, but as the Moon moves into Leo, embrace adventure and new opportunities.

Capricorn: Emotional reflection is key early in the day, but by evening, focus on stepping into leadership roles and pursuing your personal ambitions.

Aquarius: The day begins with introspection, but as the energy shifts, focus on expressing your creativity and connecting with others in meaningful ways.

Pisces: Emotional reflection is important early in the day, but later, use your heightened confidence to pursue creative projects and personal growth.

For those born on April 15: Born under the transition from Cancer to Leo, these individuals are emotionally intuitive yet confident and creative. In 2025, they'll thrive by balancing their emotional well-being with bold actions and personal growth. It's a year for both self-care and self-expression.

Daily Insights: The Moon in Leo emphasizes self-expression, creativity, and confidence. It's a day for stepping into the spotlight, embracing leadership, and pursuing your passions. With Mars in Capricorn, there's also a sense of discipline, making it a great time for combining ambition with creativity.

Aries: Your confidence is high today. Use this energy to pursue your personal goals and step into leadership roles with enthusiasm.

Taurus: Creativity flows easily today. Focus on expressing yourself through your work or hobbies, and don't be afraid to take the lead in projects.

Gemini: It's a great day for social interactions and sharing your ideas. Use your communication skills to inspire others and collaborate on creative endeavors.

Cancer: While your emotional intuition is still strong, today's energy encourages you to step out of your comfort zone and express yourself confidently.

Leo: The Moon in your sign amplifies your natural charisma and creativity. Use this energy to take bold steps toward your passions and inspire others.

Virgo: Balance creativity with practicality today. Use your disciplined nature to focus on long-term goals while expressing your unique talents.

Libra: Relationships feel exciting and dynamic today. Focus on creative ways to connect with loved ones and embrace your individuality.

Scorpio: Your passion is strong today. Use this energy to pursue personal goals with intensity and determination.

Sagittarius: Adventure and creativity are calling you today. Use this energy to explore new opportunities and express yourself freely.

Capricorn: Leadership and discipline come naturally today. Use this energy to focus on personal projects and inspire those around you.

Aquarius: Your creativity shines today. Use this energy to pursue innovative ideas and connect with others through meaningful collaborations.

Pisces: It's a day for self-expression and personal growth. Use your creativity to focus on your goals and embrace new opportunities with confidence.

For those born on April 16: Born under the Moon in Leo, these individuals are charismatic, creative, and confident. In 2025, they'll thrive by stepping into leadership roles, embracing their unique talents, and pursuing their passions with determination.

Daily Insights: The Moon in Leo continues to emphasize creativity, confidence, and self-expression, but as it transitions into Virgo later in the day, the focus shifts toward practicality, organization, and attention to detail. It's a day for balancing bold ideas with disciplined action.

Aries: Start the day with confidence and bold action, but as the Moon moves into Virgo, focus on organizing your plans and taking practical steps toward your goals.

Taurus: Creativity is highlighted in the morning, but as the day progresses, shift your focus to long-term planning and refining your ideas.

Gemini: Use the early part of the day for socializing and creative expression, but later, focus on practical tasks and organizing your thoughts.

Cancer: The day begins with self-expression, but as the energy shifts, focus on grounding yourself and taking practical steps toward your goals.

Leo: The Moon in your sign continues to enhance your creativity, but later, shift your focus to productivity and organization to ensure long-term success.

Virgo: The Moon enters your sign later today, enhancing your natural strengths in productivity and attention to detail. Use this energy to tackle important tasks.

Libra: Relationships feel exciting early in the day, but as the energy shifts, focus on balancing personal connections with practical responsibilities.

Scorpio: It's a day for balancing creativity with practicality. Start with bold actions, but later, focus on refining your plans and taking disciplined steps forward.

Sagittarius: The morning encourages adventure and self-expression, but later, shift your focus to practical matters and long-term goals.

Capricorn: Leadership and discipline guide you today. Use the early energy for creative pursuits, but by evening, focus on organizing your goals and taking action.

Aquarius: It's a day for balancing creativity and innovation with practicality. Use the morning for bold ideas, but later, focus on refining your plans.

Pisces: Emotional reflection is key early in the day, but as the energy shifts, focus on grounding yourself and taking practical steps toward your goals.

For those born on April 17: Born under the transition from Leo to Virgo, these individuals are both creative and disciplined. In 2025, they'll find success by balancing their bold ideas with practical action, focusing on both creativity and productivity to achieve their goals.

Daily Insights: The Moon in Virgo emphasizes productivity, organization, and attention to detail. It's a great day for focusing on practical tasks, refining your plans, and making steady progress toward long-term goals. With Mercury in Aries, there's also a boost in clear communication and direct action.

Aries: Focus on productivity today. Use your energy to tackle tasks that require attention to detail and make steady progress toward your goals.

Taurus: It's a day for practical actions. Use your disciplined nature to organize your thoughts and make progress on long-term goals.

Gemini: Your analytical skills are strong today. Use this energy to focus on problem-solving and refining your ideas.

Cancer: Emotional clarity comes through practical actions today. Focus on organizing your personal life and making steady progress on your goals.

Leo: After a period of creativity, today encourages you to focus on practical matters. Use your discipline to make progress on long-term plans.

Virgo: The Moon in your sign enhances your natural strengths. Use this energy to focus on productivity and tackle tasks that require precision.

Libra: It's a day for balancing relationships with practical responsibilities. Focus on creating harmony while staying productive and organized.

Scorpio: Your determination is strong today. Use this energy to focus on refining your plans and making steady progress toward your goals.

Sagittarius: Practical matters take precedence today. Use this energy to focus on your responsibilities and organize your thoughts.

Capricorn: Discipline and focus are key today. Use this energy to make significant progress on your long-term projects and goals.

Aquarius: While you're often focused on big ideas, today encourages you to focus on the details and ensure that your plans are practical.

Pisces: Emotional reflection is balanced with practicality today. Use this energy to organize your life and focus on long-term goals.

For those born on April 18: Born under the Moon in Virgo, these individuals are practical, organized, and focused on productivity. In 2025, they'll thrive by refining their plans, staying disciplined, and making steady progress toward their long-term goals.

Daily Insights: The Moon in Virgo continues to emphasize productivity and organization, but as it transitions into Libra later in the day, the energy shifts toward balance, relationships, and harmony. It's a day for balancing practical tasks with social interactions and personal connections.

Aries: The day starts with a focus on productivity, but as the Moon moves into Libra, shift your attention to your relationships and creating harmony in your life.

Taurus: Use the morning to focus on practical matters, but by evening, you'll feel more inclined to engage in social interactions and nurture your relationships.

Gemini: Productivity is high early in the day, but later, shift your focus to connecting with others and finding balance in your personal life.

Cancer: The morning encourages you to focus on emotional clarity and productivity, but as the energy shifts, focus on nurturing your relationships.

Leo: Start the day with practical tasks, but as the Moon moves into Libra, focus on balancing your personal goals with your relationships.

Virgo: The Moon in your sign enhances your productivity, but by evening, shift your attention to creating harmony in your relationships.

Libra: The day starts with a focus on productivity, but as the Moon enters your sign, you'll feel energized to focus on your relationships and personal well-being.

Scorpio: It's a day for balancing productivity with emotional growth. Use the morning for practical tasks, but later, focus on deepening your connections with others.

Sagittarius: The day begins with a focus on responsibilities, but by evening, you'll feel more inclined to explore social interactions and embrace balance.

Capricorn: Discipline and focus guide you throughout the day, but later, shift your attention to creating harmony in your relationships and personal life.

Aquarius: The day starts with practical actions, but as the energy shifts, focus on engaging with others and exploring new ideas in your relationships.

Pisces: The morning is perfect for organizing your thoughts and tasks, but by evening, focus on connecting with others and finding emotional balance.

For those born on April 19: Born under the transition from Virgo to Libra, these individuals are both practical and focused on balance. In 2025, they'll thrive by combining their disciplined approach to productivity with a focus on relationships and harmony in their personal life.

Daily Insights: The Moon in Libra brings a focus on balance, harmony, and relationships. It's a great day for social interactions, resolving conflicts, and creating equilibrium in both personal and professional life. With the Sun entering Taurus, there's also an emphasis on stability, practicality, and long-term goals.

Aries: The energy shifts today, encouraging you to focus on balance and harmony in your relationships. Use this time to create equilibrium in your personal and professional life.

Taurus: The Sun enters your sign today, bringing a sense of stability and focus on long-term goals. Balance this with nurturing your relationships and creating harmony around you.

Gemini: Relationships take center stage today. Focus on communicating clearly and finding balance in your personal interactions.

Cancer: Balance is key today. Focus on nurturing your home environment and personal relationships while keeping an eye on your goals.

Leo: Leadership and creativity are highlighted, but today encourages you to focus on balancing your ambitions with maintaining harmony in your relationships.

Virgo: It's a day for balancing your practical mindset with social interactions. Use this energy to find harmony between your responsibilities and personal life.

Libra: With the Moon in your sign, your need for balance and harmony is amplified. Focus on creating peace in your relationships and maintaining equilibrium in your life.

Scorpio: Relationships feel emotionally deep today. Use this energy to connect with others on a deeper level while maintaining harmony in your personal life.

Sagittarius: Social interactions are favored today. Use your natural charm to connect with others while ensuring balance in your personal and professional life.

Capricorn: It's a day for balancing your responsibilities with your relationships. Focus on finding harmony between your work and personal life.

Aquarius: Innovation and creativity come naturally today, but focus on creating balance in your interactions and maintaining harmony in your relationships.

Pisces: Emotional balance is important today. Use this energy to connect with loved ones and focus on creating stability in your relationships.

For those born on April 20: Born under the transition from Aries to Taurus, these individuals are both action-oriented and practical. In 2025, they'll thrive by balancing their ambition with their need for stability and long-term success. It's a year for focusing on personal growth while maintaining harmony in relationships.

Daily Insights: The Moon in Libra continues to emphasize balance, relationships, and harmony, but as it transitions into Scorpio later in the day, the focus shifts toward emotional intensity, transformation, and deeper connections. It's a day for balancing social interactions with emotional introspection.

Aries: The day begins with a focus on relationships and balance, but as the Moon moves into Scorpio, you'll feel more inclined to explore deeper emotional connections.

Taurus: Use the early part of the day to focus on social interactions and creating harmony, but later, dive into emotional reflection and personal growth.

Gemini: Relationships are in focus early in the day, but as the energy shifts, you'll feel more introspective and inclined to explore your inner world.

Cancer: Balance is important in the morning, but as the Moon moves into Scorpio, focus on emotional depth and nurturing your closest relationships.

Leo: Start the day by focusing on balance in your interactions, but later, shift your attention to emotional transformation and personal growth.

Virgo: The morning is perfect for maintaining harmony in your daily life, but by evening, focus on emotional clarity and personal reflection.

Libra: The Moon in your sign encourages you to maintain balance in your relationships, but later, you'll feel more inclined to explore emotional depth.

Scorpio: The Moon enters your sign later in the day, heightening your emotional intensity. Use this energy to focus on personal transformation and deepening your connections with others.

Sagittarius: Balance your social life in the morning, but by evening, focus on exploring your emotional world and strengthening your relationships.

Capricorn: Discipline and balance guide you in the morning, but later, shift your attention to emotional reflection and personal transformation.

Aquarius: It's a day for balancing relationships and personal goals. As the energy shifts, focus on emotional depth and meaningful connections.

Pisces: Emotional balance is important early in the day, but as the energy transitions, focus on exploring your inner self and strengthening your emotional connections.

For those born on April 21: Born under the transition from Libra to Scorpio, these individuals are both balanced and emotionally intense. In 2025, they'll thrive by balancing their relationships with personal transformation and emotional growth. It's a year for exploring deeper connections and self-reflection.

Daily Insights: The Moon in Scorpio brings emotional intensity, transformation, and a focus on deep connections. It's a day for introspection, exploring your emotional world, and working through personal transformations. With the Sun in Taurus, there's also a grounding influence, encouraging stability and long-term planning.

Aries: Your emotions run deep today. Use this energy for personal reflection and focus on emotional growth while maintaining stability in your goals.

Taurus: It's a day for introspection and emotional transformation. Focus on exploring your inner world and finding emotional clarity.

Gemini: Deep conversations and emotional reflection are favored today. Use your communication skills to connect with others on a deeper level.

Cancer: Emotional intensity is heightened today. Focus on personal transformation and nurturing your relationships with emotional depth.

Leo: It's a day for exploring your emotional needs. Use this energy to focus on personal growth and strengthening your closest relationships.

Virgo: Emotional clarity comes through introspection today. Use this energy to focus on personal transformation and emotional healing.

Libra: Relationships take on a deeper tone today. Focus on emotional connections and work on resolving any lingering issues in your relationships.

Scorpio: With the Moon in your sign, your emotional intensity is amplified. Use this energy for self-reflection and personal transformation.

Sagittarius: Emotional introspection is key today. Focus on exploring your inner world and strengthening your emotional connections.

Capricorn: Your determination is strong today. Use this energy to focus on long-term goals while exploring emotional depth and personal transformation.

Aquarius: Emotional reflection is important today. Use your innovative thinking to explore your feelings and focus on personal growth.

Pisces: Your intuition is heightened today. Use this energy for emotional healing and personal transformation through deep reflection.

For those born on April 22: Born under the Moon in Scorpio, these individuals are emotionally intense, intuitive, and transformative. In 2025, they'll thrive by focusing on personal transformation, emotional growth, and deepening their connections with others. It's a year for inner growth and exploring emotional depth.

Daily Insights: The Moon in Scorpio continues to bring emotional intensity and a focus on personal transformation. It's a day for exploring your inner world, working on emotional healing, and strengthening your closest relationships. With Mars in Capricorn, there's also a sense of determination and focus on long-term goals.

Aries: Your emotions are intense today. Use this energy for personal transformation and emotional healing while staying focused on your goals.

Taurus: It's a day for emotional reflection. Focus on exploring your inner world and working on personal growth and emotional clarity.

Gemini: Deep conversations and emotional exploration are favored today. Use your communication skills to connect with others on a profound level.

Cancer: Emotional depth is strong today. Use this energy to focus on healing and transforming your personal relationships.

Leo: It's a day for introspection and emotional reflection. Use this energy to explore your feelings and work on personal growth.

Virgo: Emotional clarity comes through introspection. Focus on healing and working through any unresolved emotional issues.

Libra: Relationships take on a deeper, more intense tone today. Focus on emotional connections and work on strengthening your bonds with loved ones.

Scorpio: The Moon in your sign amplifies your emotional intensity. Use this energy for self-reflection and personal transformation.

Sagittarius: Emotional introspection is key today. Focus on exploring your feelings and strengthening your emotional connections with others.

Capricorn: Your determination is strong today. Use this energy to focus on long-term goals while also working on emotional growth and healing.

Aquarius: Emotional reflection is important today. Use your innovative thinking to explore your emotions and focus on personal transformation.

Pisces: Your intuition is heightened today. Use this energy to focus on emotional healing and working through any unresolved issues.

For those born on April 23: Born under the Moon in Scorpio, these individuals are emotionally intense, intuitive, and transformative. In 2025, they'll thrive by focusing on personal transformation and emotional healing. It's a year for deepening relationships and exploring emotional depth.

April 24, 2025

Daily Insights: The Moon transitions into Sagittarius, bringing a sense of optimism, adventure, and personal growth. It's a great day for exploring new opportunities, learning, and expanding your horizons. With the Sun in Taurus, there's a grounding influence that encourages you to pursue long-term goals with determination.

Aries: Your adventurous spirit is strong today. Use this energy to explore new opportunities and take bold steps toward personal growth.

Taurus: After a period of introspection, today encourages you to embrace new experiences and explore opportunities for personal growth.

Gemini: It's a day for learning and exploration. Use your curiosity to engage with new ideas and connect with others in exciting ways.

Cancer: Adventure and optimism are calling you today. Focus on expanding your horizons and embracing personal growth.

Leo: Your confidence is high today. Use this energy to pursue new opportunities and take bold steps toward achieving your goals.

Virgo: It's a day for expanding your knowledge and exploring new ideas. Use your practical mindset to approach new opportunities with confidence.

Libra: Social interactions are lively today. Use this energy to connect with others, share your ideas, and embrace new experiences.

Scorpio: After a period of emotional intensity, today encourages you to focus on personal growth and exploring new opportunities.

Sagittarius: The Moon in your sign enhances your sense of adventure and optimism. It's a great day to pursue your passions and explore new possibilities.

Capricorn: While discipline is important, today encourages you to explore new ideas and take action on opportunities that excite you.

Aquarius: Your innovative ideas shine today. Use this energy to explore new possibilities and share your unique perspective with others.

Pisces: It's a day for adventure and personal growth. Use your intuition to guide you as you explore new opportunities and embrace change.

For those born on April 24: Born under the Moon in Sagittarius, these individuals are adventurous, optimistic, and eager to explore new possibilities. In 2025, they'll thrive by embracing opportunities for personal growth, learning, and expanding their horizons. It's a year for exploration and self-discovery.

Daily Insights: The Moon in Sagittarius continues to bring a sense of adventure, optimism, and personal growth. It's a great day for expanding your horizons, learning new things, and exploring new opportunities. With Mercury in Taurus, there's also a focus on clear communication and practical thinking, helping you ground your ideas in reality.

Aries: Your adventurous spirit is high today. Use this energy to explore new opportunities and focus on personal growth, while staying practical in your decision-making.

Taurus: It's a day for exploring new ideas and broadening your horizons. Use your practicality to ground any new ideas in achievable steps.

Gemini: Your curiosity is heightened today. Use this energy to engage in stimulating conversations and explore new learning opportunities.

Cancer: Adventure and optimism are your guides today. Step out of your comfort zone and embrace new experiences for personal growth.

Leo: Your confidence is amplified today. Use this energy to pursue new opportunities and take bold action toward your personal goals.

Virgo: It's a day for learning and expanding your knowledge. Use your disciplined nature to explore new topics and apply them practically.

Libra: Social interactions are lively today. Use this energy to connect with others and explore new perspectives while maintaining balance in your relationships.

Scorpio: Adventure takes center stage today. Use this energy to explore new experiences and focus on personal transformation.

Sagittarius: The Moon in your sign enhances your natural sense of adventure and optimism. It's a perfect day to pursue your passions and explore new possibilities.

Capricorn: While discipline is important, today encourages you to explore new ideas and broaden your perspectives. Embrace opportunities for growth.

Aquarius: Your innovative thinking is strong today. Use this energy to explore new possibilities and share your creative ideas with others.

Pisces: It's a day for personal growth and exploration. Use your intuition to guide you as you embrace new opportunities and expand your horizons.

For those born on April 25: Born under the Moon in Sagittarius, these individuals are adventurous, optimistic, and driven by a desire to explore new possibilities. In 2025, they'll thrive by embracing opportunities for growth and learning, while balancing their enthusiasm with practical planning.

Daily Insights: The Moon in Sagittarius continues to inspire exploration, learning, and optimism. However, as it transitions into Capricorn later in the day, the focus shifts toward discipline, practicality, and long-term planning. It's a day for balancing adventure with responsibility and setting clear goals for the future.

Aries: Start the day with a sense of adventure, but as the Moon enters Capricorn, focus on grounding your energy and setting long-term goals.

Taurus: The day begins with optimism, but later, you'll feel more inclined to focus on practical matters and organizing your long-term plans.

Gemini: Use the early part of the day for exploration and learning, but as the energy shifts, focus on refining your goals and taking practical steps toward achieving them.

Cancer: The day starts with excitement and exploration, but later, shift your focus to creating stability in your personal life and setting clear goals.

Leo: While you'll feel energized and confident early in the day, the Moon in Capricorn encourages you to focus on discipline and long-term planning later on.

Virgo: Use the morning for intellectual exploration and personal growth, but as the day progresses, focus on organizing your life and working toward your long-term ambitions.

Libra: Socializing and learning are highlighted early in the day, but by evening, you'll feel more focused on practical matters and setting goals for the future.

Scorpio: Adventure and exploration take center stage in the morning, but as the energy shifts, focus on emotional reflection and long-term planning.

Sagittarius: The Moon in your sign brings a sense of optimism and adventure, but later, as the energy shifts to Capricorn, you'll feel more inclined to focus on responsibility and long-term success.

Capricorn: The day begins with exploration, but as the Moon enters your sign, you'll feel energized to focus on practical tasks and long-term goals.

Aquarius: It's a day for balancing adventure with practicality. Use the morning for exploration, but later, focus on refining your ideas and setting clear goals.

Pisces: The day starts with exploration and optimism, but as the energy shifts, focus on grounding yourself and creating long-term stability.

For those born on April 26: Born under the transition from Sagittarius to Capricorn, these individuals are both adventurous and disciplined. In 2025, they'll find success by balancing their desire for exploration with a focus on long-term goals and responsibility. It's a year for growth through both adventure and planning.

Daily Insights: The Moon in Capricorn emphasizes discipline, responsibility, and long-term planning. It's a day for focusing on your goals, staying productive, and making steady progress toward success. With Mars in Taurus, there's a boost of determination and focus, making it a great day for practical achievements.

Aries: Focus on your long-term goals today. Use your energy to make steady progress toward your ambitions while staying disciplined.

Taurus: It's a great day for practical achievements. Use your determination and focus to work on long-term plans and build stability in your life.

Gemini: Your focus shifts toward practicality today. Use this energy to organize your ideas and take disciplined steps toward your goals.

Cancer: It's a day for focusing on stability and long-term success. Use this energy to create structure in your personal life and make progress on your goals.

Leo: Discipline and leadership are your strengths today. Use this energy to focus on long-term goals and inspire others to follow your lead.

Virgo: Productivity is high today. Use this energy to focus on tasks that require attention to detail and long-term planning.

Libra: Balance is key today. Focus on maintaining harmony in your relationships while working on your long-term goals.

Scorpio: Your determination is strong today. Use this energy to focus on your long-term ambitions and make steady progress toward achieving them.

Sagittarius: While adventure is important, today encourages you to focus on grounding yourself and working on practical goals.

Capricorn: The Moon in your sign enhances your natural discipline and determination. It's a perfect day for making significant progress on your long-term goals.

Aquarius: Focus on practical matters today. Use your innovative thinking to find creative solutions to long-term challenges.

Pisces: Emotional stability is important today. Use this energy to focus on your long-term goals and work toward creating stability in your life.

For those born on April 27: Born under the Moon in Capricorn, these individuals are disciplined, practical, and focused on long-term success. In 2025, they'll thrive by setting clear goals and working steadily toward achieving them. It's a year for personal growth through discipline and determination.

Daily Insights: The Moon in Capricorn continues to emphasize practicality, discipline, and long-term planning. However, as the Moon transitions into Aquarius later in the day, the energy shifts toward creativity, innovation, and social connections. It's a day for balancing productivity with creative exploration.

Aries: Use the morning for disciplined work, but as the Moon moves into Aquarius, embrace your creativity and explore new ideas.

Taurus: The day starts with a focus on productivity and long-term goals, but later, you'll feel more inclined to explore new possibilities and engage in social activities.

Gemini: Productivity is high early in the day, but by evening, shift your focus to connecting with others and exploring innovative ideas.

Cancer: Start the day with practical goals in mind, but later, shift your attention to creative projects and social interactions.

Leo: The morning is ideal for focused work, but as the energy shifts, you'll feel more inclined to engage in collaborative efforts and creative pursuits.

Virgo: Use the early part of the day for productivity and organization, but by evening, you'll feel more inclined to engage in creative problem-solving and social activities.

Libra: Relationships feel stable early in the day, but later, focus on finding creative solutions and connecting with others in meaningful ways.

Scorpio: Determination and discipline guide you early in the day, but by evening, you'll feel more inclined to explore new perspectives and innovative ideas.

Sagittarius: While productivity is important, the evening encourages you to explore new possibilities and engage in social interactions.

Capricorn: The Moon in your sign enhances your discipline and focus, but as the energy shifts, focus on social connections and creative exploration.

Aquarius: The evening brings a burst of creative energy. Use this time to explore innovative ideas and connect with others in meaningful ways.

Pisces: Emotional reflection is key early in the day, but as the energy shifts, focus on expressing your creativity and engaging in social interactions.

For those born on April 28: Born under the transition from Capricorn to Aquarius, these individuals are both disciplined and creative. In 2025, they'll thrive by balancing their practical mindset with their innovative ideas. It's a year for combining discipline with creativity and social connections.

Daily Insights: The Moon in Aquarius brings a focus on creativity, innovation, and social interactions. It's a great day for exploring new ideas, connecting with others, and embracing your individuality. With Mercury in Taurus, there's a balance between practical thinking and innovative solutions, making it an ideal time for creative problem-solving.

Aries: Your creativity shines today. Use this energy to explore new ideas and connect with others through meaningful collaborations.

Taurus: It's a day for combining practicality with creativity. Use your determination to bring innovative ideas into reality.

Gemini: Social interactions are stimulating today. Engage in conversations that inspire new perspectives and broaden your horizons.

Cancer: Creativity and innovation are calling you today. Use this energy to explore new ways of expressing yourself and connecting with others.

Leo: Leadership and creativity go hand in hand today. Use your confidence to take the lead in innovative projects and inspire others.

Virgo: It's a great day for exploring creative solutions. Use your analytical skills to approach challenges in innovative ways.

Libra: Relationships are dynamic and exciting today. Focus on connecting with others in unconventional ways and exploring new perspectives.

Scorpio: Your passion for personal growth is strong today. Use this energy to explore new ideas and engage in meaningful conversations.

Sagittarius: Adventure and creativity are calling you today. Focus on expanding your horizons and embracing new opportunities.

Capricorn: While discipline is important, today encourages you to explore new ideas and engage in creative thinking.

Aquarius: With the Moon in your sign, your creativity and individuality are amplified. Use this energy to pursue innovative ideas and connect with others.

Pisces: Your intuition is strong today. Use this energy to explore creative projects and connect with others in meaningful ways.

For those born on April 29: Born under the Moon in Aquarius, these individuals are creative, innovative, and socially connected. In 2025, they'll thrive by embracing their individuality, exploring new ideas, and focusing on personal growth through social connections and creative expression.

Daily Insights: The Moon in Aquarius continues to emphasize creativity, innovation, and social interactions. It's a great day for exploring unique ideas, connecting with others, and pushing boundaries. With Venus in Gemini, relationships may feel lively and intellectually stimulating, encouraging open communication and curiosity.

Aries: Your creativity is high today. Use this energy to explore new ideas and connect with others through meaningful conversations and collaborations.

Taurus: It's a day for embracing innovation. Use your practical mindset to explore creative solutions and engage with others in unique ways.

Gemini: Social interactions are exciting today. Engage in stimulating conversations and focus on connecting with others through shared interests.

Cancer: It's a day for thinking outside the box. Use your creativity to explore new ways of expressing yourself and connect with others in fresh, exciting ways.

Leo: Leadership and innovation are your strengths today. Use this energy to take charge of creative projects and inspire those around you with bold ideas.

Virgo: It's a day for exploring creative solutions to practical problems. Use your analytical skills to think innovatively and tackle challenges.

Libra: Relationships feel dynamic and intellectually stimulating today. Focus on engaging in open communication and exploring new perspectives with loved ones.

Scorpio: Your passion for personal growth is strong today. Use this energy to explore new ideas and engage in deep, meaningful conversations.

Sagittarius: Adventure and curiosity are calling you today. Use this energy to explore new opportunities and engage with others in intellectually stimulating ways.

Capricorn: While discipline is important, today encourages you to embrace creativity and innovation. Use your practical skills to bring new ideas to life.

Aquarius: The Moon in your sign enhances your creativity and individuality. Use this energy to explore new ideas and connect with others through shared passions.

Pisces: Your intuition is heightened today. Use this energy to focus on creative projects and engage in social interactions that inspire you.

For those born on April 30: Born under the Moon in Aquarius, these individuals are innovative, creative, and socially connected. In 2025, they'll thrive by exploring new ideas, embracing their individuality, and engaging with others in intellectually stimulating ways.

Daily Insights: The Moon in Aquarius continues to encourage creativity, innovation, and unique social connections, but as it transitions into Pisces later in the day, the focus shifts toward emotional reflection, intuition, and empathy. It's a day for balancing intellectual exploration with emotional depth.

Aries: Start the day with innovative ideas and social connections, but as the Moon enters Pisces, shift your focus to emotional reflection and nurturing relationships.

Taurus: The morning is great for exploring creative solutions, but later, focus on emotional healing and connecting with loved ones on a deeper level.

Gemini: Your mind is active early in the day, but as the Moon enters Pisces, focus on balancing your intellectual pursuits with emotional reflection.

Cancer: Emotional intuition is heightened as the day progresses. Use the morning for socializing, but later, focus on self-care and nurturing close relationships.

Leo: Creativity shines early in the day, but as the energy shifts, focus on your emotional well-being and connecting with those who matter most.

Virgo: Productivity is high in the morning, but by evening, you'll feel more inclined to explore your emotions and focus on personal healing.

Libra: Relationships feel dynamic early in the day, but as the Moon enters Pisces, focus on deepening your emotional connections and finding inner balance.

Scorpio: Use the morning for exploring new ideas, but later, focus on emotional growth and reflection. Your intuition is especially strong today.

Sagittarius: The day starts with excitement and creativity, but later, you'll feel more inclined to focus on emotional healing and connecting with loved ones.

Capricorn: Early productivity gives way to emotional reflection as the day progresses. Focus on grounding yourself and nurturing your relationships.

Aquarius: The Moon in your sign brings out your creativity, but as the energy shifts, focus on emotional introspection and personal growth.

Pisces: The Moon enters your sign later today, amplifying your intuition and emotional sensitivity. Use this energy to focus on self-care and emotional healing.

For those born on May 1: Born under the transition from Aquarius to Pisces, these individuals are both creative and emotionally intuitive. In 2025, they'll thrive by balancing their innovative ideas with emotional reflection, focusing on both personal growth and deepening relationships.

Daily Insights: The Moon in Pisces brings a focus on emotional reflection, intuition, and creativity. It's a great day for engaging in artistic projects, connecting with loved ones on a deeper level, and exploring your inner world. With Mercury in Taurus, there's also an emphasis on clear and practical communication.

Aries: Your intuition is strong today. Use this energy to focus on emotional reflection and nurture your relationships with empathy and understanding.

Taurus: It's a great day for combining creativity with practicality. Focus on expressing your emotions through artistic projects or clear communication.

Gemini: Emotional reflection is key today. Use this energy to connect with your inner self and engage in meaningful conversations with loved ones.

Cancer: The Moon in Pisces enhances your emotional intuition. Use this energy to focus on self-care and nurturing your close relationships.

Leo: While you're often focused on action, today encourages emotional reflection. Use this time to explore your feelings and deepen your connections.

Virgo: Balance is important today. Focus on nurturing your emotional well-being while also staying grounded in practical matters.

Libra: Relationships take on a deeper tone today. Focus on emotional connections and use your intuition to guide meaningful conversations.

Scorpio: Your emotional depth is strong today. Use this energy for self-reflection and deepening your relationships with those you care about.

Sagittarius: Adventure takes a backseat today as you focus on emotional healing and personal growth. Use this energy to explore your inner world.

Capricorn: Emotional clarity comes through reflection today. Use this energy to ground yourself and focus on creating stability in your relationships.

Aquarius: While you're often focused on innovation, today encourages you to focus on emotional growth and nurturing your personal connections.

Pisces: The Moon in your sign amplifies your intuition and emotional sensitivity. Use this energy to focus on personal healing and nurturing your relationships.

For those born on May 2: Born under the Moon in Pisces, these individuals are deeply intuitive, creative, and emotionally sensitive. In 2025, they'll thrive by focusing on emotional growth, personal healing, and expressing their creativity through artistic pursuits.

Daily Insights: The Moon in Pisces continues to emphasize emotional reflection, creativity, and intuition. It's a day for focusing on self-care, engaging in artistic projects, and connecting with others on a deeper level. With Venus in Gemini, relationships may feel intellectually stimulating, encouraging open communication and curiosity.

Aries: Emotional intuition is heightened today. Focus on nurturing your relationships and using your creativity to express your feelings.

Taurus: It's a day for balancing practicality with emotional reflection. Use this energy to focus on your emotional well-being and personal growth.

Gemini: Your communication skills are highlighted today. Use this energy to engage in meaningful conversations and explore your emotional world.

Cancer: Emotional reflection is key today. Use this energy to focus on self-care and strengthening your personal relationships.

Leo: While action is important, today encourages you to reflect on your emotions and connect with others in meaningful ways.

Virgo: Balance your practical nature with emotional reflection today. Use this energy to focus on your inner world and nurture your relationships.

Libra: Relationships take on a deeper tone today. Focus on emotional connections and use your intuition to guide your conversations.

Scorpio: Your emotional depth is amplified today. Use this energy for self-reflection and strengthening your relationships with loved ones.

Sagittarius: It's a day for focusing on emotional well-being. Use this energy to connect with your inner self and explore your feelings.

Capricorn: Emotional reflection is important today. Focus on creating stability in your personal life and deepening your relationships.

Aquarius: While you're often focused on ideas, today encourages emotional growth. Use this energy to connect with others on a deeper level.

Pisces: The Moon in your sign continues to amplify your intuition and creativity. Use this energy for emotional healing and self-expression.

For those born on May 3: Born under the Moon in Pisces, these individuals are emotionally intuitive, creative, and deeply connected to their inner world. In 2025, they'll thrive by focusing on personal healing, nurturing relationships, and expressing their creativity through meaningful projects.

Daily Insights: The Moon in Pisces continues to bring emotional depth and reflection, but as it transitions into Aries later in the day, the energy shifts toward action, motivation, and confidence. It's a day for balancing emotional introspection with bold action and setting clear goals.

Aries: The day starts with emotional reflection, but as the Moon enters your sign, you'll feel energized and ready to take bold action on your goals.

Taurus: Emotional reflection is important in the morning, but later, shift your focus to taking practical steps toward your long-term goals.

Gemini: Use the early part of the day for creative reflection, but by evening, you'll feel more inclined to take bold steps toward your ambitions.

Cancer: Emotional clarity is important early in the day, but as the energy shifts, focus on taking action and pursuing your personal goals.

Leo: Start the day with self-reflection, but as the Moon enters Aries, your confidence will rise, making it a great time to take bold action.

Virgo: Balance emotional reflection with practicality today. Use the morning for introspection, but by evening, shift your focus to your goals.

Libra: Relationships feel emotionally deep early in the day, but later, focus on balancing emotional connections with personal ambition.

Scorpio: Emotional intensity is high in the morning, but as the day progresses, shift your attention to personal growth and taking bold action.

Sagittarius: The day begins with emotional reflection, but by evening, you'll feel energized and ready to pursue your goals with enthusiasm.

Capricorn: Use the morning for emotional reflection, but as the energy shifts, focus on taking action and making steady progress toward your goals.

Aquarius: The day starts with emotional introspection, but later, focus on innovation and taking bold steps toward your personal projects.

Pisces: The Moon in your sign enhances your intuition, but as the energy shifts, focus on taking action and pursuing your personal ambitions with confidence.

For those born on May 4: Born under the transition from Pisces to Aries, these individuals are both intuitive and action-oriented. In 2025, they'll thrive by balancing emotional reflection with bold steps toward their personal goals. It's a year for personal growth through both introspection and decisive action.

Daily Insights: The Moon in Aries brings energy, motivation, and confidence. It's a day for taking bold action, pursuing your goals, and embracing new opportunities. With Mars in Capricorn, there's also a sense of discipline and focus, making it a great time to combine ambition with practicality.

Aries: The Moon in your sign gives you a burst of energy and confidence. Use this to take bold steps toward your personal goals and ambitions.

Taurus: It's a day for balancing practicality with bold action. Use your disciplined nature to make steady progress toward your goals.

Gemini: Your energy is high today. Use this to explore new ideas and take action on projects you've been considering.

Cancer: It's a day for taking bold action. Use your confidence to pursue your personal goals while maintaining balance in your emotional life.

Leo: Your leadership skills are highlighted today. Use this energy to take charge and pursue your ambitions with confidence and enthusiasm.

Virgo: Discipline and focus are your strengths today. Use this energy to tackle practical tasks and make progress on your long-term plans.

Libra: Relationships feel dynamic and exciting today. Focus on balancing your personal goals with your connections to others.

Scorpio: Your determination is strong today. Use this energy to focus on your personal goals and take bold action toward achieving them.

Sagittarius: Adventure and excitement are calling you today. Use this energy to explore new opportunities and take bold steps toward your dreams.

Capricorn: Discipline and practicality guide you today. Use this energy to focus on your long-term goals and make steady progress toward success.

Aquarius: Your innovative thinking shines today. Use this energy to explore creative projects and take bold action on your personal goals.

Pisces: It's a day for taking action on your personal ambitions. Use your intuition to guide you as you embrace new opportunities with confidence.

For those born on May 5: Born under the Moon in Aries, these individuals are confident, action-oriented, and ambitious. In 2025, they'll thrive by taking bold steps toward their goals and embracing new opportunities with enthusiasm and determination.

Daily Insights: The Moon in Aries continues to bring energy, confidence, and motivation. It's a great day for taking bold steps, embracing new opportunities, and focusing on your goals. With Venus in Gemini, communication in relationships is favored, adding a lively and curious tone to personal connections.

Aries: Your confidence is high today, and you're ready to take bold action. Use this energy to pursue your personal ambitions and connect with others.

Taurus: It's a day for balancing action with practicality. Use your determination to move forward on your goals while staying grounded in your plans.

Gemini: Your communication skills are highlighted today. Use this energy to engage in meaningful conversations and share your ideas with others.

Cancer: It's a day for stepping out of your comfort zone and embracing new opportunities. Use your confidence to take bold steps toward your goals.

Leo: Leadership and confidence come naturally today. Use this energy to take charge of projects and inspire those around you with your enthusiasm.

Virgo: It's a productive day for focusing on your goals. Use your disciplined nature to make progress on tasks that require attention to detail.

Libra: Relationships take on a lively tone today. Use your communication skills to engage with others and strengthen your personal connections.

Scorpio: Your determination is strong today. Use this energy to focus on your long-term goals and make steady progress toward achieving them.

Sagittarius: Adventure and excitement are calling you today. Use this energy to explore new opportunities and pursue your dreams with enthusiasm.

Capricorn: Discipline and focus guide you today. Use this energy to work on your long-term plans and make practical decisions for your future.

Aquarius: Your creativity shines today. Use this energy to explore new ideas and take action on personal projects that excite you.

Pisces: It's a day for taking bold steps toward your goals. Use your intuition to guide you as you move forward with confidence and determination.

For those born on May 6: Born under the Moon in Aries, these individuals are confident, action-oriented, and driven by their ambitions. In 2025, they'll thrive by taking decisive steps toward their goals and embracing new opportunities with enthusiasm and determination.

Daily Insights: The Moon in Aries continues to emphasize action and motivation, but as it transitions into Taurus later in the day, the energy shifts toward stability, practicality, and long-term planning. It's a day for balancing bold actions with careful consideration of long-term goals.

Aries: The day begins with high energy and bold actions, but as the Moon moves into Taurus, focus on grounding yourself and setting long-term goals.

Taurus: The Moon enters your sign later today, bringing a sense of stability and focus on practical matters. Use this energy to work toward your long-term ambitions.

Gemini: It's a day for balancing bold ideas with practical steps. Use the morning for exploration, but by evening, shift your focus to long-term planning.

Cancer: Start the day with confidence and action, but as the energy shifts, focus on creating stability in your personal life and making thoughtful decisions.

Leo: The morning is ideal for pursuing your passions, but as the Moon enters Taurus, focus on grounding your ideas and setting realistic goals.

Virgo: Use the early part of the day for productivity, but by evening, shift your attention to organizing your thoughts and refining your plans for the future.

Libra: Relationships feel dynamic early in the day, but as the energy shifts, focus on creating stability and balance in your personal connections.

Scorpio: The day begins with determination and bold action, but as the Moon moves into Taurus, focus on creating emotional and financial security.

Sagittarius: Adventure and action dominate the morning, but as the day progresses, shift your focus to practical matters and grounding your plans.

Capricorn: Discipline and focus guide you throughout the day, but later, shift your attention to creating stability and working on long-term goals.

Aquarius: The morning is perfect for exploring new ideas, but by evening, focus on practical solutions and setting achievable goals for the future.

Pisces: The day starts with bold action, but as the energy shifts, focus on grounding your emotions and creating stability in your personal life.

For those born on May 7: Born under the transition from Aries to Taurus, these individuals are both action-oriented and practical. In 2025, they'll find success by balancing their bold ambitions with practical planning, focusing on long-term goals while embracing new opportunities for growth.

May 8, 2025

Daily Insights: The Moon in Taurus emphasizes stability, practicality, and long-term planning. It's a great day for focusing on practical matters, setting achievable goals, and making steady progress. With Mars in Capricorn, there's a boost of determination and discipline, making it a perfect day for productivity and success.

Aries: Focus on grounding your energy today. Use your determination to make steady progress toward your long-term goals and practical matters.

Taurus: The Moon in your sign enhances your sense of stability and focus on practical goals. Use this energy to work toward your personal growth and ambitions.

Gemini: It's a day for focusing on long-term planning. Use your curiosity to explore new ideas while staying grounded in practical solutions.

Cancer: Stability and emotional security are important today. Use this energy to create a sense of comfort and progress in your personal life.

Leo: It's a great day for focusing on long-term goals. Use your leadership skills to inspire others while making steady progress on your ambitions.

Virgo: Productivity is high today. Use this energy to focus on tasks that require attention to detail and long-term planning.

Libra: Relationships feel stable and secure today. Focus on creating harmony in your personal connections while also working on your goals.

Scorpio: Your determination is strong today. Use this energy to focus on your long-term goals and make practical decisions for your future.

Sagittarius: Adventure takes a backseat today as you focus on grounding yourself and working toward practical goals.

Capricorn: Discipline and focus are your strengths today. Use this energy to make steady progress on your long-term projects and goals.

Aquarius: While creativity is important, today encourages you to focus on practical solutions and setting achievable goals for the future.

Pisces: Emotional stability is key today. Use this energy to ground yourself and focus on creating long-term security in your relationships and personal life.

For those born on May 8: Born under the Moon in Taurus, these individuals are practical, grounded, and focused on long-term success. In 2025, they'll thrive by setting clear goals and making steady progress toward achieving them, using their disciplined nature to stay focused on their ambitions.

Daily Insights: The Moon in Taurus continues to emphasize stability and practicality, but as it transitions into Gemini later in the day, the focus shifts toward communication, learning, and curiosity. It's a day for balancing practical matters with intellectual exploration and social interactions.

Aries: The day begins with a focus on practical goals, but as the Moon moves into Gemini, you'll feel more inclined to engage in conversations and explore new ideas.

Taurus: Use the morning for practical tasks, but later, shift your focus to learning and connecting with others in meaningful ways.

Gemini: The Moon enters your sign later today, bringing a burst of energy and curiosity. It's a great time for exploring new ideas and engaging in conversations.

Cancer: Start the day by focusing on stability, but as the energy shifts, you'll feel more inclined to connect with others and engage in intellectual pursuits.

Leo: The morning is ideal for working on long-term goals, but by evening, focus on socializing and sharing your ideas with others.

Virgo: Use the early part of the day for productivity, but later, shift your attention to learning and expanding your knowledge through conversations.

Libra: Relationships feel stable early in the day, but as the Moon moves into Gemini, focus on communicating openly and exploring new perspectives.

Scorpio: The day begins with determination and focus on practical matters, but later, you'll feel more inclined to engage in intellectual exploration.

Sagittarius: The morning is perfect for grounding your energy, but by evening, you'll feel more curious and eager to explore new opportunities.

Capricorn: Discipline and focus guide you early in the day, but as the energy shifts, you'll feel more inclined to engage in social interactions and learning.

Aquarius: The day starts with practicality, but by evening, your creativity and curiosity will be at their peak, making it a great time for exploring new ideas.

Pisces: Emotional stability is important early in the day, but later, focus on intellectual exploration and engaging with others through meaningful conversations.

For those born on May 9: Born under the transition from Taurus to Gemini, these individuals are both practical and curious. In 2025, they'll thrive by balancing their disciplined nature with intellectual exploration, focusing on both long-term goals and learning new things.

Daily Insights: The Moon in Gemini brings a focus on communication, learning, and curiosity. It's a great day for engaging in conversations, exploring new ideas, and connecting with others. With Mercury in Taurus, there's also an emphasis on clear and practical communication, helping to ground your ideas in reality.

Aries: Your curiosity is strong today. Use this energy to engage in conversations, explore new ideas, and take action on your personal goals.

Taurus: It's a day for balancing practicality with intellectual exploration. Use your determination to communicate your ideas clearly and work toward your goals.

Gemini: The Moon in your sign enhances your communication skills. It's a great day to share your ideas, engage with others, and explore new possibilities.

Cancer: Emotional reflection is important, but today encourages intellectual growth. Use this energy to engage in meaningful conversations and expand your knowledge.

Leo: Leadership and creativity are highlighted today. Use your confidence to inspire others and share your innovative ideas.

Virgo: Productivity is high today. Use your analytical mind to explore new ideas and engage in thoughtful conversations that challenge your thinking.

Libra: Relationships feel dynamic and intellectually stimulating today. Focus on open communication and engaging with others in meaningful ways.

Scorpio: Your determination is strong today. Use this energy to explore new perspectives and deepen your understanding of the world around you.

Sagittarius: Adventure and learning go hand in hand today. Use your curiosity to explore new opportunities and engage in conversations that inspire you.

Capricorn: It's a day for balancing your disciplined nature with intellectual exploration. Use this energy to focus on long-term planning while staying open to new ideas.

Aquarius: Your innovative thinking shines today. Use this energy to explore creative projects and share your unique perspective with others.

Pisces: While intuition is strong, today encourages intellectual exploration. Use this energy to engage in conversations that broaden your horizons.

For those born on May 10: Born under the Moon in Gemini, these individuals are curious, communicative, and eager to learn. In 2025, they'll thrive by exploring new ideas, engaging in meaningful conversations, and using their sharp minds to connect with others and solve problems.

Daily Insights: The Moon in Gemini continues to emphasize communication, learning, and curiosity. It's a great day for engaging in conversations, exploring new ideas, and connecting with others. With Venus in Gemini, relationships may feel intellectually stimulating, adding excitement to personal interactions.

Aries: Your communication skills are highlighted today. Use this energy to engage in stimulating conversations and share your ideas with confidence.

Taurus: It's a day for balancing practical goals with intellectual exploration. Use your grounded nature to communicate your thoughts clearly.

Gemini: The Moon in your sign enhances your curiosity and communication. It's a perfect day to explore new ideas and connect with others in meaningful ways.

Cancer: While emotional reflection is important, today encourages you to focus on intellectual growth and exploring new perspectives.

Leo: Leadership and creativity are key today. Use your confidence to inspire others and share your innovative ideas with enthusiasm.

Virgo: Productivity is high, and your analytical skills are sharp. Use this energy to focus on problem-solving and meaningful discussions.

Libra: Relationships feel lively and intellectually stimulating. Focus on communicating openly and exploring new perspectives with loved ones.

Scorpio: Your determination is strong today. Use this energy to engage in deep conversations and expand your understanding of the world around you.

Sagittarius: Adventure and learning are highlighted today. Use your curiosity to explore new opportunities and engage in conversations that inspire you.

Capricorn: It's a day for balancing discipline with intellectual exploration. Use your practical nature to engage in thoughtful discussions.

Aquarius: Your creativity and innovative thinking shine today. Use this energy to explore new ideas and share your unique perspective with others.

Pisces: Emotional intuition is important, but today encourages you to focus on intellectual exploration. Use this energy to engage in meaningful conversations.

For those born on May 11: Born under the Moon in Gemini, these individuals are curious, communicative, and always eager to learn. In 2025, they'll thrive by engaging in conversations, exploring new ideas, and using their sharp intellect to make meaningful connections.

Daily Insights: The Moon in Gemini continues to bring a focus on communication, curiosity, and learning, but as it transitions into Cancer later in the day, the energy shifts toward emotional well-being, nurturing relationships, and self-care. It's a day for balancing intellectual exploration with emotional connection.

Aries: The day begins with lively conversations, but as the Moon moves into Cancer, focus on emotional reflection and nurturing your personal relationships.

Taurus: Use the morning for exploring new ideas, but as the energy shifts, focus on creating emotional stability in your personal life.

Gemini: Your communication skills are heightened early in the day, but later, focus on emotional connections and strengthening your relationships with loved ones.

Cancer: The Moon enters your sign later today, heightening your emotional sensitivity. It's a great time for self-care and nurturing close relationships.

Leo: Start the day with intellectual exploration, but as the Moon moves into Cancer, shift your focus to emotional balance and personal growth.

Virgo: Productivity is high early in the day, but by evening, focus on emotional reflection and nurturing your personal well-being.

Libra: Relationships are intellectually stimulating in the morning, but later, focus on deepening emotional connections and creating harmony in your relationships.

Scorpio: Your curiosity is high early in the day, but as the energy shifts, focus on emotional healing and strengthening your relationships.

Sagittarius: The day begins with excitement and exploration, but later, shift your focus to emotional reflection and personal growth.

Capricorn: Use the morning for practical tasks and intellectual pursuits, but by evening, focus on nurturing your emotional well-being and relationships.

Aquarius: Creativity and intellectual exploration are highlighted early in the day, but as the Moon enters Cancer, focus on emotional growth and self-care.

Pisces: The day begins with curiosity, but later, you'll feel more inclined to focus on emotional healing and nurturing your close relationships.

For those born on May 12: Born under the transition from Gemini to Cancer, these individuals are both intellectually curious and emotionally intuitive. In 2025, they'll thrive by balancing their sharp minds with emotional reflection, focusing on both learning and nurturing their relationships.

Daily Insights: The Moon in Cancer emphasizes emotional well-being, self-care, and nurturing relationships. It's a great day for focusing on home life, connecting with loved ones, and creating a sense of emotional security. With the Sun in Taurus, there's also a grounding influence, helping you stay practical while tending to your emotional needs.

Aries: Emotional reflection is important today. Use this energy to focus on nurturing your relationships and creating balance in your personal life.

Taurus: It's a day for balancing emotional well-being with practical goals. Use your grounded nature to focus on self-care and long-term planning.

Gemini: Emotional connections are highlighted today. Use your communication skills to nurture your relationships and create harmony in your personal life.

Cancer: The Moon in your sign enhances your emotional intuition. Focus on self-care and strengthening your relationships with loved ones.

Leo: While you're often focused on action, today encourages emotional reflection. Use this time to nurture your personal well-being and relationships.

Virgo: Balance is key today. Focus on creating emotional stability in your life while maintaining progress on your practical goals.

Libra: Relationships take on a deeper, more emotional tone today. Focus on nurturing your connections and creating harmony in your personal life.

Scorpio: Your emotional depth is strong today. Use this energy to focus on personal healing and deepening your connections with loved ones.

Sagittarius: It's a day for focusing on emotional well-being. Use this energy to create stability in your personal life and nurture your close relationships.

Capricorn: Emotional reflection is important today. Use this energy to focus on creating stability in your relationships and personal life.

Aquarius: While you're often focused on big ideas, today encourages emotional growth. Use this energy to focus on self-care and personal relationships.

Pisces: Your intuition is heightened today. Use this energy to focus on emotional healing and strengthening your relationships.

For those born on May 13: Born under the Moon in Cancer, these individuals are emotionally intuitive, nurturing, and deeply connected to their home and family. In 2025, they'll thrive by focusing on emotional well-being, nurturing relationships, and creating stability in their personal lives.

May 14, 2025

Daily Insights: The Moon in Cancer continues to emphasize emotional reflection, nurturing relationships, and self-care. However, as the Moon transitions into Leo later in the day, the focus shifts toward self-expression, confidence, and creativity. It's a day for balancing emotional well-being with personal empowerment.

Aries: Start the day focusing on your emotional well-being, but as the Moon moves into Leo, you'll feel more confident and ready to take bold actions.

Taurus: The morning is ideal for nurturing your personal relationships, but later in the day, focus on expressing your creativity and stepping into the spotlight.

Gemini: The day starts with emotional reflection, but as the energy shifts, you'll feel more inclined to engage in social activities and express yourself.

Cancer: The Moon in your sign encourages emotional self-care, but as it enters Leo, your confidence will rise, making it a great time to focus on personal growth.

Leo: The Moon enters your sign later today, boosting your confidence and creativity. Use this energy to pursue your passions and take the lead in your projects.

Virgo: Emotional clarity is important early in the day, but as the energy shifts, focus on creative problem-solving and expressing your unique talents.

Libra: Relationships feel emotionally deep in the morning, but as the day progresses, focus on expressing yourself and embracing your individuality.

Scorpio: It's a day for balancing emotional reflection with personal empowerment. Start with self-care, but later, take bold steps toward your goals.

Sagittarius: The morning is perfect for focusing on emotional well-being, but as the Moon moves into Leo, embrace adventure and new opportunities.

Capricorn: Emotional reflection is key early in the day, but by evening, focus on stepping into leadership roles and pursuing your personal ambitions.

Aquarius: The day begins with introspection, but as the energy shifts, focus on expressing your creativity and connecting with others in meaningful ways.

Pisces: Emotional reflection is important early in the day, but later, use your heightened confidence to pursue creative projects and personal growth.

For those born on May 14: Born under the transition from Cancer to Leo, these individuals are both emotionally intuitive and confident. In 2025, they'll thrive by balancing their emotional well-being with bold actions and personal growth. It's a year for both self-care and self-expression.

Daily Insights: The Moon in Leo emphasizes self-expression, creativity, and confidence. It's a day for stepping into the spotlight, embracing leadership, and pursuing your passions. With Mars in Capricorn, there's also a sense of discipline, making it a great time for combining ambition with creativity.

Aries: Your confidence is high today. Use this energy to pursue your personal goals and step into leadership roles with enthusiasm.

Taurus: Creativity flows easily today. Focus on expressing yourself through your work or hobbies, and don't be afraid to take the lead in projects.

Gemini: It's a great day for social interactions and sharing your ideas. Use your communication skills to inspire others and collaborate on creative endeavors.

Cancer: While your emotional intuition is still strong, today's energy encourages you to step out of your comfort zone and express yourself confidently.

Leo: The Moon in your sign amplifies your natural charisma and creativity. Use this energy to take bold steps toward your passions and inspire others.

Virgo: Balance creativity with practicality today. Use your disciplined nature to focus on long-term goals while expressing your unique talents.

Libra: Relationships feel exciting and dynamic today. Focus on creative ways to connect with loved ones and embrace your individuality.

Scorpio: Your passion is strong today. Use this energy to pursue personal goals with intensity and determination.

Sagittarius: Adventure and creativity are calling you today. Use this energy to explore new opportunities and express yourself freely.

Capricorn: Leadership and discipline come naturally today. Use this energy to focus on personal projects and inspire those around you.

Aquarius: Your creativity shines today. Use this energy to pursue innovative ideas and connect with others through meaningful collaborations.

Pisces: It's a day for self-expression and personal growth. Use your creativity to focus on your goals and embrace new opportunities with confidence.

For those born on May 15: Born under the Moon in Leo, these individuals are charismatic, creative, and confident. In 2025, they'll thrive by stepping into leadership roles, embracing their unique talents, and pursuing their passions with determination.

Daily Insights: The Moon in Leo continues to emphasize confidence, self-expression, and creativity. It's a day for stepping into leadership roles, pursuing your passions, and embracing your individuality. However, as the Moon transitions into Virgo later in the day, the focus shifts toward practicality, organization, and attention to detail.

Aries: Start the day with bold actions and confidence, but as the Moon moves into Virgo, focus on organizing your plans and taking practical steps toward your goals.

Taurus: Use the morning to express your creativity and passion, but later in the day, shift your focus to practical matters and long-term planning.

Gemini: The day begins with exciting conversations and social interactions, but as the energy shifts, focus on refining your ideas and organizing your thoughts.

Cancer: Emotional reflection is important early in the day, but later, focus on practical tasks and creating stability in your personal life.

Leo: The Moon in your sign boosts your charisma and leadership skills, but as the day progresses, focus on grounding your energy and organizing your goals.

Virgo: The Moon enters your sign later today, enhancing your natural attention to detail and practicality. Use this energy to tackle important tasks.

Libra: Relationships take on a dynamic tone early in the day, but as the energy shifts, focus on balancing your emotional connections with practical responsibilities.

Scorpio: It's a day for balancing your passion with practicality. Start with bold actions, but later, focus on refining your plans and staying disciplined.

Sagittarius: The morning is filled with excitement and creativity, but later, shift your focus to practical matters and long-term goals.

Capricorn: Leadership and discipline guide you early in the day, but later, shift your attention to organizing your tasks and working on long-term projects.

Aquarius: Use the morning for creative pursuits, but as the Moon moves into Virgo, focus on practical solutions and refining your ideas.

Pisces: Emotional reflection is important early in the day, but later, focus on grounding yourself and organizing your life for greater stability.

For those born on May 16: Born under the transition from Leo to Virgo, these individuals are both creative and disciplined. In 2025, they'll thrive by balancing their bold ideas with practical action, focusing on both creativity and productivity to achieve their goals.

Daily Insights: The Moon in Virgo emphasizes productivity, organization, and attention to detail. It's a great day for focusing on practical matters, refining your plans, and making steady progress toward long-term goals. With Mercury in Taurus, communication is clear and grounded, making it an ideal time for problem-solving and setting realistic expectations.

Aries: Focus on productivity today. Use your energy to organize your plans and make steady progress toward your long-term goals.

Taurus: It's a day for practical achievements. Use your grounded nature to refine your ideas and work on long-term projects.

Gemini: Your analytical skills are strong today. Use this energy to focus on problem-solving and refining your thoughts.

Cancer: Emotional clarity comes through practicality today. Use this energy to focus on organizing your personal life and creating stability.

Leo: After a period of creativity, today encourages you to focus on practical matters. Use your discipline to make progress on long-term goals.

Virgo: The Moon in your sign enhances your natural strengths. Use this energy to focus on productivity and tackle tasks that require precision.

Libra: Relationships feel grounded today. Focus on creating harmony in your personal connections while staying productive and organized.

Scorpio: Your determination is strong today. Use this energy to focus on your long-term goals and make steady progress toward achieving them.

Sagittarius: Practical matters take precedence today. Use this energy to focus on your responsibilities and organize your thoughts.

Capricorn: Discipline and focus are key today. Use this energy to make significant progress on your long-term projects and goals.

Aquarius: While creativity is important, today encourages you to focus on practical solutions and refining your innovative ideas.

Pisces: Emotional reflection is balanced with practicality today. Use this energy to organize your life and focus on long-term goals.

For those born on May 17: Born under the Moon in Virgo, these individuals are practical, organized, and focused on productivity. In 2025, they'll thrive by refining their plans, staying disciplined, and making steady progress toward their long-term goals.

Daily Insights: The Moon in Virgo continues to emphasize practicality, productivity, and organization, but as it transitions into Libra later in the day, the focus shifts toward balance, relationships, and harmony. It's a day for balancing practical tasks with social interactions and personal connections.

Aries: The day starts with a focus on productivity, but as the Moon moves into Libra, shift your attention to your relationships and finding balance in your life.

Taurus: Use the morning to focus on practical tasks, but later, engage in social interactions and nurture your personal connections.

Gemini: Productivity is high early in the day, but by evening, you'll feel more inclined to engage with others and focus on your relationships.

Cancer: The morning is ideal for organizing your personal life, but as the energy shifts, focus on nurturing your relationships and finding emotional balance.

Leo: Start the day with practical tasks, but as the Moon moves into Libra, focus on balancing your personal goals with your relationships.

Virgo: The Moon in your sign enhances your productivity, but by evening, shift your attention to creating harmony in your relationships.

Libra: The day starts with a focus on productivity, but as the Moon enters your sign, you'll feel energized to focus on your relationships and personal well-being.

Scorpio: It's a day for balancing productivity with emotional growth. Use the morning for practical tasks, but later, focus on deepening your connections with others.

Sagittarius: The day begins with a focus on responsibilities, but by evening, you'll feel more inclined to explore social interactions and embrace balance.

Capricorn: Discipline and focus guide you throughout the day, but later, shift your attention to creating harmony in your relationships and personal life.

Aquarius: The day starts with practical actions, but as the energy shifts, focus on engaging with others and exploring new ideas in your relationships.

Pisces: The morning is perfect for organizing your thoughts and tasks, but by evening, focus on connecting with others and finding emotional balance.

For those born on May 18: Born under the transition from Virgo to Libra, these individuals are both practical and focused on balance. In 2025, they'll thrive by combining their disciplined approach to productivity with a focus on relationships and harmony in their personal life.

Daily Insights: The Moon in Libra emphasizes balance, harmony, and relationships. It's a great day for social interactions, resolving conflicts, and creating equilibrium in your personal and professional life. With the Sun in Taurus, there's also an emphasis on stability, practicality, and long-term goals.

Aries: The energy shifts today, encouraging you to focus on balance and harmony in your relationships. Use this time to create equilibrium in your personal and professional life.

Taurus: Balance is key today. Use your grounded nature to focus on maintaining harmony in your personal relationships while working toward your long-term goals.

Gemini: Relationships take center stage today. Focus on communicating clearly and finding balance in your personal interactions.

Cancer: Balance is important in both your home and professional life today. Use this energy to create harmony and resolve any lingering issues.

Leo: It's a day for balancing your personal ambitions with your relationships. Focus on nurturing your connections while pursuing your goals.

Virgo: Productivity is balanced with harmony today. Use this energy to focus on your relationships while staying organized in your personal goals.

Libra: With the Moon in your sign, your need for balance and harmony is amplified. Focus on creating peace in your relationships and maintaining equilibrium in your life.

Scorpio: Relationships feel emotionally deep today. Use this energy to connect with others on a deeper level while maintaining harmony in your personal life.

Sagittarius: Social interactions are favored today. Use your natural charm to connect with others while ensuring balance in your personal and professional life.

Capricorn: It's a day for balancing your responsibilities with your relationships. Focus on finding harmony between your work and personal life.

Aquarius: Innovation and creativity come naturally today, but focus on creating balance in your interactions and maintaining harmony in your relationships.

Pisces: Emotional balance is important today. Use this energy to connect with loved ones and focus on creating stability in your relationships.

For those born on May 19: Born under the Moon in Libra, these individuals are focused on balance, harmony, and relationships. In 2025, they'll thrive by creating equilibrium in their personal and professional lives while working toward their long-term goals with patience and determination.

Daily Insights: The Moon in Libra continues to emphasize balance, relationships, and harmony, but as it transitions into Scorpio later in the day, the focus shifts toward emotional intensity, transformation, and deep connections. It's a day for balancing social interactions with emotional introspection.

Aries: The day begins with a focus on relationships and balance, but as the Moon moves into Scorpio, you'll feel more inclined to explore deeper emotional connections.

Taurus: Use the early part of the day to focus on social interactions and creating harmony, but later, dive into emotional reflection and personal growth.

Gemini: Relationships are in focus early in the day, but as the energy shifts, you'll feel more introspective and inclined to explore your inner world.

Cancer: Balance is important in the morning, but as the Moon moves into Scorpio, focus on emotional depth and nurturing your closest relationships.

Leo: Start the day by focusing on balance in your interactions, but later, shift your attention to emotional transformation and personal growth.

Virgo: The morning is perfect for maintaining harmony in your daily life, but by evening, focus on emotional clarity and personal reflection.

Libra: The Moon in your sign encourages you to maintain balance in your relationships, but later, you'll feel more inclined to explore emotional depth.

Scorpio: The Moon enters your sign later in the day, heightening your emotional intensity. Use this energy to focus on personal transformation and deepening your connections with others.

Sagittarius: Balance your social life in the morning, but by evening, focus on exploring your emotional world and strengthening your relationships.

Capricorn: Discipline and balance guide you in the morning, but later, shift your attention to emotional reflection and personal transformation.

Aquarius: It's a day for balancing relationships and personal goals. As the energy shifts, focus on emotional depth and meaningful connections.

Pisces: Emotional balance is important early in the day, but as the energy transitions, focus on exploring your inner self and strengthening your emotional connections.

For those born on May 20: Born under the transition from Libra to Scorpio, these individuals are both balanced and emotionally intense. In 2025, they'll thrive by balancing their relationships with personal transformation and emotional growth. It's a year for exploring deeper connections and self-reflection.

Daily Insights: The Moon in Scorpio brings emotional intensity, transformation, and a focus on deep connections. It's a day for introspection, exploring your emotional world, and working through personal transformations. With the Sun entering Gemini, there's also an emphasis on communication, curiosity, and learning.

Aries: Your emotions are intense today. Use this energy for personal transformation and emotional healing while staying open to new perspectives and ideas.

Taurus: It's a day for emotional reflection and personal growth. Use your intuition to explore your inner world and focus on creating emotional stability.

Gemini: With the Sun entering your sign, your curiosity is heightened. Use this energy to engage in deep conversations and explore emotional connections.

Cancer: Emotional depth is strong today. Use this energy to nurture your relationships and focus on personal transformation.

Leo: While you're often focused on action, today encourages emotional reflection. Use this time to explore your feelings and connect with others on a deeper level.

Virgo: Balance is important today. Use this energy to focus on emotional clarity while also maintaining progress on your practical goals.

Libra: Relationships take on a deeper tone today. Focus on emotional connections and use your intuition to guide meaningful conversations.

Scorpio: With the Moon in your sign, your emotional intensity is amplified. Use this energy for self-reflection and personal transformation.

Sagittarius: Emotional introspection is key today. Use your curiosity to explore your feelings and deepen your connections with others.

Capricorn: Your determination is strong today. Use this energy to focus on emotional growth and work on long-term goals that bring stability.

Aquarius: While you're often focused on ideas, today encourages emotional reflection. Use this energy to connect with others on a deeper level.

Pisces: Your intuition is heightened today. Use this energy for emotional healing and focus on creating meaningful connections.

For those born on May 21: Born under the transition from Taurus to Gemini, these individuals are emotionally intense yet curious and communicative. In 2025, they'll thrive by exploring deeper emotional connections while using their sharp minds to engage in intellectual pursuits.

Daily Insights: The Moon in Scorpio continues to bring emotional intensity and a focus on personal transformation. It's a day for introspection, deep conversations, and emotional healing. With Mercury in Gemini, there's an emphasis on clear communication and intellectual exploration, encouraging you to balance your emotions with logic.

Aries: Your emotions are strong today, but balance them with clear communication. Use this energy to explore your inner world while staying open to new ideas.

Taurus: It's a day for emotional reflection and transformation. Use your practical nature to ground your emotions and focus on personal growth.

Gemini: Your communication skills are heightened today. Use this energy to engage in deep conversations and explore your emotional connections.

Cancer: Emotional depth is highlighted today. Use this energy to nurture your relationships and focus on personal transformation and growth.

Leo: While action is important, today encourages you to reflect on your emotions. Use this time to deepen your understanding of yourself and your relationships.

Virgo: Emotional clarity comes through introspection today. Use this energy to focus on your personal growth and long-term goals.

Libra: Relationships feel emotionally intense today. Focus on deepening your connections and finding balance between your emotions and logic.

Scorpio: The Moon in your sign enhances your emotional intensity. Use this energy for self-reflection and transformation in both your personal and emotional life.

Sagittarius: Emotional introspection is key today. Use your natural curiosity to explore your inner world and strengthen your connections with others.

Capricorn: Your determination is strong today. Use this energy to focus on emotional growth and work toward your long-term goals with clarity.

Aquarius: Emotional reflection is important today. Use this energy to focus on creating deeper connections and exploring your inner emotions.

Pisces: Your intuition is heightened today. Use this energy for emotional healing and focus on nurturing your relationships with loved ones.

For those born on May 22: Born under the Moon in Scorpio, these individuals are emotionally intense, intuitive, and deeply connected to their inner world. In 2025, they'll thrive by focusing on emotional healing, personal transformation, and deepening their relationships.

Daily Insights: The Moon in Sagittarius brings a shift toward optimism, adventure, and personal growth. It's a great day for exploring new opportunities, expanding your horizons, and engaging with others in a positive and open-minded way. With Venus in Gemini, relationships feel lively and intellectually stimulating.

Aries: Your adventurous spirit is high today. Use this energy to explore new opportunities and focus on personal growth and self-discovery.

Taurus: After a period of emotional reflection, today encourages you to embrace new experiences and explore opportunities for personal growth.

Gemini: It's a day for learning and exploration. Use your curiosity to engage in stimulating conversations and explore new ideas.

Cancer: Adventure and optimism are calling you today. Step out of your comfort zone and embrace new experiences for personal growth.

Leo: Your confidence is amplified today. Use this energy to pursue new opportunities and take bold action toward your personal goals.

Virgo: It's a great day for learning and expanding your knowledge. Use your disciplined nature to explore new topics and apply them practically.

Libra: Social interactions are lively today. Use this energy to connect with others and embrace new perspectives in your personal life.

Scorpio: After a period of emotional intensity, today encourages you to focus on personal growth and explore new opportunities with optimism.

Sagittarius: The Moon in your sign amplifies your adventurous nature. It's a perfect day to pursue your passions and embrace new possibilities.

Capricorn: While discipline is important, today encourages you to explore new ideas and broaden your horizons with an open mind.

Aquarius: Your innovative ideas shine today. Use this energy to explore new possibilities and share your unique perspective with others.

Pisces: It's a day for personal growth and exploration. Use your intuition to guide you as you embrace new opportunities and expand your horizons.

For those born on May 23: Born under the Moon in Sagittarius, these individuals are adventurous, optimistic, and eager to explore new possibilities. In 2025, they'll thrive by embracing opportunities for growth, learning, and self-discovery while maintaining a positive outlook.

Daily Insights: The Moon in Sagittarius continues to inspire exploration, optimism, and personal growth. It's a great day for learning new things, pursuing your passions, and expanding your horizons. With Mercury in Gemini, communication is clear and lively, making it a perfect time for engaging conversations and sharing ideas.

Aries: Your curiosity is strong today. Use this energy to explore new opportunities and engage in conversations that inspire personal growth.

Taurus: It's a day for balancing practicality with exploration. Use your grounded nature to explore new ideas while staying focused on your long-term goals.

Gemini: Communication is your strength today. Use this energy to engage in meaningful conversations and explore new ideas with an open mind.

Cancer: Adventure and learning are calling you today. Step out of your comfort zone and embrace new experiences for personal growth and development.

Leo: Your confidence and leadership are highlighted today. Use this energy to take bold actions toward your goals and inspire those around you.

Virgo: It's a great day for learning and expanding your knowledge. Use your analytical skills to explore new topics and gain valuable insights.

Libra: Relationships feel lively and intellectually stimulating. Use this energy to engage in conversations that deepen your connections and broaden your perspective.

Scorpio: After a period of emotional depth, today encourages you to focus on personal growth and embrace new opportunities for self-discovery.

Sagittarius: The Moon in your sign amplifies your natural curiosity and sense of adventure. It's a perfect day for exploring new ideas and pursuing your passions.

Capricorn: While discipline is important, today encourages you to explore new possibilities and broaden your horizons with optimism.

Aquarius: Your innovative thinking shines today. Use this energy to explore creative projects and engage in conversations that inspire new ideas.

Pisces: It's a day for personal exploration and learning. Use your intuition to guide you as you explore new opportunities and expand your knowledge.

For those born on May 24: Born under the Moon in Sagittarius, these individuals are adventurous, curious, and eager to learn. In 2025, they'll thrive by embracing new experiences, pursuing personal growth, and expanding their knowledge through exploration.

Daily Insights: The Moon in Sagittarius continues to inspire exploration and learning, but as it transitions into Capricorn later in the day, the focus shifts toward discipline, practicality, and long-term planning. It's a day for balancing adventure with responsibility and setting clear goals for the future.

Aries: Start the day with a sense of adventure, but as the Moon moves into Capricorn, focus on grounding your energy and setting long-term goals.

Taurus: The day begins with optimism, but later, you'll feel more inclined to focus on practical matters and organizing your long-term plans.

Gemini: Use the early part of the day for exploration and learning, but as the energy shifts, focus on refining your goals and taking practical steps toward achieving them.

Cancer: The day starts with excitement and exploration, but later, shift your focus to creating stability in your personal life and setting clear goals.

Leo: While you'll feel energized and confident early in the day, the Moon in Capricorn encourages you to focus on discipline and long-term planning later on.

Virgo: Use the morning for intellectual exploration and personal growth, but as the day progresses, focus on organizing your life and working toward your long-term ambitions.

Libra: Socializing and learning are highlighted early in the day, but by evening, you'll feel more focused on practical matters and setting goals for the future.

Scorpio: Adventure and exploration take center stage in the morning, but as the energy shifts, focus on emotional reflection and long-term planning.

Sagittarius: The Moon in your sign brings a sense of optimism and adventure, but later, as the energy shifts to Capricorn, you'll feel more inclined to focus on responsibility and long-term success.

Capricorn: The day begins with exploration, but as the Moon enters your sign, you'll feel energized to focus on practical tasks and long-term goals.

Aquarius: It's a day for balancing adventure with practicality. Use the morning for exploration, but later, focus on refining your ideas and setting clear goals.

Pisces: The day starts with exploration and optimism, but as the energy shifts, focus on grounding yourself and creating long-term stability.

For those born on May 25: Born under the transition from Sagittarius to Capricorn, these individuals are both adventurous and disciplined. In 2025, they'll find success by balancing their desire for exploration with a focus on long-term goals and responsibility.

Daily Insights: The Moon in Capricorn emphasizes discipline, practicality, and long-term planning. It's a great day for focusing on your goals, staying productive, and making steady progress. With Mars in Taurus, there's also a boost of determination and focus, making it an ideal day for practical achievements.

Aries: Focus on your long-term goals today. Use your energy to make steady progress toward your ambitions while staying disciplined.

Taurus: It's a great day for practical achievements. Use your determination and focus to work on long-term plans and build stability in your life.

Gemini: Your focus shifts toward practicality today. Use this energy to organize your ideas and take disciplined steps toward your goals.

Cancer: It's a day for focusing on stability and long-term success. Use this energy to create structure in your personal life and make progress on your goals.

Leo: Leadership and confidence are your strengths today. Use this energy to focus on long-term goals and inspire others to follow your lead.

Virgo: Productivity is high today. Use this energy to focus on tasks that require attention to detail and long-term planning.

Libra: Relationships feel grounded and stable today. Focus on creating harmony in your personal connections while working toward your goals.

Scorpio: Your determination is strong today. Use this energy to focus on your long-term goals and make practical decisions for your future.

Sagittarius: While adventure is important, today encourages you to focus on grounding yourself and working on practical goals.

Capricorn: The Moon in your sign enhances your natural discipline and determination. It's a perfect day for making significant progress on your long-term goals.

Aquarius: Focus on practical matters today. Use your innovative thinking to find creative solutions to long-term challenges.

Pisces: Emotional stability is important today. Use this energy to focus on your long-term goals and work toward creating stability in your life.

For those born on May 26: Born under the Moon in Capricorn, these individuals are disciplined, practical, and focused on long-term success. In 2025, they'll thrive by setting clear goals and making steady progress toward achieving them, using their disciplined nature to stay focused on their ambitions.

Daily Insights: The Moon in Capricorn continues to emphasize practicality, discipline, and long-term planning. However, as the Moon transitions into Aquarius later in the day, the focus shifts toward creativity, innovation, and social interactions. It's a day for balancing productivity with creative exploration.

Aries: Use the morning for disciplined work, but as the Moon moves into Aquarius, embrace your creativity and explore new ideas.

Taurus: The day starts with a focus on productivity and long-term goals, but later, you'll feel more inclined to explore new possibilities and engage in social activities.

Gemini: Productivity is high early in the day, but by evening, shift your focus to connecting with others and exploring innovative ideas.

Cancer: Start the day with practical goals in mind, but later, shift your attention to creative projects and social interactions.

Leo: The morning is ideal for focused work, but as the energy shifts, you'll feel more inclined to engage in collaborative efforts and creative pursuits.

Virgo: Use the early part of the day for productivity and organization, but by evening, you'll feel more inclined to engage in creative problem-solving and social activities.

Libra: Relationships feel stable early in the day, but later, focus on finding creative solutions and connecting with others in meaningful ways.

Scorpio: Determination and discipline guide you early in the day, but by evening, you'll feel more inclined to explore new perspectives and innovative ideas.

Sagittarius: While productivity is important, the evening encourages you to explore new possibilities and engage in social interactions.

Capricorn: The Moon in your sign enhances your discipline and focus, but as the energy shifts, focus on social connections and creative exploration.

Aquarius: The evening brings a burst of creative energy. Use this time to explore innovative ideas and connect with others in meaningful ways.

Pisces: Emotional reflection is key early in the day, but as the energy shifts, focus on expressing your creativity and engaging in social interactions.

For those born on May 27: Born under the transition from Capricorn to Aquarius, these individuals are both disciplined and creative. In 2025, they'll thrive by balancing their practical mindset with their innovative ideas. It's a year for combining discipline with creativity and social connections.

Daily Insights: The Moon in Aquarius brings a focus on creativity, innovation, and social interactions. It's a great day for exploring new ideas, connecting with others, and embracing your individuality. With Mercury in Gemini, communication is clear and lively, making it an ideal time for engaging conversations and sharing ideas.

Aries: Your creativity shines today. Use this energy to explore new ideas and connect with others through meaningful collaborations.

Taurus: It's a day for combining practicality with creativity. Use your determination to bring innovative ideas into reality.

Gemini: Social interactions are stimulating today. Engage in conversations that inspire new perspectives and broaden your horizons.

Cancer: Creativity and innovation are calling you today. Use this energy to explore new ways of expressing yourself and connecting with others.

Leo: Leadership and creativity go hand in hand today. Use your confidence to take the lead in innovative projects and inspire others.

Virgo: It's a great day for exploring creative solutions. Use your analytical skills to approach challenges in innovative ways.

Libra: Relationships are dynamic and exciting today. Focus on connecting with others in unconventional ways and exploring new perspectives.

Scorpio: Your passion for personal growth is strong today. Use this energy to explore new ideas and engage in meaningful conversations.

Sagittarius: Adventure and creativity are calling you today. Focus on expanding your horizons and embracing new opportunities.

Capricorn: While discipline is important, today encourages you to explore new ideas and engage in creative thinking.

Aquarius: With the Moon in your sign, your creativity and individuality are amplified. Use this energy to pursue innovative ideas and connect with others.

Pisces: Your intuition is strong today. Use this energy to explore creative projects and connect with others in meaningful ways.

For those born on May 28: Born under the Moon in Aquarius, these individuals are creative, innovative, and socially connected. In 2025, they'll thrive by embracing their individuality, exploring new ideas, and focusing on personal growth through social connections and creative expression.

Daily Insights: The Moon in Aquarius continues to emphasize creativity, innovation, and individuality, but as it transitions into Pisces later in the day, the focus shifts toward emotional reflection, intuition, and empathy. It's a day for balancing intellectual exploration with emotional depth.

Aries: Start the day with innovative ideas and social connections, but as the Moon enters Pisces, shift your focus to emotional reflection and nurturing relationships.

Taurus: The morning is great for exploring creative solutions, but later, focus on emotional healing and connecting with loved ones on a deeper level.

Gemini: Your mind is active early in the day, but as the Moon enters Pisces, focus on balancing your intellectual pursuits with emotional reflection.

Cancer: Emotional intuition is heightened as the day progresses. Use the morning for socializing, but later, focus on self-care and nurturing close relationships.

Leo: Creativity shines early in the day, but as the energy shifts, focus on your emotional well-being and connecting with those who matter most.

Virgo: Productivity is high in the morning, but by evening, you'll feel more inclined to explore your emotions and focus on personal healing.

Libra: Relationships feel dynamic early in the day, but as the Moon enters Pisces, focus on deepening your emotional connections and finding inner balance.

Scorpio: Use the morning for exploring new ideas, but later, focus on emotional growth and reflection. Your intuition is especially strong today.

Sagittarius: The day starts with excitement and creativity, but later, you'll feel more inclined to focus on emotional healing and connecting with loved ones.

Capricorn: Early productivity gives way to emotional reflection as the day progresses. Focus on grounding yourself and nurturing your relationships.

Aquarius: The Moon in your sign brings out your creativity, but as the energy shifts, focus on emotional introspection and personal growth.

Pisces: The Moon enters your sign later today, amplifying your intuition and emotional sensitivity. Use this energy to focus on self-care and emotional healing.

For those born on May 29: Born under the transition from Aquarius to Pisces, these individuals are both creative and emotionally intuitive. In 2025, they'll thrive by balancing their innovative ideas with emotional reflection, focusing on both personal growth and deepening relationships.

Daily Insights: The Moon in Pisces brings a focus on emotional reflection, intuition, and creativity. It's a great day for engaging in artistic projects, connecting with loved ones on a deeper level, and exploring your inner world. With Mercury in Gemini, communication remains lively, making it a good day for expressing your emotions through words.

Aries: Your intuition is strong today. Use this energy to focus on emotional reflection and nurture your relationships with empathy and understanding.

Taurus: It's a great day for combining creativity with practicality. Focus on expressing your emotions through artistic projects or clear communication.

Gemini: Emotional reflection is key today. Use this energy to connect with your inner self and engage in meaningful conversations with loved ones.

Cancer: The Moon in Pisces enhances your emotional intuition. Use this energy to focus on self-care and strengthening your personal relationships.

Leo: While you're often focused on action, today encourages emotional reflection. Use this time to explore your feelings and deepen your connections.

Virgo: Balance your practical nature with emotional reflection today. Use this energy to focus on your inner world and nurture your relationships.

Libra: Relationships take on a deeper tone today. Focus on emotional connections and use your intuition to guide your conversations.

Scorpio: Your emotional depth is amplified today. Use this energy for self-reflection and strengthening your relationships with loved ones.

Sagittarius: It's a day for focusing on emotional well-being. Use this energy to connect with your inner self and explore your feelings.

Capricorn: Emotional reflection is important today. Focus on creating stability in your personal life and deepening your relationships.

Aquarius: While you're often focused on big ideas, today encourages emotional growth. Use this energy to focus on self-care and personal relationships.

Pisces: The Moon in your sign amplifies your intuition and emotional sensitivity. Use this energy to focus on personal healing and nurturing your relationships.

For those born on May 30: Born under the Moon in Pisces, these individuals are emotionally intuitive, creative, and deeply connected to their inner world. In 2025, they'll thrive by focusing on personal healing, nurturing relationships, and expressing their creativity through meaningful projects.

Daily Insights: The Moon in Pisces continues to emphasize emotional depth, intuition, and creativity. It's a day for self-reflection, engaging in artistic projects, and nurturing close relationships. With Venus in Gemini, communication in relationships remains lively and curious, encouraging meaningful conversations and open dialogue.

Aries: Your emotions are strong today. Use this energy to reflect on your inner world and focus on nurturing your personal relationships with empathy.

Taurus: It's a day for balancing practicality with emotional reflection. Use this energy to focus on emotional healing and expressing yourself creatively.

Gemini: Your communication skills are highlighted today. Use this energy to engage in deep conversations and explore your emotional connections.

Cancer: Emotional reflection is important today. Use this time to nurture your personal well-being and strengthen your close relationships.

Leo: While you're often focused on action, today encourages you to reflect on your emotions. Use this energy to deepen your connections with loved ones.

Virgo: It's a day for emotional clarity and reflection. Focus on balancing your practical nature with your emotional well-being.

Libra: Relationships take on a deeper, more emotional tone today. Use this energy to strengthen your emotional connections and engage in meaningful conversations.

Scorpio: Your emotional depth is highlighted today. Use this energy for self-reflection and to focus on personal growth and healing.

Sagittarius: It's a day for focusing on emotional well-being. Use this energy to reflect on your inner self and nurture your relationships with care.

Capricorn: Emotional reflection is important today. Use this energy to create stability in your personal life and focus on nurturing your relationships.

Aquarius: While you're often focused on new ideas, today encourages you to focus on your emotional growth. Use this energy to connect with others on a deeper level.

Pisces: The Moon in your sign enhances your emotional intuition. Use this energy for self-care, personal healing, and strengthening your relationships with loved ones.

For those born on May 31: Born under the Moon in Pisces, these individuals are emotionally intuitive, creative, and deeply connected to their inner world. In 2025, they'll thrive by focusing on personal healing, nurturing relationships, and expressing their creativity through meaningful projects.

Daily Insights: The Moon transitions into Aries, bringing energy, confidence, and a focus on action. It's a day for taking bold steps toward your goals, embracing new opportunities, and focusing on personal ambitions. With the Sun in Gemini, communication and curiosity are also highlighted, making it a great time for exploring new ideas.

Aries: The Moon in your sign brings a boost of energy and confidence. Use this to take bold steps toward your personal goals and embrace new opportunities.

Taurus: It's a day for action and confidence. Use this energy to push forward on your goals while staying grounded in your practical plans.

Gemini: Communication and action are your strengths today. Use this energy to pursue new ideas, engage in meaningful conversations, and take action on your plans.

Cancer: Confidence and emotional reflection are balanced today. Use this energy to take bold steps toward personal growth while maintaining emotional balance.

Leo: Your leadership skills are highlighted today. Use your energy and confidence to inspire others and take charge of projects that excite you.

Virgo: It's a day for balancing action with practical steps. Use your disciplined nature to take bold actions while staying focused on your long-term goals.

Libra: Relationships take on a dynamic tone today. Use your confidence to communicate openly and strengthen your connections with others.

Scorpio: Your determination is strong today. Use this energy to take bold steps toward your long-term goals and focus on personal growth.

Sagittarius: Adventure and action are calling you today. Use your enthusiasm to explore new opportunities and embrace exciting challenges.

Capricorn: Discipline and focus guide you today. Use this energy to take practical steps toward achieving your long-term goals and ambitions.

Aquarius: Your creativity and confidence shine today. Use this energy to explore new ideas and take bold actions toward personal growth.

Pisces: It's a day for taking action on your personal ambitions. Use your intuition to guide you as you embrace new opportunities with confidence.

For those born on June 1: Born under the Moon in Aries, these individuals are confident, action-oriented, and ambitious. In 2025, they'll thrive by taking bold steps toward their goals and embracing new opportunities with enthusiasm and determination.

Daily Insights: The Moon in Aries continues to bring energy, motivation, and a focus on personal goals. It's a great day for taking decisive actions, embracing challenges, and pursuing your ambitions. With Mercury in Gemini, communication is clear and lively, making it a good time for sharing ideas and connecting with others.

Aries: Your confidence and motivation are high today. Use this energy to push forward on your personal goals and take bold actions with confidence.

Taurus: It's a day for balancing bold actions with practicality. Use your grounded nature to take steady steps toward your long-term goals.

Gemini: Communication and action are your strengths today. Use this energy to engage in meaningful conversations and take action on new ideas.

Cancer: Confidence and emotional balance are key today. Use this energy to focus on personal growth and take bold steps toward your ambitions.

Leo: Leadership and action are highlighted today. Use your natural confidence to take charge of projects and inspire those around you.

Virgo: It's a productive day for focusing on your goals. Use your disciplined nature to take bold actions while staying organized and practical.

Libra: Relationships feel dynamic and exciting today. Focus on communicating openly and taking action to strengthen your personal connections.

Scorpio: Your determination is strong today. Use this energy to focus on your long-term goals and take decisive actions toward achieving them.

Sagittarius: Adventure and excitement are calling you today. Use your enthusiasm to explore new opportunities and take bold steps toward your dreams.

Capricorn: Discipline and focus guide you today. Use this energy to take practical steps toward your long-term goals and ambitions.

Aquarius: Your creativity and innovative thinking shine today. Use this energy to explore new ideas and take bold actions toward your personal goals.

Pisces: It's a day for taking action on your personal ambitions. Use your intuition to guide you as you embrace new opportunities with confidence.

For those born on June 2: Born under the Moon in Aries, these individuals are energetic, driven, and focused on taking bold actions toward their goals. In 2025, they'll thrive by pursuing new opportunities with confidence and determination, making significant progress toward their ambitions.

Daily Insights: The Moon in Aries continues to provide energy, confidence, and motivation, but as it transitions into Taurus later in the day, the focus shifts toward stability, practicality, and long-term planning. It's a day for balancing bold actions with careful consideration of your long-term goals.

Aries: The day starts with high energy and motivation, but as the Moon moves into Taurus, focus on grounding yourself and setting practical goals for the future.

Taurus: The Moon enters your sign later today, bringing a sense of stability and focus on practical matters. Use this energy to work toward your long-term ambitions.

Gemini: It's a day for balancing bold ideas with practical steps. Use the morning for exploration, but by evening, shift your focus to long-term planning.

Cancer: Start the day with confidence and action, but as the energy shifts, focus on creating stability in your personal life and making thoughtful decisions.

Leo: The morning is ideal for pursuing your passions, but as the Moon enters Taurus, focus on grounding your ideas and setting realistic goals.

Virgo: Use the early part of the day for productivity, but by evening, shift your attention to organizing your thoughts and refining your plans for the future.

Libra: Relationships feel dynamic early in the day, but as the energy shifts, focus on creating stability and balance in your personal connections.

Scorpio: The day begins with determination and bold action, but as the Moon moves into Taurus, focus on creating emotional and financial security.

Sagittarius: Adventure and action dominate the morning, but as the day progresses, shift your focus to practical matters and grounding your plans.

Capricorn: Discipline and focus guide you throughout the day, but later, shift your attention to creating stability and working on long-term goals.

Aquarius: The morning is perfect for exploring new ideas, but by evening, focus on practical solutions and setting achievable goals for the future.

Pisces: The day starts with bold action, but as the energy shifts, focus on grounding your emotions and creating stability in your personal life.

For those born on June 3: Born under the transition from Aries to Taurus, these individuals are both action-oriented and practical. In 2025, they'll find success by balancing their bold ambitions with practical planning, focusing on long-term goals while embracing new opportunities for growth.

Daily Insights: The Moon in Taurus emphasizes stability, practicality, and long-term planning. It's a great day for focusing on practical matters, setting achievable goals, and making steady progress. With Mars in Capricorn, there's a boost of determination and focus, making it a perfect day for productivity and success.

Aries: Focus on grounding your energy today. Use your determination to make steady progress toward your long-term goals and practical matters.

Taurus: The Moon in your sign enhances your sense of stability and focus on practical goals. Use this energy to work toward your personal growth and ambitions.

Gemini: It's a day for focusing on long-term planning. Use your curiosity to explore new ideas while staying grounded in practical solutions.

Cancer: Stability and emotional security are important today. Use this energy to create a sense of comfort and progress in your personal life.

Leo: It's a great day for focusing on long-term goals. Use your leadership skills to inspire others while making steady progress on your ambitions.

Virgo: Productivity is high today. Use this energy to focus on tasks that require attention to detail and long-term planning.

Libra: Relationships feel stable and secure today. Focus on creating harmony in your personal connections while also working on your goals.

Scorpio: Your determination is strong today. Use this energy to focus on your long-term goals and make practical decisions for your future.

Sagittarius: Adventure takes a backseat today as you focus on grounding yourself and working toward practical goals.

Capricorn: Discipline and focus are your strengths today. Use this energy to make steady progress on your long-term projects and goals.

Aquarius: While creativity is important, today encourages you to focus on practical solutions and setting achievable goals for the future.

Pisces: Emotional stability is key today. Use this energy to ground yourself and focus on creating long-term security in your relationships and personal life.

For those born on June 4: Born under the Moon in Taurus, these individuals are practical, grounded, and focused on long-term success. In 2025, they'll thrive by setting clear goals and making steady progress toward achieving them, using their disciplined nature to stay focused on their ambitions.

June 5, 2025

Daily Insights: The Moon in Taurus continues to emphasize stability and practicality, but as it transitions into Gemini later in the day, the focus shifts toward communication, learning, and curiosity. It's a day for balancing practical matters with intellectual exploration and social interactions.

Aries: The day begins with a focus on practical goals, but as the Moon moves into Gemini, you'll feel more inclined to engage in conversations and explore new ideas.

Taurus: Use the morning for practical tasks, but later, shift your focus to learning and connecting with others in meaningful ways.

Gemini: The Moon enters your sign later today, bringing a burst of energy and curiosity. It's a great time for exploring new ideas and engaging in conversations.

Cancer: Start the day by focusing on stability, but as the energy shifts, you'll feel more inclined to connect with others and engage in intellectual pursuits.

Leo: The morning is ideal for working on long-term goals, but by evening, focus on socializing and sharing your ideas with others.

Virgo: Use the early part of the day for productivity, but later, shift your attention to learning and expanding your knowledge through conversations.

Libra: Relationships feel stable early in the day, but as the Moon moves into Gemini, focus on communicating openly and exploring new perspectives.

Scorpio: The day begins with determination and focus on practical matters, but later, you'll feel more inclined to engage in intellectual exploration.

Sagittarius: The morning is perfect for grounding your energy, but by evening, you'll feel more curious and eager to explore new opportunities.

Capricorn: Discipline and focus guide you early in the day, but as the energy shifts, you'll feel more inclined to engage in social interactions and learning.

Aquarius: The day starts with practical actions, but as the Moon moves into Gemini, focus on engaging with others and exploring new ideas.

Pisces: The morning is perfect for organizing your thoughts and tasks, but by evening, focus on connecting with others and finding emotional balance.

For those born on June 5: Born under the transition from Taurus to Gemini, these individuals are both practical and curious. In 2025, they'll thrive by balancing their disciplined approach with intellectual exploration, focusing on both long-term goals and learning new things.

June 6, 2025

Daily Insights: The Moon in Gemini brings a focus on communication, learning, and curiosity. It's a great day for engaging in conversations, exploring new ideas, and connecting with others. With Mercury in Gemini, there's an added emphasis on clear and lively communication, making it an ideal time for intellectual exploration.

Aries: Your curiosity is strong today. Use this energy to engage in conversations, explore new ideas, and take action on your personal goals.

Taurus: It's a day for balancing practicality with intellectual exploration. Use your grounded nature to communicate your thoughts clearly and explore new perspectives.

Gemini: The Moon in your sign enhances your communication skills. Use this energy to connect with others, share your ideas, and explore new opportunities.

Cancer: It's a day for focusing on learning and intellectual growth. Use this energy to connect with your inner self and engage in meaningful conversations.

Leo: Leadership and creativity are highlighted today. Use your confidence to inspire others and share your innovative ideas with enthusiasm.

Virgo: Your analytical skills are sharp today. Use this energy to focus on problem-solving and exploring new ideas through conversation.

Libra: Relationships feel dynamic and intellectually stimulating. Focus on engaging with loved ones in meaningful conversations and exploring new perspectives.

Scorpio: Your emotional depth is strong today. Use this energy to engage in deep conversations and explore new ideas that challenge your thinking.

Sagittarius: Adventure and learning go hand in hand today. Use your curiosity to explore new opportunities and engage in conversations that inspire you.

Capricorn: It's a day for balancing discipline with intellectual exploration. Use this energy to engage in thoughtful discussions and refine your long-term goals.

Aquarius: Your creativity and innovative thinking shine today. Use this energy to explore new ideas and engage in collaborative conversations.

Pisces: It's a day for intellectual exploration and emotional reflection. Use this energy to connect with others in meaningful ways and share your ideas.

For those born on June 6: Born under the Moon in Gemini, these individuals are curious, communicative, and eager to explore new ideas. In 2025, they'll thrive by engaging in conversations, learning new things, and using their sharp minds to make meaningful connections with others.

Daily Insights: The Moon in Gemini continues to emphasize communication, learning, and curiosity, but as it transitions into Cancer later in the day, the focus shifts toward emotional well-being, nurturing relationships, and self-care. It's a day for balancing intellectual exploration with emotional connection.

Aries: The day begins with lively conversations, but as the Moon moves into Cancer, shift your focus to emotional reflection and nurturing your relationships.

Taurus: Use the morning for exploring new ideas, but as the energy shifts, focus on creating emotional stability in your personal life.

Gemini: Your communication skills are heightened early in the day, but later, focus on emotional connections and strengthening your relationships with loved ones.

Cancer: The Moon enters your sign later today, heightening your emotional sensitivity. It's a great time for self-care and nurturing close relationships.

Leo: Start the day with intellectual exploration, but as the Moon moves into Cancer, shift your focus to emotional balance and personal growth.

Virgo: Productivity is high early in the day, but by evening, focus on emotional reflection and nurturing your personal well-being.

Libra: Relationships are intellectually stimulating in the morning, but later, focus on deepening emotional connections and creating harmony in your relationships.

Scorpio: Your curiosity is high early in the day, but as the energy shifts, focus on emotional healing and strengthening your relationships.

Sagittarius: The day begins with excitement and exploration, but later, shift your focus to emotional reflection and personal growth.

Capricorn: Use the morning for practical tasks and intellectual pursuits, but by evening, focus on nurturing your emotional well-being and relationships.

Aquarius: Creativity and intellectual exploration are highlighted early in the day, but as the Moon enters Cancer, focus on emotional growth and self-care.

Pisces: The day begins with curiosity, but later, you'll feel more inclined to focus on emotional healing and nurturing your close relationships.

For those born on June 7: Born under the transition from Gemini to Cancer, these individuals are both intellectually curious and emotionally intuitive. In 2025, they'll thrive by balancing their sharp minds with emotional reflection, focusing on both learning and nurturing their relationships.

Daily Insights: The Moon in Cancer emphasizes emotional well-being, self-care, and nurturing relationships. It's a great day for focusing on home life, connecting with loved ones, and creating a sense of emotional security. With Venus in Gemini, relationships may feel intellectually stimulating, adding excitement to personal connections.

Aries: Emotional reflection is important today. Use this energy to focus on nurturing your relationships and creating balance in your personal life.

Taurus: It's a day for balancing emotional well-being with practical goals. Use your grounded nature to focus on self-care and long-term planning.

Gemini: Emotional connections are highlighted today. Use your communication skills to nurture your relationships and create harmony in your personal life.

Cancer: The Moon in your sign enhances your emotional intuition. Focus on self-care and strengthening your relationships with loved ones.

Leo: While you're often focused on action, today encourages emotional reflection. Use this time to nurture your personal well-being and relationships.

Virgo: Balance is key today. Focus on creating emotional stability in your life while maintaining progress on your practical goals.

Libra: Relationships take on a deeper, more emotional tone today. Focus on nurturing your connections and creating harmony in your personal life.

Scorpio: Your emotional depth is strong today. Use this energy to focus on personal healing and deepening your connections with loved ones.

Sagittarius: It's a day for focusing on emotional well-being. Use this energy to create stability in your personal life and nurture your close relationships.

Capricorn: Emotional reflection is important today. Use this energy to focus on creating stability in your relationships and personal life.

Aquarius: While you're often focused on big ideas, today encourages emotional growth. Use this energy to focus on self-care and personal relationships.

Pisces: Your intuition is heightened today. Use this energy to focus on emotional healing and strengthening your relationships.

For those born on June 8: Born under the Moon in Cancer, these individuals are emotionally intuitive, nurturing, and deeply connected to their home and family. In 2025, they'll thrive by focusing on emotional well-being, nurturing relationships, and creating stability in their personal lives.

Daily Insights: The Moon in Cancer continues to emphasize emotional reflection, nurturing relationships, and self-care. However, as the Moon transitions into Leo later in the day, the focus shifts toward self-expression, confidence, and creativity. It's a day for balancing emotional well-being with personal empowerment.

Aries: Start the day focusing on your emotional well-being, but as the Moon moves into Leo, you'll feel more confident and ready to take bold actions.

Taurus: The morning is ideal for nurturing your personal relationships, but later in the day, focus on expressing your creativity and stepping into the spotlight.

Gemini: The day starts with emotional reflection, but as the energy shifts, you'll feel more inclined to engage in social activities and express yourself.

Cancer: The Moon in your sign encourages emotional self-care, but as it enters Leo, your confidence will rise, making it a great time to focus on personal growth.

Leo: The Moon enters your sign later today, boosting your confidence and creativity. Use this energy to pursue your passions and take the lead in your projects.

Virgo: Emotional clarity is important early in the day, but as the energy shifts, focus on creative problem-solving and expressing your unique talents.

Libra: Relationships feel emotionally deep in the morning, but as the day progresses, focus on expressing yourself and embracing your individuality.

Scorpio: It's a day for balancing emotional reflection with personal empowerment. Start with self-care, but later, take bold steps toward your goals.

Sagittarius: The morning is perfect for focusing on emotional well-being, but as the Moon moves into Leo, embrace adventure and new opportunities.

Capricorn: Emotional reflection is key early in the day, but by evening, focus on stepping into leadership roles and pursuing your personal ambitions.

Aquarius: The day begins with introspection, but as the energy shifts, focus on expressing your creativity and connecting with others in meaningful ways.

Pisces: Emotional reflection is important early in the day, but later, use your heightened confidence to pursue creative projects and personal growth.

For those born on June 9: Born under the transition from Cancer to Leo, these individuals are both emotionally intuitive and confident. In 2025, they'll thrive by balancing their emotional well-being with bold actions and personal growth. It's a year for both self-care and self-expression.

Daily Insights: The Moon in Leo emphasizes self-expression, creativity, and confidence. It's a day for stepping into the spotlight, embracing leadership, and pursuing your passions. With Mars in Capricorn, there's also a sense of discipline, making it a great time for combining ambition with creativity.

Aries: Your confidence is high today. Use this energy to pursue your personal goals and step into leadership roles with enthusiasm.

Taurus: Creativity flows easily today. Focus on expressing yourself through your work or hobbies, and don't be afraid to take the lead in projects.

Gemini: It's a great day for social interactions and sharing your ideas. Use your communication skills to inspire others and collaborate on creative endeavors.

Cancer: While your emotional intuition is still strong, today's energy encourages you to step out of your comfort zone and express yourself confidently.

Leo: The Moon in your sign amplifies your natural charisma and creativity. Use this energy to take bold steps toward your passions and inspire others.

Virgo: Balance creativity with practicality today. Use your disciplined nature to focus on long-term goals while expressing your unique talents.

Libra: Relationships feel exciting and dynamic today. Focus on creative ways to connect with loved ones and embrace your individuality.

Scorpio: Your passion is strong today. Use this energy to pursue personal goals with intensity and determination.

Sagittarius: Adventure and creativity are calling you today. Use this energy to explore new opportunities and express yourself freely.

Capricorn: Leadership and discipline come naturally today. Use this energy to focus on personal projects and inspire those around you.

Aquarius: Your creativity shines today. Use this energy to pursue innovative ideas and connect with others through meaningful collaborations.

Pisces: It's a day for self-expression and personal growth. Use your creativity to focus on your goals and embrace new opportunities with confidence.

For those born on June 10: Born under the Moon in Leo, these individuals are charismatic, creative, and confident. In 2025, they'll thrive by stepping into leadership roles, embracing their unique talents, and pursuing their passions with determination.

Daily Insights: The Moon in Leo continues to emphasize confidence, creativity, and leadership. It's a day for taking bold actions, expressing yourself, and pursuing your passions. However, as the Moon transitions into Virgo later in the day, the focus shifts toward practicality, organization, and attention to detail.

Aries: Start the day with bold actions and confidence, but as the Moon moves into Virgo, focus on organizing your plans and taking practical steps toward your goals.

Taurus: Use the morning to express your creativity and passion, but later in the day, shift your focus to practical matters and long-term planning.

Gemini: The day begins with exciting conversations and social interactions, but as the energy shifts, focus on refining your ideas and organizing your thoughts.

Cancer: Emotional reflection is important early in the day, but later, focus on practical tasks and creating stability in your personal life.

Leo: The Moon in your sign boosts your charisma and leadership skills, but as the day progresses, focus on grounding your energy and organizing your goals.

Virgo: The Moon enters your sign later today, enhancing your natural attention to detail and practicality. Use this energy to tackle important tasks.

Libra: Relationships take on a dynamic tone early in the day, but as the energy shifts, focus on balancing your emotional connections with practical responsibilities.

Scorpio: It's a day for balancing your passion with practicality. Start with bold actions, but later, focus on refining your plans and staying disciplined.

Sagittarius: The morning is filled with excitement and creativity, but later, shift your focus to practical matters and long-term goals.

Capricorn: Leadership and discipline guide you early in the day, but later, shift your attention to organizing your tasks and working on long-term projects.

Aquarius: Use the morning for creative pursuits, but as the Moon moves into Virgo, focus on practical solutions and refining your ideas.

Pisces: Emotional reflection is important early in the day, but later, focus on grounding yourself and organizing your life for greater stability.

For those born on June 11: Born under the transition from Leo to Virgo, these individuals are both creative and disciplined. In 2025, they'll thrive by balancing their bold ideas with practical action, focusing on both creativity and productivity to achieve their goals.

Daily Insights: The Moon in Virgo emphasizes productivity, organization, and attention to detail. It's a great day for focusing on practical matters, refining your plans, and making steady progress toward long-term goals. With Mercury in Gemini, communication is clear and grounded, making it an ideal time for problem-solving and setting realistic expectations.

Aries: Focus on productivity today. Use your energy to organize your plans and make steady progress toward your long-term goals.

Taurus: It's a day for practical achievements. Use your grounded nature to refine your ideas and work on long-term projects.

Gemini: Your analytical skills are strong today. Use this energy to focus on problem-solving and refining your thoughts.

Cancer: Emotional clarity comes through practicality today. Use this energy to focus on organizing your personal life and creating stability.

Leo: After a period of creativity, today encourages you to focus on practical matters. Use your discipline to make progress on long-term goals.

Virgo: The Moon in your sign enhances your natural strengths. Use this energy to focus on productivity and tackle tasks that require precision.

Libra: Relationships feel grounded today. Focus on creating harmony in your personal connections while staying productive and organized.

Scorpio: Your determination is strong today. Use this energy to focus on your long-term goals and make steady progress toward achieving them.

Sagittarius: Practical matters take precedence today. Use this energy to focus on your responsibilities and organize your thoughts.

Capricorn: Discipline and focus are key today. Use this energy to make significant progress on your long-term projects and goals.

Aquarius: While creativity is important, today encourages you to focus on practical solutions and refining your innovative ideas.

Pisces: Emotional reflection is balanced with practicality today. Use this energy to organize your life and focus on long-term goals.

For those born on June 12: Born under the Moon in Virgo, these individuals are practical, organized, and focused on productivity. In 2025, they'll thrive by refining their plans, staying disciplined, and making steady progress toward their long-term goals.

Daily Insights: The Moon in Virgo continues to emphasize practicality, productivity, and organization, but as it transitions into Libra later in the day, the focus shifts toward balance, relationships, and harmony. It's a day for balancing practical tasks with social interactions and personal connections.

Aries: The day starts with a focus on productivity, but as the Moon moves into Libra, shift your attention to your relationships and finding balance in your life.

Taurus: Use the morning to focus on practical tasks, but later, engage in social interactions and nurture your personal connections.

Gemini: Productivity is high early in the day, but by evening, you'll feel more inclined to engage with others and focus on your relationships.

Cancer: The morning is ideal for organizing your personal life, but as the energy shifts, focus on nurturing your relationships and finding emotional balance.

Leo: Start the day with practical tasks, but as the Moon moves into Libra, focus on balancing your personal goals with your relationships.

Virgo: The Moon in your sign enhances your productivity, but by evening, shift your attention to creating harmony in your relationships.

Libra: The day starts with a focus on productivity, but as the Moon enters your sign, you'll feel energized to focus on your relationships and personal well-being.

Scorpio: It's a day for balancing productivity with emotional growth. Use the morning for practical tasks, but later, focus on deepening your connections with others.

Sagittarius: The day begins with a focus on responsibilities, but by evening, you'll feel more inclined to explore social interactions and embrace balance.

Capricorn: Discipline and focus guide you throughout the day, but later, shift your attention to creating harmony in your relationships and personal life.

Aquarius: The day starts with practical actions, but as the energy shifts, focus on engaging with others and exploring new ideas in your relationships.

Pisces: The morning is perfect for organizing your thoughts and tasks, but by evening, focus on connecting with others and finding emotional balance.

For those born on June 13: Born under the transition from Virgo to Libra, these individuals are both practical and focused on balance. In 2025, they'll thrive by combining their disciplined approach to productivity with a focus on relationships and harmony in their personal life.

Daily Insights: The Moon in Libra emphasizes balance, harmony, and relationships. It's a great day for social interactions, resolving conflicts, and creating equilibrium in your personal and professional life. With the Sun in Gemini, communication is lively, making it a good time for engaging conversations.

Aries: The energy shifts today, encouraging you to focus on balance and harmony in your relationships. Use this time to create equilibrium in your personal and professional life.

Taurus: Balance is key today. Use your grounded nature to focus on maintaining harmony in your personal relationships while working toward your long-term goals.

Gemini: Relationships take center stage today. Focus on communicating clearly and finding balance in your personal interactions.

Cancer: Balance is important in both your home and professional life today. Use this energy to create harmony and resolve any lingering issues.

Leo: It's a day for balancing your personal ambitions with your relationships. Focus on nurturing your connections while pursuing your goals.

Virgo: Productivity is balanced with harmony today. Use this energy to focus on your relationships while staying organized in your personal goals.

Libra: With the Moon in your sign, your need for balance and harmony is amplified. Focus on creating peace in your relationships and maintaining equilibrium in your life.

Scorpio: Relationships feel emotionally deep today. Use this energy to connect with others on a deeper level while maintaining harmony in your personal life.

Sagittarius: Social interactions are favored today. Use your natural charm to connect with others while ensuring balance in your personal and professional life.

Capricorn: It's a day for balancing your responsibilities with your relationships. Focus on finding harmony between your work and personal life.

Aquarius: Innovation and creativity come naturally today, but focus on creating balance in your interactions and maintaining harmony in your relationships.

Pisces: Emotional balance is important today. Use this energy to connect with loved ones and focus on creating stability in your relationships.

For those born on June 14: Born under the Moon in Libra, these individuals are focused on balance, harmony, and relationships. In 2025, they'll thrive by creating equilibrium in their personal and professional lives while working toward their long-term goals with patience and determination.

Daily Insights: The Moon in Libra continues to emphasize balance, relationships, and harmony, but as it transitions into Scorpio later in the day, the focus shifts toward emotional intensity, transformation, and deep connections. It's a day for balancing social interactions with emotional introspection.

Aries: The day begins with a focus on relationships and balance, but as the Moon moves into Scorpio, you'll feel more inclined to explore deeper emotional connections.

Taurus: Use the early part of the day to focus on social interactions and creating harmony, but later, dive into emotional reflection and personal growth.

Gemini: Relationships are in focus early in the day, but as the energy shifts, you'll feel more introspective and inclined to explore your inner world.

Cancer: Balance is important in the morning, but as the Moon moves into Scorpio, focus on emotional depth and nurturing your closest relationships.

Leo: Start the day by focusing on balance in your interactions, but later, shift your attention to emotional transformation and personal growth.

Virgo: The morning is perfect for maintaining harmony in your daily life, but by evening, focus on emotional clarity and personal reflection.

Libra: The Moon in your sign encourages you to maintain balance in your relationships, but later, you'll feel more inclined to explore emotional depth.

Scorpio: The Moon enters your sign later in the day, heightening your emotional intensity. Use this energy to focus on personal transformation and deepening your connections with others.

Sagittarius: Balance your social life in the morning, but by evening, focus on exploring your emotional world and strengthening your relationships.

Capricorn: Discipline and balance guide you in the morning, but later, shift your attention to emotional reflection and personal transformation.

Aquarius: It's a day for balancing relationships and personal goals. As the energy shifts, focus on emotional depth and meaningful connections.

Pisces: Emotional balance is important early in the day, but as the energy transitions, focus on exploring your inner self and strengthening your emotional connections.

For those born on June 15: Born under the transition from Libra to Scorpio, these individuals are both balanced and emotionally intense. In 2025, they'll thrive by balancing their relationships with personal transformation and emotional growth. It's a year for exploring deeper connections and self-reflection.

Daily Insights: The Moon in Scorpio continues to bring emotional intensity and transformation. It's a day for introspection, deep emotional connections, and personal transformation. With Venus in Gemini, communication in relationships is highlighted, encouraging meaningful conversations and open dialogue.

Aries: Your emotions are intense today. Use this energy for personal transformation and emotional healing while staying open to meaningful conversations.

Taurus: It's a day for emotional reflection and personal growth. Use your intuition to explore your inner world and focus on creating emotional security.

Gemini: Communication is your strength today. Use this energy to engage in deep conversations and explore your emotional connections.

Cancer: Emotional depth is strong today. Use this energy to nurture your relationships and focus on personal transformation and growth.

Leo: While action is important, today encourages you to reflect on your emotions. Use this time to deepen your understanding of yourself and your relationships.

Virgo: Balance your practical nature with emotional reflection today. Use this energy to explore your inner world and nurture your relationships.

Libra: Relationships feel emotionally deep today. Focus on creating harmony in your emotional connections and engaging in meaningful conversations.

Scorpio: The Moon in your sign enhances your emotional intensity. Use this energy for self-reflection and personal transformation.

Sagittarius: It's a day for emotional introspection. Use your curiosity to explore your inner world and strengthen your emotional connections.

Capricorn: Your determination is strong today. Use this energy to focus on emotional growth and work toward long-term goals that bring stability.

Aquarius: Emotional reflection is important today. Use this energy to focus on creating deeper connections and exploring your inner emotions.

Pisces: Your intuition is heightened today. Use this energy for emotional healing and focus on nurturing your relationships with loved ones.

For those born on June 16: Born under the Moon in Scorpio, these individuals are emotionally intense, intuitive, and deeply connected to their inner world. In 2025, they'll thrive by focusing on emotional healing, personal transformation, and deepening their relationships.

Daily Insights: The Moon in Scorpio continues to bring emotional intensity and focus on personal transformation. However, as it transitions into Sagittarius later in the day, the focus shifts toward optimism, adventure, and exploration. It's a day for balancing introspection with excitement for new possibilities.

Aries: Start the day with emotional reflection, but as the Moon moves into Sagittarius, shift your focus to new opportunities and personal growth.

Taurus: The morning is ideal for emotional introspection, but later in the day, focus on expanding your horizons and embracing new experiences.

Gemini: Emotional reflection is important early in the day, but as the energy shifts, focus on engaging with others and exploring new ideas.

Cancer: The morning is perfect for nurturing your relationships, but later, focus on stepping out of your comfort zone and embracing new possibilities.

Leo: Emotional depth is important early in the day, but as the Moon moves into Sagittarius, focus on taking bold steps toward your personal goals.

Virgo: The day starts with emotional clarity, but later, focus on exploring new ideas and expanding your knowledge.

Libra: Relationships feel emotionally deep early in the day, but later, focus on creating harmony and embracing new perspectives.

Scorpio: The Moon in your sign enhances your emotional intensity, but as the day progresses, focus on personal growth and exploring new opportunities.

Sagittarius: The Moon enters your sign later in the day, bringing a boost of optimism and excitement. Use this energy to pursue new passions.

Capricorn: Start the day with emotional reflection, but as the energy shifts, focus on setting new goals and expanding your horizons.

Aquarius: The morning is perfect for exploring emotional depth, but by evening, shift your focus to creativity and embracing new ideas.

Pisces: Emotional intuition is heightened early in the day, but as the energy shifts, focus on personal growth and exploring new possibilities.

For those born on June 17: Born under the transition from Scorpio to Sagittarius, these individuals are emotionally intense but adventurous. In 2025, they'll thrive by balancing emotional reflection with personal growth and embracing new experiences.

June 18, 2025

Daily Insights: The Moon in Sagittarius brings a sense of adventure, optimism, and personal growth. It's a day for exploring new opportunities, learning, and expanding your horizons. With Mercury in Gemini, communication is lively, making it a great time for engaging in stimulating conversations.

Aries: Your adventurous spirit is high today. Use this energy to explore new opportunities and focus on personal growth.

Taurus: It's a day for balancing stability with exploration. Use your grounded nature to pursue new experiences while staying focused on long-term goals.

Gemini: Communication is your strength today. Use this energy to engage in stimulating conversations and explore new ideas.

Cancer: Adventure and learning are calling you today. Step out of your comfort zone and embrace new experiences for personal growth.

Leo: Your confidence and leadership are highlighted today. Use this energy to take bold actions toward your goals and inspire those around you.

Virgo: It's a great day for learning and expanding your knowledge. Use your analytical mind to explore new topics and gain valuable insights.

Libra: Relationships feel dynamic and intellectually stimulating. Focus on engaging in conversations that deepen your connections and broaden your perspective.

Scorpio: After a period of emotional intensity, today encourages you to focus on personal growth and embrace new opportunities for self-discovery.

Sagittarius: The Moon in your sign enhances your sense of adventure and optimism. It's a perfect day to pursue your passions and explore new possibilities.

Capricorn: While discipline is important, today encourages you to explore new ideas and broaden your horizons with an open mind.

Aquarius: Your innovative thinking shines today. Use this energy to explore new possibilities and share your unique perspective with others.

Pisces: It's a day for personal growth and exploration. Use your intuition to guide you as you embrace new opportunities and expand your horizons.

For those born on June 18: Born under the Moon in Sagittarius, these individuals are adventurous, curious, and eager to learn. In 2025, they'll thrive by exploring new opportunities, pursuing personal growth, and embracing new possibilities.

Daily Insights: The Moon in Sagittarius continues to inspire optimism, exploration, and learning. It's a day for expanding your knowledge, pursuing your passions, and embracing new experiences. With Venus in Gemini, relationships feel lively and intellectually stimulating, encouraging open communication.

Aries: Your sense of adventure is strong today. Use this energy to explore new possibilities and pursue your personal goals with enthusiasm.

Taurus: It's a day for balancing practicality with exploration. Use your grounded nature to pursue new ideas while staying focused on long-term goals.

Gemini: Communication is highlighted today. Use this energy to engage in meaningful conversations and explore new ideas with curiosity.

Cancer: Adventure and learning are calling you today. Step out of your comfort zone and embrace new experiences for personal growth and development.

Leo: Leadership and action are your strengths today. Use this energy to take bold steps toward your goals and inspire those around you.

Virgo: It's a great day for learning and expanding your knowledge. Use your analytical skills to approach challenges with an open mind.

Libra: Relationships feel dynamic and exciting today. Focus on engaging in conversations that broaden your perspective and deepen your connections.

Scorpio: After a period of emotional intensity, today encourages you to focus on personal growth and embracing new possibilities for self-discovery.

Sagittarius: The Moon in your sign enhances your natural sense of adventure. Use this energy to explore new ideas and pursue your passions.

Capricorn: While discipline is important, today encourages you to explore new ideas and broaden your horizons with optimism and enthusiasm.

Aquarius: Your creativity and innovative thinking shine today. Use this energy to explore new ideas and share your unique perspective with others.

Pisces: It's a day for personal growth and exploration. Use your intuition to guide you as you embrace new opportunities and expand your horizons.

For those born on June 19: Born under the Moon in Sagittarius, these individuals are adventurous, optimistic, and always eager to learn. In 2025, they'll thrive by pursuing new opportunities for growth, expanding their knowledge, and embracing exciting new possibilities.

Daily Insights: The Moon in Sagittarius continues to bring optimism and adventure, but as it transitions into Capricorn later in the day, the focus shifts toward discipline, practicality, and long-term planning. It's a day for balancing exploration with responsibility and setting clear goals for the future.

Aries: Start the day with a sense of adventure, but as the Moon moves into Capricorn, focus on grounding yourself and setting long-term goals.

Taurus: The day begins with optimism and excitement, but later, you'll feel more inclined to focus on practical matters and organizing your long-term plans.

Gemini: Use the early part of the day for exploration and learning, but as the energy shifts, focus on refining your goals and taking practical steps toward achieving them.

Cancer: Adventure is important early in the day, but as the Moon moves into Capricorn, focus on creating stability in your personal life and making thoughtful decisions.

Leo: The morning is ideal for pursuing your passions, but as the Moon enters Capricorn, focus on grounding your ideas and setting realistic goals.

Virgo: Use the early part of the day for intellectual exploration, but later, shift your focus to organizing your thoughts and refining your plans for

Libra: The morning is perfect for social interactions and learning, but as the Moon moves into Capricorn, focus on bringing balance to your relationships and setting practical goals.

Scorpio: Start the day with a sense of excitement and adventure, but by evening, you'll feel more inclined to focus on long-term stability and emotional security.

Sagittarius: The Moon in your sign brings optimism early in the day, but as it transitions into Capricorn, focus on practical steps and responsibility to achieve your goals.

Capricorn: The Moon enters your sign later today, bringing a sense of discipline and focus. Use this energy to work on long-term projects and set achievable goals.

Aquarius: Adventure and learning are highlighted in the morning, but as the energy shifts, focus on practical solutions and refining your innovative ideas.

Pisces: The day begins with curiosity and exploration, but as the Moon moves into Capricorn, focus on grounding yourself and making long-term decisions for stability.

For those born on June 20: Born under the transition from Sagittarius to Capricorn, these individuals are both adventurous and practical. In 2025, they'll find success by balancing their enthusiasm for exploration with a focus on long-term goals and responsibility.

Daily Insights: The Moon in Capricorn emphasizes discipline, practicality, and long-term planning. It's a great day for focusing on your goals, staying productive, and making steady progress. With Mars in Capricorn, there's extra determination and focus, making it an ideal time to work on your ambitions.

Aries: Focus on your long-term goals today. Use your energy to make steady progress while staying disciplined and grounded.

Taurus: It's a day for practical achievements. Use your determination to work on long-term projects and create stability in your life.

Gemini: It's a productive day for organizing your thoughts and refining your plans. Use this energy to stay focused and disciplined.

Cancer: Emotional reflection and stability are key today. Use this energy to focus on your long-term personal and professional goals.

Leo: Confidence and leadership are highlighted today. Use your focus to take charge of important projects and inspire those around you.

Virgo: It's a great day for focusing on productivity and long-term planning. Use your disciplined nature to tackle important tasks.

Libra: Relationships feel stable today. Focus on creating harmony in your personal connections while staying productive with your goals.

Scorpio: Your determination is strong today. Use this energy to focus on long-term goals and make practical decisions for the future.

Sagittarius: Adventure takes a backseat today as you focus on creating stability and working toward your long-term goals.

Capricorn: The Moon in your sign enhances your natural discipline and focus. Use this energy to make significant progress on your ambitions.

Aquarius: While creativity is important, today encourages you to focus on practical solutions and refining your ideas for long-term success.

Pisces: It's a day for balancing emotional reflection with practical goals. Use this energy to create stability in your life and focus on long-term achievements.

For those born on June 21: Born under the Moon in Capricorn, these individuals are disciplined, practical, and focused on achieving long-term success. In 2025, they'll thrive by setting clear goals and making steady progress toward their ambitions.

Daily Insights: The Moon in Capricorn continues to bring focus on discipline, productivity, and long-term goals, but as it transitions into Aquarius later in the day, the energy shifts toward creativity, innovation, and social interactions. It's a day for balancing practical work with creative exploration.

Aries: Use the morning for disciplined work, but as the Moon moves into Aquarius, embrace your creativity and explore new ideas.

Taurus: The day starts with a focus on productivity, but later, shift your attention to social interactions and creative thinking.

Gemini: Productivity is high early in the day, but by evening, you'll feel more inclined to engage in conversations and explore new possibilities.

Cancer: Start the day with practical goals, but as the Moon enters Aquarius, focus on creativity and exploring new opportunities.

Leo: The morning is perfect for focusing on your goals, but as the day progresses, embrace new ways of thinking and collaborating with others.

Virgo: Use the early part of the day for productivity, but later, shift your focus to creative problem-solving and engaging with others.

Libra: Relationships feel stable early in the day, but later, focus on innovative solutions and exploring new perspectives in your connections.

Scorpio: Determination guides you early in the day, but as the energy shifts, focus on expanding your mind and embracing creative ideas.

Sagittarius: The day starts with a focus on responsibilities, but later, you'll feel more curious and eager to explore new possibilities.

Capricorn: The Moon in your sign enhances your focus on discipline, but as it moves into Aquarius, explore creative ideas and social opportunities.

Aquarius: The evening brings a burst of creativity and innovation. Use this time to explore new projects and connect with others.

Pisces: Emotional reflection is key early in the day, but as the Moon enters Aquarius, focus on expressing your creativity and exploring new possibilities.

For those born on June 22: Born under the transition from Capricorn to Aquarius, these individuals are both disciplined and innovative. In 2025, they'll thrive by balancing practicality with creativity, focusing on both long-term goals and exploring new ideas.

Daily Insights: The Moon in Aquarius brings a focus on creativity, innovation, and social interactions. It's a day for exploring new ideas, collaborating with others, and embracing your individuality. With Mercury in Gemini, communication is clear and lively, making it a perfect time for engaging conversations and sharing ideas.

Aries: Your creativity shines today. Use this energy to explore new ideas and connect with others through meaningful collaborations.

Taurus: It's a day for balancing practicality with creativity. Use your determination to bring innovative ideas into reality.

Gemini: Social interactions are stimulating today. Engage in conversations that inspire new perspectives and broaden your horizons.

Cancer: Creativity and innovation are calling you today. Use this energy to explore new ways of expressing yourself and connecting with others.

Leo: Leadership and creativity go hand in hand today. Use your confidence to take the lead in innovative projects and inspire others.

Virgo: It's a great day for exploring creative solutions. Use your analytical skills to approach challenges in innovative ways.

Libra: Relationships are dynamic and exciting today. Focus on connecting with others in unconventional ways and exploring new perspectives.

Scorpio: Your passion for personal growth is strong today. Use this energy to explore new ideas and engage in meaningful conversations.

Sagittarius: Adventure and creativity are calling you today. Focus on expanding your horizons and embracing new opportunities.

Capricorn: While discipline is important, today encourages you to explore new ideas and engage in creative thinking.

Aquarius: With the Moon in your sign, your creativity and individuality are amplified. Use this energy to pursue innovative ideas and connect with others.

Pisces: Your intuition is strong today. Use this energy to explore creative projects and connect with others in meaningful ways.

For those born on June 23: Born under the Moon in Aquarius, these individuals are creative, innovative, and socially connected. In 2025, they'll thrive by embracing their individuality, exploring new ideas, and focusing on personal growth through social connections and creative expression.

Daily Insights: The Moon in Aquarius continues to emphasize creativity, innovation, and individuality, but as it transitions into Pisces later in the day, the focus shifts toward emotional reflection, intuition, and empathy. It's a day for balancing intellectual exploration with emotional depth.

Aries: Start the day with innovative ideas and social connections, but as the Moon enters Pisces, shift your focus to emotional reflection and nurturing relationships.

Taurus: The morning is great for exploring creative solutions, but later, focus on emotional healing and connecting with loved ones on a deeper level.

Gemini: Your mind is active early in the day, but as the Moon enters Pisces, focus on balancing your intellectual pursuits with emotional reflection.

Cancer: Emotional intuition is heightened as the day progresses. Use the morning for socializing, but later, focus on self-care and nurturing close relationships.

Leo: Creativity shines early in the day, but as the energy shifts, focus on your emotional well-being and connecting with those who matter most.

Virgo: Productivity is high in the morning, but by evening, you'll feel more inclined to explore your emotions and focus on personal healing.

Libra: Relationships feel dynamic early in the day, but as the Moon enters Pisces, focus on deepening your emotional connections and finding inner balance.

Scorpio: Use the morning for exploring new ideas, but later, focus on emotional growth and reflection. Your intuition is especially strong today.

Sagittarius: The day starts with excitement and creativity, but later, you'll feel more inclined to focus on emotional healing and connecting with loved ones.

Capricorn: Early productivity gives way to emotional reflection as the day progresses. Focus on grounding yourself and nurturing your relationships.

Aquarius: The Moon in your sign brings out your creativity, but as the energy shifts, focus on emotional introspection and personal growth.

Pisces: The Moon enters your sign later today, amplifying your intuition and emotional sensitivity. Use this energy to focus on self-care and emotional healing.

For those born on June 24: Born under the transition from Aquarius to Pisces, these individuals are both creative and emotionally intuitive. In 2025, they'll thrive by balancing their innovative ideas with emotional reflection, focusing on both personal growth and deepening relationships.

Daily Insights: The Moon in Pisces brings a focus on emotional reflection, intuition, and creativity. It's a great day for engaging in artistic projects, connecting with loved ones on a deeper level, and exploring your inner world. With Mercury in Gemini, communication remains lively, making it a good day for expressing your emotions through words.

Aries: Your intuition is strong today. Use this energy to focus on emotional reflection and nurture your relationships with empathy and understanding.

Taurus: It's a great day for combining creativity with practicality. Focus on expressing your emotions through artistic projects or clear communication.

Gemini: Emotional reflection is key today. Use this energy to connect with your inner self and engage in meaningful conversations with loved ones.

Cancer: The Moon in Pisces enhances your emotional intuition. Use this energy to focus on self-care and strengthening your personal relationships.

Leo: While you're often focused on action, today encourages emotional reflection. Use this time to explore your feelings and deepen your connections.

Virgo: Balance your practical nature with emotional reflection today. Use this energy to focus on your inner world and nurture your relationships.

Libra: Relationships take on a deeper tone today. Focus on emotional connections and use your intuition to guide your conversations.

Scorpio: Your emotional depth is amplified today. Use this energy for self-reflection and strengthening your relationships with loved ones.

Sagittarius: It's a day for focusing on emotional well-being. Use this energy to connect with your inner self and explore your feelings.

Capricorn: Emotional reflection is important today. Focus on creating stability in your personal life and deepening your relationships.

Aquarius: While you're often focused on big ideas, today encourages emotional growth. Use this energy to focus on self-care and personal relationships.

Pisces: The Moon in your sign amplifies your intuition and emotional sensitivity. Use this energy to focus on personal healing and nurturing your relationships with loved ones.

For those born on June 25: Born under the Moon in Pisces, these individuals are emotionally intuitive, creative, and deeply connected to their inner world. In 2025, they'll thrive by focusing on personal healing, nurturing relationships, and expressing their creativity through meaningful projects.

Daily Insights: The Moon in Pisces continues to enhance emotional sensitivity, creativity, and intuition. It's a great day for self-reflection, nurturing relationships, and engaging in creative projects. With Mars in Capricorn, there's a grounded energy that helps you take practical steps toward your long-term goals, even while embracing your emotions.

Aries: Your intuition is heightened today. Use this energy to reflect on your inner self and focus on nurturing your personal relationships.

Taurus: It's a great day for balancing practicality with emotional reflection. Use your grounded nature to connect with your feelings and work on your long-term goals.

Gemini: Emotional connections are highlighted today. Use your communication skills to deepen relationships and explore your inner world.

Cancer: The Moon in Pisces enhances your natural emotional depth. Use this energy to focus on self-care and strengthen your relationships with loved ones.

Leo: While you're often action-oriented, today encourages emotional reflection. Use this time to explore your feelings and connect with those around you.

Virgo: Balance practicality with emotional insight today. Use your disciplined nature to explore your inner world and nurture your personal connections.

Libra: Relationships feel emotionally deep today. Focus on creating harmony in your personal life and nurturing your emotional well-being.

Scorpio: Your emotional intensity is strong today. Use this energy for self-reflection and focus on personal transformation and healing.

Sagittarius: It's a day for focusing on emotional well-being. Use this energy to connect with your inner self and explore your emotional depth.

Capricorn: While practicality is key, today encourages emotional reflection. Use this time to focus on balancing your responsibilities with your personal growth.

Aquarius: While your mind often focuses on big ideas, today encourages emotional introspection. Use this energy to connect with your feelings and nurture your relationships.

Pisces: The Moon in your sign amplifies your emotional sensitivity and intuition. Use this energy for personal healing and deepening your relationships with loved ones.

For those born on June 26: Born under the Moon in Pisces, these individuals are emotionally intuitive, creative, and deeply connected to their inner world. In 2025, they'll thrive by focusing on personal healing, nurturing relationships, and expressing their creativity in meaningful ways.

Daily Insights: The Moon in Pisces continues to encourage emotional reflection, but as it transitions into Aries later in the day, the focus shifts toward action, confidence, and bold steps forward. It's a day for balancing emotional introspection with taking decisive actions toward your goals.

Aries: Start the day with emotional reflection, but as the Moon enters your sign, shift your focus to taking bold actions and pursuing your personal goals.

Taurus: Use the morning for emotional introspection, but later, focus on taking practical steps toward your long-term ambitions.

Gemini: Emotional reflection is key early in the day, but as the energy shifts, focus on engaging with others and taking action on your ideas.

Cancer: Start the day by nurturing your emotional well-being, but as the Moon moves into Aries, focus on stepping out of your comfort zone and embracing new challenges.

Leo: Emotional reflection is important early in the day, but as the Moon enters Aries, your confidence will rise, making it a great time to take bold actions.

Virgo: Use the early part of the day for emotional clarity, but by evening, shift your focus to organizing your thoughts and taking action toward your goals.

Libra: Relationships feel emotionally deep in the morning, but later, focus on communicating openly and taking action to strengthen your connections.

Scorpio: Emotional depth is important early in the day, but as the Moon moves into Aries, focus on taking bold steps toward personal growth and transformation.

Sagittarius: Start the day with emotional introspection, but later, shift your focus to adventure and exploring new opportunities with confidence.

Capricorn: Emotional reflection is key early in the day, but as the Moon enters Aries, shift your attention to taking practical steps toward your long-term goals.

Aquarius: The morning is perfect for emotional reflection, but by evening, focus on pursuing new ideas and taking bold actions with confidence.

Pisces: The Moon in your sign enhances your emotional intuition early in the day, but as the energy shifts, focus on taking decisive actions toward your ambitions.

For those born on June 27: Born under the transition from Pisces to Aries, these individuals are both emotionally intuitive and action-oriented. In 2025, they'll thrive by balancing emotional introspection with taking bold steps toward their personal goals and ambitions.

Daily Insights: The Moon in Aries brings a surge of energy, confidence, and motivation. It's a great day for taking bold steps, embracing new opportunities, and focusing on personal goals. With the Sun in Cancer, there's also an emphasis on nurturing relationships and emotional well-being, making it a day for balancing personal ambition with emotional connections.

Aries: Your confidence is high today. Use this energy to pursue your personal goals and take bold actions with enthusiasm.

Taurus: It's a day for balancing bold actions with practicality. Use your determination to make steady progress toward your long-term goals.

Gemini: Communication and action are your strengths today. Use this energy to engage in meaningful conversations and take action on your ideas.

Cancer: Confidence and emotional reflection are key today. Use this energy to focus on personal growth and take bold steps toward your ambitions.

Leo: Leadership and action are highlighted today. Use your natural confidence to take charge of projects and inspire those around you.

Virgo: It's a productive day for focusing on your goals. Use your disciplined nature to take bold actions while staying organized and practical.

Libra: Relationships feel dynamic and exciting today. Focus on communicating openly and taking action to strengthen your personal connections.

Scorpio: Your determination is strong today. Use this energy to focus on your long-term goals and take decisive actions toward achieving them.

Sagittarius: Adventure and excitement are calling you today. Use your enthusiasm to explore new opportunities and take bold steps toward your dreams.

Capricorn: Discipline and focus guide you today. Use this energy to take practical steps toward your long-term goals and ambitions.

Aquarius: Your creativity and innovative thinking shine today. Use this energy to explore new ideas and take bold actions toward your personal goals.

Pisces: It's a day for taking action on your personal ambitions. Use your intuition to guide you as you embrace new opportunities with confidence.

For those born on June 28: Born under the Moon in Aries, these individuals are confident, action-oriented, and driven. In 2025, they'll thrive by taking bold steps toward their personal goals and embracing new opportunities with enthusiasm.

Daily Insights: The Moon in Aries continues to bring energy, motivation, and a focus on personal goals. It's a great day for taking decisive actions, embracing challenges, and pursuing your ambitions. With Mercury in Gemini, communication is clear and lively, making it a good time for sharing ideas and connecting with others.

Aries: Your confidence and motivation are high today. Use this energy to push forward on your personal goals and take bold actions with confidence.

Taurus: It's a day for balancing bold actions with practicality. Use your grounded nature to take steady steps toward your long-term goals.

Gemini: Communication is your strength today. Use this energy to engage in meaningful conversations and explore new ideas with curiosity.

Cancer: Confidence and emotional balance are key today. Use this energy to focus on personal growth and take bold steps toward your ambitions.

Leo: Leadership and action are highlighted today. Use your natural confidence to take charge of projects and inspire those around you.

Virgo: Productivity is high today. Use your disciplined nature to focus on practical tasks and take bold actions toward your goals.

Libra: Relationships feel dynamic today. Focus on open communication and take action to strengthen your personal connections.

Scorpio: Your determination is strong today. Use this energy to take decisive steps toward achieving your long-term goals.

Sagittarius: Adventure and excitement are calling you today. Use your enthusiasm to explore new opportunities and take bold steps toward your dreams.

Capricorn: Discipline and focus guide you today. Use this energy to take practical steps toward your long-term goals and ambitions.

Aquarius: Your creativity and innovative thinking shine today. Use this energy to explore new ideas and take bold actions toward your personal goals.

Pisces: It's a day for taking action on your personal ambitions. Use your intuition to guide you as you embrace new opportunities with confidence.

For those born on June 29: Born under the Moon in Aries, these individuals are energetic, motivated, and focused on achieving their goals. In 2025, they'll thrive by embracing challenges, taking bold actions, and pursuing their ambitions with enthusiasm.

Daily Insights: The Moon in Aries continues to provide energy, confidence, and motivation, but as it transitions into Taurus later in the day, the focus shifts toward stability, practicality, and long-term planning. It's a day for balancing bold actions with careful consideration of your long-term goals.

Aries: The day starts with high energy and motivation, but as the Moon moves into Taurus, focus on grounding yourself and setting practical goals for the future.

Taurus: The Moon enters your sign later today, bringing a sense of stability and focus on practical matters. Use this energy to work toward your long-term ambitions.

Gemini: It's a day for balancing bold ideas with practical steps. Use the morning for exploration, but by evening, shift your focus to long-term planning.

Cancer: Start the day with confidence and action, but as the energy shifts, focus on creating stability in your personal life and making thoughtful decisions.

Leo: The morning is ideal for pursuing your passions, but as the Moon enters Taurus, focus on grounding your ideas and setting realistic goals.

Virgo: Use the early part of the day for intellectual exploration, but by evening, shift your focus to organizing your thoughts and refining your plans for the future.

Libra: Relationships feel dynamic early in the day, but as the energy shifts, focus on bringing balance and stability into your personal connections.

Scorpio: The day begins with excitement and exploration, but later, you'll feel more inclined to focus on creating emotional and financial security.

Sagittarius: The Moon in Aries brings adventure and bold action, but as it moves into Taurus, focus on grounding your plans and working toward stability.

Capricorn: Discipline and focus guide you throughout the day, but later, shift your attention to creating stability and working on long-term goals.

Aquarius: The morning is perfect for exploring new ideas, but by evening, focus on practical solutions and setting achievable goals for the future.

Pisces: The day starts with bold action, but as the Moon moves into Taurus, focus on grounding your emotions and creating stability in your personal life.

For those born on June 30: Born under the transition from Aries to Taurus, these individuals are both action-oriented and practical. In 2025, they'll thrive by balancing their bold ambitions with practical planning, focusing on long-term goals while embracing new opportunities for growth.

Daily Insights: The Moon in Taurus emphasizes stability, practicality, and long-term planning. It's a great day for focusing on practical matters, setting achievable goals, and making steady progress. With Mars in Capricorn, there's a boost of determination and focus, making it an ideal time for productivity and success.

Aries: Focus on grounding your energy today. Use your determination to make steady progress toward your long-term goals and practical matters.

Taurus: The Moon in your sign enhances your sense of stability and focus on practical goals. Use this energy to work toward your personal growth and ambitions.

Gemini: It's a day for focusing on long-term planning. Use your curiosity to explore new ideas while staying grounded in practical solutions.

Cancer: Stability and emotional security are important today. Use this energy to create a sense of comfort and progress in your personal life.

Leo: It's a great day for focusing on long-term goals. Use your leadership skills to inspire others while making steady progress on your ambitions.

Virgo: Productivity is high today. Use this energy to focus on tasks that require attention to detail and long-term planning.

Libra: Relationships feel grounded today. Focus on creating harmony in your personal connections while working toward your goals.

Scorpio: Your determination is strong today. Use this energy to focus on your long-term goals and make practical decisions for the future.

Sagittarius: Adventure takes a backseat today as you focus on grounding yourself and working toward practical goals.

Capricorn: Discipline and focus are your strengths today. Use this energy to make steady progress on your long-term projects and goals.

Aquarius: While creativity is important, today encourages you to focus on practical solutions and setting achievable goals for the future.

Pisces: Emotional stability is key today. Use this energy to ground yourself and focus on creating long-term security in your relationships and personal life.

For those born on July 1: Born under the Moon in Taurus, these individuals are practical, grounded, and focused on long-term success. In 2025, they'll thrive by setting clear goals and making steady progress toward achieving them, using their disciplined nature to stay focused on their ambitions.

July 2, 2025

Daily Insights: The Moon in Taurus continues to emphasize stability and practicality, but as it transitions into Gemini later in the day, the focus shifts toward communication, learning, and curiosity. It's a day for balancing practical matters with intellectual exploration and social interactions.

Aries: Use the morning for practical goals, but as the Moon moves into Gemini, shift your focus to communication and exploring new ideas.

Taurus: Start the day with stability and focus on long-term planning, but by evening, engage in social interactions and intellectual pursuits.

Gemini: The Moon enters your sign later today, bringing a burst of energy and curiosity. It's a great time for exploring new ideas and engaging in conversations.

Cancer: The day starts with a focus on stability, but as the energy shifts, focus on connecting with others and exploring new perspectives.

Leo: Use the morning for practical work, but as the Moon enters Gemini, engage with others and share your ideas freely.

Virgo: The early part of the day is productive, but by evening, focus on engaging with new ideas and refining your long-term plans.

Libra: Relationships feel stable early in the day, but as the Moon moves into Gemini, focus on open communication and exploring new perspectives with loved ones.

Scorpio: The day begins with determination and focus, but later, you'll feel more inclined to explore social interactions and new opportunities.

Sagittarius: Start the day with practicality, but as the Moon enters Gemini, shift your focus to learning and intellectual exploration.

Capricorn: Discipline guides you early in the day, but by evening, shift your attention to communication and engaging with others.

Aquarius: The day starts with practical tasks, but later, explore new ideas and engage with others in stimulating conversations.

Pisces: Emotional reflection is key early in the day, but as the Moon moves into Gemini, focus on socializing and expressing your ideas clearly.

For those born on July 2: Born under the transition from Taurus to Gemini, these individuals are both practical and curious. In 2025, they'll thrive by balancing their disciplined approach with intellectual exploration, focusing on both long-term goals and learning new things.

Daily Insights: The Moon in Gemini brings a focus on communication, learning, and curiosity. It's a great day for engaging in conversations, exploring new ideas, and connecting with others. With Mercury in Gemini, there's an added emphasis on clear and lively communication, making it an ideal time for intellectual exploration.

Aries: Your curiosity is strong today. Use this energy to engage in conversations, explore new ideas, and take action on your personal goals.

Taurus: It's a day for balancing practicality with intellectual exploration. Use your grounded nature to communicate your thoughts clearly and explore new perspectives.

Gemini: The Moon in your sign enhances your communication skills. Use this energy to connect with others, share your ideas, and explore new opportunities.

Cancer: It's a day for focusing on learning and intellectual growth. Use this energy to connect with your inner self and engage in meaningful conversations.

Leo: Leadership and creativity are highlighted today. Use your confidence to inspire others and share your innovative ideas with enthusiasm.

Virgo: Your analytical skills are sharp today. Use this energy to focus on problem-solving and exploring new ideas through conversation.

Libra: Relationships feel dynamic and intellectually stimulating. Focus on engaging with loved ones in meaningful conversations and exploring new perspectives.

Scorpio: Your emotional depth is strong today. Use this energy to engage in deep conversations and explore new ideas that challenge your thinking.

Sagittarius: Adventure and learning go hand in hand today. Use your curiosity to explore new opportunities and engage in conversations that inspire you.

Capricorn: It's a day for balancing discipline with intellectual exploration. Use this energy to engage in thoughtful discussions and refine your long-term goals.

Aquarius: Your creativity and innovative thinking shine today. Use this energy to explore new ideas and engage in collaborative conversations.

Pisces: It's a day for intellectual exploration and emotional reflection. Use this energy to connect with others in meaningful ways and share your ideas.

For those born on July 3: Born under the Moon in Gemini, these individuals are curious, communicative, and eager to explore new ideas. In 2025, they'll thrive by engaging in conversations, learning new things, and using their sharp minds to make meaningful connections with others.

Daily Insights: The Moon in Gemini continues to emphasize communication, learning, and curiosity, but as it transitions into Cancer later in the day, the focus shifts toward emotional well-being, nurturing relationships, and self-care. It's a day for balancing intellectual exploration with emotional connection.

Aries: The day begins with lively conversations, but as the Moon moves into Cancer, shift your focus to emotional reflection and nurturing your relationships.

Taurus: Use the morning for exploring new ideas, but as the energy shifts, focus on creating emotional stability in your personal life.

Gemini: Your communication skills are heightened early in the day, but later, focus on emotional connections and strengthening your relationships with loved ones.

Cancer: The Moon enters your sign later today, heightening your emotional sensitivity. It's a great time for self-care and nurturing close relationships.

Leo: Start the day with intellectual exploration, but as the Moon moves into Cancer, shift your focus to emotional balance and personal growth.

Virgo: Productivity is high early in the day, but by evening, focus on emotional reflection and nurturing your personal well-being.

Libra: Relationships are intellectually stimulating in the morning, but later, focus on deepening emotional connections and creating harmony in your relationships.

Scorpio: Your curiosity is high early in the day, but as the energy shifts, focus on emotional healing and strengthening your relationships.

Sagittarius: The day begins with excitement and exploration, but later, shift your focus to emotional reflection and personal growth.

Capricorn: Use the morning for practical tasks and intellectual pursuits, but by evening, focus on nurturing your emotional well-being and relationships.

Aquarius: Creativity and intellectual exploration are highlighted early in the day, but as the Moon enters Cancer, focus on emotional growth and self-care.

Pisces: The day begins with curiosity and intellectual exploration, but as the Moon moves into Cancer, focus on emotional healing and nurturing your close relationships.

For those born on July 4: Born under the transition from Gemini to Cancer, these individuals are both intellectually curious and emotionally intuitive. In 2025, they'll thrive by balancing their sharp minds with emotional reflection, focusing on both learning and nurturing their relationships.

Daily Insights: The Moon in Cancer emphasizes emotional reflection, nurturing relationships, and self-care. It's a great day for focusing on home life, connecting with loved ones, and creating a sense of emotional security. With Venus in Gemini, relationships feel lively and intellectually stimulating, adding excitement to personal connections.

Aries: Emotional reflection is important today. Use this energy to focus on nurturing your relationships and creating balance in your personal life.

Taurus: It's a day for balancing emotional well-being with practical goals. Use your grounded nature to focus on self-care and long-term planning.

Gemini: Emotional connections are highlighted today. Use your communication skills to nurture your relationships and create harmony in your personal life.

Cancer: The Moon in your sign enhances your emotional intuition. Focus on self-care and strengthening your relationships with loved ones.

Leo: While you're often focused on action, today encourages emotional reflection. Use this time to nurture your personal well-being and relationships.

Virgo: Balance is key today. Focus on creating emotional stability in your life while maintaining progress on your practical goals.

Libra: Relationships take on a deeper, more emotional tone today. Focus on nurturing your connections and creating harmony in your personal life.

Scorpio: Your emotional depth is strong today. Use this energy to focus on personal healing and deepening your connections with loved ones.

Sagittarius: It's a day for focusing on emotional well-being. Use this energy to create stability in your personal life and nurture your close relationships.

Capricorn: Emotional reflection is important today. Use this energy to focus on creating stability in your relationships and personal life.

Aquarius: While you're often focused on big ideas, today encourages emotional growth. Use this energy to focus on self-care and personal relationships.

Pisces: Your intuition is heightened today. Use this energy to focus on emotional healing and strengthening your relationships with loved ones.

For those born on July 5: Born under the Moon in Cancer, these individuals are emotionally intuitive, nurturing, and deeply connected to their home and family. In 2025, they'll thrive by focusing on emotional well-being, nurturing relationships, and creating stability in their personal lives.

July 6, 2025

Daily Insights: The Moon in Cancer continues to emphasize emotional reflection, nurturing relationships, and self-care. However, as the Moon transitions into Leo later in the day, the focus shifts toward self-expression, confidence, and creativity. It's a day for balancing emotional well-being with personal empowerment.

Aries: Start the day focusing on your emotional well-being, but as the Moon moves into Leo, you'll feel more confident and ready to take bold actions.

Taurus: The morning is ideal for nurturing your personal relationships, but later, focus on expressing your creativity and stepping into the spotlight.

Gemini: The day starts with emotional reflection, but as the energy shifts, you'll feel more inclined to engage in social activities and express yourself.

Cancer: The Moon in your sign encourages emotional self-care, but as it enters Leo, your confidence will rise, making it a great time to focus on personal growth.

Leo: The Moon enters your sign later today, boosting your confidence and creativity. Use this energy to pursue your passions and take the lead in your projects.

Virgo: Emotional clarity is important early in the day, but as the energy shifts, focus on creative problem-solving and expressing your unique talents.

Libra: Relationships feel emotionally deep in the morning, but as the day progresses, focus on expressing yourself and embracing your individuality.

Scorpio: It's a day for balancing emotional reflection with personal empowerment. Start with self-care, but later, take bold steps toward your goals.

Sagittarius: The morning is perfect for focusing on emotional well-being, but as the Moon moves into Leo, embrace adventure and new opportunities.

Capricorn: Emotional reflection is key early in the day, but by evening, focus on stepping into leadership roles and pursuing your personal ambitions.

Aquarius: The day begins with introspection, but as the energy shifts, focus on expressing your creativity and connecting with others in meaningful ways.

Pisces: Emotional reflection is important early in the day, but later, use your heightened confidence to pursue creative projects and personal growth.

For those born on July 6: Born under the transition from Cancer to Leo, these individuals are both emotionally intuitive and confident. In 2025, they'll thrive by balancing their emotional well-being with bold actions and personal growth. It's a year for both self-care and self-expression.

Daily Insights: The Moon in Leo emphasizes self-expression, creativity, and confidence. It's a day for stepping into the spotlight, embracing leadership, and pursuing your passions. With Mars in Capricorn, there's also a sense of discipline, making it a great time for combining ambition with creativity.

Aries: Your confidence is high today. Use this energy to pursue your personal goals and step into leadership roles with enthusiasm.

Taurus: Creativity flows easily today. Focus on expressing yourself through your work or hobbies, and don't be afraid to take the lead in projects.

Gemini: It's a great day for social interactions and sharing your ideas. Use your communication skills to inspire others and collaborate on creative endeavors.

Cancer: While your emotional intuition is still strong, today's energy encourages you to step out of your comfort zone and express yourself confidently.

Leo: The Moon in your sign amplifies your natural charisma and creativity. Use this energy to take bold steps toward your passions and inspire others.

Virgo: Balance creativity with practicality today. Use your disciplined nature to focus on long-term goals while expressing your unique talents.

Libra: Relationships feel exciting and dynamic today. Focus on creative ways to connect with loved ones and embrace your individuality.

Scorpio: Your passion is strong today. Use this energy to pursue personal goals with intensity and determination.

Sagittarius: Adventure and creativity are calling you today. Use this energy to explore new opportunities and express yourself freely.

Capricorn: Leadership and discipline come naturally today. Use this energy to focus on personal projects and inspire those around you.

Aquarius: Your creativity shines today. Use this energy to pursue innovative ideas and connect with others through meaningful collaborations.

Pisces: It's a day for self-expression and personal growth. Use your creativity to focus on your goals and embrace new opportunities with confidence.

For those born on July 7: Born under the Moon in Leo, these individuals are charismatic, creative, and confident. In 2025, they'll thrive by stepping into leadership roles, embracing their unique talents, and pursuing their passions with determination.

Daily Insights: The Moon in Leo continues to amplify confidence, creativity, and leadership, but as it transitions into Virgo later in the day, the focus shifts toward practicality, organization, and attention to detail. It's a day for balancing bold actions with practical steps to ensure long-term success.

Aries: Start the day with bold actions and confidence, but as the Moon moves into Virgo, focus on organizing your plans and taking practical steps toward your goals.

Taurus: Use the morning to express your creativity and passion, but later in the day, shift your focus to practical matters and long-term planning.

Gemini: The day begins with exciting conversations and social interactions, but as the energy shifts, focus on refining your ideas and organizing your thoughts.

Cancer: Emotional reflection is important early in the day, but later, focus on practical tasks and creating stability in your personal life.

Leo: The Moon in your sign boosts your charisma and leadership skills, but as the day progresses, focus on grounding your energy and organizing your goals.

Virgo: The Moon enters your sign later today, enhancing your natural attention to detail and practicality. Use this energy to tackle important tasks.

Libra: Relationships take on a dynamic tone early in the day, but as the energy shifts, focus on balancing your emotional connections with practical responsibilities.

Scorpio: It's a day for balancing your passion with practicality. Start with bold actions, but later, focus on refining your plans and staying disciplined.

Sagittarius: The morning is filled with excitement and creativity, but later, shift your focus to practical matters and long-term goals.

Capricorn: Leadership and discipline guide you early in the day, but later, shift your attention to organizing your tasks and working on long-term projects.

Aquarius: Use the morning for creative pursuits, but as the Moon moves into Virgo, focus on practical solutions and refining your ideas.

Pisces: Emotional reflection is important early in the day, but later, focus on grounding yourself and organizing your life for greater stability.

For those born on July 8: Born under the transition from Leo to Virgo, these individuals are both creative and disciplined. In 2025, they'll thrive by balancing their bold ideas with practical action, focusing on both creativity and productivity to achieve their goals.

Daily Insights: The Moon in Virgo emphasizes productivity, organization, and attention to detail. It's a great day for focusing on practical matters, refining your plans, and making steady progress toward long-term goals. With Mercury in Gemini, communication is clear and grounded, making it an ideal time for problem-solving and setting realistic expectations.

Aries: Focus on productivity today. Use your energy to organize your plans and make steady progress toward your long-term goals.

Taurus: It's a day for practical achievements. Use your grounded nature to refine your ideas and work on long-term projects.

Gemini: Your analytical skills are strong today. Use this energy to focus on problem-solving and refining your thoughts.

Cancer: Emotional clarity comes through practicality today. Use this energy to focus on organizing your personal life and creating stability.

Leo: After a period of creativity, today encourages you to focus on practical matters. Use your discipline to make progress on long-term goals.

Virgo: The Moon in your sign enhances your natural strengths. Use this energy to focus on productivity and tackle tasks that require precision.

Libra: Relationships feel grounded today. Focus on creating harmony in your personal connections while staying productive and organized.

Scorpio: Your determination is strong today. Use this energy to focus on your long-term goals and make practical decisions for the future.

Sagittarius: Practical matters take precedence today. Use this energy to focus on your responsibilities and organize your thoughts.

Capricorn: Discipline and focus are key today. Use this energy to make significant progress on your long-term projects and goals.

Aquarius: While creativity is important, today encourages you to focus on practical solutions and refining your innovative ideas.

Pisces: Emotional reflection is balanced with practicality today. Use this energy to organize your life and focus on long-term goals.

For those born on July 9: Born under the Moon in Virgo, these individuals are practical, organized, and focused on productivity. In 2025, they'll thrive by refining their plans, staying disciplined, and making steady progress toward their long-term goals.

Daily Insights: The Moon in Virgo continues to emphasize practicality, productivity, and organization, but as it transitions into Libra later in the day, the focus shifts toward balance, relationships, and harmony. It's a day for balancing practical tasks with social interactions and personal connections.

Aries: The day starts with a focus on productivity, but as the Moon moves into Libra, shift your attention to your relationships and finding balance in your life.

Taurus: Use the morning to focus on practical tasks, but later, engage in social interactions and nurture your personal connections.

Gemini: Productivity is high early in the day, but by evening, you'll feel more inclined to engage with others and focus on your relationships.

Cancer: The morning is ideal for organizing your personal life, but as the energy shifts, focus on nurturing your relationships and finding emotional balance.

Leo: Start the day with practical tasks, but as the Moon moves into Libra, focus on balancing your personal goals with your relationships.

Virgo: The Moon in your sign enhances your productivity, but by evening, shift your attention to creating harmony in your relationships.

Libra: The day starts with a focus on productivity, but as the Moon enters your sign, you'll feel energized to focus on your relationships and personal well-being.

Scorpio: It's a day for balancing productivity with emotional growth. Use the morning for practical tasks, but later, focus on deepening your connections with others.

Sagittarius: The day begins with a focus on responsibilities, but by evening, you'll feel more inclined to explore social interactions and embrace balance.

Capricorn: Discipline and focus guide you throughout the day, but later, shift your attention to creating harmony in your relationships and personal life.

Aquarius: The day starts with practical actions, but as the energy shifts, focus on engaging with others and exploring new ideas in your relationships.

Pisces: The morning is perfect for organizing your thoughts and tasks, but by evening, focus on connecting with others and finding emotional balance.

For those born on July 10: Born under the transition from Virgo to Libra, these individuals are both practical and focused on balance. In 2025, they'll thrive by combining their disciplined approach to productivity with a focus on relationships and harmony in their personal life.

Daily Insights: The Moon in Libra emphasizes balance, harmony, and relationships. It's a great day for social interactions, resolving conflicts, and creating equilibrium in your personal and professional life. With the Sun in Cancer, emotions may feel more intense, but it's an ideal time for nurturing connections.

Aries: The energy shifts today, encouraging you to focus on balance and harmony in your relationships. Use this time to create equilibrium in your personal and professional life.

Taurus: Balance is key today. Use your grounded nature to focus on maintaining harmony in your personal relationships while working toward your long-term goals.

Gemini: Relationships take center stage today. Focus on communicating clearly and finding balance in your personal interactions.

Cancer: Balance is important in both your home and professional life today. Use this energy to create harmony and resolve any lingering issues.

Leo: It's a day for balancing your personal ambitions with your relationships. Focus on nurturing your connections while pursuing your goals.

Virgo: Productivity is balanced with harmony today. Use this energy to focus on your relationships while staying organized in your personal goals.

Libra: With the Moon in your sign, your need for balance and harmony is amplified. Focus on creating peace in your relationships and maintaining equilibrium in your life.

Scorpio: Relationships feel emotionally deep today. Use this energy to connect with others on a deeper level while maintaining harmony in your personal life.

Sagittarius: Social interactions are favored today. Use your natural charm to connect with others while ensuring balance in your personal and professional life.

Capricorn: It's a day for balancing your responsibilities with your relationships. Focus on finding harmony between your work and personal life.

Aquarius: Innovation and creativity come naturally today, but focus on creating balance in your interactions and maintaining harmony in your relationships.

Pisces: Emotional balance is important today. Use this energy to connect with loved ones and focus on creating stability in your relationships.

For those born on July 11: Born under the Moon in Libra, these individuals are focused on balance, harmony, and relationships. In 2025, they'll thrive by creating equilibrium in their personal and professional lives while working toward their long-term goals with patience and determination.

Daily Insights: The Moon in Libra continues to emphasize balance and harmony, but as it transitions into Scorpio later in the day, the focus shifts toward emotional depth, transformation, and intense connections. It's a day for balancing social interactions with emotional introspection.

Aries: The day begins with a focus on relationships and balance, but as the Moon moves into Scorpio, you'll feel more inclined to explore deeper emotional connections.

Taurus: Use the early part of the day to focus on social interactions and creating harmony, but later, dive into emotional reflection and personal growth.

Gemini: Relationships are in focus early in the day, but as the energy shifts, you'll feel more introspective and inclined to explore your inner world.

Cancer: Balance is important in the morning, but as the Moon moves into Scorpio, focus on emotional depth and nurturing your closest relationships.

Leo: Start the day by focusing on balance in your interactions, but later, shift your attention to emotional transformation and personal growth.

Virgo: The morning is perfect for maintaining harmony in your daily life, but by evening, focus on emotional clarity and personal reflection.

Libra: The Moon in your sign encourages you to maintain balance in your relationships, but later, you'll feel more inclined to explore emotional depth.

Scorpio: The Moon enters your sign later in the day, heightening your emotional intensity. Use this energy to focus on personal transformation and deepening your connections with others.

Sagittarius: Balance your social life in the morning, but by evening, focus on exploring your emotional world and strengthening your relationships.

Capricorn: Discipline and balance guide you in the morning, but later, shift your attention to emotional reflection and personal transformation.

Aquarius: It's a day for balancing relationships and personal goals. As the energy shifts, focus on emotional depth and meaningful connections.

Pisces: Emotional balance is important early in the day, but as the energy transitions, focus on exploring your inner self and strengthening your emotional connections.

For those born on July 12: Born under the transition from Libra to Scorpio, these individuals are both balanced and emotionally intense. In 2025, they'll thrive by balancing their relationships with personal transformation and emotional growth. It's a year for exploring deeper connections and self-reflection.

Daily Insights: The Moon in Scorpio emphasizes emotional depth, transformation, and introspection. It's a day for exploring your inner world, focusing on personal growth, and deepening your connections with others. With Venus in Gemini, communication is still lively, encouraging meaningful conversations and emotional openness.

Aries: Emotional reflection is key today. Use this energy to focus on personal growth and explore deeper connections with those around you.

Taurus: It's a day for emotional transformation. Use your grounded nature to explore your inner world and focus on healing and growth.

Gemini: Communication is highlighted today. Use this energy to engage in deep conversations and explore your emotional connections.

Cancer: Emotional depth is strong today. Use this energy to nurture your relationships and focus on personal transformation and healing.

Leo: While action is important, today encourages emotional reflection. Use this time to deepen your understanding of yourself and your relationships.

Virgo: Balance your practical nature with emotional reflection today. Use this energy to explore your inner world and nurture your personal connections.

Libra: Relationships feel emotionally deep today. Focus on creating harmony in your emotional connections and engaging in meaningful conversations.

Scorpio: The Moon in your sign enhances your emotional intensity. Use this energy for self-reflection and personal transformation.

Sagittarius: It's a day for emotional introspection. Use your curiosity to explore your inner world and strengthen your emotional connections.

Capricorn: Your determination is strong today. Use this energy to focus on emotional growth and work toward long-term goals that bring stability.

Aquarius: Emotional reflection is important today. Use this energy to focus on creating deeper connections and exploring your inner emotions.

Pisces: Your intuition is heightened today. Use this energy for emotional healing and focus on nurturing your relationships with loved ones.

For those born on July 13: Born under the Moon in Scorpio, these individuals are emotionally intense, intuitive, and deeply connected to their inner world. In 2025, they'll thrive by focusing on personal transformation, emotional healing, and deepening their relationships.

Daily Insights: The Moon in Scorpio continues to bring emotional intensity, focus, and transformation. However, as it transitions into Sagittarius later in the day, the energy shifts toward optimism, adventure, and exploration. It's a day for balancing introspection with excitement for new possibilities.

Aries: Start the day with emotional reflection, but as the Moon moves into Sagittarius, shift your focus to new opportunities and personal growth.

Taurus: The morning is ideal for emotional introspection, but later in the day, focus on expanding your horizons and embracing new experiences.

Gemini: Emotional reflection is important early in the day, but as the energy shifts, focus on engaging with others and exploring new ideas.

Cancer: The morning is perfect for nurturing your relationships, but later, focus on stepping out of your comfort zone and embracing new possibilities.

Leo: Emotional depth is important early in the day, but as the Moon moves into Sagittarius, focus on taking bold steps toward your personal goals.

Virgo: The day starts with emotional clarity, but later, focus on exploring new ideas and expanding your knowledge.

Libra: Relationships feel emotionally deep early in the day, but later, focus on creating harmony and embracing new perspectives.

Scorpio: The Moon in your sign enhances your emotional intensity, but as the day progresses, focus on personal growth and exploring new opportunities.

Sagittarius: The Moon enters your sign later in the day, bringing a boost of optimism and excitement. Use this energy to pursue new passions.

Capricorn: Start the day with emotional reflection, but as the energy shifts, focus on setting new goals and expanding your horizons.

Aquarius: The morning is perfect for exploring emotional depth, but by evening, shift your focus to creativity and embracing new ideas.

Pisces: Emotional intuition is heightened early in the day, but as the energy shifts, focus on personal growth and exploring new possibilities.

For those born on July 14: Born under the transition from Scorpio to Sagittarius, these individuals are emotionally intense but adventurous. In 2025, they'll thrive by balancing emotional reflection with personal growth and embracing new experiences.

Daily Insights: The Moon in Sagittarius brings a sense of adventure, optimism, and personal growth. It's a day for exploring new opportunities, learning, and expanding your horizons. With Mercury in Gemini, communication is lively, making it a great time for engaging in stimulating conversations.

Aries: Your adventurous spirit is high today. Use this energy to explore new opportunities and focus on personal growth.

Taurus: It's a day for balancing stability with exploration. Use your grounded nature to pursue new experiences while staying focused on long-term goals.

Gemini: Communication is your strength today. Use this energy to engage in stimulating conversations and explore new ideas.

Cancer: Adventure and learning are calling you today. Step out of your comfort zone and embrace new experiences for personal growth.

Leo: Your confidence and leadership are highlighted today. Use this energy to take bold actions toward your goals and inspire those around you.

Virgo: It's a great day for learning and expanding your knowledge. Use your analytical mind to explore new topics and gain valuable insights.

Libra: Relationships feel dynamic and intellectually stimulating. Focus on engaging in conversations that deepen your connections and broaden your perspective.

Scorpio: After a period of emotional intensity, today encourages you to focus on personal growth and embrace new opportunities for self-discovery.

Sagittarius: The Moon in your sign enhances your sense of adventure and optimism. It's a perfect day to pursue your passions and explore new possibilities.

Capricorn: While discipline is important, today encourages you to explore new ideas and broaden your horizons with an open mind.

Aquarius: Your innovative thinking shines today. Use this energy to explore new possibilities and share your unique perspective with others.

Pisces: It's a day for personal growth and exploration. Use your intuition to guide you as you embrace new opportunities and expand your horizons.

For those born on July 15: Born under the Moon in Sagittarius, these individuals are adventurous, curious, and eager to learn. In 2025, they'll thrive by exploring new opportunities, pursuing personal growth, and embracing new possibilities.

Daily Insights: The Moon in Sagittarius continues to inspire optimism, exploration, and learning. It's a day for expanding your knowledge, pursuing your passions, and embracing new experiences. With Venus in Gemini, relationships feel lively and intellectually stimulating, encouraging open communication.

Aries: Your sense of adventure is strong today. Use this energy to explore new possibilities and pursue your personal goals with enthusiasm.

Taurus: It's a day for balancing practicality with exploration. Use your grounded nature to pursue new ideas while staying focused on long-term goals.

Gemini: Communication is highlighted today. Use this energy to engage in meaningful conversations and explore new ideas with curiosity.

Cancer: Adventure and learning are calling you today. Step out of your comfort zone and embrace new experiences for personal growth and development.

Leo: Leadership and action are your strengths today. Use this energy to take bold steps toward your goals and inspire those around you.

Virgo: It's a great day for learning and expanding your knowledge. Use your analytical skills to approach challenges with an open mind.

Libra: Relationships feel dynamic and exciting today. Focus on engaging in conversations that broaden your perspective and deepen your connections.

Scorpio: After a period of emotional intensity, today encourages you to focus on personal growth and embracing new possibilities for self-discovery.

Sagittarius: The Moon in your sign enhances your natural sense of adventure. Use this energy to explore new ideas and pursue your passions.

Capricorn: While discipline is important, today encourages you to explore new ideas and broaden your horizons with optimism and enthusiasm.

Aquarius: Your creativity and innovative thinking shine today. Use this energy to explore new ideas and share your unique perspective with others.

Pisces: It's a day for personal growth and exploration. Use your intuition to guide you as you embrace new opportunities and expand your horizons.

For those born on July 16: Born under the Moon in Sagittarius, these individuals are adventurous, optimistic, and always eager to learn. In 2025, they'll thrive by pursuing new opportunities for growth, expanding their knowledge, and embracing exciting new possibilities.

Daily Insights: The Moon in Sagittarius continues to bring optimism and adventure, but as it transitions into Capricorn later in the day, the focus shifts toward discipline, practicality, and long-term planning. It's a day for balancing exploration with responsibility and setting clear goals for the future.

Aries: Start the day with a sense of adventure, but as the Moon moves into Capricorn, focus on grounding yourself and setting long-term goals.

Taurus: The day begins with optimism and excitement, but later, you'll feel more inclined to focus on practical matters and organizing your long-term plans.

Gemini: Use the early part of the day for exploration and learning, but as the energy shifts, focus on refining your goals and taking practical steps toward achieving them.

Cancer: Adventure is important early in the day, but as the Moon moves into Capricorn, focus on creating stability in your personal life and making thoughtful decisions.

Leo: The morning is ideal for pursuing your passions, but as the Moon enters Capricorn, focus on grounding your ideas and setting realistic goals.

Virgo: Use the early part of the day for intellectual exploration, but later, shift your focus to organizing your thoughts and refining your plans for the future.

Libra: Relationships feel dynamic early in the day, but as the energy shifts, focus on creating harmony and balance in your connections, while also setting practical goals.

Scorpio: The morning is filled with excitement and creativity, but later, shift your focus to practical matters and long-term goals.

Sagittarius: The Moon in your sign brings optimism early in the day, but as it transitions into Capricorn, focus on practical steps and responsibility to achieve your goals.

Capricorn: The Moon enters your sign later today, bringing a sense of discipline and focus. Use this energy to work on long-term projects and set achievable goals.

Aquarius: Adventure and learning are highlighted in the morning, but as the Moon enters Capricorn, focus on practical solutions and refining your innovative ideas.

Pisces: The morning is perfect for exploration and creativity, but by evening, focus on grounding yourself and making long-term decisions for stability.

For those born on July 17: Born under the transition from Sagittarius to Capricorn, these individuals are both adventurous and practical. In 2025, they'll thrive by balancing their enthusiasm for exploration with a focus on long-term goals and responsibility.

Daily Insights: The Moon in Capricorn emphasizes discipline, practicality, and long-term planning. It's a great day for focusing on your goals, staying productive, and making steady progress. With Mars in Capricorn, there's extra determination and focus, making it a perfect time for tackling ambitious projects.

Aries: Focus on your long-term goals today. Use your energy to make steady progress while staying disciplined and grounded.

Taurus: It's a day for practical achievements. Use your determination to work on long-term projects and create stability in your life.

Gemini: It's a productive day for organizing your thoughts and refining your plans. Use this energy to stay focused and disciplined.

Cancer: Emotional reflection and stability are key today. Use this energy to focus on your long-term personal and professional goals.

Leo: Confidence and leadership are highlighted today. Use your focus to take charge of important projects and inspire those around you.

Virgo: It's a great day for focusing on productivity and long-term planning. Use your disciplined nature to tackle important tasks.

Libra: Relationships feel stable today. Focus on creating harmony in your personal connections while staying productive with your goals.

Scorpio: Your determination is strong today. Use this energy to focus on long-term goals and make practical decisions for the future.

Sagittarius: Adventure takes a backseat today as you focus on creating stability and working toward your long-term goals.

Capricorn: The Moon in your sign enhances your natural discipline and focus. Use this energy to make significant progress on your ambitions.

Aquarius: While creativity is important, today encourages you to focus on practical solutions and refining your ideas for long-term success.

Pisces: Emotional reflection is balanced with practicality today. Use this energy to organize your life and focus on long-term goals.

For those born on July 18: Born under the Moon in Capricorn, these individuals are disciplined, practical, and focused on achieving long-term success. In 2025, they'll thrive by setting clear goals and making steady progress toward achieving them, using their disciplined nature to stay focused on their ambitions.

Daily Insights: The Moon in Capricorn continues to emphasize discipline, productivity, and long-term goals, but as it transitions into Aquarius later in the day, the focus shifts toward creativity, innovation, and social connections. It's a day for balancing practical work with creative exploration.

Aries: Use the morning for disciplined work, but as the Moon moves into Aquarius, embrace your creativity and explore new ideas.

Taurus: The day starts with a focus on productivity, but later, shift your attention to social interactions and creative thinking.

Gemini: Productivity is high early in the day, but by evening, you'll feel more inclined to engage in conversations and explore new possibilities.

Cancer: Start the day with practical goals, but as the Moon enters Aquarius, focus on creativity and exploring new opportunities.

Leo: The morning is perfect for focusing on your goals, but as the day progresses, embrace new ways of thinking and collaborating with others.

Virgo: Use the early part of the day for productivity, but later, shift your focus to creative problem-solving and engaging with others.

Libra: Relationships feel stable early in the day, but later, focus on innovative solutions and exploring new perspectives in your connections.

Scorpio: Determination guides you early in the day, but as the energy shifts, focus on expanding your mind and embracing creative ideas.

Sagittarius: The day starts with a focus on responsibilities, but later, you'll feel more curious and eager to explore new possibilities.

Capricorn: The Moon in your sign enhances your focus on discipline, but as it moves into Aquarius, explore creative ideas and social opportunities.

Aquarius: The evening brings a burst of creativity and innovation. Use this time to explore new projects and connect with others.

Pisces: Emotional reflection is key early in the day, but as the Moon enters Aquarius, focus on socializing and expressing your creativity.

For those born on July 19: Born under the transition from Capricorn to Aquarius, these individuals are both disciplined and creative. In 2025, they'll thrive by balancing practicality with innovation, focusing on both long-term goals and exploring new possibilities.

July 20, 2025

Daily Insights: The Moon in Aquarius brings a focus on creativity, innovation, and social connections. It's a great day for engaging with others, exploring new ideas, and embracing your individuality. With Venus in Gemini, relationships feel lively and intellectually stimulating, making it a perfect time for meaningful conversations.

Aries: Your creativity shines today. Use this energy to explore new ideas and connect with others through meaningful collaborations.

Taurus: It's a day for balancing practicality with creativity. Use your determination to bring innovative ideas into reality.

Gemini: Social interactions are stimulating today. Engage in conversations that inspire new perspectives and broaden your horizons.

Cancer: Creativity and innovation are calling you today. Use this energy to explore new ways of expressing yourself and connecting with others.

Leo: Leadership and creativity go hand in hand today. Use your confidence to take the lead in innovative projects and inspire others.

Virgo: It's a great day for exploring creative solutions. Use your analytical skills to approach challenges in innovative ways.

Libra: Relationships are dynamic and exciting today. Focus on connecting with others in unconventional ways and exploring new perspectives.

Scorpio: Your passion for personal growth is strong today. Use this energy to explore new ideas and engage in meaningful conversations.

Sagittarius: Adventure and creativity are calling you today. Focus on expanding your horizons and embracing new opportunities.

Capricorn: While discipline is important, today encourages you to explore new ideas and engage in creative thinking.

Aquarius: With the Moon in your sign, your creativity and individuality are amplified. Use this energy to pursue innovative ideas and connect with others.

Pisces: Your intuition is strong today. Use this energy to explore creative projects and connect with others in meaningful ways.

For those born on July 20: Born under the Moon in Aquarius, these individuals are creative, innovative, and socially connected. In 2025, they'll thrive by embracing their individuality, exploring new ideas, and focusing on personal growth through social connections and creative expression.

Daily Insights: The Moon in Aquarius continues to emphasize creativity, innovation, and individuality, but as it transitions into Pisces later in the day, the focus shifts toward emotional reflection, intuition, and empathy. It's a day for balancing intellectual exploration with emotional depth.

Aries: Start the day with innovative ideas and social connections, but as the Moon enters Pisces, shift your focus to emotional reflection and nurturing relationships.

Taurus: The morning is great for exploring creative solutions, but later, focus on emotional healing and connecting with loved ones on a deeper level.

Gemini: Your mind is active early in the day, but as the Moon enters Pisces, focus on balancing your intellectual pursuits with emotional reflection.

Cancer: Emotional intuition is heightened as the day progresses. Use the morning for socializing, but later, focus on self-care and nurturing close relationships.

Leo: Creativity shines early in the day, but as the energy shifts, focus on your emotional well-being and connecting with those who matter most.

Virgo: Productivity is high in the morning, but by evening, you'll feel more inclined to explore your emotions and focus on personal healing.

Libra: Relationships feel dynamic early in the day, but as the Moon enters Pisces, focus on deepening your emotional connections and finding inner balance.

Scorpio: Use the morning for exploring new ideas, but later, focus on emotional growth and reflection. Your intuition is especially strong today.

Sagittarius: The day starts with excitement and creativity, but later, you'll feel more inclined to focus on emotional healing and connecting with loved ones.

Capricorn: Early productivity gives way to emotional reflection as the day progresses. Focus on grounding yourself and nurturing your relationships.

Aquarius: The Moon in your sign brings out your creativity, but as the energy shifts, focus on emotional introspection and personal growth.

Pisces: The Moon enters your sign later today, amplifying your intuition and emotional sensitivity. Use this energy to focus on self-care and emotional healing.

For those born on July 21: Born under the transition from Aquarius to Pisces, these individuals are both creative and emotionally intuitive. In 2025, they'll thrive by balancing intellectual exploration with emotional reflection, focusing on both personal growth and deepening relationships.

Daily Insights: The Moon in Pisces continues to enhance emotional sensitivity, creativity, and intuition. It's a great day for self-reflection, nurturing relationships, and engaging in creative projects. With Mars in Capricorn, there's a grounded energy that helps you take practical steps toward your long-term goals, even while embracing your emotions.

Aries: Your intuition is heightened today. Use this energy to reflect on your inner self and focus on nurturing your personal relationships.

Taurus: It's a great day for balancing practicality with emotional reflection. Use your grounded nature to connect with your feelings and work on your long-term goals.

Gemini: Emotional connections are highlighted today. Use your communication skills to deepen relationships and explore your inner world.

Cancer: The Moon in Pisces enhances your natural emotional depth. Use this energy to focus on self-care and strengthen your relationships with loved ones.

Leo: While you're often action-oriented, today encourages emotional reflection. Use this time to explore your feelings and connect with those around you.

Virgo: Balance practicality with emotional insight today. Use your disciplined nature to explore your inner world and nurture your personal connections.

Libra: Relationships feel emotionally deep today. Focus on creating harmony in your personal life and nurturing your emotional well-being.

Scorpio: Your emotional intensity is strong today. Use this energy for self-reflection and focus on personal transformation and healing.

Sagittarius: It's a day for focusing on emotional well-being. Use this energy to connect with your inner self and explore your emotional depth.

Capricorn: While practicality is key, today encourages emotional reflection. Use this time to focus on balancing your responsibilities with your personal growth.

Aquarius: While your mind often focuses on big ideas, today encourages emotional introspection. Use this energy to connect with your feelings and nurture your relationships.

Pisces: The Moon in your sign amplifies your emotional sensitivity and intuition. Use this energy for personal healing and deepening your relationships with loved ones.

For those born on July 22: Born under the Moon in Pisces, these individuals are emotionally intuitive, creative, and deeply connected to their inner world. In 2025, they'll thrive by focusing on personal healing, nurturing relationships, and expressing their creativity in meaningful ways.

Daily Insights: The Moon in Pisces continues to encourage emotional reflection, but as it transitions into Aries later in the day, the focus shifts toward action, confidence, and bold steps forward. It's a day for balancing emotional introspection with taking decisive actions toward your goals.

Aries: Start the day with emotional reflection, but as the Moon enters your sign, shift your focus to taking bold actions and pursuing your personal goals.

Taurus: Use the morning for emotional introspection, but later, focus on taking practical steps toward your long-term ambitions.

Gemini: Emotional reflection is key early in the day, but as the energy shifts, focus on engaging with others and taking action on your ideas.

Cancer: Start the day by nurturing your emotional well-being, but as the Moon moves into Aries, focus on stepping out of your comfort zone and embracing new challenges.

Leo: Emotional reflection is important early in the day, but as the Moon enters Aries, your confidence will rise, making it a great time to take bold actions.

Virgo: Use the early part of the day for emotional clarity, but by evening, shift your focus to organizing your thoughts and taking action toward your goals.

Libra: Relationships feel emotionally deep in the morning, but later, focus on communicating openly and taking action to strengthen your connections.

Scorpio: Emotional depth is important early in the day, but as the Moon moves into Aries, focus on taking bold steps toward personal growth and transformation.

Sagittarius: Start the day with emotional introspection, but later, shift your focus to adventure and exploring new opportunities with confidence.

Capricorn: Emotional reflection is key early in the day, but as the Moon enters Aries, shift your attention to taking practical steps toward your long-term goals.

Aquarius: The morning is perfect for emotional reflection, but by evening, focus on pursuing new ideas and taking bold actions with confidence.

Pisces: The Moon in your sign enhances your emotional intuition early in the day, but as the energy shifts, focus on taking decisive actions toward your ambitions.

For those born on July 23: Born under the transition from Pisces to Aries, these individuals are both emotionally intuitive and action-oriented. In 2025, they'll thrive by balancing emotional introspection with taking bold steps toward their personal goals and ambitions.

Daily Insights: The Moon in Aries brings a surge of energy, confidence, and motivation. It's a great day for taking bold steps, embracing new opportunities, and focusing on personal goals. With the Sun in Leo, there's also an emphasis on creativity and self-expression, making it a day for bold actions and embracing your true self.

Aries: Your confidence is high today. Use this energy to pursue your personal goals and take bold actions with enthusiasm.

Taurus: It's a day for balancing bold actions with practicality. Use your determination to make steady progress toward your long-term goals.

Gemini: Communication and action are your strengths today. Use this energy to engage in meaningful conversations and take action on your ideas.

Cancer: Confidence and emotional reflection are key today. Use this energy to focus on personal growth and take bold steps toward your ambitions.

Leo: Leadership and action are highlighted today. Use your natural confidence to take charge of projects and inspire those around you.

Virgo: It's a productive day for focusing on your goals. Use your disciplined nature to take bold actions while staying organized and practical.

Libra: Relationships feel dynamic and exciting today. Focus on communicating openly and taking action to strengthen your personal connections.

Scorpio: Your determination is strong today. Use this energy to focus on your long-term goals and take decisive actions toward achieving them.

Sagittarius: Adventure and excitement are calling you today. Use your enthusiasm to explore new opportunities and take bold steps toward your dreams.

Capricorn: Discipline and focus guide you today. Use this energy to take practical steps toward your long-term goals and ambitions.

Aquarius: Your creativity and innovative thinking shine today. Use this energy to explore new ideas and take bold actions toward your personal goals.

Pisces: It's a day for taking action on your personal ambitions. Use your intuition to guide you as you embrace new opportunities with confidence.

For those born on July 24: Born under the Moon in Aries, these individuals are confident, action-oriented, and driven. In 2025, they'll thrive by taking bold steps toward their personal goals and embracing new opportunities with enthusiasm.

Daily Insights: The Moon in Aries continues to bring energy, motivation, and a focus on personal goals. It's a great day for taking decisive actions, embracing challenges, and pursuing your ambitions. With Mercury in Leo, communication is bold and creative, making it a perfect time for expressing your ideas with confidence.

Aries: Your confidence and motivation are high today. Use this energy to push forward on your personal goals and take bold actions with confidence.

Taurus: It's a day for balancing bold actions with practicality. Use your grounded nature to take steady steps toward your long-term goals.

Gemini: Communication is your strength today. Use this energy to engage in meaningful conversations and explore new ideas with curiosity.

Cancer: Confidence and emotional balance are key today. Use this energy to focus on personal growth and take bold steps toward your ambitions.

Leo: Leadership and action are highlighted today. Use your natural confidence to take charge of projects and inspire those around you.

Virgo: Productivity is high today. Use your disciplined nature to focus on practical tasks and take bold actions toward your goals.

Libra: Relationships feel dynamic today. Focus on open communication and take action to strengthen your personal connections.

Scorpio: Your determination is strong today. Use this energy to take decisive steps toward achieving your long-term goals.

Sagittarius: Adventure and excitement are calling you today. Use your enthusiasm to explore new opportunities and take bold steps toward your dreams.

Capricorn: Discipline and focus guide you today. Use this energy to take practical steps toward your long-term goals and ambitions.

Aquarius: Your creativity and innovative thinking shine today. Use this energy to explore new ideas and take bold actions toward your personal goals.

Pisces: It's a day for taking action on your personal ambitions. Use your intuition to guide you as you embrace new opportunities with confidence.

For those born on July 25: Born under the Moon in Aries, these individuals are energetic, motivated, and focused on achieving their goals. In 2025, they'll thrive by embracing challenges, taking bold actions, and pursuing their ambitions with enthusiasm.

Daily Insights: The Moon in Aries continues to provide energy, confidence, and motivation, but as it transitions into Taurus later in the day, the focus shifts toward stability, practicality, and long-term planning. It's a day for balancing bold actions with careful consideration of your long-term goals.

Aries: The day starts with high energy and motivation, but as the Moon moves into Taurus, focus on grounding yourself and setting practical goals for the future.

Taurus: The Moon enters your sign later today, bringing a sense of stability and focus on practical matters. Use this energy to work toward your long-term ambitions.

Gemini: It's a day for balancing bold ideas with practical steps. Use the morning for exploration, but by evening, shift your focus to long-term planning.

Cancer: The morning is perfect for pursuing your ambitions with confidence, but as the Moon moves into Taurus, focus on grounding your emotions and working toward long-term stability in your personal life.

Leo: Start the day with creative energy and bold actions, but as the energy shifts, focus on setting practical goals that will lead to long-term success.

Virgo: Use the early part of the day to act on your bold ideas, but later in the day, shift your attention to organizing your long-term plans and ensuring stability.

Libra: Relationships feel dynamic in the morning, but by evening, focus on creating harmony and long-term emotional stability in your personal connections.

Scorpio: Your energy is strong in the morning for taking bold steps, but later, focus on grounding yourself and creating stability in your professional and personal life.

Sagittarius: Adventure is calling you in the morning, but as the Moon enters Taurus, shift your focus to setting realistic goals and making steady progress.

Capricorn: The morning is filled with confidence and motivation, but by evening, focus on your long-term goals and ensure that your actions are practical and grounded.

Aquarius: Creativity and innovation are your strengths in the morning, but as the day progresses, shift your attention to setting practical steps for future success.

Pisces: Use the morning for emotional reflection and taking action on personal goals, but later, focus on grounding yourself and ensuring emotional and practical stability in your life.

For those born on July 26: Born under the transition from Aries to Taurus, these individuals are energetic and driven but also practical and grounded. In 2025, they'll thrive by balancing their bold ambitions with careful long-term planning and steady progress toward success.

Daily Insights: The Moon in Taurus brings a focus on stability, practicality, and long-term planning. It's a great day for working on your goals methodically, taking slow and steady steps toward success. With Mars in Capricorn, there's an added boost of discipline, making it an ideal time for productivity and laying the groundwork for future ambitions.

Aries: Focus on grounding yourself today. Use your energy to set practical goals and work methodically toward your long-term ambitions.

Taurus: The Moon in your sign amplifies your sense of stability and focus. Use this energy to work on practical matters and ensure you're making steady progress.

Gemini: It's a day for long-term planning. Use your intellectual curiosity to refine your goals and take practical steps to move toward them.

Cancer: Stability is key today. Focus on grounding your emotions and working toward long-term stability in your personal and professional life.

Leo: While creativity is important, today encourages you to focus on practical goals. Use your leadership skills to guide others in achieving long-term success.

Virgo: It's a productive day for focusing on practical matters. Use your disciplined nature to ensure that you're making steady progress on your goals.

Libra: Relationships feel stable and grounded today. Focus on creating harmony in your personal connections while working toward long-term success.

Scorpio: Your determination is strong today. Use this energy to focus on your long-term goals and ensure you're making practical decisions for the future.

Sagittarius: Adventure takes a backseat today as you focus on creating stability and working toward practical goals in your personal and professional life.

Capricorn: Discipline and focus are your strengths today. Use this energy to make steady progress on your long-term projects and goals.

Aquarius: While creativity and innovation are important, today encourages you to focus on practical solutions and laying the groundwork for future success.

Pisces: Emotional stability is key today. Use this energy to ground yourself and work on practical steps to ensure long-term security in your life.

For those born on July 27: Born under the Moon in Taurus, these individuals are practical, grounded, and focused on long-term success. In 2025, they'll thrive by setting clear goals and making steady progress toward them, using their disciplined nature to stay focused on their ambitions.

Daily Insights: The Moon in Taurus continues to emphasize stability, practicality, and long-term goals, but as it transitions into Gemini later in the day, the focus shifts toward communication, learning, and curiosity. It's a day for balancing practical work with intellectual exploration and social connections.

Aries: Use the morning to focus on grounding yourself and working toward long-term goals, but later in the day, shift your focus to communication and exploring new ideas.

Taurus: Start the day with stability and practicality, but by evening, embrace social interactions and intellectual exploration.

Gemini: The Moon enters your sign later today, bringing a burst of energy and curiosity. It's a great time for exploring new ideas and engaging in conversations.

Cancer: The day begins with a focus on stability, but as the energy shifts, focus on connecting with others and exploring new perspectives.

Leo: Use the morning for practical work, but as the Moon enters Gemini, engage with others and share your ideas freely.

Virgo: The early part of the day is productive, but by evening, focus on engaging with new ideas and refining your long-term plans.

Libra: Relationships feel stable early in the day, but as the Moon moves into Gemini, focus on open communication and exploring new perspectives with loved ones.

Scorpio: The day begins with determination and focus, but later, you'll feel more inclined to explore social interactions and new opportunities.

Sagittarius: Start the day with practicality, but as the Moon enters Gemini, shift your focus to learning and intellectual exploration.

Capricorn: Discipline guides you early in the day, but by evening, shift your attention to communication and engaging with others.

Aquarius: The day starts with practical tasks, but later, explore new ideas and engage with others in stimulating conversations.

Pisces: Emotional reflection is key early in the day, but as the Moon moves into Gemini, focus on socializing and expressing your ideas clearly.

For those born on July 28: Born under the transition from Taurus to Gemini, these individuals are both practical and curious. In 2025, they'll thrive by balancing their disciplined approach with intellectual exploration, focusing on both long-term goals and learning new things.

Daily Insights: The Moon in Gemini brings a focus on communication, learning, and curiosity. It's a great day for engaging in conversations, exploring new ideas, and connecting with others. With Mercury in Leo, there's an added emphasis on creativity and bold expression, making it an ideal time for sharing ideas confidently.

Aries: Your curiosity is strong today. Use this energy to engage in conversations, explore new ideas, and take action on your personal goals.

Taurus: It's a day for balancing practicality with intellectual exploration. Use your grounded nature to communicate your thoughts clearly and explore new perspectives.

Gemini: The Moon in your sign enhances your communication skills. Use this energy to connect with others, share your ideas, and explore new opportunities.

Cancer: It's a day for focusing on learning and intellectual growth. Use this energy to connect with your inner self and engage in meaningful conversations.

Leo: Leadership and creativity are highlighted today. Use your confidence to inspire others and share your innovative ideas with enthusiasm.

Virgo: Your analytical skills are sharp today. Use this energy to focus on problem-solving and exploring new ideas through conversation.

Libra: Relationships feel dynamic and intellectually stimulating. Focus on engaging with loved ones in meaningful conversations and exploring new perspectives.

Scorpio: Your emotional depth is strong today. Use this energy to engage in deep conversations and explore new ideas that challenge your thinking.

Sagittarius: Adventure and learning go hand in hand today. Use your curiosity to explore new opportunities and engage in conversations that inspire you.

Capricorn: It's a day for balancing discipline with intellectual exploration. Use this energy to engage in thoughtful discussions and refine your long-term goals.

Aquarius: Your creativity and innovative thinking shine today. Use this energy to explore new ideas and engage in collaborative conversations.

Pisces: It's a day for intellectual exploration and emotional reflection. Use this energy to connect with others in meaningful ways and share your ideas.

For those born on July 29: Born under the Moon in Gemini, these individuals are curious, communicative, and eager to explore new ideas. In 2025, they'll thrive by engaging in conversations, learning new things, and using their sharp minds to make meaningful connections with others.

Daily Insights: The Moon in Gemini continues to emphasize communication, learning, and curiosity, but as it transitions into Cancer later in the day, the focus shifts toward emotional well-being, nurturing relationships, and self-care. It's a day for balancing intellectual exploration with emotional connection.

Aries: The day begins with lively conversations, but as the Moon moves into Cancer, shift your focus to emotional reflection and nurturing your relationships.

Taurus: Use the morning for exploring new ideas, but as the energy shifts, focus on creating emotional stability in your personal life.

Gemini: Your communication skills are heightened early in the day, but later, focus on emotional connections and strengthening your relationships with loved ones.

Cancer: The Moon enters your sign later today, heightening your emotional sensitivity. It's a great time for self-care and nurturing close relationships.

Leo: Start the day with intellectual exploration, but as the Moon moves into Cancer, shift your focus to emotional balance and personal growth.

Virgo: Productivity is high early in the day, but by evening, focus on emotional reflection and nurturing your personal well-being.

Libra: Relationships are intellectually stimulating in the morning, but later, focus on deepening emotional connections and creating harmony in your relationships.

Scorpio: Your curiosity is high early in the day, but as the energy shifts, focus on emotional healing and strengthening your relationships.

Sagittarius: The day begins with excitement and exploration, but later, shift your focus to emotional reflection and personal growth.

Capricorn: Use the morning for practical tasks and intellectual pursuits, but by evening, focus on nurturing your emotional well-being and relationships.

Aquarius: Creativity and intellectual exploration are highlighted early in the day, but as the Moon enters Cancer, focus on emotional growth and self-care.

Pisces: The day begins with curiosity, but later, you'll feel more inclined to focus on emotional healing and nurturing your close relationships.

For those born on July 30: Born under the transition from Gemini to Cancer, these individuals are both intellectually curious and emotionally intuitive. In 2025, they'll thrive by balancing their sharp minds with emotional reflection, focusing on both learning and nurturing their relationships.

Daily Insights: The Moon in Cancer brings a focus on emotional reflection, nurturing relationships, and self-care. It's a day for connecting with loved ones, focusing on home life, and creating a sense of emotional security. With Venus in Leo, relationships may feel passionate and exciting, adding a creative spark to your connections.

Aries: Emotional reflection is important today. Use this energy to nurture your relationships and create balance in your personal life.

Taurus: It's a day for balancing emotional well-being with practical goals. Use your grounded nature to focus on self-care and long-term planning.

Gemini: Emotional connections are highlighted today. Use your communication skills to nurture your relationships and create harmony in your personal life.

Cancer: The Moon in your sign enhances your emotional intuition. Focus on self-care and strengthening your relationships with loved ones.

Leo: While you're often focused on action, today encourages emotional reflection. Use this time to nurture your personal well-being and relationships.

Virgo: Balance is key today. Focus on creating emotional stability in your life while maintaining progress on your practical goals.

Libra: Relationships take on a deeper, more emotional tone today. Focus on nurturing your connections and creating harmony in your personal life.

Scorpio: Your emotional depth is strong today. Use this energy to focus on personal healing and deepening your connections with loved ones.

Sagittarius: It's a day for focusing on emotional well-being. Use this energy to create stability in your personal life and nurture your close relationships.

Capricorn: Emotional reflection is important today. Use this energy to focus on creating stability in your relationships and personal life.

Aquarius: While your mind is often focused on big ideas, today encourages emotional growth. Use this energy to focus on self-care and personal relationships.

Pisces: Your intuition is heightened today. Use this energy for emotional healing and nurturing your relationships with loved ones.

For those born on July 31: Born under the Moon in Cancer, these individuals are emotionally intuitive, nurturing, and deeply connected to their home and family. In 2025, they'll thrive by focusing on emotional well-being, nurturing relationships, and creating stability in their personal lives.

Daily Insights: The Moon in Cancer continues to emphasize emotional reflection, self-care, and nurturing relationships. It's a day for focusing on your emotional well-being and connecting with loved ones. As the Sun is in Leo, there's also a blend of emotional depth with creative self-expression, making it a great time for balancing emotions with personal ambitions.

Aries: Emotional balance is important today. Use this energy to nurture your relationships and take time for self-care while maintaining your confidence in personal goals.

Taurus: Focus on emotional well-being today. Use your grounded nature to strengthen your personal connections and create a sense of stability.

Gemini: Communication is highlighted today. Use this energy to have meaningful conversations and nurture emotional connections with loved ones.

Cancer: The Moon in your sign enhances your emotional intuition. Take time for self-care and focus on deepening your relationships with those close to you.

Leo: While your leadership and creativity are strong, today encourages emotional reflection. Use this energy to nurture your inner self and find balance between ambition and emotional well-being.

Virgo: Emotional clarity is key today. Use this energy to focus on organizing your personal life and deepening emotional bonds with loved ones.

Libra: Relationships take on a more nurturing tone today. Focus on creating emotional harmony and balance in your personal and professional connections.

Scorpio: Emotional reflection is important today. Use this energy to focus on healing and deepening your emotional connections with those you care about.

Sagittarius: It's a day for focusing on emotional well-being and creating stability in your personal life. Take time to connect with your inner self and nurture your relationships.

Capricorn: Emotional reflection is key today. Use this energy to ground yourself and focus on nurturing both your relationships and your personal goals.

Aquarius: While creativity is important, today encourages emotional introspection. Use this energy to connect with loved ones and focus on self-care.

Pisces: The Moon in Cancer heightens your emotional sensitivity today. Use this energy to focus on healing, nurturing your relationships, and self-care.

For those born on August 1: Born under the Moon in Cancer, these individuals are emotionally intuitive and deeply connected to their personal relationships. In 2025, they'll thrive by focusing on nurturing their emotional well-being and creating harmony in their personal life.

Daily Insights: The Moon in Cancer encourages continued focus on emotional well-being, but as it transitions into Leo later in the day, the energy shifts toward confidence, creativity, and self-expression. It's a day for balancing emotional reflection with bold actions toward your personal goals.

Aries: Start the day with emotional reflection, but as the Moon enters Leo, shift your focus to taking bold steps toward your personal goals.

Taurus: The day begins with a focus on emotional stability, but later, embrace creative expression and personal empowerment.

Gemini: Emotional connections are key early in the day, but as the energy shifts, focus on communication and expressing your unique ideas.

Cancer: The morning is ideal for nurturing your emotional well-being, but as the Moon enters Leo, focus on stepping into the spotlight and pursuing your personal ambitions.

Leo: The Moon enters your sign later today, amplifying your confidence and creativity. Use this energy to take bold steps toward your goals and lead with enthusiasm.

Virgo: The day starts with emotional clarity, but later, shift your focus to expressing your creativity and finding new ways to approach your long-term goals.

Libra: Relationships feel emotionally deep in the morning, but as the day progresses, focus on embracing creativity and finding balance in your personal connections.

Scorpio: The morning is perfect for emotional introspection, but later, focus on taking bold steps toward personal transformation and expressing your true self.

Sagittarius: Start the day by reflecting on your emotional well-being, but as the Moon enters Leo, embrace new adventures and creative opportunities.

Capricorn: The morning is ideal for grounding yourself emotionally, but as the energy shifts, focus on stepping into leadership roles and expressing your creative talents.

Aquarius: Use the morning for emotional reflection, but later, focus on exploring new ideas and expressing yourself confidently in social settings.

Pisces: Emotional sensitivity is high early in the day, but as the Moon moves into Leo, shift your focus to personal empowerment and creative expression.

For those born on August 2: Born under the transition from Cancer to Leo, these individuals are emotionally intuitive and confident. In 2025, they'll thrive by balancing their emotional well-being with bold actions toward their personal goals, stepping into leadership roles and expressing their creativity.

Daily Insights: The Moon in Leo brings a surge of confidence, creativity, and leadership. It's a great day for expressing your true self, taking bold actions, and pursuing your passions. With Mars in Capricorn, there's a balance of discipline and ambition, making it an ideal time for working toward your goals with confidence.

Aries: Your confidence is high today. Use this energy to take bold actions toward your personal goals and express yourself creatively.

Taurus: Creativity flows easily today. Focus on expressing your unique ideas and working toward your long-term goals with determination.

Gemini: Communication and self-expression are your strengths today. Use this energy to connect with others and share your innovative ideas.

Cancer: The Moon in Leo encourages you to step out of your comfort zone and pursue your personal goals with confidence and creativity.

Leo: The Moon in your sign amplifies your natural leadership and creativity. Use this energy to take bold steps toward your passions and inspire others.

Virgo: Balance creativity with practicality today. Use your disciplined nature to focus on long-term goals while expressing your unique talents.

Libra: Relationships feel dynamic and exciting today. Focus on creative ways to connect with loved ones and embrace your individuality.

Scorpio: Your passion is strong today. Use this energy to pursue personal goals with intensity and determination.

Sagittarius: Adventure and creativity are calling you today. Use this energy to explore new opportunities and express yourself freely.

Capricorn: Leadership and discipline come naturally today. Use this energy to focus on personal projects and inspire those around you.

Aquarius: Your creativity shines today. Use this energy to pursue innovative ideas and connect with others through meaningful collaborations.

Pisces: It's a day for self-expression and personal growth. Use your creativity to focus on your goals and embrace new opportunities with confidence.

For those born on August 3: Born under the Moon in Leo, these individuals are charismatic, creative, and confident. In 2025, they'll thrive by stepping into leadership roles, embracing their unique talents, and pursuing their passions with determination.

Daily Insights: The Moon in Leo continues to amplify confidence, creativity, and leadership, but as it transitions into Virgo later in the day, the focus shifts toward practicality, organization, and attention to detail. It's a day for balancing bold actions with practical steps to ensure long-term success.

Aries: Start the day with bold actions and confidence, but as the Moon moves into Virgo, focus on organizing your plans and taking practical steps toward your goals.

Taurus: Use the morning to express your creativity and passion, but later in the day, shift your focus to practical matters and long-term planning.

Gemini: The day begins with exciting conversations and social interactions, but as the energy shifts, focus on refining your ideas and organizing your thoughts.

Cancer: Emotional reflection is important early in the day, but later, focus on practical tasks and creating stability in your personal life.

Leo: The Moon in your sign boosts your charisma and leadership skills, but as the day progresses, focus on grounding your energy and organizing your goals.

Virgo: The Moon enters your sign later today, enhancing your natural attention to detail and practicality. Use this energy to tackle important tasks.

Libra: Relationships take on a dynamic tone early in the day, but as the energy shifts, focus on balancing your emotional connections with practical responsibilities.

Scorpio: It's a day for balancing your passion with practicality. Start with bold actions, but later, focus on refining your plans and staying disciplined.

Sagittarius: The morning is filled with excitement and creativity, but later, shift your focus to practical matters and long-term goals.

Capricorn: Leadership and discipline guide you early in the day, but later, shift your attention to organizing your tasks and working on long-term projects.

Aquarius: Use the morning for creative pursuits, but as the Moon moves into Virgo, focus on practical solutions and refining your ideas.

Pisces: Emotional reflection is important early in the day, but later, focus on grounding yourself and organizing your life for greater stability.

For those born on August 4: Born under the transition from Leo to Virgo, these individuals are both creative and disciplined. In 2025, they'll thrive by balancing their bold ideas with practical action, focusing on both creativity and productivity to achieve their goals.

Daily Insights: The Moon in Virgo emphasizes productivity, organization, and attention to detail. It's a great day for focusing on practical matters, refining your plans, and making steady progress toward long-term goals. With Mercury in Gemini, communication is clear and grounded, making it an ideal time for problem-solving and setting realistic expectations.

Aries: Focus on productivity today. Use your energy to organize your plans and make steady progress toward your long-term goals.

Taurus: It's a day for practical achievements. Use your grounded nature to refine your ideas and work on long-term projects.

Gemini: Your analytical skills are strong today. Use this energy to focus on problem-solving and refining your thoughts to make steady progress on your goals.

Cancer: Emotional clarity comes through practicality today. Use this energy to focus on organizing your personal life and creating stability.

Leo: After a period of creativity, today encourages you to focus on practical matters. Use your discipline to make progress on long-term goals.

Virgo: The Moon in your sign enhances your natural strengths. Use this energy to focus on productivity and tackle tasks that require precision.

Libra: Relationships feel grounded today. Focus on creating harmony in your personal connections while staying productive and organized.

Scorpio: Your determination is strong today. Use this energy to focus on your long-term goals and make practical decisions for the future.

Sagittarius: Practical matters take precedence today. Use this energy to focus on your responsibilities and organize your thoughts.

Capricorn: Discipline and focus are key today. Use this energy to make significant progress on your long-term projects and goals.

Aquarius: While creativity is important, today encourages you to focus on practical solutions and refining your innovative ideas.

Pisces: Emotional reflection is balanced with practicality today. Use this energy to organize your life and focus on long-term goals.

For those born on August 5: Born under the Moon in Virgo, these individuals are practical, organized, and focused on productivity. In 2025, they'll thrive by refining their plans, staying disciplined, and making steady progress toward their long-term goals.

Daily Insights: The Moon in Virgo continues to emphasize productivity, organization, and attention to detail. It's a great day for refining your goals, making practical decisions, and focusing on personal and professional growth. With the Sun in Leo, there's also a sense of creativity in the air, making it a good time for blending practicality with creative thinking.

Aries: Stay focused on the details today. Use your energy to fine-tune your plans and make practical progress on your personal goals.

Taurus: It's a productive day for you. Use your grounded nature to focus on long-term projects and ensure everything is organized and in order.

Gemini: Your sharp mind is perfect for problem-solving today. Use this energy to refine your ideas and organize your thoughts for future action.

Cancer: Emotional clarity comes through practicality today. Focus on organizing your personal life and building emotional security.

Leo: While your natural confidence is strong, today encourages practicality. Use this energy to ground your creative ideas and make them a reality.

Virgo: The Moon in your sign amplifies your natural productivity. Use this energy to stay organized and focus on tasks that require your attention to detail.

Libra: Relationships feel stable and grounded today. Focus on creating harmony in your interactions while staying productive and focused.

Scorpio: Your determination is strong today. Use this energy to focus on refining your long-term goals and making practical decisions for the future.

Sagittarius: Today is about practical matters. Use this energy to focus on your responsibilities and stay disciplined in working toward your goals.

Capricorn: Productivity is high today. Use your disciplined nature to stay focused on long-term projects and ensure progress is being made.

Aquarius: While creativity is important, today encourages you to stay grounded. Use this energy to refine your innovative ideas and ensure they are practical.

Pisces: Emotional reflection is balanced with practicality today. Use this energy to organize your life and make steady progress toward your long-term goals.

For those born on August 6: Born under the Moon in Virgo, these individuals are detail-oriented, productive, and practical. In 2025, they'll thrive by focusing on refining their plans and ensuring that they're making steady progress toward their long-term goals.

Daily Insights: The Moon in Virgo continues to encourage practicality and productivity, but as it transitions into Libra later in the day, the focus shifts toward balance, relationships, and harmony. It's a day for balancing work with personal connections and finding equilibrium in all areas of life.

Aries: The morning is perfect for productivity, but as the Moon moves into Libra, focus on balancing your work with your personal relationships.

Taurus: Start the day by focusing on practical matters, but by evening, shift your attention to socializing and finding balance in your life.

Gemini: Use the early part of the day to organize your thoughts and tasks, but later, engage in conversations and create harmony in your relationships.

Cancer: It's a day for emotional clarity and balance. Start with practical tasks, but as the energy shifts, focus on nurturing your relationships and finding harmony.

Leo: Your leadership and creativity are important, but as the Moon moves into Libra, focus on balancing your goals with your relationships.

Virgo: The Moon in your sign enhances your productivity early in the day, but by evening, shift your focus to creating harmony in your personal connections.

Libra: The day starts with a focus on productivity, but as the Moon enters your sign, you'll feel more inclined to focus on relationships and creating balance in your life.

Scorpio: It's a day for balancing productivity with emotional depth. Use the morning for practical tasks, but later, focus on connecting with loved ones.

Sagittarius: Responsibilities take center stage early in the day, but as the energy shifts, focus on social interactions and bringing balance to your personal life.

Capricorn: Discipline guides you early in the day, but by evening, shift your attention to creating harmony in your relationships and finding equilibrium.

Aquarius: The morning is perfect for creative pursuits, but as the Moon moves into Libra, focus on balancing your social life and work goals.

Pisces: Emotional clarity is important early in the day, but as the Moon enters Libra, focus on connecting with others and creating balance in your relationships.

For those born on August 7: Born under the transition from Virgo to Libra, these individuals are both productive and focused on harmony. In 2025, they'll thrive by balancing their attention to detail with creating harmonious relationships and personal connections.

Daily Insights: The Moon in Libra emphasizes balance, harmony, and relationships. It's a great day for social interactions, resolving conflicts, and creating equilibrium in your personal and professional life. With Venus in Leo, relationships may feel passionate and exciting, making it an ideal time for creative and romantic pursuits.

Aries: Focus on finding balance in your relationships today. Use this energy to create harmony in your personal and professional life.

Taurus: Balance is important today. Focus on maintaining harmony in your relationships while working toward your personal goals.

Gemini: Relationships take center stage today. Focus on communicating clearly and creating harmony in your interactions.

Cancer: It's a day for balancing your emotional needs with your relationships. Use this energy to create equilibrium in your personal connections.

Leo: While confidence and leadership come naturally, today encourages you to focus on your relationships and ensure balance in your personal life.

Virgo: Balance productivity with harmony today. Use this energy to focus on both your work goals and your relationships.

Libra: With the Moon in your sign, balance and harmony are highlighted. Use this energy to create peace in your relationships and your personal life.

Scorpio: Relationships feel emotionally deep today. Use this energy to connect with others on a deeper level while maintaining balance in your life.

Sagittarius: Social interactions are favored today. Use your natural charm to connect with others while ensuring harmony in your personal life.

Capricorn: It's a day for balancing your responsibilities with your relationships. Focus on finding harmony between your work and personal life.

Aquarius: Creativity and innovation come naturally today, but focus on creating balance in your interactions and ensuring harmony in your relationships.

Pisces: Emotional balance is important today. Use this energy to connect with loved ones and focus on creating stability in your relationships.

For those born on August 8: Born under the Moon in Libra, these individuals are focused on balance, harmony, and relationships. In 2025, they'll thrive by creating equilibrium in their personal and professional lives while working toward their goals with patience and determination.

Daily Insights: The Moon in Libra continues to emphasize balance and harmony, but as it transitions into Scorpio later in the day, the focus shifts toward emotional depth, transformation, and intense connections. It's a day for balancing social interactions with emotional introspection.

Aries: The day begins with a focus on relationships and balance, but as the Moon moves into Scorpio, you'll feel more inclined to explore deeper emotional connections.

Taurus: Use the early part of the day to focus on social interactions and creating harmony, but later, dive into emotional reflection and personal growth.

Gemini: Relationships are in focus early in the day, but as the energy shifts, you'll feel more introspective and inclined to explore your inner world.

Cancer: Balance is important in the morning, but as the Moon moves into Scorpio, focus on emotional depth and nurturing your closest relationships.

Leo: Start the day by focusing on balance in your interactions, but later, shift your attention to emotional transformation and personal growth.

Virgo: The morning is perfect for maintaining harmony in your daily life, but by evening, focus on emotional clarity and personal reflection.

Libra: The Moon in your sign encourages you to maintain balance in your relationships, but later, you'll feel more inclined to explore emotional depth.

Scorpio: The Moon enters your sign later in the day, heightening your emotional intensity. Use this energy to focus on personal transformation and deepening your connections with others.

Sagittarius: Balance your social life in the morning, but by evening, focus on exploring your emotional world and strengthening your relationships.

Capricorn: Discipline and balance guide you in the morning, but later, shift your attention to emotional reflection and personal transformation.

Aquarius: It's a day for balancing relationships and personal goals. As the energy shifts, focus on emotional depth and meaningful connections.

Pisces: Emotional balance is important early in the day, but as the energy transitions, focus on exploring your inner self and strengthening your emotional connections.

For those born on August 9: Born under the transition from Libra to Scorpio, these individuals are both balanced and emotionally intense. In 2025, they'll thrive by balancing their relationships with personal transformation and emotional growth. It's a year for exploring deeper connections and self-reflection.

August 10, 2025

Daily Insights: The Moon in Scorpio emphasizes emotional depth, transformation, and introspection. It's a day for exploring your inner world, focusing on personal growth, and deepening your connections with others. With Mercury in Gemini, communication is still lively, encouraging meaningful conversations and emotional openness.

Aries: Emotional reflection is key today. Use this energy to focus on personal growth and explore deeper connections with those around you.

Taurus: It's a day for emotional transformation. Use your grounded nature to explore your inner world and focus on healing and growth.

Gemini: Communication is highlighted today. Use this energy to engage in deep conversations and explore your emotional connections.

Cancer: Emotional depth is strong today. Use this energy to nurture your relationships and focus on personal transformation and healing.

Leo: While action is important, today encourages emotional reflection. Use this time to deepen your understanding of yourself and your relationships.

Virgo: Balance your practical nature with emotional reflection today. Use this energy to explore your inner world and nurture your personal connections.

Libra: Relationships feel emotionally deep today. Focus on creating harmony in your emotional connections and engaging in meaningful conversations.

Scorpio: The Moon in your sign enhances your emotional intensity. Use this energy for self-reflection and personal transformation.

Sagittarius: It's a day for emotional introspection. Use your curiosity to explore your inner world and strengthen your emotional connections.

Capricorn: Your determination is strong today. Use this energy to focus on emotional growth and work toward long-term goals that bring stability.

Aquarius: Emotional reflection is important today. Use this energy to focus on creating deeper connections and exploring your inner emotions.

Pisces: Your intuition is heightened today. Use this energy for emotional healing and focus on nurturing your relationships with loved ones.

For those born on August 10: Born under the Moon in Scorpio, these individuals are emotionally intense, intuitive, and deeply connected to their inner world. In 2025, they'll thrive by focusing on personal transformation, emotional healing, and deepening their relationships.

Daily Insights: The Moon in Scorpio continues to bring emotional intensity and focus on personal transformation. However, as it transitions into Sagittarius later in the day, the focus shifts toward optimism, adventure, and exploration. It's a day for balancing introspection with excitement for new possibilities.

Aries: Start the day with emotional reflection, but as the Moon moves into Sagittarius, shift your focus to new opportunities and personal growth.

Taurus: The morning is ideal for emotional introspection, but later in the day, focus on expanding your horizons and embracing new experiences.

Gemini: Emotional reflection is important early in the day, but as the energy shifts, focus on engaging with others and exploring new ideas.

Cancer: The morning is perfect for nurturing your relationships, but later, focus on stepping out of your comfort zone and embracing new possibilities.

Leo: Emotional depth is important early in the day, but as the Moon moves into Sagittarius, focus on taking bold steps toward your personal goals.

Virgo: The day starts with emotional clarity, but later, focus on exploring new ideas and expanding your knowledge.

Libra: Relationships feel emotionally deep early in the day, but later, focus on creating harmony and embracing new perspectives.

Scorpio: The Moon in your sign enhances your emotional intensity, but as the day progresses, focus on personal growth and exploring new opportunities.

Sagittarius: The Moon enters your sign later in the day, bringing a boost of optimism and excitement. Use this energy to pursue new passions.

Capricorn: Start the day with emotional reflection, but as the energy shifts, focus on setting new goals and expanding your horizons.

Aquarius: The morning is perfect for exploring emotional depth, but by evening, shift your focus to creativity and embracing new ideas.

Pisces: Emotional intuition is heightened early in the day, but as the energy shifts, focus on personal growth and exploring new possibilities.

For those born on August 11: Born under the transition from Scorpio to Sagittarius, these individuals are emotionally intense but adventurous. In 2025, they'll thrive by balancing emotional reflection with personal growth and embracing new experiences.

Daily Insights: The Moon in Sagittarius brings a sense of adventure, optimism, and personal growth. It's a day for exploring new opportunities, learning, and expanding your horizons. With Mercury in Gemini, communication is lively, making it a great time for engaging in stimulating conversations.

Aries: Your adventurous spirit is high today. Use this energy to explore new opportunities and focus on personal growth.

Taurus: It's a day for balancing stability with exploration. Use your grounded nature to pursue new experiences while staying focused on long-term goals.

Gemini: Communication is your strength today. Use this energy to engage in stimulating conversations and explore new ideas.

Cancer: Adventure and learning are calling you today. Step out of your comfort zone and embrace new experiences for personal growth.

Leo: Your confidence and leadership are highlighted today. Use this energy to take bold actions toward your goals and inspire those around you.

Virgo: It's a great day for learning and expanding your knowledge. Use your analytical mind to explore new topics and gain valuable insights.

Libra: Relationships feel dynamic and intellectually stimulating. Focus on engaging in conversations that deepen your connections and broaden your perspective.

Scorpio: After a period of emotional intensity, today encourages you to focus on personal growth and embrace new opportunities for self-discovery.

Sagittarius: The Moon in your sign enhances your sense of adventure and optimism. It's a perfect day to pursue your passions and explore new possibilities.

Capricorn: While discipline is important, today encourages you to explore new ideas and broaden your horizons with an open mind.

Aquarius: Your innovative thinking shines today. Use this energy to explore new possibilities and share your unique perspective with others.

Pisces: It's a day for personal growth and exploration. Use your intuition to guide you as you embrace new opportunities and expand your horizons.

For those born on August 12: Born under the Moon in Sagittarius, these individuals are adventurous, curious, and eager to learn. In 2025, they'll thrive by exploring new opportunities, pursuing personal growth, and embracing new possibilities.

Daily Insights: The Moon in Sagittarius continues to inspire optimism, exploration, and learning. It's a day for expanding your knowledge, pursuing your passions, and embracing new experiences. With Venus in Gemini, relationships feel lively and intellectually stimulating, encouraging open communication.

Aries: Your sense of adventure is strong today. Use this energy to explore new possibilities and pursue your personal goals with enthusiasm.

Taurus: It's a day for balancing practicality with exploration. Use your grounded nature to pursue new ideas while staying focused on long-term goals.

Gemini: Communication is highlighted today. Use this energy to engage in meaningful conversations and explore new ideas with curiosity.

Cancer: Adventure and learning are calling you today. Step out of your comfort zone and embrace new experiences for personal growth and development.

Leo: Leadership and action are your strengths today. Use this energy to take bold steps toward your goals and inspire those around you.

Virgo: It's a great day for learning and expanding your knowledge. Use your analytical skills to approach challenges with an open mind.

Libra: Relationships feel dynamic and exciting today. Focus on engaging in conversations that broaden your perspective and deepen your connections.

Scorpio: After a period of emotional intensity, today encourages you to focus on personal growth and embracing new possibilities for self-discovery.

Sagittarius: The Moon in your sign enhances your natural sense of adventure. Use this energy to explore new ideas and pursue your passions.

Capricorn: While discipline is important, today encourages you to explore new ideas and broaden your horizons with optimism and enthusiasm.

Aquarius: Your creativity and innovative thinking shine today. Use this energy to explore new ideas and share your unique perspective with others.

Pisces: It's a day for personal growth and exploration. Use your intuition to guide you as you embrace new opportunities and expand your horizons.

For those born on August 13: Born under the Moon in Sagittarius, these individuals are adventurous, optimistic, and always eager to learn. In 2025, they'll thrive by pursuing new opportunities for growth, expanding their knowledge, and embracing exciting new possibilities.

Daily Insights: The Moon in Sagittarius continues to bring optimism and adventure, but as it transitions into Capricorn later in the day, the focus shifts toward discipline, practicality, and long-term planning. It's a day for balancing exploration with responsibility and setting clear goals for the future.

Aries: Start the day with a sense of adventure, but as the Moon moves into Capricorn, focus on grounding yourself and setting long-term goals.

Taurus: The day begins with optimism and excitement, but later, you'll feel more inclined to focus on practical matters and organizing your long-term plans.

Gemini: Use the early part of the day for exploration and learning, but as the energy shifts, focus on refining your goals and taking practical steps toward achieving them.

Cancer: Adventure is important early in the day, but as the Moon moves into Capricorn, focus on creating stability in your personal life and making thoughtful decisions.

Leo: The morning is ideal for pursuing your passions, but as the Moon enters Capricorn, focus on grounding your ideas and setting realistic goals.

Virgo: Use the early part of the day for intellectual exploration, but later, shift your focus to organizing your thoughts and refining your plans for the future.

Libra: Relationships feel dynamic early in the day, but as the energy shifts, focus on creating harmony and balance in your connections, while also setting practical goals.

Scorpio: The morning is filled with excitement and creativity, but later, shift your focus to practical matters and long-term goals.

Sagittarius: The Moon in your sign brings optimism early in the day, but as it transitions into Capricorn, focus on practical steps and responsibility to achieve your goals.

Capricorn: The Moon enters your sign later today, bringing a sense of discipline and focus. Use this energy to work on long-term projects and set achievable goals.

Aquarius: Adventure and learning are highlighted in the morning, but as the Moon enters Capricorn, focus on practical solutions and refining your innovative ideas for long-term success.

Pisces: The morning is perfect for exploring new possibilities, but as the day progresses, focus on grounding yourself and setting practical goals for the future.

For those born on August 14: Born under the transition from Sagittarius to Capricorn, these individuals are both adventurous and practical. In 2025, they'll thrive by balancing their enthusiasm for exploration with a focus on long-term goals and responsibility.

Daily Insights: The Moon in Capricorn emphasizes discipline, practicality, and long-term planning. It's a great day for focusing on your goals, staying productive, and making steady progress. With Mars in Capricorn, there's extra determination and focus, making it an ideal time for working on ambitious projects and achieving success.

Aries: Focus on your long-term goals today. Use your energy to make steady progress while staying disciplined and grounded.

Taurus: It's a day for practical achievements. Use your determination to work on long-term projects and create stability in your life.

Gemini: It's a productive day for organizing your thoughts and refining your plans. Use this energy to stay focused and disciplined.

Cancer: Emotional reflection and stability are key today. Use this energy to focus on your long-term personal and professional goals.

Leo: Confidence and leadership are highlighted today. Use your focus to take charge of important projects and inspire those around you.

Virgo: It's a great day for focusing on productivity and long-term planning. Use your disciplined nature to tackle important tasks.

Libra: Relationships feel stable today. Focus on creating harmony in your personal connections while staying productive with your goals.

Scorpio: Your determination is strong today. Use this energy to focus on long-term goals and make practical decisions for the future.

Sagittarius: Adventure takes a backseat today as you focus on creating stability and working toward your long-term goals.

Capricorn: The Moon in your sign enhances your natural discipline and focus. Use this energy to make significant progress on your ambitions.

Aquarius: While creativity is important, today encourages you to focus on practical solutions and refining your ideas for long-term success.

Pisces: Emotional reflection is balanced with practicality today. Use this energy to organize your life and focus on long-term goals.

For those born on August 15: Born under the Moon in Capricorn, these individuals are disciplined, practical, and focused on achieving long-term success. In 2025, they'll thrive by setting clear goals and making steady progress toward their ambitions, using their disciplined nature to stay focused.

Daily Insights: The Moon in Capricorn continues to emphasize discipline, productivity, and long-term goals, but as it transitions into Aquarius later in the day, the focus shifts toward creativity, innovation, and social connections. It's a day for balancing practical work with creative exploration.

Aries: Use the morning for disciplined work, but as the Moon moves into Aquarius, embrace your creativity and explore new ideas.

Taurus: The day starts with a focus on productivity, but later, shift your attention to social interactions and creative thinking.

Gemini: Productivity is high early in the day, but by evening, you'll feel more inclined to engage in conversations and explore new possibilities.

Cancer: Start the day with practical goals, but as the Moon enters Aquarius, focus on creativity and exploring new opportunities.

Leo: The morning is perfect for focusing on your goals, but as the day progresses, embrace new ways of thinking and collaborating with others.

Virgo: Use the early part of the day for productivity, but later, shift your focus to creative problem-solving and engaging with others.

Libra: Relationships feel stable early in the day, but later, focus on innovative solutions and exploring new perspectives in your connections.

Scorpio: Determination guides you early in the day, but as the energy shifts, focus on expanding your mind and embracing creative ideas.

Sagittarius: The day starts with a focus on responsibilities, but later, you'll feel more curious and eager to explore new possibilities.

Capricorn: The Moon in your sign enhances your focus on discipline, but as it moves into Aquarius, explore creative ideas and social opportunities.

Aquarius: The evening brings a burst of creativity and innovation. Use this time to explore new projects and connect with others.

Pisces: Emotional reflection is key early in the day, but as the Moon enters Aquarius, focus on socializing and expressing your creativity.

For those born on August 16: Born under the transition from Capricorn to Aquarius, these individuals are both disciplined and creative. In 2025, they'll thrive by balancing practicality with innovation, focusing on both long-term goals and exploring new possibilities.

Daily Insights: The Moon in Aquarius brings a focus on creativity, innovation, and social connections. It's a great day for engaging with others, exploring new ideas, and embracing your individuality. With Venus in Gemini, relationships feel lively and intellectually stimulating, making it a perfect time for meaningful conversations.

Aries: Your creativity shines today. Use this energy to explore new ideas and connect with others through meaningful collaborations.

Taurus: It's a day for balancing practicality with creativity. Use your determination to bring innovative ideas into reality.

Gemini: Social interactions are stimulating today. Engage in conversations that inspire new perspectives and broaden your horizons.

Cancer: Creativity and innovation are calling you today. Use this energy to explore new ways of expressing yourself and connecting with others.

Leo: Leadership and creativity go hand in hand today. Use your confidence to take the lead in innovative projects and inspire others.

Virgo: It's a great day for exploring creative solutions. Use your analytical skills to approach challenges in innovative ways.

Libra: Relationships are dynamic and exciting today. Focus on connecting with others in unconventional ways and exploring new perspectives.

Scorpio: Your passion for personal growth is strong today. Use this energy to explore new ideas and engage in meaningful conversations.

Sagittarius: Adventure and creativity are calling you today. Focus on expanding your horizons and embracing new opportunities.

Capricorn: While discipline is important, today encourages you to explore new ideas and engage in creative thinking.

Aquarius: With the Moon in your sign, your creativity and individuality are amplified. Use this energy to pursue innovative ideas and connect with others.

Pisces: Your intuition is strong today. Use this energy to explore creative projects and connect with others in meaningful ways.

For those born on August 17: Born under the Moon in Aquarius, these individuals are creative, innovative, and socially connected. In 2025, they'll thrive by embracing their individuality, exploring new ideas, and focusing on personal growth through social connections and creative expression.

Daily Insights: The Moon in Aquarius continues to emphasize creativity, innovation, and individuality, but as it transitions into Pisces later in the day, the focus shifts toward emotional reflection, intuition, and empathy. It's a day for balancing intellectual exploration with emotional depth.

Aries: Start the day with innovative ideas and social connections, but as the Moon enters Pisces, shift your focus to emotional reflection and nurturing relationships.

Taurus: The morning is great for exploring creative solutions, but later, focus on emotional healing and connecting with loved ones on a deeper level.

Gemini: Your mind is active early in the day, but as the Moon enters Pisces, focus on balancing your intellectual pursuits with emotional reflection.

Cancer: Emotional intuition is heightened as the day progresses. Use the morning for socializing, but later, focus on self-care and nurturing close relationships.

Leo: Creativity shines early in the day, but as the energy shifts, focus on your emotional well-being and connecting with those who matter most.

Virgo: Productivity is high in the morning, but by evening, you'll feel more inclined to explore your emotions and focus on personal healing.

Libra: Relationships feel dynamic early in the day, but as the Moon enters Pisces, focus on deepening your emotional connections and finding inner balance.

Scorpio: Use the morning for exploring new ideas, but later, focus on emotional growth and reflection. Your intuition is especially strong today.

Sagittarius: The day starts with excitement and creativity, but later, you'll feel more inclined to focus on emotional healing and connecting with loved ones.

Capricorn: Early productivity gives way to emotional reflection as the day progresses. Focus on grounding yourself and nurturing your relationships.

Aquarius: The Moon in your sign brings out your creativity, but as the energy shifts, focus on emotional introspection and personal growth.

Pisces: The Moon enters your sign later today, amplifying your intuition and emotional sensitivity. Use this energy to focus on self-care and emotional healing.

For those born on August 18: Born under the transition from Aquarius to Pisces, these individuals are both creative and emotionally intuitive. In 2025, they'll thrive by balancing intellectual exploration with emotional reflection, focusing on both personal growth and deepening relationships.

Daily Insights: The Moon in Pisces brings a focus on emotional reflection, intuition, and creativity. It's a great day for engaging in artistic projects, connecting with loved ones on a deeper level, and exploring your inner world. With Mercury in Gemini, communication remains lively, making it a good day for expressing your emotions through words.

Aries: Your intuition is strong today. Use this energy to focus on emotional reflection and nurture your relationships with empathy and understanding.

Taurus: It's a great day for combining creativity with practicality. Focus on expressing your emotions through artistic projects or clear communication.

Gemini: Emotional reflection is key today. Use this energy to connect with your inner self and engage in meaningful conversations with loved ones.

Cancer: The Moon in Pisces enhances your emotional intuition. Use this energy to focus on self-care and strengthening your personal relationships.

Leo: While you're often focused on action, today encourages emotional reflection. Use this time to explore your feelings and deepen your connections.

Virgo: Balance your practical nature with emotional reflection today. Use this energy to focus on your inner world and nurture your relationships with empathy.

Libra: Relationships feel emotionally deep today. Focus on connecting with loved ones and creating harmony in your emotional connections.

Scorpio: Your emotional intensity is strong today. Use this energy for self-reflection and focus on healing and strengthening your emotional bonds.

Sagittarius: It's a day for emotional introspection. Use this energy to explore your inner world and strengthen your emotional connections with loved ones.

Capricorn: While you're often focused on discipline, today encourages emotional reflection. Use this time to connect with your feelings and focus on personal healing.

Aquarius: While your mind is often focused on innovation, today encourages emotional growth. Use this energy to nurture your close relationships and engage in self-care.

Pisces: The Moon in your sign amplifies your emotional sensitivity and intuition. Use this energy for personal healing and deepening your emotional connections with others.

For those born on August 19: Born under the Moon in Pisces, these individuals are emotionally intuitive, creative, and deeply connected to their inner world. In 2025, they'll thrive by focusing on emotional healing, nurturing relationships, and expressing their creativity through meaningful projects.

Daily Insights: The Moon in Pisces continues to emphasize emotional reflection, creativity, and intuition. It's a great day for focusing on your inner world, nurturing relationships, and exploring creative pursuits. With Venus in Leo, there's also a heightened sense of passion and creativity in relationships, making it a perfect day for expressing love and appreciation.

Aries: Your emotions are heightened today. Use this energy to reflect on your personal relationships and express your feelings with clarity and empathy.

Taurus: Focus on balancing your practical side with emotional reflection. It's a good day for nurturing close relationships and working on creative projects.

Gemini: Your communication skills are highlighted today, especially in matters of the heart. Use this energy to engage in deep conversations and express your emotions openly.

Cancer: The Moon in Pisces enhances your emotional sensitivity. Use this time to focus on self-care and nurture your relationships with loved ones.

Leo: Your passion and creativity shine today. Use this energy to express your feelings boldly and nurture your romantic relationships.

Virgo: Balance practicality with emotional reflection today. Use this energy to focus on your inner world and strengthen your personal connections.

Libra: Relationships feel emotionally deep and fulfilling today. Focus on creating harmony in your personal life and nurturing your emotional well-being.

Scorpio: Your emotional depth is strong today. Use this energy for self-reflection, personal transformation, and healing emotional wounds.

Sagittarius: It's a day for focusing on emotional well-being. Use this energy to connect with your inner self and nurture your relationships with loved ones.

Capricorn: While you're often focused on goals, today encourages emotional reflection. Use this time to connect with your feelings and focus on personal growth.

Aquarius: While creativity is important, today encourages you to focus on emotional connections. Use this energy to nurture your relationships and express your feelings.

Pisces: The Moon in your sign amplifies your emotional sensitivity and intuition. Use this energy for personal healing and deepening your emotional connections.

For those born on August 20: Born under the Moon in Pisces, these individuals are emotionally intuitive, creative, and compassionate. In 2025, they'll thrive by focusing on their emotional well-being, nurturing relationships, and expressing their creativity through meaningful projects.

Daily Insights: The Moon in Pisces continues to bring emotional sensitivity, but as it transitions into Aries later in the day, the energy shifts toward action, confidence, and bold decisions. It's a day for balancing emotional reflection with taking bold steps toward your goals.

Aries: Start the day with emotional reflection, but as the Moon enters your sign, focus on taking bold actions and pursuing your personal goals with confidence.

Taurus: The morning is perfect for emotional introspection, but as the energy shifts, focus on taking practical steps toward your long-term goals.

Gemini: Emotional reflection is key early in the day, but as the energy shifts, focus on engaging with others and taking action on your ideas.

Cancer: The morning is ideal for nurturing your emotional well-being, but as the Moon moves into Aries, embrace new challenges and step out of your comfort zone.

Leo: Emotional reflection is important early in the day, but as the Moon enters Aries, your confidence will rise, making it a great time to take bold actions.

Virgo: Use the early part of the day for emotional clarity, but later, shift your focus to organizing your thoughts and taking action on your plans.

Libra: Relationships feel emotionally deep in the morning, but as the energy shifts, focus on communicating openly and taking action to strengthen your connections.

Scorpio: Emotional depth is important early in the day, but as the Moon moves into Aries, focus on taking bold steps toward personal growth and transformation.

Sagittarius: Start the day with emotional introspection, but later, shift your focus to adventure and exploring new opportunities with confidence.

Capricorn: Emotional reflection is key early in the day, but as the Moon enters Aries, focus on taking practical steps toward your long-term goals.

Aquarius: The morning is perfect for emotional reflection, but as the energy shifts, focus on pursuing new ideas and taking bold actions with confidence.

Pisces: The Moon in your sign enhances your emotional intuition early in the day, but as the energy shifts, focus on taking decisive actions toward your ambitions.

For those born on August 21: Born under the transition from Pisces to Aries, these individuals are emotionally intuitive and action-oriented. In 2025, they'll thrive by balancing emotional reflection with taking bold steps toward their personal goals and ambitions.

Daily Insights: The Moon in Aries brings a surge of energy, confidence, and motivation. It's a great day for taking bold steps, embracing new opportunities, and focusing on personal goals. With Mercury in Leo, communication is bold and creative, making it a perfect time for expressing your ideas with confidence.

Aries: Your confidence and motivation are high today. Use this energy to push forward on your personal goals and take bold actions with enthusiasm.

Taurus: It's a day for balancing bold actions with practicality. Use your grounded nature to take steady steps toward your long-term goals.

Gemini: Communication is your strength today. Use this energy to engage in meaningful conversations and explore new ideas with curiosity.

Cancer: Confidence and emotional reflection are key today. Use this energy to focus on personal growth and take bold steps toward your ambitions.

Leo: Leadership and action are highlighted today. Use your natural confidence to take charge of projects and inspire those around you.

Virgo: Productivity is high today. Use your disciplined nature to focus on practical tasks and take bold actions toward your goals.

Libra: Relationships feel dynamic today. Focus on open communication and take action to strengthen your personal connections.

Scorpio: Your determination is strong today. Use this energy to take decisive steps toward achieving your long-term goals.

Sagittarius: Adventure and excitement are calling you today. Use your enthusiasm to explore new opportunities and take bold steps toward your dreams.

Capricorn: Discipline and focus guide you today. Use this energy to take practical steps toward your long-term goals and ambitions.

Aquarius: Your creativity and innovative thinking shine today. Use this energy to explore new ideas and take bold actions toward your personal goals.

Pisces: It's a day for taking action on your personal ambitions. Use your intuition to guide you as you embrace new opportunities with confidence.

For those born on August 22: Born under the Moon in Aries, these individuals are confident, action-oriented, and driven. In 2025, they'll thrive by taking bold steps toward their personal goals and embracing new opportunities with enthusiasm.

Daily Insights: The Moon in Aries continues to bring energy, motivation, and a focus on personal goals. It's a great day for taking decisive actions, embracing challenges, and pursuing your ambitions. With Mars in Capricorn, there's an added boost of discipline and determination, making it a powerful day for working on long-term projects.

Aries: Your confidence and motivation are high today. Use this energy to push forward on your personal goals and take bold actions with confidence.

Taurus: It's a day for balancing bold actions with practicality. Use your grounded nature to take steady steps toward your long-term goals.

Gemini: Communication and action are your strengths today. Use this energy to engage in meaningful conversations and explore new ideas.

Cancer: Confidence and emotional reflection are key today. Use this energy to focus on personal growth and take bold steps toward your ambitions.

Leo: Leadership and action are highlighted today. Use your natural confidence to take charge of projects and inspire those around you.

Virgo: Productivity is high today. Use your disciplined nature to focus on practical tasks and take bold actions toward your goals.

Libra: Relationships feel dynamic and exciting today. Focus on open communication and take action to strengthen your personal connections.

Scorpio: Your determination is strong today. Use this energy to take decisive steps toward achieving your long-term goals.

Sagittarius: Adventure and excitement are calling you today. Use your enthusiasm to explore new opportunities and take bold steps toward your dreams.

Capricorn: Discipline and focus guide you today. Use this energy to make steady progress on your long-term goals and ambitions.

Aquarius: Your creativity and innovative thinking shine today. Use this energy to explore new ideas and take bold actions toward your personal goals.

Pisces: It's a day for taking action on your personal ambitions. Use your intuition to guide you as you embrace new opportunities with confidence.

For those born on August 23: Born under the Moon in Aries, these individuals are energetic, motivated, and focused on achieving their goals. In 2025, they'll thrive by embracing challenges, taking bold actions, and pursuing their ambitions with enthusiasm.

Daily Insights: The Moon in Aries continues to provide energy, confidence, and motivation, but as it transitions into Taurus later in the day, the focus shifts toward stability, practicality, and long-term planning. It's a day for balancing bold actions with careful consideration of your long-term goals.

Aries: The day starts with high energy and motivation, but as the Moon moves into Taurus, focus on grounding yourself and setting practical goals for the future.

Taurus: The Moon enters your sign later today, bringing a sense of stability and focus on practical matters. Use this energy to work toward your long-term ambitions.

Gemini: It's a day for balancing bold ideas with practical steps. Use the morning for exploration, but by evening, shift your focus to long-term planning.

Cancer: The morning is perfect for pursuing your ambitions with confidence, but as the Moon moves into Taurus, focus on grounding your emotions and working toward long-term stability in your personal life.

Leo: Start the day with creative energy and bold actions, but as the energy shifts, focus on setting practical goals that will lead to long-term success.

Virgo: Use the early part of the day to act on your bold ideas, but later in the day, shift your attention to organizing your long-term plans and ensuring stability.

Libra: Relationships feel dynamic in the morning, but by evening, focus on creating harmony and long-term emotional stability in your personal connections.

Scorpio: Your energy is strong in the morning for taking bold steps, but later, focus on grounding yourself and creating stability in your professional and personal life.

Sagittarius: Adventure is calling you in the morning, but as the Moon enters Taurus, shift your focus to setting realistic goals and making steady progress.

Capricorn: The morning is filled with confidence and motivation, but by evening, focus on your long-term goals and ensure that your actions are practical and grounded.

Aquarius: Creativity and innovation are your strengths in the morning, but as the day progresses, shift your attention to setting practical steps for future success.

Pisces: Use the morning for emotional reflection and taking action on personal goals, but later, focus on grounding yourself and ensuring emotional and practical stability in your life.

For those born on August 24: Born under the transition from Aries to Taurus, these individuals are energetic and driven but also practical and grounded. In 2025, they'll thrive by balancing their bold ambitions with careful long-term planning and steady progress toward success.

Daily Insights: The Moon in Taurus emphasizes stability, practicality, and long-term planning. It's a great day for working on your goals methodically, taking slow and steady steps toward success. With Mars in Capricorn, there's an added boost of discipline, making it an ideal time for productivity and laying the groundwork for future ambitions.

Aries: Focus on grounding yourself today. Use your energy to set practical goals and work methodically toward your long-term ambitions.

Taurus: The Moon in your sign amplifies your sense of stability and focus. Use this energy to work on practical matters and ensure you're making steady progress.

Gemini: It's a day for long-term planning. Use your intellectual curiosity to refine your goals and take practical steps to move toward them.

Cancer: Stability is key today. Focus on grounding your emotions and working toward long-term stability in your personal and professional life.

Leo: While creativity is important, today encourages you to focus on practical goals. Use your leadership skills to guide others in achieving long-term success.

Virgo: It's a productive day for focusing on practical matters. Use your disciplined nature to ensure that you're making steady progress on your goals.

Libra: Relationships feel stable and grounded today. Focus on creating harmony in your personal connections while working toward long-term success.

Scorpio: Your determination is strong today. Use this energy to focus on your long-term goals and ensure you're making practical decisions for the future.

Sagittarius: Adventure takes a backseat today as you focus on creating stability and working toward practical goals in your personal and professional life.

Capricorn: Discipline and focus are your strengths today. Use this energy to make steady progress on your long-term projects and goals.

Aquarius: While creativity and innovation are important, today encourages you to focus on practical solutions and laying the groundwork for future success.

Pisces: Emotional stability is key today. Use this energy to ground yourself and work on practical steps to ensure long-term security in your life.

For those born on August 25: Born under the Moon in Taurus, these individuals are practical, grounded, and focused on long-term success. In 2025, they'll thrive by setting clear goals and making steady progress toward them, using their disciplined nature to stay focused on their ambitions.

Daily Insights: The Moon in Taurus continues to emphasize stability, practicality, and long-term goals, but as it transitions into Gemini later in the day, the focus shifts toward communication, learning, and curiosity. It's a day for balancing practical work with intellectual exploration and social connections.

Aries: Use the morning to focus on grounding yourself and working toward long-term goals, but later in the day, shift your focus to communication and exploring new ideas.

Taurus: Start the day with stability and practicality, but by evening, embrace social interactions and intellectual exploration.

Gemini: The Moon enters your sign later today, bringing a burst of energy and curiosity. It's a great time for exploring new ideas and engaging in conversations.

Cancer: The day begins with a focus on stability, but as the energy shifts, focus on connecting with others and exploring new perspectives.

Leo: Use the morning for practical work, but as the Moon enters Gemini, engage with others and share your ideas freely.

Virgo: The early part of the day is productive, but by evening, focus on engaging with new ideas and refining your long-term plans.

Libra: Relationships feel stable early in the day, but as the Moon moves into Gemini, focus on open communication and exploring new perspectives with loved ones.

Scorpio: The day begins with determination and focus, but later, you'll feel more inclined to explore social interactions and new opportunities.

Sagittarius: Start the day with practicality, but as the Moon enters Gemini, shift your focus to learning and intellectual exploration.

Capricorn: Discipline guides you early in the day, but by evening, shift your attention to communication and engaging with others.

Aquarius: The day starts with practical tasks, but later, explore new ideas and engage with others in stimulating conversations.

Pisces: Emotional reflection is key early in the day, but as the Moon moves into Gemini, focus on socializing and expressing your ideas clearly.

For those born on August 26: Born under the transition from Taurus to Gemini, these individuals are both practical and curious. In 2025, they'll thrive by balancing their disciplined approach with intellectual exploration, focusing on both long-term goals and learning new things.

Daily Insights: The Moon in Gemini brings a focus on communication, learning, and curiosity. It's a great day for engaging in conversations, exploring new ideas, and connecting with others. With Mercury in Leo, there's an added emphasis on creativity and bold expression, making it an ideal time for sharing ideas confidently.

Aries: Your curiosity is strong today. Use this energy to engage in conversations, explore new ideas, and take action on your personal goals.

Taurus: It's a day for balancing practicality with intellectual exploration. Use your grounded nature to communicate your thoughts clearly and explore new perspectives.

Gemini: The Moon in your sign enhances your communication skills. Use this energy to connect with others, share your ideas, and explore new opportunities.

Cancer: It's a day for focusing on learning and intellectual growth. Use this energy to connect with your inner self and engage in meaningful conversations.

Leo: Leadership and creativity are highlighted today. Use your confidence to inspire others and share your innovative ideas with enthusiasm.

Virgo: Your analytical skills are sharp today. Use this energy to focus on problem-solving and exploring new ideas through conversation.

Libra: Relationships feel dynamic and intellectually stimulating. Focus on engaging with loved ones in meaningful conversations and exploring new perspectives.

Scorpio: Your emotional depth is strong today. Use this energy to engage in deep conversations and explore new ideas that challenge your thinking.

Sagittarius: Adventure and learning go hand in hand today. Use your curiosity to explore new opportunities and engage in conversations that inspire you.

Capricorn: It's a day for balancing discipline with intellectual exploration. Use this energy to engage in thoughtful discussions and refine your long-term goals.

Aquarius: Your creativity and innovative thinking shine today. Use this energy to explore new ideas and engage in collaborative conversations.

Pisces: It's a day for intellectual exploration and emotional reflection. Use this energy to connect with others in meaningful ways and share your ideas.

For those born on August 27: Born under the Moon in Gemini, these individuals are curious, communicative, and eager to explore new ideas. In 2025, they'll thrive by engaging in conversations, learning new things, and using their sharp minds to make meaningful connections with others.

Daily Insights: The Moon in Gemini continues to emphasize communication, learning, and curiosity, but as it transitions into Cancer later in the day, the focus shifts toward emotional well-being, nurturing relationships, and self-care. It's a day for balancing intellectual exploration with emotional connection.

Aries: The day begins with lively conversations, but as the Moon moves into Cancer, shift your focus to emotional reflection and nurturing your relationships.

Taurus: Use the morning for exploring new ideas, but as the energy shifts, focus on creating emotional stability in your personal life.

Gemini: Your communication skills are heightened early in the day, but later, focus on emotional connections and strengthening your relationships with loved ones.

Cancer: The Moon enters your sign later today, heightening your emotional sensitivity. It's a great time for self-care and nurturing close relationships.

Leo: Start the day with intellectual exploration, but as the Moon moves into Cancer, shift your focus to emotional balance and personal growth.

Virgo: Productivity is high early in the day, but by evening, focus on emotional reflection and nurturing your personal well-being.

Libra: Relationships are intellectually stimulating in the morning, but later, focus on deepening emotional connections and creating harmony in your relationships.

Scorpio: Your curiosity is high early in the day, but as the energy shifts, focus on emotional healing and strengthening your relationships.

Sagittarius: The day begins with excitement and exploration, but later, shift your focus to emotional reflection and personal growth.

Capricorn: Use the morning for practical tasks and intellectual pursuits, but by evening, focus on nurturing your emotional well-being and relationships.

Aquarius: Creativity and intellectual exploration are highlighted early in the day, but as the Moon enters Cancer, focus on emotional growth and self-care.

Pisces: The day begins with curiosity, but later, you'll feel more inclined to focus on emotional healing and nurturing your close relationships.

For those born on August 28: Born under the transition from Gemini to Cancer, these individuals are both intellectually curious and emotionally intuitive. In 2025, they'll thrive by balancing their sharp minds with emotional reflection, focusing on both learning and nurturing their relationships.

Daily Insights: The Moon in Cancer emphasizes emotional reflection, nurturing relationships, and self-care. It's a great day for focusing on your emotional well-being and connecting with loved ones. With Venus in Leo, there's also a blend of emotional depth and creative self-expression, making it a great time for balancing emotions with personal ambitions.

Aries: Emotional balance is important today. Use this energy to nurture your relationships and take time for self-care while maintaining confidence in your personal goals.

Taurus: Focus on emotional well-being today. Use your grounded nature to strengthen your personal connections and create stability in your relationships.

Gemini: Communication is highlighted today. Use this energy to have meaningful conversations and nurture emotional connections with loved ones.

Cancer: The Moon in your sign enhances your emotional intuition. Take time for self-care and focus on deepening your relationships with those close to you.

Leo: While your leadership and creativity are strong, today encourages emotional reflection. Use this energy to nurture your inner self and balance ambition with emotional well-being.

Virgo: Emotional clarity is key today. Use this energy to focus on organizing your personal life and deepening emotional bonds with loved ones.

Libra: Relationships take on a more nurturing tone today. Focus on creating emotional harmony and balance in your personal and professional connections.

Scorpio: Emotional reflection is important today. Use this energy to focus on healing and deepening your emotional connections with those you care about.

Sagittarius: It's a day for focusing on emotional well-being and creating stability in your personal life. Take time to connect with your inner self and nurture your relationships.

Capricorn: Emotional reflection is key today. Use this energy to ground yourself and focus on nurturing both your relationships and your personal goals.

Aquarius: While creativity is important, today encourages emotional introspection. Use this energy to connect with loved ones and focus on self-care.

Pisces: The Moon in Cancer heightens your emotional sensitivity today. Use this energy to focus on healing, nurturing your relationships, and self-care.

For those born on August 29: Born under the Moon in Cancer, these individuals are emotionally intuitive, nurturing, and deeply connected to their home and family. In 2025, they'll thrive by focusing on their emotional well-being, nurturing relationships, and creating stability in their personal lives.

Daily Insights: The Moon in Cancer continues to emphasize emotional well-being, but as it transitions into Leo later in the day, the focus shifts toward confidence, creativity, and self-expression. It's a day for balancing emotional reflection with taking bold actions toward your personal goals.

Aries: Start the day with emotional reflection, but as the Moon enters Leo, shift your focus to taking bold steps toward your personal goals.

Taurus: The day begins with a focus on emotional stability, but later, embrace creative expression and personal empowerment.

Gemini: Emotional connections are key early in the day, but as the energy shifts, focus on communication and expressing your unique ideas.

Cancer: The morning is ideal for nurturing your emotional well-being, but as the Moon enters Leo, focus on stepping into the spotlight and pursuing your personal ambitions.

Leo: The Moon enters your sign later today, amplifying your confidence and creativity. Use this energy to take bold steps toward your goals and lead with enthusiasm.

Virgo: The day starts with emotional clarity, but later, shift your focus to expressing your creativity and finding new ways to approach your long-term goals.

Libra: Relationships feel emotionally deep in the morning, but as the day progresses, focus on embracing creativity and finding balance in your personal connections.

Scorpio: The morning is perfect for emotional introspection, but later, focus on taking bold steps toward personal transformation and expressing your true self.

Sagittarius: Start the day by reflecting on your emotional well-being, but as the Moon enters Leo, embrace new adventures and creative opportunities.

Capricorn: The morning is ideal for grounding yourself emotionally, but as the energy shifts, focus on stepping into leadership roles and expressing your creative talents.

Aquarius: Use the morning for emotional reflection, but later, focus on exploring new ideas and expressing yourself confidently in social settings.

Pisces: Emotional sensitivity is high early in the day, but as the Moon moves into Leo, shift your focus to personal empowerment and creative expression.

For those born on August 30: Born under the transition from Cancer to Leo, these individuals are emotionally intuitive and confident. In 2025, they'll thrive by balancing their emotional well-being with bold actions toward their personal goals, stepping into leadership roles and expressing their creativity.

Daily Insights: The Moon in Leo brings a surge of confidence, creativity, and leadership. It's a great day for expressing your true self, taking bold actions, and pursuing your passions. With Mars in Capricorn, there's a balance of discipline and ambition, making it an ideal time for working toward your goals with confidence.

Aries: Your confidence is high today. Use this energy to pursue your personal goals and take bold actions with enthusiasm.

Taurus: Creativity flows easily today. Focus on expressing your unique ideas and working toward your long-term goals with determination.

Gemini: Communication and self-expression are your strengths today. Use this energy to connect with others and share your innovative ideas.

Cancer: The Moon in Leo encourages you to step out of your comfort zone and pursue your personal goals with confidence and creativity.

Leo: The Moon in your sign amplifies your natural leadership and creativity. Use this energy to take bold steps toward your passions and inspire others.

Virgo: Balance creativity with practicality today. Use your disciplined nature to focus on long-term goals while expressing your unique talents.

Libra: Relationships feel dynamic and exciting today. Focus on creative ways to connect with loved ones and embrace your individuality.

Scorpio: Your passion is strong today. Use this energy to pursue personal goals with intensity and determination.

Sagittarius: Adventure and creativity are calling you today. Use this energy to explore new opportunities and express yourself freely.

Capricorn: Leadership and discipline come naturally today. Use this energy to focus on personal projects and inspire those around you.

Aquarius: Your creativity shines today. Use this energy to pursue innovative ideas and connect with others through meaningful collaborations.

Pisces: It's a day for self-expression and personal growth. Use your creativity to focus on your goals and embrace new opportunities with confidence.

For those born on August 31: Born under the Moon in Leo, these individuals are charismatic, creative, and confident. In 2025, they'll thrive by stepping into leadership roles, embracing their unique talents, and pursuing their passions with determination.

Daily Insights: The Moon in Leo continues to highlight confidence, creativity, and self-expression. It's a day for pursuing your passions and stepping into leadership roles. With the Sun also in Virgo, there's a blend of creativity and practicality, making it a great time to focus on personal goals while staying organized.

Aries: Your confidence is high today. Use this energy to take bold steps toward your personal ambitions while maintaining focus on long-term goals.

Taurus: Creativity is flowing, but balance it with practicality. Focus on steady progress while expressing your ideas in innovative ways.

Gemini: Communication and self-expression are your strengths today. Use this energy to engage with others and share your bold ideas with confidence.

Cancer: Step out of your comfort zone and embrace new opportunities. Focus on pursuing your personal passions and expressing yourself creatively.

Leo: The Moon in your sign enhances your natural leadership and creativity. Use this energy to take bold actions and inspire those around you.

Virgo: Balance creativity with practicality today. Use your organizational skills to turn your creative ideas into tangible results.

Libra: Relationships feel dynamic and exciting. Focus on connecting with others through creative expression and engaging in stimulating conversations.

Scorpio: Your determination is strong today. Use this energy to pursue your personal goals with intensity while balancing creativity and discipline.

Sagittarius: Adventure and creativity are calling you today. Use this energy to explore new opportunities and embrace your unique talents.

Capricorn: Leadership and discipline guide you today. Use this energy to take control of your projects and inspire those around you to reach their potential.

Aquarius: Your innovative thinking is highlighted. Use this energy to focus on creative projects and express your unique perspective confidently.

Pisces: It's a day for self-expression and personal growth. Use your creativity to focus on your long-term goals and explore new opportunities with confidence.

For those born on September 1: Born under the Moon in Leo, these individuals are creative, charismatic, and confident. In 2025, they'll thrive by stepping into leadership roles, embracing their unique talents, and pursuing their passions with determination.

Daily Insights: The Moon in Leo continues to enhance confidence and creativity, but as it transitions into Virgo later in the day, the focus shifts toward practicality, organization, and attention to detail. It's a day for balancing bold ideas with disciplined actions to achieve long-term success.

Aries: Start the day with bold actions, but as the Moon moves into Virgo, shift your focus to organizing your plans and refining your goals.

Taurus: The day begins with creative expression, but later, focus on practical steps toward your long-term goals.

Gemini: Use the morning for creative pursuits and communication, but as the energy shifts, focus on organizing your ideas and refining your plans.

Cancer: Confidence and creativity guide you early in the day, but later, shift your focus to emotional balance and practical tasks.

Leo: The Moon in your sign enhances your leadership, but as it moves into Virgo, focus on grounding your energy and organizing your long-term goals.

Virgo: The Moon enters your sign later today, amplifying your attention to detail and practical nature. Use this energy to refine your plans and focus on productivity.

Libra: The morning is great for engaging in creative conversations, but later, focus on balancing your personal goals with practical responsibilities.

Scorpio: Start the day by pursuing your passions, but as the Moon moves into Virgo, shift your focus to refining your long-term plans and staying disciplined.

Sagittarius: The day starts with excitement and creativity, but later, shift your focus to practical tasks and responsibilities.

Capricorn: Discipline and leadership guide you in the morning, but later, shift your attention to organizing your goals and refining your long-term plans.

Aquarius: The morning is ideal for creative expression, but as the Moon moves into Virgo, focus on refining your ideas and ensuring they are practical.

Pisces: Start the day with emotional reflection and creativity, but later, focus on organizing your personal life and making practical decisions.

For those born on September 2: Born under the transition from Leo to Virgo, these individuals are both creative and practical. In 2025, they'll thrive by balancing their bold ideas with disciplined actions, focusing on both creativity and productivity to achieve their goals.

September 3, 2025

Daily Insights: The Moon in Virgo emphasizes productivity, organization, and attention to detail. It's a great day for focusing on practical matters, refining your plans, and making steady progress toward your long-term goals. With Mercury in Leo, there's still room for creative communication, making it a perfect day for blending creativity with discipline.

Aries: Stay focused on your goals today. Use your energy to organize your thoughts and make steady progress toward your long-term ambitions.

Taurus: It's a day for practical achievements. Use your grounded nature to refine your ideas and work steadily on long-term projects.

Gemini: Your analytical skills are strong today. Use this energy to focus on problem-solving and refining your ideas.

Cancer: Balance emotional reflection with practical tasks today. Focus on organizing your personal life and creating emotional stability.

Leo: After a period of creativity, today encourages you to focus on practical matters. Use your energy to refine your long-term plans.

Virgo: The Moon in your sign enhances your natural strengths. Use this energy to focus on productivity and tackle tasks that require precision.

Libra: Relationships feel stable today. Focus on balancing your personal goals with your relationships while staying productive.

Scorpio: Your determination is strong today. Use this energy to focus on long-term goals and ensure that you're making practical decisions.

Sagittarius: Practical matters take precedence today. Use this energy to focus on your responsibilities and stay disciplined in achieving your goals.

Capricorn: Discipline and focus are your strengths today. Use this energy to make significant progress on your long-term projects and goals.

Aquarius: While creativity is important, today encourages you to focus on practical solutions and refining your innovative ideas.

Pisces: Emotional reflection is balanced with practicality today. Use this energy to organize your life and make steady progress toward your goals.

For those born on September 3: Born under the Moon in Virgo, these individuals are practical, detail-oriented, and highly productive. In 2025, they'll thrive by refining their plans, staying disciplined, and making steady progress toward their long-term goals.

September 4, 2025

Daily Insights: The Moon in Virgo continues to emphasize productivity, but as it transitions into Libra later in the day, the focus shifts toward balance, relationships, and harmony. It's a day for balancing work with social interactions and ensuring that all areas of your life are in equilibrium.

Aries: The morning is perfect for productivity, but as the Moon moves into Libra, focus on balancing your work with your personal relationships.

Taurus: Start the day with practical tasks, but later, shift your focus to nurturing relationships and creating balance in your life.

Gemini: The day begins with a focus on organization, but as the energy shifts, engage in meaningful conversations and strengthen your relationships.

Cancer: The morning is ideal for organizing your life, but as the Moon enters Libra, focus on nurturing your relationships and finding harmony.

Leo: The day starts with practical tasks, but later, focus on balancing your creative pursuits with your relationships.

Virgo: The Moon in your sign enhances your productivity early in the day, but by evening, focus on maintaining balance in your personal life.

Libra: The day starts with productivity, but as the Moon enters your sign, focus on nurturing relationships and finding balance in all areas of life.

Scorpio: It's a day for balancing productivity with emotional depth. Use the morning for practical tasks, but later, focus on nurturing your relationships.

Sagittarius: Responsibilities guide you in the morning, but by evening, focus on social interactions and bringing balance to your personal life.

Capricorn: Discipline and focus guide you in the morning, but later, shift your attention to maintaining harmony in your relationships.

Aquarius: The morning is perfect for creativity and productivity, but as the Moon moves into Libra, focus on balancing your work and social life.

Pisces: Emotional reflection is key early in the day, but as the Moon enters Libra, focus on nurturing relationships and finding inner balance.

For those born on September 4: Born under the transition from Virgo to Libra, these individuals are both productive and focused on balance. In 2025, they'll thrive by balancing their attention to detail with creating harmonious relationships and personal connections.

Daily Insights: The Moon in Libra emphasizes balance, harmony, and relationships. It's a great day for social interactions, resolving conflicts, and creating equilibrium in your personal and professional life. With Venus in Leo, relationships may feel passionate and exciting, making it an ideal time for romantic and creative pursuits.

Aries: Focus on finding balance in your relationships today. Use this energy to create harmony in your personal and professional life.

Taurus: Balance is key today. Focus on maintaining harmony in your relationships while working toward your long-term goals.

Gemini: Relationships take center stage today. Focus on communicating clearly and creating harmony in your personal interactions.

Cancer: It's a day for balancing emotional needs with your relationships. Use this energy to create equilibrium in your personal connections.

Leo: While your confidence is strong, today encourages you to focus on your relationships and ensuring balance in your personal life.

Virgo: Balance productivity with harmony today. Use this energy to focus on both your work goals and your relationships.

Libra: With the Moon in your sign, balance and harmony are highlighted. Use this energy to create peace in your relationships and personal life.

Scorpio: Relationships feel emotionally deep today. Use this energy to connect with others on a deeper level while maintaining balance in your life.

Sagittarius: Social interactions are favored today. Use your natural charm to connect with others while ensuring harmony in your personal life.

Capricorn: It's a day for balancing your responsibilities with your relationships. Focus on finding harmony between your work and personal life.

Aquarius: Creativity and innovation come naturally today, but focus on creating balance in your interactions and ensuring harmony in your relationships.

Pisces: Emotional balance is important today. Use this energy to connect with loved ones and focus on creating stability in your relationships.

For those born on September 5: Born under the Moon in Libra, these individuals are focused on balance, harmony, and relationships. In 2025, they'll thrive by creating equilibrium in their personal and professional lives while working toward their goals with patience and determination.

Daily Insights: The Moon in Libra continues to emphasize balance and harmony, but as it transitions into Scorpio later in the day, the focus shifts toward emotional depth, transformation, and intense connections. It's a day for balancing social interactions with emotional introspection.

Aries: The day begins with a focus on relationships and balance, but as the Moon moves into Scorpio, you'll feel more inclined to explore deeper emotional connections.

Taurus: Use the early part of the day to focus on social interactions and creating harmony, but later, dive into emotional reflection and personal growth.

Gemini: Relationships are in focus early in the day, but as the energy shifts, you'll feel more introspective and inclined to explore your inner world.

Cancer: Balance is important in the morning, but as the Moon moves into Scorpio, focus on emotional depth and nurturing your closest relationships.

Leo: Start the day by focusing on balance in your interactions, but later, shift your attention to emotional transformation and personal growth.

Virgo: The morning is perfect for maintaining harmony in your daily life, but by evening, focus on emotional clarity and personal reflection.

Libra: The Moon in your sign encourages you to maintain balance in your relationships, but later, you'll feel more inclined to explore emotional depth.

Scorpio: The Moon enters your sign later in the day, heightening your emotional intensity. Use this energy to focus on personal transformation and deepening your connections with others.

Sagittarius: Balance your social life in the morning, but by evening, focus on exploring your emotional world and strengthening your relationships.

Capricorn: Discipline and balance guide you in the morning, but later, shift your attention to emotional reflection and personal transformation.

Aquarius: It's a day for balancing relationships and personal goals. As the energy shifts, focus on emotional depth and meaningful connections.

Pisces: Emotional balance is important early in the day, but as the energy transitions, focus on exploring your inner self and strengthening your emotional connections.

For those born on September 6: Born under the transition from Libra to Scorpio, these individuals are both balanced and emotionally intense. In 2025, they'll thrive by balancing their relationships with personal transformation and emotional growth. It's a year for exploring deeper connections and self-reflection.

Daily Insights: The Moon in Scorpio emphasizes emotional depth, transformation, and introspection. It's a day for exploring your inner world, focusing on personal growth, and deepening your connections with others. With Mercury in Gemini, communication is still lively, encouraging meaningful conversations and emotional openness.

Aries: Emotional reflection is key today. Use this energy to focus on personal growth and explore deeper connections with those around you.

Taurus: It's a day for emotional transformation. Use your grounded nature to explore your inner world and focus on healing and growth.

Gemini: Communication is highlighted today. Use this energy to engage in deep conversations and explore your emotional connections.

Cancer: Emotional depth is strong today. Use this energy to nurture your relationships and focus on personal transformation and healing.

Leo: While action is important, today encourages emotional reflection. Use this time to deepen your understanding of yourself and your relationships.

Virgo: Balance your practical nature with emotional reflection today. Use this energy to explore your inner world and nurture your personal connections.

Libra: Relationships feel emotionally deep today. Focus on creating harmony in your emotional connections and engaging in meaningful conversations.

Scorpio: The Moon in your sign enhances your emotional intensity. Use this energy for self-reflection and personal transformation.

Sagittarius: It's a day for emotional introspection. Use your curiosity to explore your inner world and strengthen your emotional connections.

Capricorn: Your determination is strong today. Use this energy to focus on emotional growth and work toward long-term goals that bring stability.

Aquarius: Emotional reflection is important today. Use this energy to focus on creating deeper connections and exploring your inner emotions.

Pisces: Your intuition is heightened today. Use this energy for emotional healing and focus on nurturing your relationships with loved ones.

For those born on September 7: Born under the Moon in Scorpio, these individuals are emotionally intense, intuitive, and deeply connected to their inner world. In 2025, they'll thrive by focusing on personal transformation, emotional healing, and deepening their relationships.

Daily Insights: The Moon in Scorpio continues to bring emotional intensity and focus on personal transformation. However, as it transitions into Sagittarius later in the day, the focus shifts toward optimism, adventure, and exploration. It's a day for balancing introspection with excitement for new possibilities.

Aries: Start the day with emotional reflection, but as the Moon moves into Sagittarius, shift your focus to new opportunities and personal growth.

Taurus: The morning is ideal for emotional introspection, but later in the day, focus on expanding your horizons and embracing new experiences.

Gemini: Emotional reflection is important early in the day, but as the energy shifts, focus on engaging with others and exploring new ideas.

Cancer: The morning is perfect for nurturing your relationships, but later, focus on stepping out of your comfort zone and embracing new possibilities.

Leo: Emotional depth is important early in the day, but as the Moon moves into Sagittarius, focus on taking bold steps toward your personal goals.

Virgo: The day starts with emotional clarity, but later, focus on exploring new ideas and expanding your knowledge.

Libra: Relationships feel emotionally deep early in the day, but later, focus on creating harmony and embracing new perspectives.

Scorpio: The Moon in your sign enhances your emotional intensity, but as the day progresses, focus on personal growth and exploring new opportunities.

Sagittarius: The Moon enters your sign later in the day, bringing a boost of optimism and excitement. Use this energy to pursue new passions.

Capricorn: Start the day with emotional reflection, but as the energy shifts, focus on setting new goals and expanding your horizons.

Aquarius: The morning is perfect for exploring emotional depth, but by evening, shift your focus to creativity and embracing new ideas.

Pisces: Emotional intuition is heightened early in the day, but as the energy shifts, focus on personal growth and exploring new possibilities.

For those born on September 8: Born under the transition from Scorpio to Sagittarius, these individuals are emotionally intense but adventurous. In 2025, they'll thrive by balancing emotional reflection with personal growth and embracing new experiences.

Daily Insights: The Moon in Sagittarius brings a sense of adventure, optimism, and personal growth. It's a day for exploring new opportunities, learning, and expanding your horizons. With Mercury in Gemini, communication is lively, making it a great time for engaging in stimulating conversations.

Aries: Your adventurous spirit is high today. Use this energy to explore new opportunities and focus on personal growth.

Taurus: It's a day for balancing stability with exploration. Use your grounded nature to pursue new experiences while staying focused on long-term goals.

Gemini: Communication is your strength today. Use this energy to engage in stimulating conversations and explore new ideas.

Cancer: Adventure and learning are calling you today. Step out of your comfort zone and embrace new experiences for personal growth.

Leo: Your confidence and leadership are highlighted today. Use this energy to take bold actions toward your goals and inspire those around you.

Virgo: It's a great day for learning and expanding your knowledge. Use your analytical mind to explore new topics and gain valuable insights.

Libra: Relationships feel dynamic and intellectually stimulating. Focus on engaging in conversations that deepen your connections and broaden your perspective.

Scorpio: After a period of emotional intensity, today encourages you to focus on personal growth and embrace new opportunities for self-discovery.

Sagittarius: The Moon in your sign enhances your sense of adventure and optimism. It's a perfect day to pursue your passions and explore new possibilities.

Capricorn: While discipline is important, today encourages you to explore new ideas and broaden your horizons with an open mind.

Aquarius: Your innovative thinking shines today. Use this energy to explore new possibilities and share your unique perspective with others.

Pisces: It's a day for personal growth and exploration. Use your intuition to guide you as you embrace new opportunities and expand your horizons.

For those born on September 9: Born under the Moon in Sagittarius, these individuals are adventurous, curious, and eager to explore new horizons. In 2025, they'll thrive by embracing new experiences, pursuing personal growth, and seeking knowledge in their quest for understanding and self-discovery.

Daily Insights: The Moon in Sagittarius continues to bring a sense of adventure and optimism. It's a great day for exploring new ideas, pursuing personal growth, and expanding your horizons. With Venus in Leo, relationships are filled with passion and creativity, making it a perfect time for romantic and social interactions.

Aries: Your adventurous side is strong today. Use this energy to explore new opportunities and embrace personal growth with enthusiasm.

Taurus: It's a day for balancing practicality with exploration. Use your grounded nature to pursue new experiences while staying focused on your long-term goals.

Gemini: Communication is lively today. Use this energy to engage in stimulating conversations and share your innovative ideas with others.

Cancer: Adventure and learning are calling you today. Step out of your comfort zone and embrace new opportunities for personal growth and development.

Leo: Your leadership and confidence are highlighted today. Use this energy to inspire those around you and take bold actions toward your goals.

Virgo: It's a great day for learning and expanding your knowledge. Use your analytical skills to explore new subjects and gain fresh insights.

Libra: Relationships feel dynamic and exciting today. Focus on engaging in meaningful conversations and exploring new perspectives with loved ones.

Scorpio: Emotional reflection gives way to adventure today. Use this energy to explore new experiences and focus on personal transformation.

Sagittarius: The Moon in your sign amplifies your natural sense of adventure and optimism. It's the perfect time to pursue your passions and embrace new possibilities.

Capricorn: While discipline is important, today encourages you to explore new ideas and broaden your horizons with an open mind.

Aquarius: Creativity and innovation are your strengths today. Use this energy to explore new possibilities and engage in collaborative projects.

Pisces: It's a day for personal growth and exploration. Use your intuition to guide you as you embrace new opportunities and expand your horizons.

For those born on September 10: Born under the Moon in Sagittarius, these individuals are adventurous, optimistic, and eager to learn. In 2025, they'll thrive by seeking new experiences, embracing personal growth, and pursuing their passions with enthusiasm and curiosity.

September 11, 2025

Daily Insights: The Moon in Sagittarius continues to bring adventure and optimism, but as it transitions into Capricorn later in the day, the focus shifts toward discipline, practicality, and long-term planning. It's a day for balancing exploration with responsibility and setting clear goals for the future.

Aries: Start the day with a sense of adventure, but as the Moon moves into Capricorn, focus on grounding yourself and setting long-term goals.

Taurus: The day begins with optimism and exploration, but later, you'll feel more inclined to focus on practical matters and organizing your long-term plans.

Gemini: Use the early part of the day for exploration and learning, but as the energy shifts, focus on refining your goals and taking practical steps toward achieving them.

Cancer: Adventure is important early in the day, but as the Moon moves into Capricorn, focus on creating stability in your personal life and making thoughtful decisions.

Leo: The morning is ideal for pursuing your passions, but as the Moon enters Capricorn, focus on grounding your ideas and setting realistic goals.

Virgo: Use the early part of the day for intellectual exploration, but later, shift your focus to organizing your thoughts and refining your plans for the future.

Libra: Relationships feel dynamic early in the day, but as the energy shifts, focus on creating harmony and setting practical goals in your personal life.

Scorpio: The morning is filled with excitement and creativity, but later, shift your focus to practical matters and long-term planning.

Sagittarius: The Moon in your sign brings optimism early in the day, but as it transitions into Capricorn, focus on practical steps and responsibility to achieve your goals.

Capricorn: The Moon enters your sign later today, bringing a sense of discipline and focus. Use this energy to work on long-term projects and set achievable goals.

Aquarius: Adventure and learning are highlighted in the morning, but as the Moon enters Capricorn, focus on practical solutions and refining your long-term plans.

Pisces: The day starts with emotional exploration, but later, focus on grounding yourself and setting practical goals for the future.

For those born on September 11: Born under the transition from Sagittarius to Capricorn, these individuals are adventurous yet practical. In 2025, they'll thrive by balancing their love for exploration with the discipline needed to achieve long-term goals.

September 12, 2025

Daily Insights: The Moon in Capricorn brings a focus on discipline, productivity, and long-term goals. It's a day for working methodically toward your ambitions and making steady progress. With Mars in Capricorn, there's extra determination and focus, making it a perfect time for tackling ambitious projects.

Aries: Focus on your long-term goals today. Use your energy to make steady progress while staying disciplined and grounded.

Taurus: It's a day for practical achievements. Use your determination to work on long-term projects and create stability in your life.

Gemini: It's a productive day for organizing your thoughts and refining your plans. Use this energy to stay focused and disciplined.

Cancer: Emotional reflection and stability are key today. Use this energy to focus on your long-term personal and professional goals.

Leo: Confidence and leadership are highlighted today. Use your focus to take charge of important projects and inspire those around you.

Virgo: It's a great day for focusing on productivity and long-term planning. Use your disciplined nature to tackle important tasks.

Libra: Relationships feel stable today. Focus on creating harmony in your personal connections while staying productive with your goals.

Scorpio: Your determination is strong today. Use this energy to focus on your long-term goals and ensure you're making practical decisions for the future.

Sagittarius: Adventure takes a backseat today as you focus on creating stability and working toward your long-term goals.

Capricorn: The Moon in your sign enhances your natural discipline and focus. Use this energy to make significant progress on your ambitions.

Aquarius: While creativity is important, today encourages you to focus on practical solutions and refining your ideas for long-term success.

Pisces: Emotional reflection is balanced with practicality today. Use this energy to organize your life and focus on long-term goals.

For those born on September 12: Born under the Moon in Capricorn, these individuals are disciplined, practical, and focused on long-term success. In 2025, they'll thrive by setting clear goals and making steady progress toward achieving them, using their disciplined nature to stay focused on their ambitions.

September 13, 2025

Daily Insights: The Moon in Capricorn continues to emphasize discipline, productivity, and long-term planning, but as it transitions into Aquarius later in the day, the focus shifts toward creativity, innovation, and social connections. It's a day for balancing practical work with creative exploration and collaboration.

Aries: Use the morning for disciplined work, but as the Moon moves into Aquarius, embrace your creativity and explore new ideas.

Taurus: The day starts with a focus on productivity, but later, shift your attention to social interactions and creative thinking.

Gemini: Productivity is high early in the day, but by evening, you'll feel more inclined to engage in conversations and explore new possibilities.

Cancer: Start the day with practical goals, but as the Moon enters Aquarius, focus on creativity and exploring new opportunities.

Leo: The morning is perfect for focusing on your goals, but as the day progresses, embrace new ways of thinking and collaborating with others.

Virgo: Use the early part of the day for productivity, but later, shift your focus to creative problem-solving and engaging with others.

Libra: Relationships feel stable early in the day, but later, focus on innovative solutions and exploring new perspectives in your connections.

Scorpio: Determination guides you early in the day, but as the energy shifts, focus on expanding your mind and embracing creative ideas.

Sagittarius: The day starts with a focus on responsibilities, but later, you'll feel more curious and eager to explore new possibilities.

Capricorn: The Moon in your sign enhances your focus on discipline, but as it moves into Aquarius, explore creative ideas and social opportunities.

Aquarius: The evening brings a burst of creativity and innovation. Use this time to explore new projects and connect with others.

Pisces: Emotional reflection is key early in the day, but as the Moon enters Aquarius, focus on socializing and expressing your creativity.

For those born on September 13: Born under the transition from Capricorn to Aquarius, these individuals are both disciplined and creative. In 2025, they'll thrive by balancing practicality with innovation, focusing on both long-term goals and exploring new possibilities.

Daily Insights: The Moon in Aquarius brings a focus on creativity, innovation, and social connections. It's a great day for engaging with others, exploring new ideas, and embracing your individuality. With Venus in Leo, relationships feel lively and intellectually stimulating, making it a perfect time for meaningful conversations.

Aries: Your creativity shines today. Use this energy to explore new ideas and connect with others through meaningful collaborations.

Taurus: It's a day for balancing practicality with creativity. Use your determination to bring innovative ideas into reality.

Gemini: Social interactions are stimulating today. Engage in conversations that inspire new perspectives and broaden your horizons.

Cancer: Creativity and innovation are calling you today. Use this energy to explore new ways of expressing yourself and connecting with others.

Leo: Leadership and creativity go hand in hand today. Use your confidence to take the lead in innovative projects and inspire others with your bold ideas.

Virgo: It's a great day for exploring creative solutions. Use your analytical skills to approach challenges in innovative ways.

Libra: Relationships are dynamic and exciting today. Focus on connecting with others in unconventional ways and exploring new perspectives in your personal connections.

Scorpio: Your passion for personal growth is strong today. Use this energy to explore new ideas and engage in meaningful conversations.

Sagittarius: Adventure and creativity are calling you today. Focus on expanding your horizons and embracing new opportunities.

Capricorn: While discipline is important, today encourages you to explore new ideas and engage in creative thinking.

Aquarius: With the Moon in your sign, your creativity and individuality are amplified. Use this energy to pursue innovative ideas and connect with others.

Pisces: Your intuition is strong today. Use this energy to explore creative projects and connect with others in meaningful ways.

For those born on September 14: Born under the Moon in Aquarius, these individuals are creative, innovative, and socially connected. In 2025, they'll thrive by embracing their individuality, exploring new ideas, and focusing on personal growth through social connections and creative expression.

Daily Insights: The Moon in Aquarius continues to emphasize creativity, innovation, and individuality, but as it transitions into Pisces later in the day, the focus shifts toward emotional reflection, intuition, and empathy. It's a day for balancing intellectual exploration with emotional depth.

Aries: Start the day with innovative ideas and social connections, but as the Moon enters Pisces, shift your focus to emotional reflection and nurturing relationships.

Taurus: The morning is great for exploring creative solutions, but later, focus on emotional healing and connecting with loved ones on a deeper level.

Gemini: Your mind is active early in the day, but as the Moon enters Pisces, focus on balancing your intellectual pursuits with emotional reflection.

Cancer: Emotional intuition is heightened as the day progresses. Use the morning for socializing, but later, focus on self-care and nurturing close relationships.

Leo: Creativity shines early in the day, but as the energy shifts, focus on your emotional well-being and connecting with those who matter most.

Virgo: Productivity is high in the morning, but by evening, you'll feel more inclined to explore your emotions and focus on personal healing.

Libra: Relationships feel dynamic early in the day, but as the Moon enters Pisces, focus on deepening your emotional connections and finding inner balance.

Scorpio: Use the morning for exploring new ideas, but later, focus on emotional growth and reflection. Your intuition is especially strong today.

Sagittarius: The day starts with excitement and creativity, but later, you'll feel more inclined to focus on emotional healing and connecting with loved ones.

Capricorn: Early productivity gives way to emotional reflection as the day progresses. Focus on grounding yourself and nurturing your relationships.

Aquarius: The Moon in your sign brings out your creativity, but as the energy shifts, focus on emotional introspection and personal growth.

Pisces: The Moon enters your sign later today, amplifying your intuition and emotional sensitivity. Use this energy to focus on self-care and emotional healing.

For those born on September 15: Born under the transition from Aquarius to Pisces, these individuals are both creative and emotionally intuitive. In 2025, they'll thrive by balancing intellectual exploration with emotional reflection, focusing on both personal growth and deepening relationships.

Daily Insights: The Moon in Pisces brings a focus on emotional reflection, intuition, and creativity. It's a great day for engaging in artistic projects, connecting with loved ones on a deeper level, and exploring your inner world. With Mercury in Gemini, communication remains lively, making it a good day for expressing your emotions through words.

Aries: Your intuition is strong today. Use this energy to focus on emotional reflection and nurture your relationships with empathy and understanding.

Taurus: It's a great day for combining creativity with practicality. Focus on expressing your emotions through artistic projects or clear communication.

Gemini: Emotional reflection is key today. Use this energy to connect with your inner self and engage in meaningful conversations with loved ones.

Cancer: The Moon in Pisces enhances your emotional intuition. Use this energy to focus on self-care and strengthening your personal relationships.

Leo: While you're often focused on action, today encourages emotional reflection. Use this time to explore your feelings and deepen your connections.

Virgo: Balance your practical nature with emotional reflection today. Use this energy to focus on your inner world and nurture your relationships.

Libra: Relationships feel emotionally deep today. Focus on connecting with loved ones and creating harmony in your emotional connections.

Scorpio: Your emotional intensity is strong today. Use this energy for self-reflection and focus on healing and strengthening your emotional bonds.

Sagittarius: It's a day for emotional introspection. Use this energy to explore your inner world and strengthen your emotional connections with loved ones.

Capricorn: While you're often focused on discipline, today encourages emotional reflection. Use this time to connect with your feelings and focus on personal healing.

Aquarius: While your mind is often focused on innovation, today encourages emotional growth. Use this energy to nurture your close relationships and engage in self-care.

Pisces: The Moon in your sign amplifies your emotional sensitivity and intuition. Use this energy for personal healing and deepening your emotional connections with others.

For those born on September 16: Born under the Moon in Pisces, these individuals are emotionally intuitive, creative, and compassionate. In 2025, they'll thrive by focusing on their emotional well-being, nurturing relationships, and expressing their creativity through meaningful projects.

Daily Insights: The Moon in Pisces continues to emphasize emotional reflection and creativity, but as it transitions into Aries later in the day, the focus shifts toward action, confidence, and bold decisions. It's a day for balancing emotional reflection with taking bold steps toward your goals.

Aries: Start the day with emotional reflection, but as the Moon enters your sign, focus on taking bold actions and pursuing your personal goals with confidence.

Taurus: The morning is perfect for emotional introspection, but as the energy shifts, focus on taking practical steps toward your long-term goals.

Gemini: Emotional reflection is key early in the day, but as the energy shifts, focus on engaging with others and taking action on your ideas.

Cancer: The morning is ideal for nurturing your emotional well-being, but as the Moon moves into Aries, embrace new challenges and step out of your comfort zone.

Leo: Emotional reflection is important early in the day, but as the Moon enters Aries, your confidence will rise, making it a great time to take bold actions.

Virgo: Use the early part of the day for emotional clarity, but later, shift your focus to organizing your thoughts and taking action on your plans.

Libra: Relationships feel emotionally deep in the morning, but as the energy shifts, focus on communicating openly and taking action to strengthen your connections.

Scorpio: Emotional depth is important early in the day, but as the Moon moves into Aries, focus on taking bold steps toward personal growth and transformation.

Sagittarius: Start the day with emotional introspection, but later, shift your focus to adventure and exploring new opportunities with confidence.

Capricorn: Emotional reflection is key early in the day, but as the Moon enters Aries, focus on taking practical steps toward your long-term goals.

Aquarius: The morning is perfect for emotional reflection, but as the energy shifts, focus on pursuing new ideas and taking bold actions with confidence.

Pisces: The Moon in your sign enhances your emotional intuition early in the day, but as the energy shifts, focus on taking decisive actions toward your ambitions.

For those born on September 17: Born under the transition from Pisces to Aries, these individuals are emotionally intuitive and action-oriented. In 2025, they'll thrive by balancing emotional reflection with taking bold steps toward their personal goals and ambitions.

Daily Insights: The Moon in Aries brings a surge of energy, confidence, and motivation. It's a great day for taking bold steps, embracing new opportunities, and focusing on personal goals. With Mercury in Leo, communication is bold and creative, making it a perfect time for expressing your ideas with confidence.

Aries: Your confidence and motivation are high today. Use this energy to push forward on your personal goals and take bold actions with enthusiasm.

Taurus: It's a day for balancing bold actions with practicality. Use your grounded nature to take steady steps toward your long-term goals.

Gemini: Communication is your strength today. Use this energy to engage in meaningful conversations and explore new ideas.

Cancer: Confidence and emotional reflection are key today. Use this energy to focus on personal growth and take bold steps toward your ambitions.

Leo: Leadership and action are highlighted today. Use your natural confidence to take charge of projects and inspire those around you.

Virgo: Productivity is high today. Use your disciplined nature to focus on practical tasks and take bold actions toward your goals.

Libra: Relationships feel dynamic and exciting today. Focus on open communication and take action to strengthen your personal connections.

Scorpio: Your determination is strong today. Use this energy to take decisive steps toward achieving your long-term goals.

Sagittarius: Adventure and excitement are calling you today. Use your enthusiasm to explore new opportunities and take bold steps toward your dreams.

Capricorn: Discipline and focus guide you today. Use this energy to take practical steps toward achieving your long-term goals and ambitions.

Aquarius: Your creativity and innovative thinking shine today. Use this energy to explore new ideas and take bold actions toward your personal goals.

Pisces: It's a day for taking action on your personal ambitions. Use your intuition to guide you as you embrace new opportunities with confidence.

For those born on September 18: Born under the Moon in Aries, these individuals are confident, action-oriented, and driven. In 2025, they'll thrive by taking bold steps toward their personal goals and embracing new opportunities with enthusiasm.

September 19, 2025

Daily Insights: The Moon in Aries continues to bring energy, motivation, and a focus on personal goals. It's a great day for taking decisive actions, embracing challenges, and pursuing your ambitions. With Mars in Capricorn, there's an added boost of discipline and determination, making it a powerful day for working on long-term projects.

Aries: Your confidence and motivation are high today. Use this energy to push forward on your personal goals and take bold actions with confidence.

Taurus: It's a day for balancing bold actions with practicality. Use your grounded nature to take steady steps toward your long-term goals.

Gemini: Communication and action are your strengths today. Use this energy to engage in meaningful conversations and explore new ideas.

Cancer: Confidence and emotional reflection are key today. Use this energy to focus on personal growth and take bold steps toward your ambitions.

Leo: Leadership and action are highlighted today. Use your natural confidence to take charge of projects and inspire those around you.

Virgo: Productivity is high today. Use your disciplined nature to focus on practical tasks and take bold actions toward your goals.

Libra: Relationships feel dynamic and exciting today. Focus on open communication and take action to strengthen your personal connections.

Scorpio: Your determination is strong today. Use this energy to take decisive steps toward achieving your long-term goals.

Sagittarius: Adventure and excitement are calling you today. Use your enthusiasm to explore new opportunities and take bold steps toward your dreams.

Capricorn: Discipline and focus guide you today. Use this energy to make steady progress on your long-term goals and ambitions.

Aquarius: Your creativity and innovative thinking shine today. Use this energy to explore new ideas and take bold actions toward your personal goals.

Pisces: It's a day for taking action on your personal ambitions. Use your intuition to guide you as you embrace new opportunities with confidence.

For those born on September 19: Born under the Moon in Aries, these individuals are energetic, motivated, and focused on achieving their goals. In 2025, they'll thrive by embracing challenges, taking bold actions, and pursuing their ambitions with enthusiasm.

Daily Insights: The Moon in Aries continues to provide energy, confidence, and motivation, but as it transitions into Taurus later in the day, the focus shifts toward stability, practicality, and long-term planning. It's a day for balancing bold actions with careful consideration of your long-term goals.

Aries: The day starts with high energy and motivation, but as the Moon moves into Taurus, focus on grounding yourself and setting practical goals for the future.

Taurus: The Moon enters your sign later today, bringing a sense of stability and focus on practical matters. Use this energy to work toward your long-term ambitions.

Gemini: It's a day for balancing bold ideas with practical steps. Use the morning for exploration, but by evening, shift your focus to long-term planning.

Cancer: The morning is ideal for pursuing your ambitions with confidence, but as the Moon moves into Taurus, focus on grounding your emotions and working toward long-term stability in your personal life.

Leo: Start the day with creative energy and bold actions, but as the energy shifts, focus on setting practical goals that will lead to long-term success.

Virgo: Use the early part of the day to act on your bold ideas, but later in the day, shift your attention to organizing your long-term plans and ensuring stability.

Libra: Relationships feel dynamic in the morning, but by evening, focus on creating harmony and long-term emotional stability in your personal connections.

Scorpio: Your energy is strong in the morning for taking bold steps, but later, focus on grounding yourself and creating stability in your professional and personal life.

Sagittarius: Adventure is calling you in the morning, but as the Moon enters Taurus, shift your focus to setting realistic goals and making steady progress.

Capricorn: The morning is filled with confidence and motivation, but by evening, focus on your long-term goals and ensure that your actions are practical and grounded.

Aquarius: Creativity and innovation are your strengths in the morning, but as the day progresses, shift your attention to setting practical steps for future success.

Pisces: Use the morning for emotional reflection and taking action on personal goals, but later, focus on grounding yourself and ensuring emotional and practical stability in your life.

For those born on September 20: Born under the transition from Aries to Taurus, these individuals are energetic and driven but also practical and grounded. In 2025, they'll thrive by balancing their bold ambitions with careful long-term planning and steady progress toward success.

Daily Insights: The Moon in Taurus emphasizes stability, practicality, and long-term planning. It's a great day for working on your goals methodically, taking slow and steady steps toward success. With Mars in Capricorn, there's an added boost of discipline, making it an ideal time for productivity and laying the groundwork for future ambitions.

Aries: Focus on grounding yourself today. Use your energy to set practical goals and work methodically toward your long-term ambitions.

Taurus: The Moon in your sign amplifies your sense of stability and focus. Use this energy to work on practical matters and ensure you're making steady progress.

Gemini: It's a day for long-term planning. Use your intellectual curiosity to refine your goals and take practical steps to move toward them.

Cancer: Stability is key today. Focus on grounding your emotions and working toward long-term stability in your personal and professional life.

Leo: While creativity is important, today encourages you to focus on practical goals. Use your leadership skills to guide others in achieving long-term success.

Virgo: It's a productive day for focusing on practical matters. Use your disciplined nature to ensure that you're making steady progress on your goals.

Libra: Relationships feel stable and grounded today. Focus on creating harmony in your personal connections while working toward long-term success.

Scorpio: Your determination is strong today. Use this energy to focus on your long-term goals and ensure you're making practical decisions for the future.

Sagittarius: Adventure takes a backseat today as you focus on creating stability and working toward practical goals in your personal and professional life.

Capricorn: Discipline and focus are your strengths today. Use this energy to make steady progress on your long-term projects and goals.

Aquarius: While creativity and innovation are important, today encourages you to focus on practical solutions and laying the groundwork for future success.

Pisces: Emotional stability is key today. Use this energy to ground yourself and work on practical steps to ensure long-term security in your life.

For those born on September 21: Born under the Moon in Taurus, these individuals are practical, grounded, and focused on long-term success. In 2025, they'll thrive by setting clear goals and making steady progress toward them, using their disciplined nature to stay focused on their ambitions.

September 22, 2025

Daily Insights: The Moon in Taurus continues to emphasize stability, practicality, and long-term goals, but as it transitions into Gemini later in the day, the focus shifts toward communication, learning, and curiosity. It's a day for balancing practical work with intellectual exploration and social connections.

Aries: Use the morning to focus on grounding yourself and working toward long-term goals, but later in the day, shift your focus to communication and exploring new ideas.

Taurus: Start the day with stability and practicality, but by evening, embrace social interactions and intellectual exploration.

Gemini: The Moon enters your sign later today, bringing a burst of energy and curiosity. It's a great time for exploring new ideas and engaging in conversations.

Cancer: The day begins with a focus on stability, but as the energy shifts, focus on connecting with others and exploring new perspectives.

Leo: Use the morning for practical work, but as the Moon enters Gemini, engage with others and share your ideas freely.

Virgo: The early part of the day is productive, but by evening, focus on engaging with new ideas and refining your long-term plans.

Libra: Relationships feel stable early in the day, but as the Moon moves into Gemini, focus on open communication and exploring new perspectives with loved ones.

Scorpio: The day begins with determination and focus, but later, you'll feel more inclined to explore social interactions and new opportunities.

Sagittarius: Start the day with practicality, but as the Moon enters Gemini, shift your focus to learning and intellectual exploration.

Capricorn: Discipline guides you early in the day, but by evening, shift your attention to communication and engaging with others.

Aquarius: The day starts with practical tasks, but later, explore new ideas and engage with others in stimulating conversations.

Pisces: Emotional reflection is key early in the day, but as the Moon moves into Gemini, focus on socializing and expressing your ideas clearly.

For those born on September 22: Born under the transition from Taurus to Gemini, these individuals are both practical and curious. In 2025, they'll thrive by balancing their disciplined approach with intellectual exploration, focusing on both long-term goals and learning new things.

Daily Insights: The Moon in Gemini brings a focus on communication, learning, and curiosity. It's a great day for engaging in conversations, exploring new ideas, and connecting with others. With Mercury in Leo, there's an added emphasis on creativity and bold expression, making it an ideal time for sharing ideas confidently.

Aries: Your curiosity is strong today. Use this energy to engage in conversations, explore new ideas, and take action on your personal goals.

Taurus: It's a day for balancing practicality with intellectual exploration. Use your grounded nature to communicate your thoughts clearly and explore new perspectives.

Gemini: The Moon in your sign enhances your communication skills. Use this energy to connect with others, share your ideas, and explore new opportunities.

Cancer: It's a day for focusing on learning and intellectual growth. Use this energy to connect with your inner self and engage in meaningful conversations.

Leo: Leadership and creativity are highlighted today. Use your confidence to inspire others and share your innovative ideas with enthusiasm.

Virgo: Your analytical skills are sharp today. Use this energy to focus on problem-solving and exploring new ideas through conversation.

Libra: Relationships feel dynamic and intellectually stimulating. Focus on engaging with loved ones in meaningful conversations and exploring new perspectives.

Scorpio: Your emotional depth is strong today. Use this energy to engage in deep conversations and explore new ideas that challenge your thinking.

Sagittarius: Adventure and learning go hand in hand today. Use your curiosity to explore new opportunities and engage in conversations that inspire you.

Capricorn: It's a day for balancing discipline with intellectual exploration. Use this energy to engage in thoughtful discussions and refine your long-term goals.

Aquarius: Your creativity and innovative thinking shine today. Use this energy to explore new ideas and engage in collaborative conversations.

Pisces: It's a day for intellectual exploration and emotional reflection. Use this energy to connect with others in meaningful ways and share your ideas.

For those born on September 23: Born under the Moon in Gemini, these individuals are curious, communicative, and eager to explore new ideas. In 2025, they'll thrive by engaging in conversations, learning new things, and using their sharp minds to make meaningful connections with others.

September 24, 2025

Daily Insights: The Moon in Gemini continues to emphasize communication, learning, and curiosity, but as it transitions into Cancer later in the day, the focus shifts toward emotional well-being, nurturing relationships, and self-care. It's a day for balancing intellectual exploration with emotional connection.

Aries: The day begins with lively conversations, but as the Moon moves into Cancer, shift your focus to emotional reflection and nurturing your relationships.

Taurus: Use the morning for exploring new ideas, but as the energy shifts, focus on creating emotional stability in your personal life.

Gemini: Your communication skills are heightened early in the day, but later, focus on emotional connections and strengthening your relationships with loved ones.

Cancer: The Moon enters your sign later today, heightening your emotional sensitivity. It's a great time for self-care and nurturing close relationships.

Leo: Start the day with intellectual exploration, but as the Moon moves into Cancer, shift your focus to emotional balance and personal growth.

Virgo: Productivity is high early in the day, but by evening, focus on emotional reflection and nurturing your personal well-being.

Libra: Relationships are intellectually stimulating in the morning, but later, focus on deepening emotional connections and finding inner balance.

Scorpio: Your curiosity is high early in the day, but as the energy shifts, focus on emotional healing and strengthening your relationships.

Sagittarius: The day starts with excitement and exploration, but later, shift your focus to emotional reflection and personal growth.

Capricorn: Use the morning for practical tasks and intellectual pursuits, but by evening, focus on nurturing your emotional well-being and relationships.

Aquarius: Creativity and intellectual exploration are highlighted early in the day, but as the Moon moves into Cancer, focus on emotional growth and self-care.

Pisces: The day begins with curiosity, but later, you'll feel more inclined to focus on emotional healing and nurturing your close relationships.

For those born on September 24: Born under the transition from Gemini to Cancer, these individuals are both intellectually curious and emotionally intuitive. In 2025, they'll thrive by balancing their sharp minds with emotional reflection, focusing on both learning and nurturing their relationships.

September 25, 2025

Daily Insights: The Moon in Cancer emphasizes emotional reflection, nurturing relationships, and self-care. It's a great day for focusing on your emotional well-being and connecting with loved ones. With Venus in Leo, there's also a blend of emotional depth and creative self-expression, making it a great time for balancing emotions with personal ambitions.

Aries: Emotional balance is important today. Use this energy to nurture your relationships and take time for self-care while maintaining confidence in your personal goals.

Taurus: Focus on emotional well-being today. Use your grounded nature to strengthen your personal connections and create stability in your relationships.

Gemini: Communication is highlighted today. Use this energy to have meaningful conversations and nurture emotional connections with loved ones.

Cancer: The Moon in your sign enhances your emotional intuition. Take time for self-care and focus on deepening your relationships with those close to you.

Leo: While your leadership and creativity are strong, today encourages emotional reflection. Use this energy to nurture your inner self and balance ambition with emotional well-being.

Virgo: Emotional clarity is key today. Use this energy to focus on organizing your personal life and deepening emotional bonds with loved ones.

Libra: Relationships take on a more nurturing tone today. Focus on creating emotional harmony and balance in your personal and professional connections.

Scorpio: Emotional reflection is important today. Use this energy to focus on healing and deepening your emotional connections with those you care about.

Sagittarius: It's a day for focusing on emotional well-being and creating stability in your personal life. Take time to connect with your inner self and nurture your relationships.

Capricorn: Emotional reflection is key today. Use this energy to ground yourself and focus on nurturing both your relationships and your personal goals.

Aquarius: While creativity is important, today encourages emotional introspection. Use this energy to connect with loved ones and focus on self-care.

Pisces: The Moon in Cancer heightens your emotional sensitivity today. Use this energy to focus on healing, nurturing your relationships, and self-care.

For those born on September 25: Born under the Moon in Cancer, these individuals are emotionally intuitive, nurturing, and deeply connected to their home and family. In 2025, they'll thrive by focusing on their emotional well-being, nurturing relationships, and creating stability in their personal lives.

Daily Insights: The Moon in Cancer continues to emphasize emotional well-being, but as it transitions into Leo later in the day, the focus shifts toward confidence, creativity, and self-expression. It's a day for balancing emotional reflection with taking bold actions toward your personal goals.

Aries: Start the day with emotional reflection, but as the Moon enters Leo, shift your focus to taking bold steps toward your personal goals.

Taurus: The day begins with a focus on emotional stability, but later, embrace creative expression and personal empowerment.

Gemini: Emotional connections are key early in the day, but as the energy shifts, focus on communication and expressing your unique ideas.

Cancer: The morning is ideal for nurturing your emotional well-being, but as the Moon enters Leo, focus on stepping into the spotlight and pursuing your personal ambitions.

Leo: The Moon enters your sign later today, amplifying your confidence and creativity. Use this energy to take bold steps toward your goals and lead with enthusiasm.

Virgo: The day starts with emotional clarity, but later, shift your focus to expressing your creativity and finding new ways to approach your long-term goals.

Libra: Relationships feel emotionally deep in the morning, but as the day progresses, focus on embracing creativity and finding balance in your personal connections.

Scorpio: The morning is perfect for emotional introspection, but later, focus on taking bold steps toward personal transformation and expressing your true self.

Sagittarius: Start the day by reflecting on your emotional well-being, but as the Moon enters Leo, embrace new adventures and creative opportunities.

Capricorn: The morning is ideal for grounding yourself emotionally, but as the energy shifts, focus on stepping into leadership roles and expressing your creative talents.

Aquarius: Use the morning for emotional reflection, but later, focus on exploring new ideas and expressing yourself confidently in social settings.

Pisces: Emotional sensitivity is high early in the day, but as the Moon moves into Leo, shift your focus to personal empowerment and creative expression.

For those born on September 26: Born under the transition from Cancer to Leo, these individuals are emotionally intuitive and confident. In 2025, they'll thrive by balancing their emotional well-being with bold actions toward their personal goals, stepping into leadership roles and expressing their creativity.

Daily Insights: The Moon in Leo brings a surge of confidence, creativity, and leadership. It's a great day for expressing your true self, taking bold actions, and pursuing your passions. With Mars in Capricorn, there's a balance of discipline and ambition, making it an ideal time for working toward your goals with confidence.

Aries: Your confidence is high today. Use this energy to pursue your personal goals and take bold actions with enthusiasm.

Taurus: Creativity flows easily today. Focus on expressing your unique ideas and working toward your long-term goals with determination.

Gemini: Communication and self-expression are your strengths today. Use this energy to connect with others and share your innovative ideas.

Cancer: The Moon in Leo encourages you to step out of your comfort zone and pursue your personal goals with confidence and creativity.

Leo: The Moon in your sign amplifies your natural leadership and creativity. Use this energy to take bold steps toward your passions and inspire others.

Virgo: Balance creativity with practicality today. Use your disciplined nature to focus on long-term goals while expressing your unique talents.

Libra: Relationships feel dynamic and exciting today. Focus on creative ways to connect with loved ones and embrace your individuality.

Scorpio: Your passion is strong today. Use this energy to pursue personal goals with intensity and determination.

Sagittarius: Adventure and creativity are calling you today. Use this energy to explore new opportunities and express yourself freely.

Capricorn: Leadership and discipline come naturally today. Use this energy to focus on personal projects and inspire those around you.

Aquarius: Your creativity shines today. Use this energy to pursue innovative ideas and connect with others through meaningful collaborations.

Pisces: It's a day for self-expression and personal growth. Use your creativity to focus on your goals and embrace new opportunities with confidence.

For those born on September 27: Born under the Moon in Leo, these individuals are charismatic, creative, and confident. In 2025, they'll thrive by stepping into leadership roles, embracing their unique talents, and pursuing their passions with determination.

Daily Insights: The Moon in Leo continues to highlight confidence and creativity, but as it transitions into Virgo later in the day, the focus shifts toward practicality, organization, and attention to detail. It's a day for balancing bold ideas with disciplined actions to achieve long-term success.

Aries: Start the day with bold actions, but as the Moon moves into Virgo, shift your focus to organizing your plans and refining your goals.

Taurus: The day begins with creative expression, but later, focus on practical steps toward your long-term goals.

Gemini: Use the morning for creative pursuits and communication, but as the energy shifts, focus on organizing your ideas and refining your plans.

Cancer: Confidence and creativity guide you early in the day, but later, shift your focus to emotional balance and practical tasks.

Leo: The Moon in your sign enhances your leadership, but as it moves into Virgo, focus on grounding your energy and organizing your long-term goals.

Virgo: The Moon enters your sign later today, amplifying your attention to detail and practical nature. Use this energy to refine your plans and focus on productivity.

Libra: The morning is great for engaging in creative conversations, but later, focus on balancing your personal goals with practical responsibilities.

Scorpio: Start the day by pursuing your passions, but as the Moon moves into Virgo, shift your focus to refining your long-term plans and staying disciplined.

Sagittarius: The day starts with excitement and creativity, but later, shift your focus to practical tasks and responsibilities.

Capricorn: Discipline and leadership guide you in the morning, but later, shift your attention to organizing your goals and refining your long-term plans.

Aquarius: The morning is ideal for creative expression, but as the Moon moves into Virgo, focus on refining your ideas and ensuring they are practical.

Pisces: Start the day with emotional reflection and creativity, but later, focus on organizing your personal life and making practical decisions.

For those born on September 28: Born under the transition from Leo to Virgo, these individuals are both creative and practical. In 2025, they'll thrive by balancing their bold ideas with disciplined actions, focusing on both creativity and productivity to achieve their goals.

Daily Insights: The Moon in Virgo emphasizes productivity, organization, and attention to detail. It's a great day for focusing on practical matters, refining your plans, and making steady progress toward your long-term goals. With Mercury in Leo, there's still room for creative communication, making it a perfect day for blending creativity with discipline.

Aries: Stay focused on your goals today. Use your energy to organize your thoughts and make steady progress toward your long-term ambitions.

Taurus: It's a day for practical achievements. Use your grounded nature to refine your ideas and work steadily on long-term projects.

Gemini: Your analytical skills are strong today. Use this energy to focus on problem-solving and refining your ideas.

Cancer: Balance emotional reflection with practical tasks today. Focus on organizing your personal life and creating emotional stability.

Leo: After a period of creativity, today encourages you to focus on practical matters. Use your energy to refine your long-term plans.

Virgo: The Moon in your sign enhances your natural strengths. Use this energy to focus on productivity and tackle tasks that require precision.

Libra: Relationships feel stable today. Focus on balancing your personal goals with your relationships while staying productive.

Scorpio: Your determination is strong today. Use this energy to focus on long-term goals and ensure you're making practical decisions for the future.

Sagittarius: Practical matters take precedence today. Use this energy to focus on your responsibilities and stay disciplined in achieving your goals.

Capricorn: Discipline and focus are your strengths today. Use this energy to make significant progress on your long-term projects and goals.

Aquarius: While creativity is important, today encourages you to focus on practical solutions and refining your innovative ideas.

Pisces: Emotional reflection is balanced with practicality today. Use this energy to organize your life and make steady progress toward your goals.

For those born on September 29: Born under the Moon in Virgo, these individuals are practical, detail-oriented, and highly productive. In 2025, they'll thrive by refining their plans, staying disciplined, and making steady progress toward their long-term goals.

Daily Insights: The Moon in Virgo continues to emphasize productivity, but as it transitions into Libra later in the day, the focus shifts toward balance, relationships, and harmony. It's a day for balancing work with social interactions and ensuring that all areas of your life are in equilibrium.

Aries: The morning is perfect for productivity, but as the Moon moves into Libra, focus on balancing your work with your personal relationships.

Taurus: Start the day with practical tasks, but later, shift your focus to nurturing relationships and creating balance in your life.

Gemini: The day begins with a focus on organization, but as the energy shifts, engage in meaningful conversations and strengthen your relationships.

Cancer: The morning is ideal for organizing your life, but as the Moon enters Libra, focus on nurturing your relationships and finding harmony.

Leo: The day starts with practical tasks, but later, focus on balancing your creative pursuits with your relationships.

Virgo: The Moon in your sign enhances your productivity early in the day, but by evening, focus on maintaining balance in your personal life.

Libra: The day starts with productivity, but as the Moon enters your sign, focus on nurturing relationships and finding balance in all areas of life.

Scorpio: It's a day for balancing productivity with emotional depth. Use the morning for practical tasks, but later, focus on nurturing your relationships.

Sagittarius: Responsibilities guide you in the morning, but by evening, focus on social interactions and bringing balance to your personal life.

Capricorn: Discipline and focus guide you in the morning, but later, shift your attention to maintaining harmony in your relationships.

Aquarius: The morning is perfect for creativity and productivity, but as the Moon moves into Libra, focus on balancing your work and social life.

Pisces: Emotional reflection is key early in the day, but as the Moon enters Libra, focus on nurturing relationships and finding inner balance.

For those born on September 30: Born under the transition from Virgo to Libra, these individuals are both productive and focused on balance. In 2025, they'll thrive by balancing their attention to detail with creating harmonious relationships and personal connections.

Daily Insights: The Moon in Libra continues to emphasize balance, relationships, and harmony. It's a great day for focusing on social interactions, resolving conflicts, and creating equilibrium in your personal and professional life. With Venus in Leo, relationships may feel passionate and exciting, making it an ideal time for romantic and creative pursuits.

Aries: Focus on finding balance in your relationships today. Use this energy to create harmony in your personal and professional life.

Taurus: Balance is key today. Focus on maintaining harmony in your relationships while working toward your long-term goals.

Gemini: Relationships take center stage today. Focus on communicating clearly and creating harmony in your personal interactions.

Cancer: It's a day for balancing emotional needs with your relationships. Use this energy to create equilibrium in your personal connections.

Leo: While your confidence is strong, today encourages you to focus on your relationships and ensuring balance in your personal life.

Virgo: Balance productivity with harmony today. Use this energy to focus on both your work goals and your relationships.

Libra: With the Moon in your sign, balance and harmony are highlighted. Use this energy to create peace in your relationships and personal life.

Scorpio: Relationships feel emotionally deep today. Use this energy to connect with others on a deeper level while maintaining balance in your life.

Sagittarius: Social interactions are favored today. Use your natural charm to connect with others while ensuring harmony in your personal life.

Capricorn: It's a day for balancing your responsibilities with your relationships. Focus on finding harmony between your work and personal life.

Aquarius: Creativity and innovation come naturally today, but focus on creating balance in your interactions and ensuring harmony in your relationships.

Pisces: Emotional balance is important today. Use this energy to connect with loved ones and focus on creating stability in your relationships.

For those born on October 1: Born under the Moon in Libra, these individuals are focused on balance, harmony, and relationships. In 2025, they'll thrive by creating equilibrium in their personal and professional lives while working toward their goals with patience and determination.

Daily Insights: The Moon in Libra continues to emphasize balance and harmony, but as it transitions into Scorpio later in the day, the focus shifts toward emotional depth, transformation, and intense connections. It's a day for balancing social interactions with emotional introspection.

Aries: The day begins with a focus on relationships and balance, but as the Moon moves into Scorpio, you'll feel more inclined to explore deeper emotional connections.

Taurus: Use the early part of the day to focus on social interactions and creating harmony, but later, dive into emotional reflection and personal growth.

Gemini: Relationships are in focus early in the day, but as the energy shifts, you'll feel more introspective and inclined to explore your inner world.

Cancer: Balance is important in the morning, but as the Moon moves into Scorpio, focus on emotional depth and nurturing your closest relationships.

Leo: Start the day by focusing on balance in your interactions, but later, shift your attention to emotional transformation and personal growth.

Virgo: The morning is perfect for maintaining harmony in your daily life, but by evening, focus on emotional clarity and personal reflection.

Libra: The Moon in your sign encourages you to maintain balance in your relationships, but later, you'll feel more inclined to explore emotional depth.

Scorpio: The Moon enters your sign later in the day, heightening your emotional intensity. Use this energy to focus on personal transformation and deepening your connections with others.

Sagittarius: Balance your social life in the morning, but by evening, focus on exploring your emotional world and strengthening your relationships.

Capricorn: Discipline and balance guide you in the morning, but later, shift your attention to emotional reflection and personal transformation.

Aquarius: It's a day for balancing relationships and personal goals. As the energy shifts, focus on emotional depth and meaningful connections.

Pisces: Emotional balance is important early in the day, but as the energy transitions, focus on exploring your inner self and strengthening your emotional connections.

For those born on October 2: Born under the transition from Libra to Scorpio, these individuals are both balanced and emotionally intense. In 2025, they'll thrive by balancing their relationships with personal transformation and emotional growth. It's a year for exploring deeper connections and self-reflection.

Daily Insights: The Moon in Scorpio emphasizes emotional depth, transformation, and introspection. It's a day for exploring your inner world, focusing on personal growth, and deepening your connections with others. With Mercury in Gemini, communication is still lively, encouraging meaningful conversations and emotional openness.

Aries: Emotional reflection is key today. Use this energy to focus on personal growth and explore deeper connections with those around you.

Taurus: It's a day for emotional transformation. Use your grounded nature to explore your inner world and focus on healing and growth.

Gemini: Communication is highlighted today. Use this energy to engage in deep conversations and explore your emotional connections.

Cancer: Emotional depth is strong today. Use this energy to nurture your relationships and focus on personal transformation and healing.

Leo: While action is important, today encourages emotional reflection. Use this time to deepen your understanding of yourself and your relationships.

Virgo: Balance your practical nature with emotional reflection today. Use this energy to explore your inner world and nurture your personal connections.

Libra: Relationships feel emotionally deep today. Focus on creating harmony in your emotional connections and engaging in meaningful conversations.

Scorpio: The Moon in your sign enhances your emotional intensity. Use this energy for self-reflection and personal transformation.

Sagittarius: It's a day for emotional introspection. Use your curiosity to explore your inner world and strengthen your emotional connections.

Capricorn: Your determination is strong today. Use this energy to focus on emotional growth and work toward long-term goals that bring stability.

Aquarius: Emotional reflection is important today. Use this energy to focus on creating deeper connections and exploring your inner emotions.

Pisces: Your intuition is heightened today. Use this energy for emotional healing and focus on nurturing your relationships with loved ones.

For those born on October 3: Born under the Moon in Scorpio, these individuals are emotionally intense, intuitive, and deeply connected to their inner world. In 2025, they'll thrive by focusing on personal transformation, emotional healing, and deepening their relationships.

Daily Insights: The Moon in Scorpio continues to bring emotional intensity and focus on personal transformation. However, as it transitions into Sagittarius later in the day, the focus shifts toward optimism, adventure, and exploration. It's a day for balancing introspection with excitement for new possibilities.

Aries: Start the day with emotional reflection, but as the Moon moves into Sagittarius, shift your focus to new opportunities and personal growth.

Taurus: The morning is ideal for emotional introspection, but later in the day, focus on expanding your horizons and embracing new experiences.

Gemini: Emotional reflection is important early in the day, but as the energy shifts, focus on engaging with others and exploring new ideas.

Cancer: The morning is perfect for nurturing your relationships, but later, focus on stepping out of your comfort zone and embracing new possibilities.

Leo: Emotional depth is important early in the day, but as the Moon moves into Sagittarius, focus on taking bold steps toward your personal goals.

Virgo: The day starts with emotional clarity, but later, focus on exploring new ideas and expanding your knowledge.

Libra: Relationships feel emotionally deep early in the day, but later, focus on creating harmony and embracing new perspectives.

Scorpio: The Moon in your sign enhances your emotional intensity, but as the day progresses, focus on personal growth and exploring new opportunities.

Sagittarius: The Moon enters your sign later in the day, bringing a boost of optimism and excitement. Use this energy to pursue new passions.

Capricorn: Start the day with emotional reflection, but as the energy shifts, focus on setting new goals and expanding your horizons.

Aquarius: The morning is perfect for exploring emotional depth, but by evening, shift your focus to creativity and embracing new ideas.

Pisces: Emotional intuition is heightened early in the day, but as the energy shifts, focus on personal growth and exploring new possibilities.

For those born on October 4: Born under the transition from Scorpio to Sagittarius, these individuals are emotionally intense but adventurous. In 2025, they'll thrive by balancing emotional reflection with personal growth and embracing new experiences.

Daily Insights: The Moon in Sagittarius brings a sense of adventure, optimism, and personal growth. It's a day for exploring new opportunities, learning, and expanding your horizons. With Mercury in Gemini, communication is lively, making it a great time for engaging in stimulating conversations.

Aries: Your adventurous spirit is high today. Use this energy to explore new opportunities and focus on personal growth.

Taurus: It's a day for balancing stability with exploration. Use your grounded nature to pursue new experiences while staying focused on long-term goals.

Gemini: Communication is your strength today. Use this energy to engage in stimulating conversations and explore new ideas.

Cancer: Adventure and learning are calling you today. Step out of your comfort zone and embrace new experiences for personal growth.

Leo: Your confidence and leadership are highlighted today. Use this energy to take bold actions toward your goals and inspire those around you.

Virgo: It's a great day for learning and expanding your knowledge. Use your analytical mind to explore new topics and gain valuable insights.

Libra: Relationships feel dynamic and intellectually stimulating. Focus on engaging in conversations that deepen your connections and broaden your perspective.

Scorpio: After a period of emotional intensity, today encourages you to focus on personal growth and embrace new opportunities for self-discovery.

Sagittarius: The Moon in your sign enhances your sense of adventure and optimism. It's a perfect day to pursue your passions and explore new possibilities.

Capricorn: While discipline is important, today encourages you to explore new ideas and broaden your horizons with an open mind.

Aquarius: Your innovative thinking shines today. Use this energy to explore new possibilities and share your unique perspective with others.

Pisces: It's a day for personal growth and exploration. Use your intuition to guide you as you embrace new opportunities and expand your horizons.

For those born on October 5: Born under the Moon in Sagittarius, these individuals are adventurous, curious, and eager to explore new horizons. In 2025, they'll thrive by embracing new experiences, pursuing personal growth, and seeking knowledge in their quest for understanding and self-discovery.

Daily Insights: The Moon in Sagittarius continues to bring adventure and optimism, but as it transitions into Capricorn later in the day, the focus shifts toward discipline, practicality, and long-term planning. It's a day for balancing exploration with responsibility and setting clear goals for the future.

Aries: Start the day with a sense of adventure, but as the Moon moves into Capricorn, focus on grounding yourself and setting long-term goals.

Taurus: The day begins with optimism and exploration, but later, you'll feel more inclined to focus on practical matters and organizing your long-term plans.

Gemini: Use the early part of the day for exploration and learning, but as the energy shifts, focus on refining your goals and taking practical steps toward achieving them.

Cancer: Adventure is important early in the day, but as the Moon moves into Capricorn, focus on creating stability in your personal life and making thoughtful decisions.

Leo: The morning is ideal for pursuing your passions, but as the Moon enters Capricorn, focus on grounding your ideas and setting realistic goals.

Virgo: Use the early part of the day for intellectual exploration, but later, shift your focus to organizing your thoughts and refining your plans for the future.

Libra: Relationships feel dynamic early in the day, but as the energy shifts, focus on creating harmony and setting practical goals in your personal life.

Scorpio: The morning is filled with excitement and creativity, but later, shift your focus to practical matters and long-term planning.

Sagittarius: The Moon in your sign brings optimism early in the day, but as it transitions into Capricorn, focus on practical steps and responsibility to achieve your goals.

Capricorn: The Moon enters your sign later today, bringing a sense of discipline and focus. Use this energy to work on long-term projects and set achievable goals.

Aquarius: Adventure and learning are highlighted in the morning, but as the Moon enters Capricorn, focus on practical solutions and refining your long-term plans.

Pisces: The day starts with emotional exploration, but later, focus on grounding yourself and setting practical goals for the future.

For those born on October 6: Born under the transition from Sagittarius to Capricorn, these individuals are adventurous yet practical. In 2025, they'll thrive by balancing their love for exploration with the discipline needed to achieve long-term goals.

Daily Insights: The Moon in Capricorn brings a focus on discipline, productivity, and long-term goals. It's a day for working methodically toward your ambitions and making steady progress. With Mars in Capricorn, there's extra determination and focus, making it a perfect time for tackling ambitious projects.

Aries: Focus on your long-term goals today. Use your energy to make steady progress while staying disciplined and grounded.

Taurus: It's a day for practical achievements. Use your determination to work on long-term projects and create stability in your life.

Gemini: It's a productive day for organizing your thoughts and refining your plans. Use this energy to stay focused and disciplined.

Cancer: Emotional reflection and stability are key today. Use this energy to focus on your long-term personal and professional goals.

Leo: Confidence and leadership are highlighted today. Use your focus to take charge of important projects and inspire those around you.

Virgo: It's a great day for focusing on productivity and long-term planning. Use your disciplined nature to tackle important tasks.

Libra: Relationships feel stable today. Focus on creating harmony in your personal connections while staying productive with your goals.

Scorpio: Your determination is strong today. Use this energy to focus on your long-term goals and ensure you're making practical decisions for the future.

Sagittarius: Adventure takes a backseat today as you focus on creating stability and working toward your long-term goals.

Capricorn: The Moon in your sign enhances your natural discipline and focus. Use this energy to make significant progress on your ambitions.

Aquarius: While creativity is important, today encourages you to focus on practical solutions and refining your ideas for long-term success.

Pisces: Emotional reflection is balanced with practicality today. Use this energy to organize your life and focus on long-term goals.

For those born on October 7: Born under the Moon in Capricorn, these individuals are disciplined, practical, and focused on long-term success. In 2025, they'll thrive by setting clear goals and making steady progress toward achieving them, using their disciplined nature to stay focused on their ambitions.

Daily Insights: The Moon in Capricorn continues to emphasize discipline, productivity, and long-term planning, but as it transitions into Aquarius later in the day, the focus shifts toward creativity, innovation, and social connections. It's a day for balancing practical work with creative exploration and collaboration.

Aries: Use the morning for disciplined work, but as the Moon moves into Aquarius, embrace your creativity and explore new ideas.

Taurus: The day starts with a focus on productivity, but later, shift your attention to social interactions and creative thinking.

Gemini: Productivity is high early in the day, but by evening, you'll feel more inclined to engage in conversations and explore new possibilities.

Cancer: Start the day with practical goals, but as the Moon enters Aquarius, focus on creativity and exploring new opportunities.

Leo: The morning is perfect for focusing on your goals, but as the day progresses, embrace new ways of thinking and collaborating with others.

Virgo: Use the early part of the day for productivity, but later, shift your focus to creative problem-solving and engaging with others.

Libra: Relationships feel stable early in the day, but later, focus on innovative solutions and exploring new perspectives in your connections.

Scorpio: Determination guides you early in the day, but as the energy shifts, focus on expanding your mind and embracing creative ideas.

Sagittarius: The day starts with a focus on responsibilities, but later, you'll feel more curious and eager to explore new possibilities.

Capricorn: The Moon in your sign enhances your focus on discipline, but as it moves into Aquarius, explore creative ideas and social opportunities.

Aquarius: The evening brings a burst of creativity and innovation. Use this time to explore new projects and connect with others.

Pisces: Emotional reflection is key early in the day, but as the Moon enters Aquarius, focus on socializing and expressing your creativity.

For those born on October 8: Born under the transition from Capricorn to Aquarius, these individuals are both disciplined and creative. In 2025, they'll thrive by balancing practicality with innovation, focusing on both long-term goals and exploring new possibilities.

Daily Insights: The Moon in Aquarius brings a focus on creativity, innovation, and social connections. It's a great day for engaging with others, exploring new ideas, and embracing your individuality. With Venus in Leo, relationships feel lively and intellectually stimulating, making it a perfect time for meaningful conversations.

Aries: Your creativity shines today. Use this energy to explore new ideas and connect with others through meaningful collaborations.

Taurus: It's a day for balancing practicality with creativity. Use your determination to bring innovative ideas into reality.

Gemini: Social interactions are stimulating today. Engage in conversations that inspire new perspectives and broaden your horizons.

Cancer: Creativity and innovation are calling you today. Use this energy to explore new ways of expressing yourself and connecting with others.

Leo: Leadership and creativity go hand in hand today. Use your confidence to take the lead in innovative projects and inspire others with your bold ideas.

Virgo: It's a great day for exploring creative solutions. Use your analytical skills to approach challenges in innovative ways.

Libra: Relationships are dynamic and exciting today. Focus on connecting with others in unconventional ways and exploring new perspectives in your personal connections.

Scorpio: Your passion for personal growth is strong today. Use this energy to explore new ideas and engage in meaningful conversations.

Sagittarius: Adventure and creativity are calling you today. Focus on expanding your horizons and embracing new opportunities.

Capricorn: While discipline is important, today encourages you to explore new ideas and engage in creative thinking.

Aquarius: With the Moon in your sign, your creativity and individuality are amplified. Use this energy to pursue innovative ideas and connect with others.

Pisces: Your intuition is strong today. Use this energy to explore creative projects and connect with others in meaningful ways.

For those born on October 9: Born under the Moon in Aquarius, these individuals are creative, innovative, and socially connected. In 2025, they'll thrive by embracing their individuality, exploring new ideas, and focusing on personal growth through social connections and creative expression.

Daily Insights: The Moon in Aquarius continues to emphasize creativity and innovation, but as it transitions into Pisces later in the day, the focus shifts toward emotional reflection, intuition, and empathy. It's a day for balancing intellectual exploration with emotional depth.

Aries: Start the day with innovative ideas and social connections, but as the Moon enters Pisces, shift your focus to emotional reflection and nurturing relationships.

Taurus: The morning is great for exploring creative solutions, but later, focus on emotional healing and connecting with loved ones on a deeper level.

Gemini: Your mind is active early in the day, but as the Moon enters Pisces, focus on balancing your intellectual pursuits with emotional reflection.

Cancer: Emotional intuition is heightened as the day progresses. Use the morning for socializing, but later, focus on self-care and nurturing close relationships.

Leo: Creativity shines early in the day, but as the energy shifts, focus on your emotional well-being and connecting with those who matter most.

Virgo: Productivity is high in the morning, but by evening, you'll feel more inclined to explore your emotions and focus on personal healing.

Libra: Relationships feel dynamic early in the day, but as the Moon enters Pisces, focus on deepening your emotional connections and finding inner balance.

Scorpio: Use the morning for exploring new ideas, but later, focus on emotional growth and reflection. Your intuition is especially strong today.

Sagittarius: The day starts with excitement and creativity, but later, you'll feel more inclined to focus on emotional healing and connecting with loved ones.

Capricorn: Early productivity gives way to emotional reflection as the day progresses. Focus on grounding yourself and nurturing your relationships.

Aquarius: The Moon in your sign brings out your creativity, but as the energy shifts, focus on emotional introspection and personal growth.

Pisces: The Moon enters your sign later today, amplifying your intuition and emotional sensitivity. Use this energy to focus on self-care and emotional healing.

For those born on October 10: Born under the transition from Aquarius to Pisces, these individuals are both creative and emotionally intuitive. In 2025, they'll thrive by balancing intellectual exploration with emotional reflection, focusing on both personal growth and deepening relationships.

Daily Insights: The Moon in Pisces brings a focus on emotional reflection, intuition, and creativity. It's a great day for engaging in artistic projects, connecting with loved ones on a deeper level, and exploring your inner world. With Mercury in Gemini, communication remains lively, making it a good day for expressing your emotions through words.

Aries: Your intuition is strong today. Use this energy to focus on emotional reflection and nurture your relationships with empathy and understanding.

Taurus: It's a great day for combining creativity with practicality. Focus on expressing your emotions through artistic projects or clear communication.

Gemini: Emotional reflection is key today. Use this energy to connect with your inner self and engage in meaningful conversations with loved ones.

Cancer: The Moon in Pisces enhances your emotional intuition. Use this energy to focus on self-care and strengthening your personal relationships.

Leo: While you're often focused on action, today encourages emotional reflection. Use this time to explore your feelings and deepen your connections.

Virgo: Balance your practical nature with emotional reflection today. Use this energy to focus on your inner world and nurture your relationships.

Libra: Relationships feel emotionally deep today. Focus on connecting with loved ones and creating harmony in your emotional connections.

Scorpio: Your emotional intensity is strong today. Use this energy for self-reflection and focus on healing and strengthening your emotional bonds.

Sagittarius: It's a day for emotional introspection. Use this energy to explore your inner world and strengthen your emotional connections with loved ones.

Capricorn: While you're often focused on discipline, today encourages emotional reflection. Use this time to connect with your feelings and focus on personal healing.

Aquarius: While your mind is often focused on innovation, today encourages emotional growth. Use this energy to nurture your close relationships and engage in self-care.

Pisces: The Moon in your sign amplifies your emotional sensitivity and intuition. Use this energy for personal healing and deepening your emotional connections with others.

For those born on October 11: Born under the Moon in Pisces, these individuals are emotionally intuitive, creative, and compassionate. In 2025, they'll thrive by focusing on their emotional well-being, nurturing relationships, and expressing their creativity through meaningful projects.

Daily Insights: The Moon in Pisces continues to emphasize emotional reflection and creativity, but as it transitions into Aries later in the day, the focus shifts toward action, confidence, and bold decisions. It's a day for balancing emotional reflection with taking bold steps toward your goals.

Aries: Start the day with emotional reflection, but as the Moon enters your sign, focus on taking bold actions and pursuing your personal goals with confidence.

Taurus: The morning is perfect for emotional introspection, but as the energy shifts, focus on taking practical steps toward your long-term goals.

Gemini: Emotional reflection is key early in the day, but as the energy shifts, focus on engaging with others and taking action on your ideas.

Cancer: The morning is ideal for nurturing your emotional well-being, but as the Moon moves into Aries, embrace new challenges and step out of your comfort zone.

Leo: Emotional reflection is important early in the day, but as the Moon enters Aries, your confidence will rise, making it a great time to take bold actions.

Virgo: Use the early part of the day for emotional clarity, but later, shift your focus to organizing your thoughts and taking action on your plans.

Libra: Relationships feel emotionally deep in the morning, but as the energy shifts, focus on communicating openly and taking action to strengthen your connections.

Scorpio: Emotional depth is important early in the day, but as the Moon moves into Aries, focus on taking bold steps toward personal growth and transformation.

Sagittarius: Start the day with emotional introspection, but later, shift your focus to adventure and exploring new opportunities with confidence.

Capricorn: Emotional reflection is key early in the day, but as the Moon enters Aries, focus on taking practical steps toward your long-term goals.

Aquarius: The morning is perfect for emotional reflection, but as the energy shifts, focus on pursuing new ideas and taking bold actions with confidence.

Pisces: The Moon in your sign enhances your emotional intuition early in the day, but as the energy shifts, focus on taking decisive actions toward your ambitions.

For those born on October 12: Born under the transition from Pisces to Aries, these individuals are emotionally intuitive and action-oriented. In 2025, they'll thrive by balancing emotional reflection with taking bold steps toward their personal goals and ambitions.

Daily Insights: The Moon in Aries brings a surge of energy, confidence, and motivation. It's a great day for taking bold steps, embracing new opportunities, and focusing on personal goals. With Mercury in Leo, communication is bold and creative, making it a perfect time for expressing your ideas with confidence.

Aries: Your confidence and motivation are high today. Use this energy to push forward on your personal goals and take bold actions with enthusiasm.

Taurus: It's a day for balancing bold actions with practicality. Use your grounded nature to take steady steps toward your long-term goals.

Gemini: Communication and action are your strengths today. Use this energy to engage in meaningful conversations and explore new ideas.

Cancer: Confidence and emotional reflection are key today. Use this energy to focus on personal growth and take bold steps toward your ambitions.

Leo: Leadership and action are highlighted today. Use your natural confidence to take charge of projects and inspire those around you.

Virgo: Productivity is high today. Use your disciplined nature to focus on practical tasks and take bold actions toward your goals.

Libra: Relationships feel dynamic and exciting today. Focus on open communication and take action to strengthen your personal connections.

Scorpio: Your determination is strong today. Use this energy to take decisive steps toward achieving your long-term goals.

Sagittarius: Adventure and excitement are calling you today. Use your enthusiasm to explore new opportunities and take bold steps toward your dreams.

Capricorn: Discipline and focus guide you today. Use this energy to make steady progress on your long-term goals and ambitions.

Aquarius: Your creativity and innovative thinking shine today. Use this energy to explore new ideas and take bold actions toward your personal goals.

Pisces: It's a day for taking action on your personal ambitions. Use your intuition to guide you as you embrace new opportunities with confidence.

For those born on October 13: Born under the Moon in Aries, these individuals are confident, action-oriented, and driven. In 2025, they'll thrive by taking bold steps toward their personal goals and embracing new opportunities with enthusiasm.

Daily Insights: The Moon in Aries continues to bring energy, motivation, and a focus on personal goals. It's a great day for taking decisive actions, embracing challenges, and pursuing your ambitions. With Mars in Capricorn, there's an added boost of discipline and determination, making it a powerful day for working on long-term projects.

Aries: Your confidence and motivation are high today. Use this energy to push forward on your personal goals and take bold actions with confidence.

Taurus: It's a day for balancing bold actions with practicality. Use your grounded nature to take steady steps toward your long-term goals.

Gemini: Communication and action are your strengths today. Use this energy to engage in meaningful conversations and explore new ideas.

Cancer: Confidence and emotional reflection are key today. Use this energy to focus on personal growth and take bold steps toward your ambitions.

Leo: Leadership and action are highlighted today. Use your natural confidence to take charge of projects and inspire those around you.

Virgo: Productivity is high today. Use your disciplined nature to focus on practical tasks and take bold actions toward your goals.

Libra: Relationships feel dynamic and exciting today. Focus on open communication and take action to strengthen your personal connections.

Scorpio: Your determination is strong today. Use this energy to take decisive steps toward achieving your long-term goals.

Sagittarius: Adventure and excitement are calling you today. Use your enthusiasm to explore new opportunities and take bold steps toward your dreams.

Capricorn: Discipline and focus guide you today. Use this energy to make steady progress on your long-term projects and goals.

Aquarius: Your creativity and innovative thinking shine today. Use this energy to explore new ideas and take bold actions toward your personal goals.

Pisces: It's a day for taking action on your personal ambitions. Use your intuition to guide you as you embrace new opportunities with confidence.

For those born on October 14: Born under the Moon in Aries, these individuals are energetic, motivated, and focused on achieving their goals. In 2025, they'll thrive by embracing challenges, taking bold actions, and pursuing their ambitions with enthusiasm.

Daily Insights: The Moon in Aries continues to provide energy, confidence, and motivation, but as it transitions into Taurus later in the day, the focus shifts toward stability, practicality, and long-term planning. It's a day for balancing bold actions with careful consideration of your long-term goals.

Aries: The day starts with high energy and motivation, but as the Moon moves into Taurus, focus on grounding yourself and setting practical goals for the future.

Taurus: The Moon enters your sign later today, bringing a sense of stability and focus on practical matters. Use this energy to work toward your long-term ambitions.

Gemini: It's a day for balancing bold ideas with practical steps. Use the morning for exploration, but by evening, shift your focus to long-term planning.

Cancer: The morning is ideal for pursuing your ambitions with confidence, but as the Moon moves into Taurus, focus on grounding your emotions and working toward long-term stability in your personal life.

Leo: Start the day with creative energy and bold actions, but as the energy shifts, focus on setting practical goals that will lead to long-term success.

Virgo: Use the early part of the day to act on your bold ideas, but later in the day, shift your attention to organizing your long-term plans and ensuring stability.

Libra: Relationships feel dynamic in the morning, but by evening, focus on creating harmony and long-term emotional stability in your personal connections.

Scorpio: Your energy is strong in the morning for taking bold steps, but later, focus on grounding yourself and creating stability in your professional and personal life.

Sagittarius: Adventure is calling you in the morning, but as the Moon enters Taurus, shift your focus to setting realistic goals and making steady progress.

Capricorn: The morning is filled with confidence and motivation, but by evening, focus on your long-term goals and ensure that your actions are practical and grounded.

Aquarius: Creativity and innovation are your strengths in the morning, but as the day progresses, shift your attention to setting practical steps for future success.

Pisces: Use the morning for emotional reflection and taking action on personal goals, but later, focus on grounding yourself and ensuring emotional and practical stability in your life.

For those born on October 15: Born under the transition from Aries to Taurus, these individuals are energetic and driven but also practical and grounded. In 2025, they'll thrive by balancing their bold ambitions with careful long-term planning and steady progress toward success.

Daily Insights: The Moon in Taurus emphasizes stability, practicality, and long-term planning. It's a great day for working on your goals methodically, taking slow and steady steps toward success. With Mars in Capricorn, there's an added boost of discipline, making it an ideal time for productivity and laying the groundwork for future ambitions.

Aries: Focus on grounding yourself today. Use your energy to set practical goals and work methodically toward your long-term ambitions.

Taurus: The Moon in your sign amplifies your sense of stability and focus. Use this energy to work on practical matters and ensure you're making steady progress.

Gemini: It's a day for long-term planning. Use your intellectual curiosity to refine your goals and take practical steps to move toward them.

Cancer: Stability is key today. Focus on grounding your emotions and working toward long-term stability in your personal and professional life.

Leo: While creativity is important, today encourages you to focus on practical goals. Use your leadership skills to guide others in achieving long-term success.

Virgo: It's a productive day for focusing on practical matters. Use your disciplined nature to ensure that you're making steady progress on your goals.

Libra: Relationships feel stable and grounded today. Focus on creating harmony in your personal connections while working toward long-term success.

Scorpio: Your determination is strong today. Use this energy to focus on your long-term goals and ensure you're making practical decisions for the future.

Sagittarius: Adventure takes a backseat today as you focus on creating stability and working toward practical goals in your personal and professional life.

Capricorn: Discipline and focus are your strengths today. Use this energy to make steady progress on your long-term projects and goals.

Aquarius: While creativity and innovation are important, today encourages you to focus on practical solutions and laying the groundwork for future success.

Pisces: Emotional stability is key today. Use this energy to ground yourself and work on practical steps to ensure long-term security in your life.

For those born on October 16: Born under the Moon in Taurus, these individuals are practical, grounded, and focused on long-term success. In 2025, they'll thrive by setting clear goals and making steady progress toward them, using their disciplined nature to stay focused on their ambitions.

Daily Insights: The Moon in Taurus continues to emphasize stability, practicality, and long-term goals, but as it transitions into Gemini later in the day, the focus shifts toward communication, learning, and curiosity. It's a day for balancing practical work with intellectual exploration and social connections.

Aries: Use the morning to focus on grounding yourself and working toward long-term goals, but later in the day, shift your focus to communication and exploring new ideas.

Taurus: Start the day with stability and practicality, but by evening, embrace social interactions and intellectual exploration.

Gemini: The Moon enters your sign later today, bringing a burst of energy and curiosity. It's a great time for exploring new ideas and engaging in conversations.

Cancer: The day begins with a focus on stability, but as the energy shifts, focus on connecting with others and exploring new perspectives.

Leo: Use the morning for practical work, but as the Moon enters Gemini, engage with others and share your ideas freely.

Virgo: The early part of the day is productive, but by evening, focus on engaging with new ideas and refining your long-term plans.

Libra: Relationships feel stable early in the day, but as the Moon moves into Gemini, focus on open communication and exploring new perspectives with loved ones.

Scorpio: The day begins with determination and focus, but later, you'll feel more inclined to explore social interactions and new opportunities.

Sagittarius: Start the day with practicality, but as the Moon enters Gemini, shift your focus to learning and intellectual exploration.

Capricorn: Discipline guides you early in the day, but by evening, shift your attention to communication and engaging with others.

Aquarius: The day starts with practical tasks, but later, explore new ideas and engage with others in stimulating conversations.

Pisces: Emotional reflection is key early in the day, but as the Moon moves into Gemini, focus on socializing and expressing your ideas clearly.

For those born on October 17: Born under the transition from Taurus to Gemini, these individuals are both practical and curious. In 2025, they'll thrive by balancing their disciplined approach with intellectual exploration, focusing on both long-term goals and learning new things.

Daily Insights: The Moon in Gemini brings a focus on communication, learning, and curiosity. It's a great day for engaging in conversations, exploring new ideas, and connecting with others. With Mercury in Leo, there's an added emphasis on creativity and bold expression, making it an ideal time for sharing ideas confidently.

Aries: Your curiosity is strong today. Use this energy to engage in conversations, explore new ideas, and take action on your personal goals.

Taurus: It's a day for balancing practicality with intellectual exploration. Use your grounded nature to communicate your thoughts clearly and explore new perspectives.

Gemini: The Moon in your sign enhances your communication skills. Use this energy to connect with others, share your ideas, and explore new opportunities.

Cancer: It's a day for focusing on learning and intellectual growth. Use this energy to connect with your inner self and engage in meaningful conversations.

Leo: Leadership and creativity are highlighted today. Use your confidence to inspire others and share your innovative ideas with enthusiasm.

Virgo: Your analytical skills are sharp today. Use this energy to focus on problem-solving and exploring new ideas through conversation.

Libra: Relationships feel dynamic and intellectually stimulating. Focus on engaging with loved ones in meaningful conversations and exploring new perspectives.

Scorpio: Your emotional depth is strong today. Use this energy to engage in deep conversations and explore new ideas that challenge your thinking.

Sagittarius: Adventure and learning go hand in hand today. Use your curiosity to explore new opportunities and engage in conversations that inspire you.

Capricorn: It's a day for balancing discipline with intellectual exploration. Use this energy to engage in thoughtful discussions and refine your long-term goals.

Aquarius: Your creativity and innovative thinking shine today. Use this energy to explore new ideas and engage in collaborative conversations.

Pisces: It's a day for intellectual exploration and emotional reflection. Use this energy to connect with others in meaningful ways and share your ideas.

For those born on October 18: Born under the Moon in Gemini, these individuals are curious, communicative, and eager to explore new ideas. In 2025, they'll thrive by engaging in conversations, learning new things, and using their sharp minds to make meaningful connections with others.

Daily Insights: The Moon in Gemini continues to emphasize communication, learning, and curiosity, but as it transitions into Cancer later in the day, the focus shifts toward emotional well-being, nurturing relationships, and self-care. It's a day for balancing intellectual exploration with emotional connection.

Aries: The day begins with lively conversations, but as the Moon moves into Cancer, shift your focus to emotional reflection and nurturing your relationships.

Taurus: Use the morning for exploring new ideas, but as the energy shifts, focus on creating emotional stability in your personal life.

Gemini: Your communication skills are heightened early in the day, but later, focus on emotional connections and strengthening your relationships with loved ones.

Cancer: The Moon enters your sign later today, heightening your emotional sensitivity. It's a great time for self-care and nurturing close relationships.

Leo: Start the day with intellectual exploration, but as the Moon moves into Cancer, shift your focus to emotional balance and personal growth.

Virgo: Productivity is high early in the day, but by evening, focus on emotional reflection and nurturing your personal well-being.

Libra: Relationships are intellectually stimulating in the morning, but later, focus on deepening emotional connections and creating harmony in your relationships.

Scorpio: Your curiosity is high early in the day, but as the energy shifts, focus on emotional healing and strengthening your relationships.

Sagittarius: The day starts with excitement and exploration, but later, shift your focus to emotional reflection and personal growth.

Capricorn: Use the morning for practical tasks and intellectual pursuits, but by evening, focus on nurturing your emotional well-being and relationships.

Aquarius: Creativity and intellectual exploration are highlighted early in the day, but as the Moon enters Cancer, focus on emotional growth and self-care.

Pisces: The day begins with curiosity, but later, you'll feel more inclined to focus on emotional healing and nurturing your close relationships.

For those born on October 19: Born under the transition from Gemini to Cancer, these individuals are both intellectually curious and emotionally intuitive. In 2025, they'll thrive by balancing their sharp minds with emotional reflection, focusing on both learning and nurturing their relationships.

Daily Insights: The Moon in Cancer emphasizes emotional reflection, nurturing relationships, and self-care. It's a great day for focusing on your emotional well-being and connecting with loved ones. With Venus in Leo, there's also a blend of emotional depth and creative self-expression, making it a great time for balancing emotions with personal ambitions.

Aries: Emotional balance is important today. Use this energy to nurture your relationships and take time for self-care while maintaining confidence in your personal goals.

Taurus: Focus on emotional well-being today. Use your grounded nature to strengthen your personal connections and create stability in your relationships.

Gemini: Communication is highlighted today. Use this energy to have meaningful conversations and nurture emotional connections with loved ones.

Cancer: The Moon in your sign enhances your emotional intuition. Take time for self-care and focus on deepening your relationships with those close to you.

Leo: While your leadership and creativity are strong, today encourages emotional reflection. Use this energy to nurture your inner self and balance ambition with emotional well-being.

Virgo: Emotional clarity is key today. Use this energy to focus on organizing your personal life and deepening emotional bonds with loved ones.

Libra: Relationships take on a more nurturing tone today. Focus on creating emotional harmony and balance in your personal and professional connections.

Scorpio: Emotional reflection is important today. Use this energy to focus on healing and deepening your emotional connections with those you care about.

Sagittarius: It's a day for focusing on emotional well-being and creating stability in your personal life. Take time to connect with your inner self and nurture your relationships.

Capricorn: Emotional reflection is key today. Use this energy to ground yourself and focus on nurturing both your relationships and your personal goals.

Aquarius: While creativity is important, today encourages emotional introspection. Use this energy to connect with loved ones and focus on self-care.

Pisces: The Moon in Cancer heightens your emotional sensitivity today. Use this energy to focus on healing, nurturing your relationships, and self-care.

For those born on October 20: Born under the Moon in Cancer, these individuals are emotionally intuitive, nurturing, and deeply connected to their home and family. In 2025, they'll thrive by focusing on their emotional well-being, nurturing relationships, and creating stability in their personal lives.

Daily Insights: The Moon in Cancer continues to emphasize emotional well-being, but as it transitions into Leo later in the day, the focus shifts toward confidence, creativity, and self-expression. It's a day for balancing emotional reflection with taking bold actions toward your personal goals.

Aries: Start the day with emotional reflection, but as the Moon enters Leo, shift your focus to taking bold steps toward your personal goals.

Taurus: The day begins with a focus on emotional stability, but later, embrace creative expression and personal empowerment.

Gemini: Emotional connections are key early in the day, but as the energy shifts, focus on communication and expressing your unique ideas.

Cancer: The morning is ideal for nurturing your emotional well-being, but as the Moon enters Leo, focus on stepping into the spotlight and pursuing your personal ambitions.

Leo: The Moon enters your sign later today, amplifying your confidence and creativity. Use this energy to take bold steps toward your goals and lead with enthusiasm.

Virgo: The day starts with emotional clarity, but later, shift your focus to expressing your creativity and finding new ways to approach your long-term goals.

Libra: Relationships feel emotionally deep in the morning, but as the day progresses, focus on embracing creativity and finding balance in your personal connections.

Scorpio: The morning is perfect for emotional introspection, but later, focus on taking bold steps toward personal transformation and expressing your true self.

Sagittarius: Start the day by reflecting on your emotional well-being, but as the Moon enters Leo, embrace new adventures and creative opportunities.

Capricorn: The morning is ideal for grounding yourself emotionally, but as the energy shifts, focus on stepping into leadership roles and expressing your creative talents.

Aquarius: Use the morning for emotional reflection, but later, focus on exploring new ideas and expressing yourself confidently in social settings.

Pisces: Emotional sensitivity is high early in the day, but as the Moon moves into Leo, shift your focus to personal empowerment and creative expression.

For those born on October 21: Born under the transition from Cancer to Leo, these individuals are emotionally intuitive and confident. In 2025, they'll thrive by balancing their emotional well-being with bold actions toward their personal goals, stepping into leadership roles and expressing their creativity.

Daily Insights: The Moon in Leo brings a surge of confidence, creativity, and leadership. It's a great day for expressing your true self, taking bold actions, and pursuing your passions. With Mars in Capricorn, there's a balance of discipline and ambition, making it an ideal time for working toward your goals with confidence.

Aries: Your confidence is high today. Use this energy to pursue your personal goals and take bold actions with enthusiasm.

Taurus: Creativity flows easily today. Focus on expressing your unique ideas and working toward your long-term goals with determination.

Gemini: Communication and self-expression are your strengths today. Use this energy to connect with others and share your innovative ideas.

Cancer: The Moon in Leo encourages you to step out of your comfort zone and pursue your personal goals with confidence and creativity.

Leo: The Moon in your sign amplifies your natural leadership and creativity. Use this energy to take bold steps toward your passions and inspire others.

Virgo: Balance creativity with practicality today. Use your disciplined nature to focus on long-term goals while expressing your unique talents.

Libra: Relationships feel dynamic and exciting today. Focus on creative ways to connect with loved ones and embrace your individuality.

Scorpio: Your passion is strong today. Use this energy to pursue personal goals with intensity and determination.

Sagittarius: Adventure and creativity are calling you today. Use this energy to explore new opportunities and express yourself freely.

Capricorn: Leadership and discipline come naturally today. Use this energy to focus on personal projects and inspire those around you.

Aquarius: Your creativity shines today. Use this energy to pursue innovative ideas and connect with others through meaningful collaborations.

Pisces: It's a day for self-expression and personal growth. Use your creativity to focus on your goals and embrace new opportunities with confidence.

For those born on October 22: Born under the Moon in Leo, these individuals are charismatic, creative, and confident. In 2025, they'll thrive by stepping into leadership roles, embracing their unique talents, and pursuing their passions with determination.

Daily Insights: The Moon in Leo continues to highlight confidence and creativity, but as it transitions into Virgo later in the day, the focus shifts toward practicality, organization, and attention to detail. It's a day for balancing bold ideas with disciplined actions to achieve long-term success.

Aries: Start the day with bold actions, but as the Moon moves into Virgo, shift your focus to organizing your plans and refining your goals.

Taurus: The day begins with creative expression, but later, focus on practical steps toward your long-term goals.

Gemini: Use the morning for creative pursuits and communication, but as the energy shifts, focus on organizing your ideas and refining your plans.

Cancer: Confidence and creativity guide you early in the day, but later, shift your focus to emotional balance and practical tasks.

Leo: The Moon in your sign enhances your leadership, but as it moves into Virgo, focus on grounding your energy and organizing your long-term goals.

Virgo: The Moon enters your sign later today, amplifying your attention to detail and practical nature. Use this energy to refine your plans and focus on productivity.

Libra: The morning is great for engaging in creative conversations, but later, focus on balancing your personal goals with practical responsibilities.

Scorpio: Start the day by pursuing your passions, but as the Moon moves into Virgo, shift your focus to refining your long-term plans and staying disciplined.

Sagittarius: The day starts with excitement and creativity, but later, shift your focus to practical tasks and responsibilities.

Capricorn: Discipline and leadership guide you in the morning, but later, shift your attention to organizing your goals and refining your long-term plans.

Aquarius: The morning is ideal for creative expression, but as the Moon moves into Virgo, focus on refining your ideas and ensuring they are practical.

Pisces: Start the day with emotional reflection and creativity, but later, focus on organizing your personal life and making practical decisions.

For those born on October 23: Born under the transition from Leo to Virgo, these individuals are both creative and practical. In 2025, they'll thrive by balancing their bold ideas with disciplined actions, focusing on both creativity and productivity to achieve their goals.

Daily Insights: The Moon in Virgo emphasizes productivity, organization, and attention to detail. It's a great day for focusing on practical matters, refining your plans, and making steady progress toward your long-term goals. With Mercury in Leo, there's still room for creative communication, making it a perfect day for blending creativity with discipline.

Aries: Stay focused on your goals today. Use your energy to organize your thoughts and make steady progress toward your long-term ambitions.

Taurus: It's a day for practical achievements. Use your grounded nature to refine your ideas and work steadily on long-term projects.

Gemini: Your analytical skills are strong today. Use this energy to focus on problem-solving and refining your ideas.

Cancer: Balance emotional reflection with practical tasks today. Focus on organizing your personal life and creating emotional stability.

Leo: After a period of creativity, today encourages you to focus on practical matters. Use your energy to refine your long-term plans.

Virgo: The Moon in your sign enhances your natural strengths. Use this energy to focus on productivity and tackle tasks that require precision.

Libra: Relationships feel stable today. Focus on balancing your personal goals with your relationships while staying productive.

Scorpio: Your determination is strong today. Use this energy to focus on long-term goals and ensure you're making practical decisions for the future.

Sagittarius: Practical matters take precedence today. Use this energy to focus on your responsibilities and stay disciplined in achieving your goals.

Capricorn: Discipline and focus are your strengths today. Use this energy to make significant progress on your long-term projects and goals.

Aquarius: While creativity is important, today encourages you to focus on practical solutions and refining your innovative ideas.

Pisces: Emotional reflection is balanced with practicality today. Use this energy to organize your life and make steady progress toward your goals.

For those born on October 24: Born under the Moon in Virgo, these individuals are practical, detail-oriented, and highly productive. In 2025, they'll thrive by refining their plans, staying disciplined, and making steady progress toward their long-term goals.

Daily Insights: The Moon in Virgo continues to emphasize productivity, but as it transitions into Libra later in the day, the focus shifts toward balance, relationships, and harmony. It's a day for balancing work with social interactions and ensuring that all areas of your life are in equilibrium.

Aries: The morning is perfect for productivity, but as the Moon moves into Libra, focus on balancing your work with your personal relationships.

Taurus: Start the day with practical tasks, but later, shift your focus to nurturing relationships and creating balance in your life.

Gemini: The day begins with a focus on organization, but as the energy shifts, engage in meaningful conversations and strengthen your relationships.

Cancer: The morning is ideal for organizing your life, but as the Moon enters Libra, focus on nurturing your relationships and finding harmony.

Leo: The day starts with practical tasks, but later, focus on balancing your creative pursuits with your relationships.

Virgo: The Moon in your sign enhances your productivity early in the day, but by evening, focus on maintaining balance in your personal life.

Libra: The day starts with productivity, but as the Moon enters your sign, focus on nurturing relationships and finding balance in all areas of life.

Scorpio: It's a day for balancing productivity with emotional depth. Use the morning for practical tasks, but later, focus on nurturing your relationships.

Sagittarius: Responsibilities guide you in the morning, but by evening, focus on social interactions and bringing balance to your personal life.

Capricorn: Discipline and focus guide you in the morning, but later, shift your attention to maintaining harmony in your relationships.

Aquarius: The morning is perfect for creativity and productivity, but as the Moon moves into Libra, focus on balancing your work and social life.

Pisces: Emotional reflection is key early in the day, but as the Moon enters Libra, focus on nurturing relationships and finding inner balance.

For those born on October 25: Born under the transition from Virgo to Libra, these individuals are both productive and focused on balance. In 2025, they'll thrive by balancing their attention to detail with creating harmonious relationships and personal connections.

Daily Insights: The Moon in Libra continues to emphasize balance, relationships, and harmony. It's a great day for focusing on social interactions, resolving conflicts, and creating equilibrium in your personal and professional life. With Venus in Leo, relationships may feel passionate and exciting, making it an ideal time for romantic and creative pursuits.

Aries: Focus on finding balance in your relationships today. Use this energy to create harmony in your personal and professional life.

Taurus: Balance is key today. Focus on maintaining harmony in your relationships while working toward your long-term goals.

Gemini: Relationships take center stage today. Focus on communicating clearly and creating harmony in your personal interactions.

Cancer: It's a day for balancing emotional needs with your relationships. Use this energy to create equilibrium in your personal connections.

Leo: While your confidence is strong, today encourages you to focus on your relationships and ensuring balance in your personal life.

Virgo: Balance productivity with harmony today. Use this energy to focus on both your work goals and your relationships.

Libra: With the Moon in your sign, balance and harmony are highlighted. Use this energy to create peace in your relationships and personal life.

Scorpio: Relationships feel emotionally deep today. Use this energy to connect with others on a deeper level while maintaining balance in your life.

Sagittarius: Social interactions are favored today. Use your natural charm to connect with others while ensuring harmony in your personal life.

Capricorn: It's a day for balancing your responsibilities with your relationships. Focus on finding harmony between your work and personal life.

Aquarius: Creativity and innovation come naturally today, but focus on creating balance in your interactions and ensuring harmony in your relationships.

Pisces: Emotional balance is important today. Use this energy to connect with loved ones and focus on creating stability in your relationships.

For those born on October 26: Born under the Moon in Libra, these individuals are focused on balance, harmony, and relationships. In 2025, they'll thrive by creating equilibrium in their personal and professional lives while working toward their goals with patience and determination.

Daily Insights: The Moon in Libra continues to bring focus on balance, relationships, and harmony, but as it transitions into Scorpio later in the day, the energy shifts toward emotional depth, transformation, and intense connections. It's a day for balancing social interactions with deep personal reflection.

Aries: Start the day by focusing on relationships and creating harmony, but as the Moon moves into Scorpio, dive deeper into your emotions and connections.

Taurus: The morning is perfect for nurturing relationships and creating balance, but as the energy shifts, focus on exploring emotional depths and personal transformation.

Gemini: Relationships are in focus early in the day, but later, shift toward introspection and exploring your emotional world.

Cancer: Start the day with balance, but as the Moon moves into Scorpio, focus on emotional clarity and deepening your closest relationships.

Leo: The day begins with a focus on balance and harmony, but later, shift toward personal growth and emotional transformation.

Virgo: The morning is ideal for keeping things in balance, but as the Moon enters Scorpio, focus on self-reflection and emotional exploration.

Libra: The Moon in your sign brings focus on harmony and balance early in the day, but as it enters Scorpio, you'll feel drawn toward emotional intensity and transformation.

Scorpio: The Moon enters your sign later today, heightening your emotional sensitivity. Use this energy to focus on personal growth and strengthening emotional connections.

Sagittarius: The morning is for socializing and creating balance, but as the energy shifts, turn inward and reflect on personal emotions and connections.

Capricorn: Balance your work and relationships in the morning, but as the Moon moves into Scorpio, focus on emotional reflection and personal growth.

Aquarius: Start the day focusing on balance and relationships, but later, turn your attention to exploring emotional depth and transformation.

Pisces: Emotional reflection and stability are key today. Use the energy later in the day to strengthen emotional bonds and engage in self-reflection.

For those born on October 27: Born under the transition from Libra to Scorpio, these individuals are balanced yet emotionally intense. In 2025, they'll thrive by focusing on relationships while embracing emotional transformation and personal growth.

Daily Insights: The Moon in Scorpio brings emotional intensity, introspection, and transformation. It's a powerful day for exploring your inner world, making deep connections with others, and focusing on personal growth. With Mercury in Virgo, communication remains grounded and practical, allowing for thoughtful conversations.

Aries: Emotional reflection is key today. Use this energy to explore personal growth and focus on deepening connections with those around you.

Taurus: The Moon in Scorpio highlights deep connections today. Use this energy to focus on relationships and personal transformation.

Gemini: Today encourages emotional depth and transformation. Use this time to explore your inner world and strengthen your relationships.

Cancer: Emotional intensity is strong today. Use this energy to nurture your closest relationships and engage in personal growth.

Leo: Emotional reflection is necessary today. Focus on understanding your emotional world and creating meaningful connections.

Virgo: Balance practicality with emotional depth today. Focus on your inner world and find healing in personal reflection.

Libra: Relationships feel intense today. Use this energy to connect on a deeper emotional level with loved ones.

Scorpio: The Moon in your sign brings emotional depth and personal transformation. Use this energy to focus on self-growth and strengthening emotional bonds.

Sagittarius: The day encourages emotional exploration. Use this time to reflect on your relationships and focus on personal growth.

Capricorn: Emotional intensity guides you today. Focus on personal transformation and deepening your relationships with those closest to you.

Aquarius: Creativity flows through your emotional depth today. Use this energy to explore new possibilities and connect with others meaningfully.

Pisces: Your emotional intuition is heightened today. Use this energy to focus on personal growth and healing.

For those born on October 28: Born under the Moon in Scorpio, these individuals are emotionally intense, intuitive, and transformative. In 2025, they'll thrive by focusing on emotional growth, deep connections, and personal transformation.

Daily Insights: The Moon in Scorpio continues to bring focus on emotional intensity and personal transformation, but as it transitions into Sagittarius later in the day, the energy shifts toward optimism, adventure, and personal freedom. It's a day for balancing introspection with the desire to explore new possibilities.

Aries: Start the day with emotional reflection, but as the Moon enters Sagittarius, shift your focus to new opportunities and personal freedom.

Taurus: Use the early part of the day for deep emotional work, but later, embrace the energy of adventure and explore new ideas.

Gemini: Emotional depth is important early in the day, but as the Moon enters Sagittarius, you'll feel more inclined to engage in learning and intellectual exploration.

Cancer: Start the day by focusing on nurturing your emotional connections, but as the energy shifts, embrace new opportunities for personal growth.

Leo: Emotional intensity gives way to adventure and personal freedom as the Moon enters Sagittarius. Focus on expanding your horizons and pursuing your goals.

Virgo: Balance emotional introspection with new possibilities today. Use the day to reflect on personal growth and seek out new experiences.

Libra: Deep relationships are key in the morning, but later, focus on adventure and broadening your perspective.

Scorpio: The Moon in your sign brings emotional depth early in the day, but as it moves into Sagittarius, explore new adventures and expand your world.

Sagittarius: The Moon enters your sign later today, bringing a sense of optimism and excitement. Use this energy to pursue your passions and explore new opportunities.

Capricorn: Emotional reflection is important in the morning, but as the energy shifts, focus on expanding your goals and seeking new adventures.

Aquarius: Early in the day, emotional exploration is key, but later, engage in new ideas and explore intellectual possibilities.

Pisces: Emotional healing and reflection are important early in the day, but later, focus on expanding your personal and professional horizons.

For those born on October 29: Born under the transition from Scorpio to Sagittarius, these individuals are emotionally deep yet adventurous. In 2025, they'll thrive by balancing emotional reflection with the pursuit of new experiences and personal growth.

Daily Insights: The Moon in Sagittarius emphasizes optimism, exploration, and personal growth. It's a great day for seeking new experiences, engaging in learning, and expanding your horizons. With Jupiter in Taurus, there's a sense of practicality balancing out the adventurous spirit, making it a good time for thoughtful exploration.

Aries: Adventure calls you today. Use this energy to explore new possibilities and focus on expanding your personal and professional goals.

Taurus: It's a day for balancing practicality with adventure. Use your grounded nature to explore new opportunities while staying focused on your long-term goals.

Gemini: Communication and learning are highlighted today. Use this energy to engage in stimulating conversations and explore new intellectual pursuits.

Cancer: Step out of your comfort zone today and embrace new experiences. Use this energy to focus on personal growth and adventure.

Leo: Confidence and leadership are emphasized today. Use this energy to take bold steps toward your goals and inspire those around you.

Virgo: It's a great day for learning and expanding your knowledge. Use your analytical mind to explore new ideas and gain fresh insights.

Libra: Relationships feel dynamic and exciting today. Focus on open communication and engage in meaningful conversations with loved ones.

Scorpio: After a period of emotional intensity, today encourages you to explore new experiences and focus on personal growth and adventure.

Sagittarius: The Moon in your sign enhances your sense of adventure and optimism. Use this energy to pursue your passions and embrace new possibilities.

Capricorn: While discipline is important, today encourages you to explore new ideas and broaden your horizons with an open mind.

Aquarius: Creativity and innovation are your strengths today. Use this energy to explore new possibilities and engage in collaborative projects.

Pisces: It's a day for personal growth and exploration. Use your intuition to guide you as you embrace new opportunities and expand your horizons.

For those born on October 30: Born under the Moon in Sagittarius, these individuals are adventurous, optimistic, and eager to explore new possibilities. In 2025, they'll thrive by embracing new experiences, expanding their horizons, and pursuing personal growth with enthusiasm.

Daily Insights: The Moon in Sagittarius continues to highlight optimism and adventure, but as it transitions into Capricorn later in the day, the focus shifts toward discipline, productivity, and long-term planning. It's a day for balancing personal freedom with responsibility and setting clear goals for the future.

Aries: Start the day with a sense of adventure, but as the Moon moves into Capricorn, focus on grounding yourself and setting practical goals.

Taurus: The morning is filled with excitement and exploration, but later, shift your attention to practical matters and refining your long-term plans.

Gemini: Adventure and learning are key early in the day, but as the energy shifts, focus on refining your ideas and setting clear goals.

Cancer: The morning is ideal for exploring new opportunities, but as the Moon enters Capricorn, shift your focus to creating emotional and practical stability.

Leo: Start the day with confidence and leadership, but later, focus on practical steps toward achieving your long-term ambitions.

Virgo: The day begins with curiosity and learning, but as the energy shifts, focus on organizing your thoughts and refining your long-term plans.

Libra: Relationships feel dynamic early in the day, but as the Moon moves into Capricorn, focus on creating balance and stability in your personal connections.

Scorpio: Start the day with curiosity and emotional exploration, but later, shift your focus to long-term planning and making steady progress on your goals.

Sagittarius: The Moon in your sign encourages adventure early in the day, but as the energy transitions, focus on setting practical steps for the future.

Capricorn: The Moon enters your sign later today, enhancing your natural discipline and focus. Use this energy to work on long-term projects and set achievable goals.

Aquarius: Early in the day, adventure and creativity flow easily, but later, focus on practical solutions and long-term goals.

Pisces: The day begins with optimism and exploration, but later, focus on grounding your emotional well-being and making steady progress on personal and professional goals.

For those born on October 31: Born under the transition from Sagittarius to Capricorn, these individuals are both adventurous and disciplined. In 2025, they'll thrive by balancing their curiosity and love for exploration with their focus on long-term success and productivity.

Daily Insights: The Moon in Capricorn brings a focus on discipline, productivity, and long-term planning. It's a great day for tackling ambitious projects, organizing your thoughts, and making steady progress toward your goals. With Venus in Virgo, attention to detail is enhanced, making it a good time for refining your plans.

Aries: Discipline and focus are key today. Use this energy to make progress on your long-term goals and stay grounded in your ambitions.

Taurus: The Moon in Capricorn amplifies your sense of stability and practicality. Use this energy to focus on building your future and refining your plans.

Gemini: It's a day for grounding your thoughts and focusing on long-term projects. Use your energy to make steady progress and refine your ideas.

Cancer: Emotional reflection and stability are key today. Use this energy to focus on long-term goals and creating emotional security in your personal life.

Leo: Leadership and discipline are emphasized today. Use this energy to focus on practical matters and long-term success.

Virgo: The Moon in Capricorn enhances your natural attention to detail. Use this energy to refine your plans and make steady progress on your goals.

Libra: Relationships feel stable today. Focus on creating harmony in your personal connections while staying productive with your long-term goals.

Scorpio: Your determination is strong today. Use this energy to focus on practical matters and long-term planning to achieve your goals.

Sagittarius: Adventure takes a backseat today as you focus on discipline and productivity. Use this energy to make steady progress on your long-term goals.

Capricorn: The Moon in your sign amplifies your discipline and determination. Use this energy to tackle ambitious projects and make significant progress.

Aquarius: Creativity is balanced with practicality today. Use this energy to refine your ideas and focus on long-term success.

Pisces: Emotional stability and practicality are important today. Use this energy to focus on grounding your emotions and working toward your long-term goals.

For those born on November 1: Born under the Moon in Capricorn, these individuals are disciplined, practical, and focused on long-term success. In 2025, they'll thrive by setting clear goals and making steady progress toward achieving them, using their disciplined nature to stay focused on their ambitions.

Daily Insights: The Moon in Capricorn continues to emphasize productivity and discipline, but as it transitions into Aquarius later in the day, the focus shifts toward creativity, innovation, and social connections. It's a day for balancing hard work with creative exploration and collaboration.

Aries: Use the morning for disciplined work, but as the Moon moves into Aquarius, embrace your creativity and explore new ideas.

Taurus: The day starts with a focus on productivity, but later, shift your attention to social interactions and creative thinking.

Gemini: Productivity is high early in the day, but by evening, you'll feel more inclined to engage in conversations and explore new possibilities.

Cancer: Start the day with practical goals, but as the Moon enters Aquarius, focus on creativity and exploring new opportunities.

Leo: The morning is perfect for focusing on your goals, but as the day progresses, embrace new ways of thinking and collaborating with others.

Virgo: Use the early part of the day for productivity, but later, shift your focus to creative problem-solving and engaging with others.

Libra: Relationships feel stable early in the day, but later, focus on innovative solutions and exploring new perspectives in your connections.

Scorpio: Determination guides you early in the day, but as the energy shifts, focus on expanding your mind and embracing creative ideas.

Sagittarius: The day starts with a focus on responsibilities, but later, you'll feel more curious and eager to explore new possibilities.

Capricorn: The Moon in your sign enhances your focus on discipline, but as it moves into Aquarius, explore creative ideas and social opportunities.

Aquarius: The evening brings a burst of creativity and innovation. Use this time to explore new projects and connect with others.

Pisces: Emotional reflection is key early in the day, but as the Moon enters Aquarius, focus on socializing and expressing your creativity.

For those born on November 2: Born under the transition from Capricorn to Aquarius, these individuals are both disciplined and creative. In 2025, they'll thrive by balancing practicality with innovation, focusing on both long-term goals and exploring new possibilities.

Daily Insights: The Moon in Aquarius brings a focus on creativity, innovation, and social connections. It's a great day for engaging with others, exploring new ideas, and embracing your individuality. With Venus in Libra, relationships feel harmonious, making it a perfect time for meaningful conversations and collaborations.

Aries: Your creativity shines today. Use this energy to explore new ideas and connect with others through meaningful collaborations.

Taurus: It's a day for balancing practicality with creativity. Use your determination to bring innovative ideas into reality.

Gemini: Social interactions are stimulating today. Engage in conversations that inspire new perspectives and broaden your horizons.

Cancer: Creativity and innovation are calling you today. Use this energy to explore new ways of expressing yourself and connecting with others.

Leo: Leadership and creativity go hand in hand today. Use your confidence to take the lead in innovative projects and inspire others with your bold ideas.

Virgo: It's a great day for exploring creative solutions. Use your analytical skills to approach challenges in innovative ways.

Libra: Relationships are dynamic and exciting today. Focus on connecting with others in unconventional ways and exploring new perspectives in your personal connections.

Scorpio: Your passion for personal growth is strong today. Use this energy to explore new ideas and engage in meaningful conversations.

Sagittarius: Adventure and creativity are calling you today. Focus on expanding your horizons and embracing new opportunities.

Capricorn: While discipline is important, today encourages you to explore new ideas and engage in creative thinking.

Aquarius: With the Moon in your sign, your creativity and individuality are amplified. Use this energy to pursue innovative ideas and connect with others.

Pisces: Your intuition is strong today. Use this energy to explore creative projects and connect with others in meaningful ways.

For those born on November 3: Born under the Moon in Aquarius, these individuals are creative, innovative, and socially connected. In 2025, they'll thrive by embracing their individuality, exploring new ideas, and focusing on personal growth through social connections and creative expression.

Daily Insights: The Moon in Aquarius continues to bring creativity and innovation, but as it transitions into Pisces later in the day, the focus shifts toward emotional reflection, intuition, and empathy. It's a day for balancing intellectual exploration with emotional depth.

Aries: Start the day with innovative ideas and social connections, but as the Moon enters Pisces, shift your focus to emotional reflection and nurturing relationships.

Taurus: The morning is great for exploring creative solutions, but later, focus on emotional healing and connecting with loved ones on a deeper level.

Gemini: Your mind is active early in the day, but as the Moon enters Pisces, focus on balancing your intellectual pursuits with emotional reflection.

Cancer: Emotional intuition is heightened as the day progresses. Use the morning for socializing, but later, focus on self-care and nurturing close relationships.

Leo: Creativity shines early in the day, but as the energy shifts, focus on your emotional well-being and connecting with those who matter most.

Virgo: Productivity is high in the morning, but by evening, you'll feel more inclined to explore your emotions and focus on personal healing.

Libra: Relationships feel dynamic early in the day, but as the Moon enters Pisces, focus on deepening your emotional connections and finding inner balance.

Scorpio: Use the morning for exploring new ideas, but later, focus on emotional growth and reflection. Your intuition is especially strong today.

Sagittarius: The day starts with excitement and creativity, but later, you'll feel more inclined to focus on emotional healing and connecting with loved ones.

Capricorn: Early productivity gives way to emotional reflection as the day progresses. Focus on grounding yourself and nurturing your relationships.

Aquarius: The Moon in your sign brings out your creativity, but as the energy shifts, focus on emotional introspection and personal growth.

Pisces: The Moon enters your sign later today, amplifying your intuition and emotional sensitivity. Use this energy to focus on self-care and emotional healing.

For those born on November 4: Born under the transition from Aquarius to Pisces, these individuals are both creative and emotionally intuitive. In 2025, they'll thrive by balancing intellectual exploration with emotional reflection, focusing on both personal growth and deepening relationships.

November 5, 2025

Daily Insights: The Moon in Pisces brings a focus on emotional reflection, intuition, and creativity. It's a great day for engaging in artistic projects, connecting with loved ones on a deeper level, and exploring your inner world. With Mercury in Gemini, communication remains lively, making it a good day for expressing your emotions through words.

Aries: Your intuition is strong today. Use this energy to focus on emotional reflection and nurture your relationships with empathy and understanding.

Taurus: It's a great day for combining creativity with practicality. Focus on expressing your emotions through artistic projects or clear communication.

Gemini: Emotional reflection is key today. Use this energy to connect with your inner self and engage in meaningful conversations with loved ones.

Cancer: The Moon in Pisces enhances your emotional intuition. Use this energy to focus on self-care and strengthening your personal relationships.

Leo: While you're often focused on action, today encourages emotional reflection. Use this time to explore your feelings and deepen your connections.

Virgo: Balance your practical nature with emotional reflection today. Use this energy to focus on your inner world and nurture your relationships.

Libra: Relationships feel emotionally deep today. Focus on connecting with loved ones and creating harmony in your emotional connections.

Scorpio: Your emotional intensity is strong today. Use this energy for self-reflection and focus on healing and strengthening your emotional bonds.

Sagittarius: It's a day for emotional introspection. Use this energy to explore your inner world and strengthen your emotional connections with loved ones.

Capricorn: While you're often focused on discipline, today encourages emotional reflection. Use this time to connect with your feelings and focus on personal healing.

Aquarius: While your mind is often focused on innovation, today encourages emotional growth. Use this energy to nurture your close relationships and engage in self-care.

Pisces: The Moon in your sign amplifies your emotional sensitivity and intuition. Use this energy for personal healing and deepening your emotional connections with others.

For those born on November 5: Born under the Moon in Pisces, these individuals are emotionally intuitive, creative, and compassionate. In 2025, they'll thrive by focusing on their emotional well-being, nurturing relationships, and expressing their creativity through meaningful projects.

Daily Insights: The Moon in Pisces continues to emphasize emotional reflection and creativity, but as it transitions into Aries later in the day, the focus shifts toward action, confidence, and bold decisions. It's a day for balancing emotional reflection with taking bold steps toward your goals.

Aries: Start the day with emotional reflection, but as the Moon enters your sign, focus on taking bold actions and pursuing your personal goals with confidence.

Taurus: The morning is perfect for emotional introspection, but as the energy shifts, focus on taking practical steps toward your long-term goals.

Gemini: Emotional reflection is key early in the day, but as the energy shifts, focus on engaging with others and taking action on your ideas.

Cancer: The morning is ideal for nurturing your emotional well-being, but as the Moon moves into Aries, embrace new challenges and step out of your comfort zone.

Leo: Emotional reflection is important early in the day, but as the Moon enters Aries, your confidence will rise, making it a great time to take bold actions.

Virgo: Use the early part of the day for emotional clarity, but later, shift your focus to organizing your thoughts and taking action on your plans.

Libra: Relationships feel emotionally deep in the morning, but as the energy shifts, focus on communicating openly and taking action to strengthen your connections.

Scorpio: Emotional depth is important early in the day, but as the Moon moves into Aries, focus on taking bold steps toward personal growth and transformation.

Sagittarius: Start the day with emotional introspection, but later, shift your focus to adventure and exploring new opportunities with confidence.

Capricorn: Emotional reflection is key early in the day, but as the Moon enters Aries, focus on taking practical steps toward your long-term goals.

Aquarius: The morning is perfect for emotional reflection, but as the energy shifts, focus on pursuing new ideas and taking bold actions with confidence.

Pisces: The Moon in your sign enhances your emotional intuition early in the day, but as the energy shifts, focus on taking decisive actions toward your ambitions.

For those born on November 6: Born under the transition from Pisces to Aries, these individuals are emotionally intuitive and action-oriented. In 2025, they'll thrive by balancing emotional reflection with taking bold steps toward their personal goals and ambitions.

November 7, 2025

Daily Insights: The Moon in Aries brings a surge of energy, confidence, and motivation. It's a great day for taking bold steps, embracing new opportunities, and focusing on personal goals. With Mercury in Leo, communication is bold and creative, making it a perfect time for expressing your ideas with confidence.

Aries: Your confidence and motivation are high today. Use this energy to push forward on your personal goals and take bold actions with enthusiasm.

Taurus: It's a day for balancing bold actions with practicality. Use your grounded nature to take steady steps toward your long-term goals.

Gemini: Communication and action are your strengths today. Use this energy to engage in meaningful conversations and explore new ideas.

Cancer: Confidence and emotional reflection are key today. Use this energy to focus on personal growth and take bold steps toward your ambitions.

Leo: Leadership and action are highlighted today. Use your natural confidence to take charge of projects and inspire those around you.

Virgo: Productivity is high today. Use your disciplined nature to focus on practical tasks and take bold actions toward your goals.

Libra: Relationships feel dynamic and exciting today. Focus on open communication and take action to strengthen your personal connections.

Scorpio: Your determination is strong today. Use this energy to take decisive steps toward achieving your long-term goals.

Sagittarius: Adventure and excitement are calling you today. Use your enthusiasm to explore new opportunities and take bold steps toward your dreams.

Capricorn: Discipline and focus guide you today. Use this energy to make steady progress on your long-term projects and goals.

Aquarius: Your creativity and innovative thinking shine today. Use this energy to explore new ideas and take bold actions toward your personal goals.

Pisces: It's a day for taking action on your personal ambitions. Use your intuition to guide you as you embrace new opportunities with confidence.

For those born on November 7: Born under the Moon in Aries, these individuals are confident, action-oriented, and driven. In 2025, they'll thrive by taking bold steps toward their personal goals and embracing new opportunities with enthusiasm.

Daily Insights: The Moon in Aries continues to bring energy, motivation, and a focus on personal goals. It's a great day for taking decisive actions, embracing challenges, and pursuing your ambitions. With Mars in Capricorn, there's an added boost of discipline and determination, making it a powerful day for working on long-term projects.

Aries: Your confidence and motivation are high today. Use this energy to push forward on your personal goals and take bold actions with confidence.

Taurus: It's a day for balancing bold actions with practicality. Use your grounded nature to take steady steps toward your long-term goals.

Gemini: Communication and action are your strengths today. Use this energy to engage in meaningful conversations and explore new ideas.

Cancer: Confidence and emotional reflection are key today. Use this energy to focus on personal growth and take bold steps toward your ambitions.

Leo: Leadership and action are highlighted today. Use your natural confidence to take charge of projects and inspire those around you.

Virgo: Productivity is high today. Use your disciplined nature to focus on practical tasks and take bold actions toward your goals.

Libra: Relationships feel dynamic and exciting today. Focus on open communication and take action to strengthen your personal connections.

Scorpio: Your determination is strong today. Use this energy to take decisive steps toward achieving your long-term goals.

Sagittarius: Adventure and excitement are calling you today. Use your enthusiasm to explore new opportunities and take bold steps toward your dreams.

Capricorn: Discipline and focus guide you today. Use this energy to make steady progress on your long-term projects and goals.

Aquarius: Your creativity and innovative thinking shine today. Use this energy to explore new ideas and take bold actions toward your personal goals.

Pisces: It's a day for taking action on your personal ambitions. Use your intuition to guide you as you embrace new opportunities with confidence.

For those born on November 8: Born under the Moon in Aries, these individuals are confident, action-oriented, and focused on achieving their goals. In 2025, they'll thrive by embracing challenges, taking bold actions, and pursuing their ambitions with determination.

Daily Insights: The Moon in Aries continues to emphasize confidence, motivation, and action, but as it transitions into Taurus later in the day, the focus shifts toward stability, practicality, and long-term planning. It's a day for balancing bold actions with careful consideration of your long-term goals.

Aries: The day begins with high energy and motivation, but as the Moon moves into Taurus, focus on grounding yourself and setting practical goals for the future.

Taurus: The Moon enters your sign later today, bringing a sense of stability and focus on practical matters. Use this energy to work steadily toward your long-term goals.

Gemini: The day starts with action-oriented energy, but later, focus on slowing down and working on practical steps toward your long-term ambitions.

Cancer: Start the day with bold actions, but as the energy shifts, focus on grounding your emotions and planning for future stability.

Leo: Confidence is high early in the day, but as the Moon enters Taurus, shift your focus to working methodically toward your long-term goals.

Virgo: The morning is ideal for taking bold steps, but later in the day, shift your attention to organizing your long-term plans and ensuring stability.

Libra: Relationships feel dynamic early in the day, but later, focus on creating harmony and stability in your connections.

Scorpio: Your determination is strong in the morning, but as the energy shifts, focus on grounding yourself and working steadily toward your goals.

Sagittarius: Adventure and excitement guide you in the morning, but as the Moon enters Taurus, focus on setting realistic goals and making steady progress.

Capricorn: Discipline and focus guide you in the morning, but by evening, focus on practical steps that ensure long-term success.

Aquarius: Creativity and bold actions are important early in the day, but later, focus on grounding your innovative ideas into practical steps.

Pisces: Emotional reflection is key early in the day, but as the energy shifts, focus on grounding yourself and ensuring emotional stability in your relationships.

For those born on November 9: Born under the transition from Aries to Taurus, these individuals are confident yet practical. In 2025, they'll thrive by balancing bold actions with careful long-term planning, focusing on both creativity and stability to achieve their goals.

Daily Insights: The Moon in Taurus emphasizes stability, practicality, and long-term planning. It's a great day for working methodically on your goals, taking slow and steady steps toward success. With Mars in Capricorn, there's a boost of discipline and determination, making it an ideal time for productivity and focus.

Aries: Focus on grounding yourself today. Use your energy to set practical goals and work methodically toward your long-term ambitions.

Taurus: The Moon in your sign amplifies your natural sense of stability. Use this energy to work on practical matters and ensure steady progress toward your goals.

Gemini: It's a day for focusing on long-term planning. Use your intellectual curiosity to refine your goals and take practical steps to move forward.

Cancer: Stability is key today. Focus on grounding your emotions and working toward creating emotional security in your life.

Leo: While creativity is important, today encourages you to focus on practical goals. Use your leadership skills to guide yourself and others toward success.

Virgo: It's a productive day for focusing on practical matters. Use your disciplined nature to ensure that you're making steady progress on your goals.

Libra: Relationships feel stable today. Focus on nurturing your personal connections and working toward harmony in your relationships.

Scorpio: Your determination is strong today. Use this energy to focus on long-term goals and ensure that you're making practical decisions for your future.

Sagittarius: Adventure takes a backseat today as you focus on practical tasks. Use this energy to make steady progress on your long-term goals.

Capricorn: Discipline and focus are your strengths today. Use this energy to make significant progress on your long-term projects.

Aquarius: Creativity and innovation are important, but today encourages you to ground your ideas in practical reality and focus on long-term goals.

Pisces: Emotional stability is key today. Use this energy to ground yourself and work steadily toward creating emotional and practical security in your life.

For those born on November 10: Born under the Moon in Taurus, these individuals are practical, grounded, and focused on long-term success. In 2025, they'll thrive by setting clear goals and making steady progress, using their disciplined nature to stay focused on achieving their ambitions.

Daily Insights: The Moon in Taurus continues to emphasize stability and practicality, but as it transitions into Gemini later in the day, the focus shifts toward communication, curiosity, and learning. It's a day for balancing practical work with intellectual exploration and social interactions.

Aries: Start the day by grounding yourself in practical tasks, but as the Moon enters Gemini, shift your focus to exploring new ideas and communicating with others.

Taurus: The morning is perfect for stability and productivity, but later, engage in social interactions and explore intellectual pursuits.

Gemini: The Moon enters your sign later today, bringing a burst of energy and curiosity. It's a great time to explore new ideas and engage in conversations.

Cancer: The day begins with a focus on grounding your emotions, but later, focus on connecting with others and exploring new perspectives.

Leo: Use the morning for practical work, but as the energy shifts, engage with others and share your creative ideas.

Virgo: Productivity is high early in the day, but later, focus on engaging in intellectual exploration and refining your long-term plans.

Libra: Relationships feel stable early in the day, but as the Moon moves into Gemini, focus on open communication and exploring new perspectives.

Scorpio: The day begins with determination and focus, but later, shift your attention to social interactions and new opportunities for learning.

Sagittarius: The morning is ideal for practical tasks, but later, embrace intellectual exploration and engage in new ideas.

Capricorn: Discipline and focus guide you early in the day, but by evening, shift your attention to communication and exploring new opportunities.

Aquarius: The morning is ideal for grounding your creative ideas, but as the Moon enters Gemini, explore new possibilities and engage in stimulating conversations.

Pisces: Emotional reflection is important early in the day, but later, focus on socializing and exploring new ideas with an open mind.

For those born on November 11: Born under the transition from Taurus to Gemini, these individuals are both practical and curious. In 2025, they'll thrive by balancing their disciplined approach with intellectual exploration, focusing on both long-term goals and new learning opportunities.

Daily Insights: The Moon in Gemini emphasizes communication, learning, and curiosity. It's a great day for engaging in conversations, exploring new ideas, and connecting with others. With Mercury in Virgo, communication remains clear and practical, making it an ideal time for sharing ideas confidently.

Aries: Your curiosity is strong today. Use this energy to engage in meaningful conversations and explore new ideas with confidence.

Taurus: It's a day for balancing practicality with intellectual exploration. Use your grounded nature to communicate your thoughts clearly and explore new perspectives.

Gemini: The Moon in your sign amplifies your communication skills. Use this energy to connect with others, share your ideas, and explore new possibilities.

Cancer: It's a day for focusing on learning and intellectual growth. Use this energy to connect with your inner self and engage in meaningful conversations.

Leo: Leadership and communication are highlighted today. Use your confidence to inspire others and share your creative ideas with enthusiasm.

Virgo: Your analytical skills are sharp today. Use this energy to focus on problem-solving and refining your ideas.

Libra: Relationships feel intellectually stimulating today. Focus on engaging in conversations that broaden your perspective and deepen your connections.

Scorpio: Your emotional depth is strong today. Use this energy to explore new ideas that challenge your thinking and deepen your understanding.

Sagittarius: Adventure and learning go hand in hand today. Use your curiosity to explore new opportunities and engage in conversations that inspire you.

Capricorn: It's a day for balancing discipline with intellectual exploration. Use this energy to refine your long-term goals and engage in thoughtful discussions.

Aquarius: Your creativity and innovative thinking shine today. Use this energy to explore new ideas and engage in collaborative conversations.

Pisces: It's a day for intellectual exploration and emotional reflection. Use this energy to connect with others in meaningful ways and share your ideas.

For those born on November 12: Born under the Moon in Gemini, these individuals are curious, communicative, and eager to explore new ideas. In 2025, they'll thrive by engaging in meaningful conversations, learning new things, and using their sharp minds to connect with others.

Daily Insights: The Moon in Gemini continues to emphasize communication and learning, but as it transitions into Cancer later in the day, the focus shifts toward emotional well-being, nurturing relationships, and self-care. It's a day for balancing intellectual exploration with emotional connection.

Aries: The day begins with curiosity and communication, but as the Moon enters Cancer, shift your focus to nurturing your emotional connections and relationships.

Taurus: Use the morning to explore new ideas, but later, focus on creating emotional stability in your personal life.

Gemini: Communication is highlighted early in the day, but as the energy shifts, focus on strengthening your emotional connections and nurturing your relationships.

Cancer: The Moon enters your sign later today, enhancing your emotional intuition. Use this energy to focus on self-care and deepening your emotional connections with loved ones.

Leo: The morning is ideal for communicating your ideas, but as the Moon enters Cancer, shift your focus to emotional balance and nurturing your relationships.

Virgo: Productivity is high early in the day, but by evening, focus on emotional reflection and nurturing your personal well-being.

Libra: Relationships are intellectually stimulating in the morning, but later, focus on creating harmony and emotional connection in your personal life.

Scorpio: Curiosity drives you early in the day, but as the energy shifts, focus on emotional healing and strengthening your closest relationships.

Sagittarius: Start the day with excitement for learning and exploring new ideas, but by evening, prioritize emotional reflection and personal growth.

Capricorn: Use the morning for practical and intellectual tasks, but as the day progresses, focus on nurturing your emotional well-being and close relationships.

Aquarius: Creativity and communication shine early in the day, but as the Moon moves into Cancer, focus on emotional self-care and nurturing your connections.

Pisces: The day begins with intellectual curiosity, but as the energy shifts, focus on emotional healing and deepening your close relationships.

For those born on November 13: Born under the transition from Gemini to Cancer, these individuals are both intellectually curious and emotionally intuitive. In 2025, they'll thrive by balancing intellectual exploration with nurturing their emotional well-being and relationships.

Daily Insights: The Moon in Cancer emphasizes emotional reflection, nurturing relationships, and self-care. It's a great day for focusing on emotional well-being and connecting with loved ones. With Venus in Virgo, there's a blend of emotional depth and practicality, making it a great time for balancing your emotions with your responsibilities.

Aries: Emotional balance is key today. Use this energy to nurture your relationships while staying grounded in your personal goals.

Taurus: Focus on emotional well-being today. Use your grounded nature to create stability in your personal life and relationships.

Gemini: Communication is important, but today also encourages you to focus on nurturing your emotional connections with loved ones.

Cancer: The Moon in your sign enhances your emotional intuition. Take time for self-care and focus on strengthening your relationships with those close to you.

Leo: While your leadership is important, today encourages emotional reflection. Use this time to nurture your inner self and focus on your emotional well-being.

Virgo: Emotional clarity and practical focus go hand in hand today. Use this energy to nurture your personal life while staying organized with your responsibilities.

Libra: Relationships feel emotionally deep today. Focus on creating harmony in your personal connections while also balancing your personal responsibilities.

Scorpio: Your emotional depth is strong today. Use this energy to focus on personal healing and deepening your relationships with those who matter most.

Sagittarius: It's a day for emotional introspection. Use this energy to connect with your inner self and focus on emotional stability in your relationships.

Capricorn: Emotional reflection is key today. Use this energy to ground yourself and focus on balancing your personal goals with emotional well-being.

Aquarius: While creativity is important, today encourages emotional introspection. Use this energy to connect with loved ones and focus on self-care.

Pisces: The Moon in Cancer heightens your emotional sensitivity today. Use this energy to focus on healing, nurturing your relationships, and self-care.

For those born on November 14: Born under the Moon in Cancer, these individuals are emotionally intuitive, nurturing, and deeply connected to their home and family. In 2025, they'll thrive by focusing on emotional well-being, nurturing relationships, and creating emotional stability in their lives.

Daily Insights: The Moon in Cancer continues to highlight emotional well-being, but as it transitions into Leo later in the day, the focus shifts toward confidence, creativity, and self-expression. It's a day for balancing emotional reflection with taking bold steps toward your personal goals.

Aries: Start the day with emotional reflection, but as the Moon moves into Leo, shift your focus to taking bold steps toward your personal ambitions.

Taurus: The day begins with emotional reflection, but as the Moon moves into Leo, focus on expressing your creativity and personal empowerment.

Gemini: Emotional connections are key early in the day, but as the energy shifts, focus on communicating your ideas with confidence.

Cancer: The morning is perfect for nurturing your emotional well-being, but as the Moon moves into Leo, embrace confidence and pursue your goals with enthusiasm.

Leo: The Moon enters your sign later today, enhancing your natural confidence and creativity. Use this energy to take bold actions and lead with enthusiasm.

Virgo: The day starts with emotional reflection, but later, shift your focus to creativity and finding new approaches to your long-term goals.

Libra: Relationships feel emotionally deep early in the day, but as the energy shifts, focus on creating balance between your emotional connections and personal growth.

Scorpio: Emotional depth is important in the morning, but as the Moon enters Leo, focus on personal transformation and expressing your true self.

Sagittarius: Start the day with emotional introspection, but later, shift your focus to exploring new adventures and expressing your creative side.

Capricorn: The morning is perfect for grounding yourself emotionally, but as the energy shifts, focus on stepping into leadership roles and pursuing your ambitions.

Aquarius: Emotional reflection is key early in the day, but later, embrace new ideas and step into the spotlight with confidence.

Pisces: Emotional sensitivity is high early in the day, but as the Moon enters Leo, focus on personal empowerment and expressing yourself with confidence.

For those born on November 15: Born under the transition from Cancer to Leo, these individuals are emotionally intuitive and confident. In 2025, they'll thrive by balancing their emotional well-being with bold actions toward their personal goals, stepping into leadership roles and expressing their creativity.

Daily Insights: The Moon in Leo brings a surge of confidence, creativity, and leadership. It's a great day for expressing yourself, taking bold actions, and pursuing your passions. With Mars in Capricorn, there's a blend of discipline and ambition, making it an ideal time for working toward your goals with confidence.

Aries: Your confidence is high today. Use this energy to pursue your personal goals and take bold actions with enthusiasm.

Taurus: Creativity flows easily today. Focus on expressing your unique ideas and working toward your long-term goals with determination.

Gemini: Communication and self-expression are your strengths today. Use this energy to connect with others and share your innovative ideas.

Cancer: The Moon in Leo encourages you to step out of your comfort zone and pursue your personal goals with confidence and creativity.

Leo: The Moon in your sign amplifies your leadership and creativity. Use this energy to take bold steps toward your passions and inspire others.

Virgo: Balance creativity with practicality today. Use your disciplined nature to focus on long-term goals while expressing your unique talents.

Libra: Relationships feel dynamic and exciting today. Focus on creative ways to connect with loved ones and embrace your individuality.

Scorpio: Your passion is strong today. Use this energy to pursue personal goals with intensity and determination.

Sagittarius: Adventure and creativity are calling you today. Use this energy to explore new opportunities and express yourself freely.

Capricorn: Leadership and discipline come naturally today. Use this energy to focus on personal projects and inspire those around you.

Aquarius: Your creativity shines today. Use this energy to pursue innovative ideas and connect with others through meaningful collaborations.

Pisces: It's a day for self-expression and personal growth. Use your creativity to focus on your goals and embrace new opportunities with confidence.

For those born on November 16: Born under the Moon in Leo, these individuals are charismatic, creative, and confident. In 2025, they'll thrive by stepping into leadership roles, embracing their unique talents, and pursuing their passions with determination.

Daily Insights: The Moon in Leo continues to highlight confidence and creativity, but as it transitions into Virgo later in the day, the focus shifts toward practicality, organization, and attention to detail. It's a day for balancing bold ideas with disciplined actions to achieve long-term success.

Aries: Start the day with bold actions, but as the Moon moves into Virgo, shift your focus to organizing your plans and refining your goals.

Taurus: The day begins with creative expression, but later, focus on practical steps toward your long-term goals.

Gemini: Use the morning for creative pursuits and communication, but as the energy shifts, focus on organizing your ideas and refining your plans.

Cancer: Confidence and creativity guide you early in the day, but later, shift your focus to emotional balance and practical tasks.

Leo: The Moon in your sign enhances your leadership, but as it moves into Virgo, focus on grounding your energy and organizing your long-term goals.

Virgo: The Moon enters your sign later today, amplifying your attention to detail and practical nature. Use this energy to refine your plans and focus on productivity.

Libra: The morning is great for engaging in creative conversations, but later, focus on balancing your personal goals with practical responsibilities.

Scorpio: Start the day by pursuing your passions, but as the Moon moves into Virgo, shift your focus to refining your long-term plans and staying disciplined.

Sagittarius: The day starts with excitement and creativity, but later, shift your focus to practical tasks and responsibilities.

Capricorn: Discipline and leadership guide you in the morning, but later, shift your attention to organizing your goals and refining your long-term plans.

Aquarius: The morning is ideal for creative expression, but as the Moon moves into Virgo, focus on refining your ideas and ensuring they are practical.

Pisces: Start the day with emotional reflection and creativity, but later, focus on organizing your personal life and making practical decisions.

For those born on November 17: Born under the transition from Leo to Virgo, these individuals are both creative and practical. In 2025, they'll thrive by balancing bold ideas with disciplined actions, focusing on both creativity and productivity to achieve their goals.

Daily Insights: The Moon in Virgo emphasizes productivity, organization, and attention to detail. It's a great day for focusing on practical matters, refining your plans, and making steady progress toward your long-term goals. With Mercury in Sagittarius, communication remains lively, making it a perfect day for blending creativity with discipline.

Aries: Stay focused on your goals today. Use your energy to organize your thoughts and make steady progress toward your long-term ambitions.

Taurus: It's a day for practical achievements. Use your grounded nature to refine your ideas and work steadily on long-term projects.

Gemini: Your analytical skills are strong today. Use this energy to focus on problem-solving and refining your ideas.

Cancer: Balance emotional reflection with practical tasks today. Focus on organizing your personal life and creating emotional stability.

Leo: After a period of creativity, today encourages you to focus on practical matters. Use your energy to refine your long-term plans.

Virgo: The Moon in your sign enhances your natural strengths. Use this energy to focus on productivity and tackle tasks that require precision.

Libra: Relationships feel stable today. Focus on balancing your personal goals with your relationships while staying productive.

Scorpio: Your determination is strong today. Use this energy to focus on long-term goals and ensure you're making practical decisions for the future.

Sagittarius: Practical matters take precedence today. Use this energy to focus on your responsibilities and stay disciplined in achieving your goals.

Capricorn: Discipline and focus are your strengths today. Use this energy to make significant progress on your long-term projects and goals.

Aquarius: While creativity is important, today encourages you to focus on practical solutions and refining your innovative ideas.

Pisces: Emotional reflection is balanced with practicality today. Use this energy to organize your life and make steady progress toward your goals.

For those born on November 18: Born under the Moon in Virgo, these individuals are practical, detail-oriented, and highly productive. In 2025, they'll thrive by refining their plans, staying disciplined, and making steady progress toward their long-term goals.

November 19, 2025

Daily Insights: The Moon in Virgo continues to emphasize productivity, but as it transitions into Libra later in the day, the focus shifts toward balance, relationships, and harmony. It's a day for balancing work with social interactions and ensuring that all areas of your life are in equilibrium.

Aries: The morning is perfect for productivity, but as the Moon moves into Libra, focus on balancing your work with your personal relationships.

Taurus: Start the day with practical tasks, but later, shift your focus to nurturing relationships and creating balance in your life.

Gemini: The day begins with a focus on organization, but as the energy shifts, engage in meaningful conversations and strengthen your relationships.

Cancer: The morning is ideal for organizing your life, but as the Moon enters Libra, focus on nurturing your relationships and finding harmony.

Leo: The day starts with practical tasks, but later, focus on balancing your creative pursuits with your relationships.

Virgo: The Moon in your sign enhances your productivity early in the day, but by evening, focus on maintaining balance in your personal life.

Libra: The day starts with productivity, but as the Moon enters your sign, focus on nurturing relationships and finding balance in all areas of life.

Scorpio: It's a day for balancing productivity with emotional depth. Use the morning for practical tasks, but later, focus on nurturing your relationships.

Sagittarius: Responsibilities guide you in the morning, but by evening, focus on social interactions and bringing balance to your personal life.

Capricorn: Discipline and focus guide you in the morning, but later, shift your attention to maintaining harmony in your relationships.

Aquarius: The morning is perfect for creativity and productivity, but as the Moon moves into Libra, focus on balancing your work and social life.

Pisces: Emotional reflection is key early in the day, but as the Moon enters Libra, focus on nurturing relationships and finding inner balance.

For those born on November 19: Born under the transition from Virgo to Libra, these individuals are both productive and focused on balance. In 2025, they'll thrive by balancing their attention to detail with creating harmonious relationships and personal connections.

November 20, 2025

Daily Insights: The Moon in Libra brings a focus on balance, relationships, and harmony. It's a great day for resolving conflicts, building stronger connections, and bringing equilibrium to all areas of your life. With Venus in Leo, relationships feel passionate, making it an ideal time for romantic and creative pursuits.

Aries: Focus on bringing balance to your relationships today. Use this energy to resolve conflicts and create harmony in your personal life.

Taurus: Balance is key today. Focus on finding harmony between your practical responsibilities and your personal relationships.

Gemini: Relationships take center stage today. Focus on communicating clearly and building harmony in your personal interactions.

Cancer: It's a day for balancing your emotional needs with your relationships. Use this energy to create emotional stability and strengthen connections.

Leo: While your confidence is high, today encourages you to focus on your relationships and creating balance in your personal life.

Virgo: Balance productivity with relationships today. Use your disciplined nature to focus on both your work goals and your personal connections.

Libra: The Moon in your sign highlights balance and harmony. Use this energy to create peace in your relationships and personal life.

Scorpio: Relationships feel emotionally deep today. Use this energy to create emotional harmony and balance in your life.

Sagittarius: Social interactions are favored today. Use your natural charm to connect with others and focus on creating harmony in your relationships.

Capricorn: It's a day for balancing your responsibilities with your relationships. Focus on finding harmony between your work and personal life.

Aquarius: Creativity and innovation are your strengths today. Use this energy to find balance in your social interactions and personal relationships.

Pisces: Emotional balance is important today. Use this energy to focus on creating stability in your relationships and your personal life.

For those born on November 20: Born under the Moon in Libra, these individuals are focused on balance, harmony, and relationships. In 2025, they'll thrive by creating equilibrium in their personal and professional lives while working toward their goals with patience and determination.

Daily Insights: The Moon in Libra continues to emphasize balance and harmony, but as it transitions into Scorpio later in the day, the focus shifts toward emotional depth, transformation, and intense connections. It's a day for balancing social interactions with deep emotional reflection.

Aries: Start the day by focusing on relationships and creating harmony, but as the Moon moves into Scorpio, dive deeper into your emotions and connections.

Taurus: The morning is perfect for nurturing relationships and creating balance, but as the energy shifts, focus on exploring emotional depths and personal transformation.

Gemini: Relationships are in focus early in the day, but later, shift toward introspection and exploring your emotional world.

Cancer: Start the day with balance, but as the Moon moves into Scorpio, focus on emotional clarity and deepening your closest relationships.

Leo: The day begins with a focus on balance and harmony, but later, shift toward personal growth and emotional transformation.

Virgo: The morning is ideal for keeping things in balance, but as the Moon enters Scorpio, focus on self-reflection and emotional exploration.

Libra: The Moon in your sign brings focus on harmony and balance early in the day, but as it enters Scorpio, you'll feel drawn toward emotional intensity and transformation.

Scorpio: The Moon enters your sign later today, heightening your emotional sensitivity. Use this energy to focus on personal growth and strengthening emotional connections.

Sagittarius: The morning is for socializing and creating balance, but as the energy shifts, turn inward and reflect on personal emotions and connections.

Capricorn: Balance your work and relationships in the morning, but as the Moon moves into Scorpio, focus on emotional reflection and personal growth.

Aquarius: Start the day focusing on balance and relationships, but later, turn your attention to exploring emotional depth and transformation.

Pisces: Emotional reflection and stability are key today. Use the energy later in the day to strengthen emotional bonds and engage in self-reflection.

For those born on November 21: Born under the transition from Libra to Scorpio, these individuals are balanced yet emotionally intense. In 2025, they'll thrive by focusing on relationships while embracing emotional transformation and personal growth.

Daily Insights: The Moon in Scorpio brings a focus on emotional depth, introspection, and transformation. It's a powerful day for exploring your inner world, making deep connections with others, and focusing on personal growth. With Mercury in Virgo, communication remains grounded and practical, encouraging meaningful and thoughtful conversations.

Aries: Emotional reflection is key today. Use this energy to explore personal growth and deepen your connections with those around you.

Taurus: The Moon in Scorpio highlights deep emotional connections. Use this energy to focus on personal transformation and strengthening relationships.

Gemini: Today encourages emotional depth and introspection. Use this time to explore your inner world and focus on personal growth.

Cancer: Emotional intensity is strong today. Use this energy to nurture your closest relationships and focus on personal transformation.

Leo: It's a day for emotional reflection and growth. Use this energy to connect with your inner self and explore deeper emotional bonds.

Virgo: Balance practicality with emotional depth today. Focus on self-reflection and making thoughtful decisions about your personal life.

Libra: Relationships feel intense and transformative today. Use this energy to connect with loved ones on a deeper emotional level.

Scorpio: The Moon in your sign brings emotional depth and personal transformation. Use this energy to focus on self-growth and deepening your connections.

Sagittarius: Emotional reflection is important today. Use this time to explore your inner world and strengthen your emotional connections.

Capricorn: Emotional intensity guides you today. Focus on personal growth and working toward long-term goals with emotional clarity.

Aquarius: Creativity flows through emotional depth today. Use this energy to explore new possibilities and connect with others meaningfully.

Pisces: Your emotional intuition is heightened today. Use this energy to focus on healing and personal growth.

For those born on November 22: Born under the Moon in Scorpio, these individuals are emotionally intense, intuitive, and transformative. In 2025, they'll thrive by focusing on emotional growth, deep connections, and personal transformation.

Daily Insights: The Moon in Scorpio continues to bring emotional intensity, but as it transitions into Sagittarius later in the day, the energy shifts toward optimism, adventure, and exploration. It's a day for balancing deep emotional reflection with the desire to explore new opportunities and embrace personal freedom.

Aries: Start the day with emotional reflection, but as the Moon enters Sagittarius, shift your focus to new opportunities and personal freedom.

Taurus: Use the early part of the day for deep emotional work, but later, embrace the energy of adventure and explore new possibilities.

Gemini: Emotional depth is important early in the day, but as the Moon enters Sagittarius, you'll feel more inclined to engage in learning and intellectual exploration.

Cancer: Focus on nurturing emotional connections in the morning, but as the energy shifts, embrace new opportunities for personal growth.

Leo: Emotional intensity gives way to adventure and personal freedom as the Moon enters Sagittarius. Focus on expanding your horizons and pursuing your goals.

Virgo: Balance emotional introspection with new possibilities today. Use the day to reflect on personal growth and seek out new experiences.

Libra: Deep relationships are key in the morning, but later, focus on broadening your perspective and exploring new opportunities.

Scorpio: The Moon in your sign brings emotional depth early in the day, but as it moves into Sagittarius, explore new adventures and expand your world.

Sagittarius: The Moon enters your sign later today, bringing a sense of optimism and excitement. Use this energy to pursue your passions and embrace new possibilities.

Capricorn: Emotional reflection is important in the morning, but as the energy shifts, focus on expanding your goals and seeking new adventures.

Aquarius: Early in the day, emotional exploration is key, but later, embrace new ideas and focus on your personal and professional growth.

Pisces: Emotional healing and reflection are important early in the day, but later, focus on expanding your personal horizons and exploring new opportunities.

For those born on November 23: Born under the transition from Scorpio to Sagittarius, these individuals are emotionally deep yet adventurous. In 2025, they'll thrive by balancing emotional reflection with the pursuit of new experiences and personal growth.

Daily Insights: The Moon in Sagittarius emphasizes optimism, exploration, and personal growth. It's a great day for seeking new experiences, engaging in learning, and expanding your horizons. With Jupiter in Taurus, there's a sense of practicality balancing out the adventurous spirit, making it a good time for thoughtful exploration.

Aries: Adventure calls you today. Use this energy to explore new possibilities and focus on expanding your personal and professional goals.

Taurus: It's a day for balancing practicality with adventure. Use your grounded nature to explore new opportunities while staying focused on your long-term goals.

Gemini: Communication and learning are highlighted today. Use this energy to engage in stimulating conversations and explore new intellectual pursuits.

Cancer: Step out of your comfort zone today and embrace new experiences. Use this energy to focus on personal growth and adventure.

Leo: Confidence and leadership are emphasized today. Use this energy to take bold steps toward your goals and inspire those around you.

Virgo: It's a great day for learning and expanding your knowledge. Use your analytical mind to explore new ideas and gain fresh insights.

Libra: Relationships feel dynamic and exciting today. Focus on open communication and engage in meaningful conversations with loved ones.

Scorpio: After a period of emotional intensity, today encourages you to explore new experiences and focus on personal growth and adventure.

Sagittarius: The Moon in your sign enhances your sense of adventure and optimism. Use this energy to pursue your passions and embrace new possibilities.

Capricorn: While discipline is important, today encourages you to explore new ideas and broaden your horizons with an open mind.

Aquarius: Creativity and innovation are your strengths today. Use this energy to explore new possibilities and engage in collaborative projects.

Pisces: It's a day for personal growth and exploration. Use your intuition to guide you as you embrace new opportunities and expand your horizons.

For those born on November 24: Born under the Moon in Sagittarius, these individuals are adventurous, optimistic, and eager to explore new possibilities. In 2025, they'll thrive by embracing new experiences, expanding their horizons, and pursuing personal growth with enthusiasm.

Daily Insights: The Moon in Sagittarius continues to highlight optimism and adventure, but as it transitions into Capricorn later in the day, the focus shifts toward discipline, productivity, and long-term planning. It's a day for balancing personal freedom with responsibility and setting clear goals for the future.

Aries: Start the day with a sense of adventure, but as the Moon moves into Capricorn, focus on grounding yourself and setting practical goals for the future.

Taurus: The morning is filled with excitement and exploration, but later, shift your attention to practical matters and refining your long-term plans.

Gemini: Adventure and learning are key early in the day, but as the energy shifts, focus on refining your ideas and setting clear goals.

Cancer: The morning is ideal for exploring new opportunities, but as the Moon enters Capricorn, shift your focus to creating emotional and practical stability.

Leo: Start the day with confidence and leadership, but later, focus on practical steps toward achieving your long-term ambitions.

Virgo: The day begins with curiosity and learning, but as the energy shifts, focus on organizing your thoughts and refining your long-term plans.

Libra: Relationships feel dynamic early in the day, but as the Moon moves into Capricorn, focus on building stability and harmony in your personal connections.

Scorpio: Start the day by exploring new possibilities, but later, shift your focus to long-term planning and making steady progress on your goals.

Sagittarius: The Moon in your sign encourages adventure early in the day, but as the energy transitions, focus on setting practical steps for the future.

Capricorn: The Moon enters your sign later today, enhancing your natural discipline and focus. Use this energy to work on long-term projects and set achievable goals.

Aquarius: Creativity and bold actions are important early in the day, but later, focus on grounding your innovative ideas into practical steps.

Pisces: The day begins with optimism and exploration, but later, focus on grounding your emotional well-being and making steady progress on personal and professional goals.

For those born on November 25: Born under the transition from Sagittarius to Capricorn, these individuals are both adventurous and disciplined. In 2025, they'll thrive by balancing their curiosity and love for exploration with their focus on long-term success and productivity.

Daily Insights: The Moon in Capricorn brings a focus on discipline, productivity, and long-term goals. It's an ideal day for working steadily toward your ambitions, organizing your plans, and making practical decisions. With Mars in Capricorn, there's an added sense of determination, making it a powerful time for tackling big projects.

Aries: Discipline and focus are key today. Use this energy to make steady progress on your long-term goals and ensure you stay grounded.

Taurus: It's a day for balancing practicality with your natural determination. Use this energy to refine your plans and work steadily toward your ambitions.

Gemini: Focus on long-term planning today. Use your intellectual curiosity to organize your ideas and take practical steps to bring them to fruition.

Cancer: Emotional stability and practical decision-making are important today. Use this energy to focus on creating emotional security in your personal life.

Leo: Confidence and leadership are highlighted today, but stay disciplined and grounded as you work toward your long-term goals.

Virgo: Your attention to detail is amplified today. Use this energy to focus on practical tasks and ensure that you're making steady progress on your plans.

Libra: Relationships feel stable and harmonious today. Focus on creating balance in your personal life while staying productive.

Scorpio: Determination and focus guide you today. Use this energy to make practical decisions that align with your long-term goals.

Sagittarius: Adventure takes a backseat today as you focus on discipline and productivity. Use this energy to work steadily toward your ambitions.

Capricorn: The Moon in your sign enhances your natural discipline and determination. Use this energy to tackle big projects and make significant progress.

Aquarius: Creativity is important, but today encourages you to ground your ideas in practical reality and focus on long-term success.

Pisces: Emotional stability and practicality go hand in hand today. Use this energy to focus on steady progress in both your personal and professional life.

For those born on November 26: Born under the Moon in Capricorn, these individuals are disciplined, practical, and goal-oriented. In 2025, they'll thrive by focusing on long-term success and making steady progress toward their ambitions, using their determination to overcome obstacles.

Daily Insights: The Moon in Capricorn continues to emphasize productivity and discipline, but as it transitions into Aquarius later in the day, the focus shifts toward creativity, innovation, and social connections. It's a day for balancing hard work with creative exploration and collaboration.

Aries: Use the morning for disciplined work, but as the Moon moves into Aquarius, embrace your creativity and explore new ideas.

Taurus: The day starts with a focus on productivity, but later, shift your attention to social interactions and creative thinking.

Gemini: Productivity is high early in the day, but by evening, you'll feel more inclined to engage in conversations and explore new possibilities.

Cancer: Start the day with practical goals, but as the Moon enters Aquarius, focus on creativity and exploring new opportunities.

Leo: The morning is perfect for focusing on your goals, but as the day progresses, embrace new ways of thinking and collaborating with others.

Virgo: Use the early part of the day for productivity, but later, shift your focus to creative problem-solving and engaging with others.

Libra: Relationships feel stable early in the day, but later, focus on innovative solutions and exploring new perspectives in your connections.

Scorpio: Determination guides you early in the day, but as the energy shifts, focus on expanding your mind and embracing creative ideas.

Sagittarius: The day starts with a focus on responsibilities, but later, you'll feel more curious and eager to explore new possibilities.

Capricorn: The Moon in your sign enhances your discipline, but as it moves into Aquarius, focus on exploring creative ideas and social opportunities.

Aquarius: The evening brings a burst of creativity and innovation. Use this time to explore new projects and connect with others.

Pisces: Emotional reflection is key early in the day, but as the Moon enters Aquarius, focus on socializing and expressing your creativity.

For those born on November 27: Born under the transition from Capricorn to Aquarius, these individuals are both disciplined and creative. In 2025, they'll thrive by balancing practicality with innovation, focusing on both long-term goals and exploring new ideas.

Daily Insights: The Moon in Aquarius emphasizes creativity, innovation, and social connections. It's a great day for engaging in conversations, exploring new ideas, and collaborating with others. With Venus in Leo, relationships feel dynamic, making it a perfect time for passionate connections and meaningful conversations.

Aries: Your creativity shines today. Use this energy to explore new ideas and connect with others through collaborative efforts.

Taurus: It's a day for balancing practicality with creativity. Use your grounded nature to bring innovative ideas into reality.

Gemini: Social interactions are stimulating today. Engage in conversations that inspire new perspectives and broaden your horizons.

Cancer: Creativity and innovation are calling you today. Use this energy to explore new ways of expressing yourself and connecting with others.

Leo: Leadership and creativity go hand in hand today. Use your confidence to take charge of projects and inspire others with your bold ideas.

Virgo: It's a great day for exploring creative solutions. Use your analytical skills to approach challenges in innovative ways.

Libra: Relationships are dynamic and exciting today. Focus on connecting with others in unconventional ways and exploring new perspectives in your personal connections.

Scorpio: Your passion for personal growth is strong today. Use this energy to explore new ideas and engage in meaningful conversations.

Sagittarius: Adventure and creativity are calling you today. Focus on expanding your horizons and embracing new opportunities.

Capricorn: While discipline is important, today encourages you to explore new ideas and engage in creative thinking.

Aquarius: With the Moon in your sign, your creativity and individuality are amplified. Use this energy to pursue innovative ideas and connect with others.

Pisces: Your intuition is strong today. Use this energy to explore creative projects and connect with others in meaningful ways.

For those born on November 28: Born under the Moon in Aquarius, these individuals are creative, innovative, and socially connected. In 2025, they'll thrive by embracing their individuality, exploring new ideas, and focusing on personal growth through social interactions.

Daily Insights: The Moon in Aquarius continues to highlight creativity and innovation, but as it transitions into Pisces later in the day, the focus shifts toward emotional reflection, intuition, and empathy. It's a day for balancing intellectual exploration with emotional depth and meaningful connections.

Aries: Start the day with creativity and exploration, but as the Moon enters Pisces, shift your focus to emotional reflection and nurturing your relationships.

Taurus: The morning is perfect for exploring creative solutions, but later, focus on emotional healing and connecting with loved ones on a deeper level.

Gemini: Social interactions are lively early in the day, but as the Moon enters Pisces, focus on balancing your intellectual pursuits with emotional reflection.

Cancer: Emotional intuition is heightened as the day progresses. Use the morning for socializing, but later, focus on self-care and deepening your connections.

Leo: Leadership and creativity shine early in the day, but as the Moon enters Pisces, turn your attention toward emotional well-being and nurturing those close to you.

Virgo: Use the morning for productivity, but as the energy shifts, focus on emotional reflection and healing. Balance work with personal care.

Libra: Relationships feel dynamic and exciting early in the day, but later, focus on creating emotional harmony and nurturing your personal connections.

Scorpio: Your creativity is strong in the morning, but as the Moon enters Pisces, focus on emotional reflection and personal transformation.

Sagittarius: Adventure and creativity guide you early in the day, but as the energy shifts, focus on personal healing and emotional connections.

Capricorn: Productivity is important in the morning, but as the Moon moves into Pisces, focus on grounding yourself emotionally and nurturing your relationships.

Aquarius: Your creativity is high early in the day, but as the Moon enters Pisces, focus on emotional growth and connecting with others meaningfully.

Pisces: The Moon enters your sign later today, enhancing your emotional intuition and sensitivity. Use this energy to focus on personal healing and nurturing your relationships.

For those born on November 29: Born under the transition from Aquarius to Pisces, these individuals are both creative and emotionally intuitive. In 2025, they'll thrive by balancing intellectual exploration with emotional reflection, focusing on both personal growth and meaningful relationships.

Daily Insights: The Moon in Pisces continues to emphasize emotional reflection, intuition, and creativity. It's a perfect day for engaging in artistic projects, deepening emotional connections, and focusing on personal healing. With Mercury in Gemini, communication remains vibrant, making it a good time for expressing your emotions through words.

Aries: Your intuition is strong today. Use this energy to nurture your relationships and engage in emotional reflection.

Taurus: Creativity flows easily today. Focus on expressing your emotions through artistic or practical outlets and spend time connecting with loved ones.

Gemini: Emotional reflection is important today. Use this energy to connect with your inner self and have meaningful conversations with others.

Cancer: The Moon in Pisces enhances your emotional sensitivity. Use this time to focus on self-care and strengthening your closest relationships.

Leo: While you're often focused on action, today encourages emotional reflection. Use this energy to explore your feelings and deepen your personal connections.

Virgo: Balance practicality with emotional reflection today. Use this time to focus on your inner world and nurture your personal relationships.

Libra: Relationships feel emotionally deep today. Focus on creating emotional harmony and connecting with loved ones on a meaningful level.

Scorpio: Your emotional intensity is strong today. Use this energy to focus on healing and strengthening your emotional bonds with those closest to you.

Sagittarius: It's a day for emotional introspection. Use this time to explore your inner world and focus on deepening your personal connections.

Capricorn: Emotional reflection is key today. Use this energy to balance your practical goals with personal care and nurturing relationships.

Aquarius: Creativity is important, but today encourages emotional introspection. Use this energy to connect with loved ones and focus on emotional growth.

Pisces: The Moon in your sign amplifies your emotional sensitivity. Use this energy for personal healing and deepening your emotional connections with others.

For those born on November 30: Born under the Moon in Pisces, these individuals are emotionally intuitive, creative, and compassionate. In 2025, they'll thrive by focusing on their emotional well-being, nurturing their relationships, and expressing their creativity in meaningful ways.

December 1, 2025

Daily Insights: The Moon in Pisces continues to highlight emotional reflection, but as it transitions into Aries later in the day, the energy shifts toward action, confidence, and bold decisions. It's a day for balancing emotional introspection with taking bold steps toward your personal goals.

Aries: Start the day with emotional reflection, but as the Moon enters your sign, shift your focus to bold actions and pursuing your goals with confidence.

Taurus: The morning is great for emotional introspection, but as the energy shifts, focus on taking practical steps toward your long-term goals.

Gemini: Emotional reflection is important early in the day, but as the Moon moves into Aries, engage in action and communication with bold confidence.

Cancer: The day begins with emotional reflection, but as the Moon moves into Aries, embrace challenges and step out of your comfort zone.

Leo: Emotional reflection is necessary early in the day, but as the Moon enters Aries, your confidence will rise, making it a great time to take bold actions.

Virgo: Use the early part of the day for emotional clarity, but later, shift your focus to organizing your thoughts and taking action on your plans.

Libra: Relationships feel emotionally deep in the morning, but as the Moon enters Aries, focus on communicating openly and taking action to strengthen your personal connections.

Scorpio: Emotional depth is important early in the day, but as the Moon moves into Aries, focus on taking bold steps toward personal growth and transformation.

Sagittarius: Start the day with emotional introspection, but later, shift your focus to adventure and explore new opportunities with confidence.

Capricorn: Emotional reflection is key early in the day, but as the Moon enters Aries, focus on taking decisive steps toward your long-term goals.

Aquarius: The morning is perfect for emotional reflection, but as the energy shifts, pursue new ideas and take bold actions toward your goals.

Pisces: The Moon in your sign enhances your emotional sensitivity early in the day, but as the Moon transitions into Aries, embrace bold steps toward your personal ambitions.

For those born on December 1: Born under the transition from Pisces to Aries, these individuals are emotionally intuitive yet action-oriented. In 2025, they'll thrive by balancing emotional reflection with bold actions toward their personal goals and ambitions.

Daily Insights: The Moon in Aries brings a surge of energy, confidence, and motivation. It's a great day for taking bold steps, embracing new opportunities, and focusing on personal ambitions. With Mars in Capricorn, there's a boost of discipline, making it an ideal time for combining bold actions with practical efforts.

Aries: Your confidence and motivation are high today. Use this energy to pursue your personal goals and take bold actions with enthusiasm.

Taurus: It's a day for balancing bold actions with practical steps. Use your grounded nature to take steady strides toward your long-term goals.

Gemini: Communication and action are your strengths today. Use this energy to engage in meaningful conversations and explore new ideas.

Cancer: Confidence and emotional reflection are key today. Use this energy to focus on personal growth and take bold steps toward your ambitions.

Leo: Leadership and action are highlighted today. Use your natural confidence to take charge of projects and inspire those around you.

Virgo: Productivity is high today. Use your disciplined nature to focus on practical tasks and take bold actions toward your goals.

Libra: Relationships feel dynamic and exciting today. Focus on open communication and take action to strengthen your personal connections.

Scorpio: Your determination is strong today. Use this energy to take decisive steps toward achieving your long-term goals.

Sagittarius: Adventure and excitement are calling you today. Use your enthusiasm to explore new opportunities and take bold steps toward your dreams.

Capricorn: Discipline and focus guide you today. Use this energy to make steady progress on your long-term projects and goals.

Aquarius: Creativity and innovative thinking shine today. Use this energy to explore new ideas and take bold actions toward your personal ambitions.

Pisces: It's a day for taking action on your personal ambitions. Use your intuition to guide you as you embrace new opportunities with confidence.

For those born on December 2: Born under the Moon in Aries, these individuals are confident, action-oriented, and driven. In 2025, they'll thrive by taking bold steps toward their personal goals and embracing new opportunities with enthusiasm.

Daily Insights: The Moon in Aries continues to highlight confidence and action, but as it transitions into Taurus later in the day, the focus shifts toward stability, practicality, and long-term planning. It's a day for balancing bold actions with careful consideration of your future goals.

Aries: The day starts with high energy and motivation, but as the Moon moves into Taurus, focus on grounding yourself and setting practical long-term goals.

Taurus: The Moon enters your sign later today, bringing a sense of stability and focus on practical matters. Use this energy to work methodically toward your ambitions.

Gemini: The morning is perfect for bold ideas and actions, but later, shift your focus to steady progress on long-term projects.

Cancer: Confidence drives you early in the day, but as the Moon moves into Taurus, focus on creating emotional stability and practical success.

Leo: The day begins with creative energy, but as the energy shifts, focus on refining your long-term goals and making steady progress.

Virgo: Use the early part of the day to act on bold ideas, but later, focus on organizing your thoughts and working steadily toward your ambitions.

Libra: Relationships are dynamic early in the day, but as the Moon enters Taurus, focus on creating harmony and long-term stability in your connections.

Scorpio: Emotional intensity is key early in the day, but later, shift your attention to long-term planning and making steady progress toward your goals.

Sagittarius: Start the day with bold steps, but as the Moon enters Taurus, focus on grounding yourself and ensuring steady progress toward your dreams.

Capricorn: Confidence and discipline guide you today. Use the morning for bold actions, but later, shift your focus to practical, long-term planning.

Aquarius: Creativity flows in the morning, but as the Moon moves into Taurus, shift your attention to grounding your ideas and making practical progress.

Pisces: Emotional reflection is key early in the day, but later, focus on grounding yourself and making steady progress toward your personal goals.

For those born on December 3: Born under the transition from Aries to Taurus, these individuals are both confident and practical. In 2025, they'll thrive by balancing bold actions with steady, long-term planning, focusing on both personal ambitions and practical achievements.

Daily Insights: The Moon in Taurus brings a focus on stability, practicality, and long-term planning. It's an ideal day for working steadily on your goals, taking deliberate steps toward success, and focusing on what brings you comfort and security. With Venus in Virgo, attention to detail is heightened, making it a perfect time for refining your plans.

Aries: Focus on grounding yourself today. Use this energy to work methodically on your long-term goals and ensure that you're making steady progress.

Taurus: The Moon in your sign enhances your sense of stability and practicality. Use this energy to focus on achieving long-term success by staying dedicated and focused.

Gemini: It's a day for balancing your curiosity with practicality. Use your creative energy to refine your ideas and work steadily toward your goals.

Cancer: Emotional reflection is important today. Use this energy to focus on creating stability in your relationships and practical success in your personal life.

Leo: While creativity is important, today encourages you to focus on steady progress. Use your confidence to inspire practical achievements.

Virgo: Productivity is high today. Use your disciplined nature to focus on refining your plans and making steady progress toward your long-term ambitions.

Libra: Relationships feel stable today. Focus on creating harmony in your personal connections while staying productive in your long-term goals.

Scorpio: Your determination is strong today. Use this energy to focus on practical steps toward achieving your long-term ambitions.

Sagittarius: Adventure takes a backseat today as you focus on grounding yourself and working steadily toward your long-term goals.

Capricorn: Discipline and focus are your strengths today. Use this energy to make significant progress on your long-term projects and goals.

Aquarius: While creativity is important, today encourages you to focus on practical solutions and refining your ideas.

Pisces: Emotional reflection is balanced with practicality today. Use this energy to focus on steady progress toward your long-term goals.

For those born on December 4: Born under the Moon in Taurus, these individuals are practical, grounded, and focused on long-term success. In 2025, they'll thrive by setting clear goals and making steady progress, using their disciplined nature to stay focused on their ambitions.

December 5, 2025

Daily Insights: The Moon in Taurus continues to emphasize stability, practicality, and long-term planning, but as it transitions into Gemini later in the day, the focus shifts toward communication, learning, and intellectual exploration. It's a day for balancing steady progress with curiosity and social interactions.

Aries: Start the day by focusing on practical tasks, but as the Moon enters Gemini, shift your attention to exploring new ideas and engaging in conversations.

Taurus: The morning is perfect for staying grounded and productive, but later, engage in intellectual pursuits and explore new opportunities.

Gemini: The Moon enters your sign later today, bringing a burst of energy and curiosity. Use this energy to engage in conversations and explore new ideas.

Cancer: Stability is key early in the day, but as the Moon moves into Gemini, focus on connecting with others and exploring new perspectives.

Leo: The day begins with a focus on practicality, but as the Moon enters Gemini, engage with others and share your creative ideas.

Virgo: Productivity is high early in the day, but later, shift your focus to learning new things and refining your long-term plans.

Libra: Relationships feel stable early in the day, but as the Moon moves into Gemini, focus on open communication and exploring new perspectives in your connections.

Scorpio: Determination and focus guide you in the morning, but as the energy shifts, explore new opportunities for intellectual and social growth.

Sagittarius: The morning is great for grounding yourself, but as the Moon moves into Gemini, focus on adventure, communication, and learning.

Capricorn: Discipline and focus guide you early in the day, but later, shift your attention to communication and exploring new opportunities.

Aquarius: Creativity and innovation are highlighted early in the day, but as the Moon enters Gemini, focus on social connections and intellectual exploration.

Pisces: Emotional reflection is key early in the day, but as the energy shifts, focus on learning new things and engaging in stimulating conversations.

For those born on December 5: Born under the transition from Taurus to Gemini, these individuals are both practical and curious. In 2025, they'll thrive by balancing their disciplined approach with intellectual exploration, focusing on both long-term success and new learning opportunities.

December 6, 2025

Daily Insights: The Moon in Gemini emphasizes communication, curiosity, and learning. It's a great day for engaging in conversations, exploring new ideas, and connecting with others. With Mercury in Sagittarius, communication is bold and lively, making it an ideal time for sharing your ideas confidently.

Aries: Your curiosity is strong today. Use this energy to engage in meaningful conversations and explore new ideas with enthusiasm.

Taurus: It's a day for balancing practicality with intellectual exploration. Use your grounded nature to communicate your thoughts clearly and explore new perspectives.

Gemini: The Moon in your sign amplifies your communication skills. Use this energy to connect with others, share your ideas, and explore new possibilities.

Cancer: Emotional reflection is important, but today also encourages you to focus on learning and connecting with others on an intellectual level.

Leo: Communication and creativity are highlighted today. Use your confidence to express your ideas and engage in meaningful conversations.

Virgo: Your analytical skills are sharp today. Use this energy to focus on problem-solving and refining your ideas.

Libra: Relationships feel intellectually stimulating today. Focus on engaging in conversations that broaden your perspective and deepen your connections.

Scorpio: Your emotional depth is strong today, but also take time to explore new ideas that challenge your thinking.

Sagittarius: Adventure and learning go hand in hand today. Use your curiosity to explore new opportunities and engage in stimulating conversations.

Capricorn: It's a day for balancing discipline with intellectual exploration. Use this energy to focus on refining your long-term goals and embracing new learning experiences.

Aquarius: Your creativity and innovative thinking shine today. Use this energy to explore new ideas and collaborate with others.

Pisces: It's a day for intellectual exploration and emotional reflection. Use this energy to connect with others in meaningful ways and share your ideas.

For those born on December 6: Born under the Moon in Gemini, these individuals are curious, communicative, and eager to explore new ideas. In 2025, they'll thrive by engaging in conversations, learning new things, and using their sharp minds to connect with others and broaden their horizons.

Daily Insights: The Moon in Gemini continues to emphasize communication and intellectual exploration, but as it transitions into Cancer later in the day, the focus shifts toward emotional well-being, nurturing relationships, and self-care. It's a day for balancing curiosity with emotional connection and personal reflection.

Aries: The day begins with lively conversations, but as the Moon enters Cancer, shift your focus to emotional reflection and nurturing your relationships.

Taurus: Use the morning for exploring new ideas, but later, focus on creating emotional stability in your personal life and nurturing your relationships.

Gemini: Communication and curiosity are highlighted early in the day, but as the energy shifts, focus on strengthening emotional connections with loved ones.

Cancer: The Moon enters your sign later today, enhancing your emotional intuition. Use this energy to focus on self-care and deepening your relationships.

Leo: Start the day with communication and creative expression, but as the Moon enters Cancer, shift your focus to emotional reflection and nurturing your personal connections.

Virgo: Productivity is high early in the day, but by evening, focus on emotional reflection and nurturing your personal well-being.

Libra: Relationships feel intellectually stimulating early in the day, but as the Moon moves into Cancer, focus on creating emotional harmony and balance in your personal life.

Scorpio: The day starts with curiosity and communication, but later, focus on emotional healing and deepening your closest relationships.

Sagittarius: The morning is ideal for exploring new opportunities, but as the Moon enters Cancer, shift your focus to emotional reflection and personal growth.

Capricorn: Use the early part of the day for intellectual pursuits, but as the energy shifts, focus on emotional reflection and grounding yourself.

Aquarius: Creativity and communication are highlighted early in the day, but later, focus on emotional introspection and self-care.

Pisces: Emotional intuition is strong today. Use this energy to nurture your relationships and focus on personal healing and reflection.

For those born on December 7: Born under the transition from Gemini to Cancer, these individuals are both intellectually curious and emotionally intuitive. In 2025, they'll thrive by balancing intellectual exploration with nurturing their emotional well-being and focusing on meaningful personal connections.

Daily Insights: The Moon in Cancer emphasizes emotional reflection, nurturing relationships, and self-care. It's a great day for focusing on emotional well-being and connecting with loved ones. With Venus in Scorpio, there's a blend of emotional depth and passion, making it a good time to focus on intense, meaningful connections.

Aries: Emotional balance is important today. Use this energy to focus on nurturing your relationships and creating harmony in your personal life.

Taurus: Focus on emotional well-being today. Use your grounded nature to create stability in your relationships and focus on self-care.

Gemini: While communication is important, today encourages you to focus on deepening your emotional connections with loved ones.

Cancer: The Moon in your sign enhances your emotional sensitivity. Take time for self-care and focus on nurturing your closest relationships.

Leo: Leadership is key, but today encourages emotional reflection. Use this time to focus on emotional growth and personal well-being.

Virgo: Balance your productivity with emotional reflection today. Use this energy to organize your personal life and nurture your relationships.

Libra: Relationships feel emotionally deep today. Focus on creating harmony and balance in your personal connections and spend time nurturing loved ones.

Scorpio: Emotional depth is strong today. Use this energy to explore personal growth and strengthen your emotional bonds with those who matter most.

Sagittarius: It's a day for emotional introspection. Use this energy to connect with your inner self and focus on creating emotional stability in your life.

Capricorn: Emotional reflection is key today. Use this energy to ground yourself and nurture your relationships while working toward your personal goals.

Aquarius: While creativity is important, today encourages emotional introspection. Use this energy to focus on personal growth and healing.

Pisces: The Moon in Cancer enhances your emotional sensitivity today. Use this energy to focus on personal healing and deepening your emotional connections.

For those born on December 8: Born under the Moon in Cancer, these individuals are emotionally intuitive, nurturing, and deeply connected to their home and family. In 2025, they'll thrive by focusing on their emotional well-being, nurturing relationships, and creating emotional stability in their lives.

Daily Insights: The Moon in Cancer continues to highlight emotional well-being, but as it transitions into Leo later in the day, the focus shifts toward confidence, creativity, and self-expression. It's a day for balancing emotional reflection with bold steps toward personal ambitions and self-expression.

Aries: Start the day with emotional reflection, but as the Moon enters Leo, shift your focus to taking bold actions and pursuing your personal goals with confidence.

Taurus: The day begins with emotional reflection, but as the Moon moves into Leo, focus on expressing your creativity and embracing personal empowerment.

Gemini: Emotional connections are key early in the day, but as the Moon moves into Leo, focus on expressing your ideas confidently and engaging with others.

Cancer: The morning is perfect for nurturing your emotional well-being, but as the Moon moves into Leo, embrace your confidence and pursue your ambitions with enthusiasm.

Leo: The Moon enters your sign later today, amplifying your natural confidence and creativity. Use this energy to take bold actions and lead with enthusiasm.

Virgo: The day starts with emotional reflection, but later, shift your focus to creativity and finding new approaches to your long-term goals.

Libra: Relationships feel emotionally deep early in the day, but as the energy shifts, focus on creating balance between your emotional connections and personal growth.

Scorpio: Emotional depth is important in the morning, but as the Moon enters Leo, focus on personal transformation and expressing your true self.

Sagittarius: Start the day with emotional introspection, but later, shift your focus to exploring new adventures and expressing your creative side.

Capricorn: The morning is perfect for grounding yourself emotionally, but as the energy shifts, focus on stepping into leadership roles and pursuing your ambitions.

Aquarius: Emotional reflection is key early in the day, but later, embrace new ideas and step into the spotlight with confidence.

Pisces: Emotional sensitivity is high early in the day, but as the Moon enters Leo, focus on personal empowerment and expressing yourself with confidence.

For those born on December 9: Born under the transition from Cancer to Leo, these individuals are emotionally intuitive and confident. In 2025, they'll thrive by balancing their emotional well-being with bold actions toward their personal goals, stepping into leadership roles and expressing their creativity.

Daily Insights: The Moon in Leo brings a surge of confidence, creativity, and leadership. It's a great day for expressing yourself, taking bold actions, and pursuing your passions. With Mars in Capricorn, there's a blend of discipline and ambition, making it an ideal time for working toward your goals with confidence.

Aries: Your confidence is high today. Use this energy to pursue your personal goals and take bold actions with enthusiasm.

Taurus: Creativity flows easily today. Focus on expressing your unique ideas and working toward your long-term goals with determination.

Gemini: Communication and self-expression are your strengths today. Use this energy to connect with others and share your innovative ideas.

Cancer: The Moon in Leo encourages you to step out of your comfort zone and pursue your personal goals with confidence and creativity.

Leo: The Moon in your sign amplifies your natural leadership and creativity. Use this energy to take bold steps toward your passions and inspire others.

Virgo: Balance creativity with practicality today. Use your disciplined nature to focus on long-term goals while expressing your unique talents.

Libra: Relationships feel dynamic and exciting today. Focus on connecting with loved ones in creative ways and embracing your individuality.

Scorpio: Your passion is strong today. Use this energy to pursue personal goals with intensity and determination.

Sagittarius: Adventure and creativity are calling you today. Use this energy to explore new opportunities and express yourself freely.

Capricorn: Leadership and discipline come naturally today. Use this energy to focus on personal projects and inspire those around you.

Aquarius: Your creativity shines today. Use this energy to pursue innovative ideas and connect with others through meaningful collaborations.

Pisces: It's a day for self-expression and personal growth. Use your creativity to focus on your goals and embrace new opportunities with confidence.

For those born on December 10: Born under the Moon in Leo, these individuals are charismatic, creative, and confident. In 2025, they'll thrive by stepping into leadership roles, embracing their unique talents, and pursuing their passions with determination.

December 11, 2025

Daily Insights: The Moon in Leo continues to highlight confidence and creativity, but as it transitions into Virgo later in the day, the focus shifts toward practicality, organization, and attention to detail. It's a day for balancing bold ideas with disciplined actions to achieve long-term success.

Aries: Start the day with bold actions, but as the Moon moves into Virgo, shift your focus to organizing your plans and refining your goals.

Taurus: The day begins with creative expression, but later, focus on practical steps toward your long-term goals.

Gemini: Use the morning for creative pursuits and communication, but as the energy shifts, focus on organizing your ideas and refining your plans.

Cancer: Confidence and creativity guide you early in the day, but later, shift your focus to emotional balance and practical tasks.

Leo: The Moon in your sign enhances your leadership, but as it moves into Virgo, focus on grounding your energy and organizing your long-term goals.

Virgo: The Moon enters your sign later today, amplifying your attention to detail and practical nature. Use this energy to refine your plans and focus on productivity.

Libra: The morning is great for engaging in creative conversations, but later, focus on balancing your personal goals with practical responsibilities.

Scorpio: Start the day by pursuing your passions, but as the Moon moves into Virgo, shift your focus to refining your long-term plans and staying disciplined.

Sagittarius: The day starts with excitement and creativity, but later, shift your focus to practical tasks and responsibilities.

Capricorn: Discipline and leadership guide you in the morning, but later, shift your attention to organizing your goals and refining your long-term plans.

Aquarius: The morning is ideal for creative expression, but as the Moon moves into Virgo, focus on refining your ideas and ensuring they are practical.

Pisces: Start the day with emotional reflection and creativity, but later, focus on organizing your personal life and making practical decisions.

For those born on December 11: Born under the transition from Leo to Virgo, these individuals are both creative and practical. In 2025, they'll thrive by balancing bold ideas with disciplined actions, focusing on both creativity and productivity to achieve their goals.

Daily Insights: The Moon in Virgo emphasizes productivity, organization, and attention to detail. It's a great day for focusing on practical matters, refining your plans, and making steady progress toward your long-term goals. With Mercury in Sagittarius, communication remains lively, making it a perfect day for blending creativity with discipline.

Aries: Stay focused on your goals today. Use your energy to organize your thoughts and make steady progress toward your long-term ambitions.

Taurus: It's a day for practical achievements. Use your grounded nature to refine your ideas and work steadily on long-term projects.

Gemini: Your analytical skills are strong today. Use this energy to focus on problem-solving and refining your ideas.

Cancer: Balance emotional reflection with practical tasks today. Focus on organizing your personal life and creating emotional stability.

Leo: After a period of creativity, today encourages you to focus on practical matters. Use your energy to refine your long-term plans.

Virgo: The Moon in your sign enhances your natural strengths. Use this energy to focus on productivity and tackle tasks that require precision.

Libra: Relationships feel stable today. Focus on balancing your personal goals with your relationships while staying productive.

Scorpio: Your determination is strong today. Use this energy to focus on long-term goals and ensure you're making practical decisions for the future.

Sagittarius: Practical matters take precedence today. Use this energy to focus on your responsibilities and stay disciplined in achieving your goals.

Capricorn: Discipline and focus are your strengths today. Use this energy to make significant progress on your long-term projects and goals.

Aquarius: While creativity is important, today encourages you to focus on practical solutions and refining your innovative ideas.

Pisces: Emotional reflection is balanced with practicality today. Use this energy to organize your life and make steady progress toward your goals.

For those born on December 12: Born under the Moon in Virgo, these individuals are practical, detail-oriented, and highly productive. In 2025, they'll thrive by refining their plans, staying disciplined, and making steady progress toward their long-term goals.

Daily Insights: The Moon in Virgo continues to emphasize productivity, but as it transitions into Libra later in the day, the focus shifts toward balance, relationships, and harmony. It's a day for balancing work with social interactions and ensuring that all areas of your life are in equilibrium.

Aries: The morning is perfect for productivity, but as the Moon moves into Libra, focus on balancing your work with your personal relationships.

Taurus: Start the day with practical tasks, but later, shift your focus to nurturing relationships and creating balance in your life.

Gemini: The day begins with a focus on organization, but as the energy shifts, engage in meaningful conversations and strengthen your relationships.

Cancer: The morning is ideal for organizing your life, but as the Moon enters Libra, focus on nurturing your relationships and finding harmony.

Leo: The day starts with practical tasks, but later, focus on balancing your creative pursuits with your relationships.

Virgo: The Moon in your sign enhances your productivity early in the day, but by evening, focus on maintaining balance in your personal life.

Libra: The day starts with productivity, but as the Moon enters your sign, focus on nurturing relationships and finding balance in all areas of life.

Scorpio: It's a day for balancing productivity with emotional depth. Use the morning for practical tasks, but later, focus on nurturing your relationships.

Sagittarius: Responsibilities guide you in the morning, but by evening, focus on social interactions and bringing balance to your personal life.

Capricorn: Discipline and focus guide you in the morning, but later, shift your attention to maintaining harmony in your relationships.

Aquarius: The morning is perfect for creativity and productivity, but as the Moon moves into Libra, focus on balancing your work and social life.

Pisces: Emotional reflection is key early in the day, but as the Moon enters Libra, focus on nurturing relationships and finding inner balance.

For those born on December 13: Born under the transition from Virgo to Libra, these individuals are both productive and focused on balance. In 2025, they'll thrive by balancing their attention to detail with creating harmonious relationships and personal connections.

Daily Insights: The Moon in Libra brings a focus on balance, relationships, and harmony. It's a great day for resolving conflicts, building stronger connections, and bringing equilibrium to all areas of your life. With Venus in Sagittarius, relationships feel dynamic and adventurous, making it an ideal time for romantic and social pursuits.

Aries: Focus on bringing balance to your relationships today. Use this energy to resolve conflicts and create harmony in your personal life.

Taurus: Balance is key today. Focus on finding harmony between your practical responsibilities and your personal relationships.

Gemini: Relationships take center stage today. Focus on communicating clearly and building harmony in your personal interactions.

Cancer: It's a day for balancing your emotional needs with your relationships. Use this energy to create emotional stability and strengthen connections.

Leo: While your confidence is high, today encourages you to focus on your relationships and creating balance in your personal life.

Virgo: Balance productivity with relationships today. Use your disciplined nature to focus on both your work goals and your personal connections.

Libra: The Moon in your sign highlights balance and harmony. Use this energy to create peace in your relationships and personal life.

Scorpio: Relationships feel emotionally deep today. Use this energy to create emotional harmony and balance in your life.

Sagittarius: Social interactions are favored today. Use your natural charm to connect with others and focus on creating harmony in your relationships.

Capricorn: It's a day for balancing your responsibilities with your relationships. Focus on finding harmony between your work and personal life.

Aquarius: Creativity and innovation are your strengths today. Use this energy to find balance in your social interactions and personal relationships.

Pisces: Emotional balance is important today. Use this energy to focus on creating stability in your relationships and your personal life.

For those born on December 14: Born under the Moon in Libra, these individuals are focused on balance, harmony, and relationships. In 2025, they'll thrive by creating equilibrium in their personal and professional lives while working toward their goals with patience and determination.

Daily Insights: The Moon in Libra continues to emphasize balance and harmony, but as it transitions into Scorpio later in the day, the focus shifts toward emotional depth, transformation, and intense connections. It's a day for balancing social interactions with deep emotional reflection.

Aries: Start the day by focusing on relationships and creating harmony, but as the Moon moves into Scorpio, dive deeper into your emotions and connections.

Taurus: The morning is perfect for nurturing relationships and creating balance, but as the energy shifts, focus on exploring emotional depths and personal transformation.

Gemini: Relationships are in focus early in the day, but later, shift toward introspection and exploring your emotional world.

Cancer: Start the day with balance, but as the Moon moves into Scorpio, focus on emotional clarity and deepening your closest relationships.

Leo: The day begins with a focus on balance and harmony, but later, shift toward personal growth and emotional transformation.

Virgo: The morning is ideal for keeping things in balance, but as the Moon enters Scorpio, focus on self-reflection and emotional exploration.

Libra: The Moon in your sign brings focus on harmony and balance early in the day, but as it enters Scorpio, you'll feel drawn toward emotional intensity and transformation.

Scorpio: The Moon enters your sign later today, heightening your emotional sensitivity. Use this energy to focus on personal growth and strengthening emotional connections.

Sagittarius: The morning is for socializing and creating balance, but as the energy shifts, turn inward and reflect on personal emotions and connections.

Capricorn: Balance your work and relationships in the morning, but as the Moon moves into Scorpio, focus on emotional reflection and personal growth.

Aquarius: Start the day focusing on balance and relationships, but later, turn your attention to exploring emotional depth and transformation.

Pisces: Emotional reflection and stability are key today. Use the energy later in the day to strengthen emotional bonds and engage in self-reflection.

For those born on December 15: Born under the transition from Libra to Scorpio, these individuals are balanced yet emotionally intense. In 2025, they'll thrive by focusing on relationships while embracing emotional transformation and personal growth.

Daily Insights: The Moon in Scorpio brings emotional depth, introspection, and transformation. It's a powerful day for exploring your inner world, making deep connections, and focusing on personal growth. With Mercury in Capricorn, communication remains grounded and practical, encouraging thoughtful and strategic conversations.

Aries: Emotional reflection is key today. Use this energy to explore your inner self and deepen your emotional connections with those around you.

Taurus: The Moon in Scorpio highlights deep connections today. Focus on your personal transformation and strengthening relationships.

Gemini: Today encourages emotional depth and introspection. Use this energy to explore your inner world and strengthen your relationships.

Cancer: Emotional intensity is strong today. Focus on nurturing your closest relationships and engaging in personal growth.

Leo: Emotional reflection is necessary today. Use this time to connect with your feelings and create meaningful connections.

Virgo: Balance your practicality with emotional depth today. Focus on personal growth and refining your long-term goals.

Libra: Relationships feel emotionally intense today. Use this energy to connect with loved ones on a deeper level.

Scorpio: The Moon in your sign amplifies your emotional intensity. Use this energy to focus on personal growth and deepening emotional bonds.

Sagittarius: Emotional introspection is key today. Use this time to explore your inner world and strengthen your closest relationships.

Capricorn: Emotional intensity guides you today. Focus on personal growth and making thoughtful decisions about your future.

Aquarius: Creativity flows through emotional depth today. Use this energy to explore new ideas and connect with others meaningfully.

Pisces: Your emotional intuition is heightened today. Use this energy to focus on personal healing and strengthening emotional connections.

For those born on December 16: Born under the Moon in Scorpio, these individuals are emotionally intense, intuitive, and focused on transformation. In 2025, they'll thrive by focusing on deep emotional growth, strengthening relationships, and embracing personal change.

Daily Insights: The Moon in Scorpio continues to bring emotional intensity and transformation, but as it transitions into Sagittarius later in the day, the energy shifts toward optimism, exploration, and adventure. It's a day for balancing deep emotional reflection with the desire to embrace new possibilities.

Aries: Start the day with emotional introspection, but as the Moon moves into Sagittarius, shift your focus to exploring new opportunities and personal growth.

Taurus: Use the early part of the day for deep emotional work, but later, embrace the energy of optimism and explore new ideas and adventures.

Gemini: Emotional depth is important early in the day, but as the Moon enters Sagittarius, you'll feel inclined to explore new opportunities and broaden your horizons.

Cancer: Focus on nurturing emotional connections in the morning, but as the energy shifts, embrace new adventures and personal growth.

Leo: Emotional intensity gives way to adventure and personal freedom as the Moon enters Sagittarius. Focus on expanding your horizons and pursuing new goals.

Virgo: Balance emotional introspection with new possibilities today. Use the day to explore new ideas and broaden your perspective.

Libra: Relationships feel deep early in the day, but later, focus on broadening your perspective and exploring new possibilities.

Scorpio: The Moon in your sign brings emotional depth early in the day, but as it moves into Sagittarius, explore new adventures and expand your world.

Sagittarius: The Moon enters your sign later today, bringing a sense of optimism and adventure. Use this energy to pursue new possibilities and embrace personal freedom.

Capricorn: Emotional reflection is important in the morning, but later, shift your focus to exploring new opportunities and expanding your goals.

Aquarius: Early in the day, emotional exploration is key, but later, shift your attention to broadening your horizons and pursuing new adventures.

Pisces: Emotional healing is key early in the day, but later, focus on exploring new opportunities and expanding your personal and professional horizons.

For those born on December 17: Born under the transition from Scorpio to Sagittarius, these individuals are emotionally intense yet adventurous. In 2025, they'll thrive by balancing emotional reflection with the pursuit of new experiences and personal growth.

December 18, 2025

Daily Insights: The Moon in Sagittarius emphasizes optimism, exploration, and personal growth. It's a great day for seeking new experiences, engaging in learning, and expanding your horizons. With Mercury in Capricorn, there's a sense of practicality balancing out the adventurous spirit, making it a good time for thoughtful exploration.

Aries: Adventure calls you today. Use this energy to explore new possibilities and focus on expanding your personal and professional goals.

Taurus: It's a day for balancing practicality with adventure. Use your grounded nature to explore new opportunities while staying focused on your long-term goals.

Gemini: Communication and learning are highlighted today. Use this energy to engage in stimulating conversations and explore new intellectual pursuits.

Cancer: Step out of your comfort zone today and embrace new experiences. Use this energy to focus on personal growth and exploration.

Leo: Confidence and leadership are emphasized today. Use this energy to take bold steps toward your goals and inspire those around you.

Virgo: It's a great day for learning and expanding your knowledge. Use your analytical mind to explore new ideas and gain fresh insights.

Libra: Relationships feel dynamic and exciting today. Focus on open communication and engage in meaningful conversations with loved ones.

Scorpio: After a period of emotional intensity, today encourages you to explore new experiences and focus on personal growth and adventure.

Sagittarius: The Moon in your sign enhances your sense of adventure and optimism. Use this energy to pursue your passions and embrace new possibilities.

Capricorn: While discipline is important, today encourages you to explore new ideas and broaden your horizons with an open mind.

Aquarius: Creativity and innovation are your strengths today. Use this energy to explore new possibilities and engage in collaborative projects.

Pisces: It's a day for personal growth and exploration. Use your intuition to guide you as you embrace new opportunities and expand your horizons.

For those born on December 18: Born under the Moon in Sagittarius, these individuals are adventurous, optimistic, and eager to explore new possibilities. In 2025, they'll thrive by embracing new experiences, expanding their horizons, and pursuing personal growth with enthusiasm.

Daily Insights: The Moon in Sagittarius continues to highlight optimism and exploration, but as it transitions into Capricorn later in the day, the focus shifts toward discipline, productivity, and long-term planning. It's a day for balancing personal freedom with responsibility and setting clear goals for the future.

Aries: Start the day with a sense of adventure, but as the Moon moves into Capricorn, focus on grounding yourself and setting practical long-term goals.

Taurus: The morning is filled with excitement and exploration, but later, shift your attention to practical matters and refining your long-term plans.

Gemini: Adventure and learning are key early in the day, but as the energy shifts, focus on refining your ideas and setting clear goals for the future.

Cancer: The morning is ideal for exploring new opportunities, but as the Moon enters Capricorn, shift your focus to creating emotional and practical stability.

Leo: Start the day with confidence and leadership, but later, focus on practical steps toward achieving your long-term ambitions.

Virgo: The day begins with curiosity and learning, but as the energy shifts, focus on organizing your thoughts and refining your long-term plans.

Libra: Relationships feel dynamic early in the day, but as the Moon moves into Capricorn, focus on building stability and harmony in your personal connections.

Scorpio: Start the day by exploring new possibilities, but later, shift your focus to long-term planning and making steady progress toward your goals.

Sagittarius: The Moon in your sign encourages adventure early in the day, but as the energy transitions, focus on setting practical steps for the future.

Capricorn: The Moon enters your sign later today, enhancing your natural discipline and focus. Use this energy to work on long-term projects and set achievable goals.

Aquarius: Creativity and bold actions are important early in the day, but later, focus on grounding your innovative ideas into practical steps.

Pisces: The day begins with optimism and exploration, but later, focus on grounding your emotional well-being and making steady progress on personal and professional goals.

For those born on December 19: Born under the transition from Sagittarius to Capricorn, these individuals are both adventurous and disciplined. In 2025, they'll thrive by balancing their curiosity and love for exploration with their focus on long-term success and productivity.

Daily Insights: The Moon in Capricorn emphasizes discipline, productivity, and long-term planning. It's an ideal day for focusing on practical tasks, setting achievable goals, and working steadily toward your ambitions. With Venus in Scorpio, relationships feel intense and transformative, adding a layer of depth to your personal connections.

Aries: Discipline and focus are key today. Use this energy to set practical long-term goals and make steady progress toward achieving them.

Taurus: The day encourages productivity and grounded actions. Focus on refining your plans and working methodically toward your ambitions.

Gemini: It's a day for balancing intellectual curiosity with practical achievements. Focus on organizing your thoughts and taking steady steps forward.

Cancer: Emotional stability and practicality are important today. Use this energy to create a sense of security in your personal and professional life.

Leo: Confidence guides you, but today encourages practical action. Use your leadership skills to take bold yet grounded steps toward your goals.

Virgo: Productivity is high today. Use your analytical skills to refine your plans and focus on long-term goals that require discipline and precision.

Libra: Relationships feel grounded today. Focus on creating harmony in your personal connections while also working steadily toward your ambitions.

Scorpio: Your determination is strong today. Use this energy to focus on long-term goals and make practical decisions that align with your ambitions.

Sagittarius: Adventure takes a backseat as you focus on grounding yourself and working toward long-term goals with practical actions.

Capricorn: The Moon in your sign enhances your discipline and determination. Use this energy to tackle big projects and make significant progress toward your goals.

Aquarius: Creativity is important, but today encourages you to ground your ideas in reality and focus on steady progress toward your long-term ambitions.

Pisces: Emotional stability is key today. Use this energy to focus on practical steps that will help you achieve your personal and professional goals.

For those born on December 20: Born under the Moon in Capricorn, these individuals are disciplined, practical, and focused on long-term success. In 2025, they'll thrive by setting clear goals, making steady progress, and using their determination to stay on track and overcome challenges.

Daily Insights: The Moon in Capricorn continues to emphasize discipline and productivity, but as it transitions into Aquarius later in the day, the focus shifts toward creativity, innovation, and social connections. It's a day for balancing practical work with creative exploration and collaboration.

Aries: Start the day with focused discipline, but as the Moon moves into Aquarius, embrace your creativity and explore new ideas.

Taurus: The morning is ideal for productivity, but later, focus on engaging with others and exploring creative solutions to long-term goals.

Gemini: Practical achievements guide you early in the day, but as the energy shifts, focus on exploring new intellectual possibilities and social connections.

Cancer: The morning is perfect for grounding yourself in practical matters, but later, embrace new opportunities for creativity and connection.

Leo: Use the early part of the day for working on your goals, but as the Moon moves into Aquarius, shift toward collaboration and innovative thinking.

Virgo: Focus on refining your plans early in the day, but as the Moon enters Aquarius, engage with others and explore creative solutions.

Libra: Relationships feel stable in the morning, but as the energy shifts, focus on exploring new perspectives and innovative approaches to personal connections.

Scorpio: Determination guides you in the morning, but as the Moon enters Aquarius, embrace creativity and explore new ideas with curiosity.

Sagittarius: The day begins with a focus on long-term goals, but later, embrace adventure and intellectual exploration.

Capricorn: The Moon in your sign enhances your productivity early in the day, but as it enters Aquarius, focus on expanding your horizons and exploring creative possibilities.

Aquarius: The Moon enters your sign later today, bringing a surge of creativity and innovation. Use this energy to explore new projects and connect with others.

Pisces: Emotional reflection is key early in the day, but as the energy shifts, focus on socializing and sharing your creative ideas with others.

For those born on December 21: Born under the transition from Capricorn to Aquarius, these individuals are both disciplined and innovative. In 2025, they'll thrive by balancing practical achievements with creative exploration, focusing on long-term success while embracing new ideas.

Daily Insights: The Moon in Aquarius emphasizes creativity, innovation, and social connections. It's a great day for engaging in conversations, exploring new ideas, and collaborating with others. With Mercury in Sagittarius, communication is bold and adventurous, making it an ideal time for sharing creative ideas confidently.

Aries: Creativity shines today. Use this energy to explore new possibilities and connect with others through collaborative efforts.

Taurus: Balance practicality with creative thinking today. Use your grounded nature to turn innovative ideas into reality.

Gemini: Social interactions are lively and engaging. Use this energy to explore new ideas and connect with others through meaningful conversations.

Cancer: Creativity and innovation call you today. Use this energy to explore new ways of expressing yourself and connecting with others.

Leo: Leadership and creativity go hand in hand today. Use your confidence to take charge of new projects and inspire others with your bold ideas.

Virgo: It's a great day for exploring creative solutions to challenges. Use your analytical skills to approach problems with fresh, innovative ideas.

Libra: Relationships feel dynamic and exciting today. Focus on connecting with others in creative ways and exploring new perspectives in your personal connections.

Scorpio: Your passion for growth is strong today. Use this energy to explore new ideas and engage in transformative conversations.

Sagittarius: Adventure and creativity are calling you today. Use this energy to explore new possibilities and embrace intellectual freedom.

Capricorn: While discipline is important, today encourages you to explore new ideas and approach your goals with creativity.

Aquarius: With the Moon in your sign, your creativity and individuality are amplified. Use this energy to pursue innovative ideas and engage with others.

Pisces: Your intuition is strong today. Use this energy to explore creative projects and connect with others in meaningful ways.

For those born on December 22: Born under the Moon in Aquarius, these individuals are creative, innovative, and socially connected. In 2025, they'll thrive by embracing their individuality, exploring new ideas, and focusing on personal growth through meaningful connections.

December 23, 2025

Daily Insights: The Moon in Aquarius continues to highlight creativity and innovation, but as it transitions into Pisces later in the day, the focus shifts toward emotional reflection, intuition, and empathy. It's a day for balancing intellectual exploration with emotional depth and meaningful connections.

Aries: Start the day with creative exploration, but as the Moon enters Pisces, shift your focus to emotional reflection and nurturing relationships.

Taurus: The morning is perfect for creative solutions, but later, focus on emotional healing and connecting with loved ones on a deeper level.

Gemini: Social interactions are lively early in the day, but as the Moon enters Pisces, focus on balancing your intellectual pursuits with emotional reflection.

Cancer: Emotional intuition is heightened as the day progresses. Use the morning for engaging with others, but later, focus on self-care and deepening your connections.

Leo: Leadership and creativity shine early in the day, but as the Moon enters Pisces, focus on emotional well-being and nurturing your personal connections.

Virgo: Productivity is high in the morning, but later, shift your focus to emotional reflection and healing. Balance work with personal care.

Libra: Relationships feel dynamic and exciting early in the day, but later, focus on creating emotional harmony and nurturing personal connections.

Scorpio: Your creativity is strong in the morning, but as the Moon enters Pisces, focus on emotional reflection and personal transformation.

Sagittarius: Adventure and creativity guide you early in the day, but later, focus on personal healing and emotional connections.

Capricorn: Productivity is important early in the day, but as the Moon moves into Pisces, focus on grounding yourself emotionally and nurturing your relationships.

Aquarius: Creativity flows easily in the morning, but later, focus on emotional growth and connecting with others meaningfully.

Pisces: The Moon enters your sign later today, enhancing your emotional intuition and sensitivity. Use this energy to focus on personal healing and deepening emotional bonds.

For those born on December 23: Born under the transition from Aquarius to Pisces, these individuals are both creative and emotionally intuitive. In 2025, they'll thrive by balancing intellectual exploration with emotional reflection, focusing on personal growth and meaningful relationships.

Daily Insights: The Moon in Pisces enhances emotional reflection, intuition, and creativity. It's a perfect day for focusing on your inner world, engaging in artistic endeavors, and nurturing close relationships. With Neptune in Pisces, the energy of the day is dreamy and imaginative, making it ideal for meditation and spiritual growth.

Aries: Your intuition is heightened today. Use this energy to focus on emotional reflection and nurture your relationships with empathy and understanding.

Taurus: It's a day for emotional and creative expression. Use your grounded nature to explore your inner world and connect with loved ones on a deeper level.

Gemini: Emotional reflection is important today. Use this energy to connect with your feelings and engage in meaningful conversations with those closest to you.

Cancer: The Moon in Pisces enhances your emotional sensitivity. Use this time for self-care and focus on strengthening your closest relationships.

Leo: Creativity and self-expression are important today. Use this energy to explore your emotions and connect with others on a meaningful level.

Virgo: Balance your practical nature with emotional reflection today. Focus on nurturing your personal life and building emotional connections with those around you.

Libra: Relationships feel emotionally deep today. Focus on creating harmony in your personal connections and nurturing your loved ones.

Scorpio: Your emotional depth is amplified today. Use this energy to focus on personal healing and strengthening your emotional bonds.

Sagittarius: It's a day for emotional introspection. Use this energy to explore your inner self and deepen your emotional connections with others.

Capricorn: Emotional reflection is key today. Use this energy to create stability in your personal life and focus on your long-term emotional well-being.

Aquarius: Creativity and emotional intuition are heightened today. Use this energy to explore new ideas and strengthen your relationships.

Pisces: The Moon in your sign amplifies your emotional intuition and creativity. Use this energy to focus on personal healing, self-care, and nurturing your relationships.

For those born on December 24: Born under the Moon in Pisces, these individuals are emotionally intuitive, creative, and compassionate. In 2025, they'll thrive by focusing on their emotional well-being, nurturing their relationships, and expressing their creativity in meaningful ways.

December 25, 2025

Daily Insights: The Moon in Pisces continues to emphasize emotional reflection and creativity, but as it transitions into Aries later in the day, the energy shifts toward action, confidence, and bold decisions. It's a day for balancing introspection with taking bold steps toward personal goals.

Aries: Start the day with emotional reflection, but as the Moon enters your sign, shift your focus to bold actions and pursuing your personal goals with confidence.

Taurus: The morning is perfect for emotional introspection, but as the Moon moves into Aries, focus on taking practical steps toward your long-term ambitions.

Gemini: Emotional reflection is key early in the day, but as the Moon moves into Aries, engage in action and communication with bold confidence.

Cancer: The day begins with emotional reflection, but as the Moon moves into Aries, embrace challenges and take decisive steps toward your goals.

Leo: Emotional reflection is necessary early in the day, but as the Moon enters Aries, your confidence will rise, making it a great time to take bold actions toward your personal ambitions.

Virgo: Use the early part of the day for emotional clarity, but later, shift your focus to organizing your thoughts and taking bold actions.

Libra: Relationships feel emotionally deep in the morning, but as the Moon enters Aries, focus on communicating openly and taking action to strengthen your personal connections.

Scorpio: Emotional depth is important early in the day, but as the Moon moves into Aries, focus on taking bold steps toward personal growth and transformation.

Sagittarius: Start the day with emotional introspection, but later, shift your focus to adventure and explore new opportunities with confidence.

Capricorn: Emotional reflection is key early in the day, but as the Moon enters Aries, focus on taking decisive steps toward your long-term goals.

Aquarius: The morning is perfect for emotional reflection, but as the energy shifts, embrace new ideas and take bold actions toward your personal ambitions.

Pisces: The Moon in your sign enhances your emotional sensitivity early in the day, but as the energy shifts, focus on bold steps toward your personal ambitions.

For those born on December 25: Born under the transition from Pisces to Aries, these individuals are emotionally intuitive yet action-oriented. In 2025, they'll thrive by balancing emotional reflection with bold steps toward their personal goals and ambitions.

Daily Insights: The Moon in Aries brings a surge of energy, confidence, and motivation. It's a great day for taking bold steps, embracing new opportunities, and focusing on personal ambitions. With Mars in Capricorn, there's a blend of discipline and practicality, making it an ideal time for working toward long-term goals.

Aries: Your confidence and motivation are high today. Use this energy to pursue your personal goals and take bold actions with enthusiasm.

Taurus: It's a day for balancing bold actions with practical steps. Use your grounded nature to take steady strides toward your long-term ambitions.

Gemini: Communication and action are your strengths today. Use this energy to engage in meaningful conversations and explore new ideas.

Cancer: Confidence and emotional reflection are key today. Use this energy to focus on personal growth and take bold steps toward your ambitions.

Leo: Leadership and creativity are emphasized today. Use your natural confidence to take charge of projects and inspire those around you.

Virgo: Productivity is high today. Use your disciplined nature to focus on practical tasks and take bold actions toward your goals.

Libra: Relationships feel dynamic and exciting today. Focus on open communication and take action to strengthen your personal connections.

Scorpio: Your determination is strong today. Use this energy to take decisive steps toward achieving your long-term goals.

Sagittarius: Adventure and excitement are calling you today. Use your enthusiasm to explore new opportunities and take bold steps toward your dreams.

Capricorn: Discipline and focus guide you today. Use this energy to make steady progress on your long-term projects and goals.

Aquarius: Creativity and innovative thinking shine today. Use this energy to explore new ideas and take bold actions toward your personal ambitions.

Pisces: It's a day for taking action on your personal ambitions. Use your intuition to guide you as you embrace new opportunities with confidence.

For those born on December 26: Born under the Moon in Aries, these individuals are confident, action-oriented, and focused on their goals. In 2025, they'll thrive by taking bold steps toward their personal ambitions and embracing new opportunities with enthusiasm.

Daily Insights: The Moon in Aries continues to highlight confidence and action, but as it transitions into Taurus later in the day, the focus shifts toward stability, practicality, and long-term planning. It's a day for balancing bold actions with careful consideration of your future goals.

Aries: The day begins with high energy and motivation, but as the Moon moves into Taurus, focus on grounding yourself and setting practical goals for the future.

Taurus: The Moon enters your sign later today, bringing a sense of stability and focus on practical matters. Use this energy to work steadily toward your long-term ambitions.

Gemini: The morning is perfect for bold actions, but as the energy shifts, focus on taking practical steps toward your long-term projects.

Cancer: Confidence guides you early in the day, but as the Moon moves into Taurus, focus on creating emotional and practical stability.

Leo: The day begins with creativity and boldness, but as the Moon transitions, focus on refining your long-term goals and making steady progress.

Virgo: Use the early part of the day to act on bold ideas, but later, shift your focus to organizing your thoughts and working steadily toward your ambitions.

Libra: Relationships feel dynamic early in the day, but as the Moon moves into Taurus, focus on creating harmony and stability in your personal connections.

Scorpio: Emotional depth is key early in the day, but later, shift your attention to long-term planning and making steady progress toward your goals.

Sagittarius: Start the day with bold actions, but as the Moon enters Taurus, focus on grounding yourself and ensuring steady progress toward your dreams.

Capricorn: Discipline and leadership guide you in the morning, but as the Moon enters Taurus, focus on setting practical goals and working toward long-term success.

Aquarius: Creativity flows easily in the morning, but as the Moon enters Taurus, shift your attention to grounding your ideas and making steady progress.

Pisces: Emotional reflection is key early in the day, but as the energy shifts, focus on grounding yourself and making practical decisions about your future.

For those born on December 27: Born under the transition from Aries to Taurus, these individuals are both confident and practical. In 2025, they'll thrive by balancing bold actions with steady, long-term planning, focusing on both personal ambitions and practical achievements.

Daily Insights: The Moon in Taurus continues to highlight stability, practicality, and long-term planning. It's an ideal day for taking steady steps toward your goals, working diligently on your projects, and focusing on what brings you comfort and security. With Venus in Capricorn, there's a sense of dedication and seriousness in relationships, making it a good time for meaningful connections.

Aries: Focus on grounding yourself today. Use this energy to work steadily on your long-term goals and ensure you're making practical progress.

Taurus: The Moon in your sign enhances your sense of stability and practicality. Use this energy to focus on achieving your ambitions through steady, methodical work.

Gemini: It's a day for balancing curiosity with practicality. Use your creative energy to refine your ideas and make steady progress on your goals.

Cancer: Emotional stability and practicality are important today. Use this energy to create security in your relationships and personal life.

Leo: Leadership is key, but today encourages steady progress. Focus on taking practical steps toward achieving your long-term ambitions.

Virgo: Productivity is high today. Use your analytical skills to refine your plans and make steady progress toward your goals.

Libra: Relationships feel grounded and stable today. Focus on creating balance and harmony in your personal connections while working toward your long-term goals.

Scorpio: Determination guides you today. Use this energy to focus on practical steps toward achieving your long-term ambitions.

Sagittarius: While you love adventure, today encourages grounding yourself and working toward long-term goals with steady actions.

Capricorn: Discipline and focus guide you today. Use this energy to make significant progress on your long-term projects and ambitions.

Aquarius: Creativity is important, but today encourages practical solutions. Use this energy to refine your ideas and make steady progress toward your goals.

Pisces: Emotional stability is key today. Use this energy to focus on personal growth and practical decisions that will benefit your future.

For those born on December 28: Born under the Moon in Taurus, these individuals are practical, grounded, and focused on long-term success. In 2025, they'll thrive by setting clear goals, working steadily toward them, and using their disciplined nature to stay on track.

December 29, 2025

Daily Insights: The Moon in Taurus continues to emphasize stability, but as it transitions into Gemini later in the day, the focus shifts toward communication, curiosity, and intellectual exploration. It's a day for balancing steady progress with lively conversations and social interactions.

Aries: The morning is perfect for focusing on your long-term goals, but as the Moon enters Gemini, shift your attention to exploring new ideas and engaging with others.

Taurus: Start the day with grounded actions, but as the Moon moves into Gemini, embrace your curiosity and engage in conversations to explore new perspectives.

Gemini: The Moon enters your sign later today, bringing a burst of energy and curiosity. Use this energy to engage in stimulating conversations and explore new opportunities.

Cancer: Emotional stability is key early in the day, but as the Moon moves into Gemini, focus on intellectual pursuits and social interactions.

Leo: The day begins with practical actions, but as the energy shifts, engage with others, share your ideas, and explore new possibilities.

Virgo: Productivity is high in the morning, but as the Moon enters Gemini, shift your focus to learning new things and refining your long-term plans.

Libra: Relationships feel grounded early in the day, but later, focus on open communication and exploring new perspectives in your connections.

Scorpio: Determination guides you early in the day, but as the energy shifts, explore new opportunities for intellectual and social growth.

Sagittarius: The morning is ideal for grounding yourself, but as the Moon enters Gemini, shift your focus to communication, learning, and adventure.

Capricorn: Discipline and focus guide you early in the day, but as the Moon enters Gemini, engage in meaningful conversations and explore new possibilities.

Aquarius: The day begins with practical thinking, but as the Moon enters Gemini, focus on social connections and intellectual exploration.

Pisces: Emotional reflection is important early in the day, but later, focus on learning new things and engaging in stimulating conversations.

For those born on December 29: Born under the transition from Taurus to Gemini, these individuals are both practical and curious. In 2025, they'll thrive by balancing their disciplined approach with intellectual exploration, focusing on both steady progress and new learning opportunities.

Daily Insights: The Moon in Gemini emphasizes communication, learning, and curiosity. It's a great day for engaging in conversations, exploring new ideas, and connecting with others. With Mercury in Sagittarius, communication remains lively and adventurous, making it a perfect time for sharing bold ideas and expanding your intellectual horizons.

Aries: Your curiosity is strong today. Use this energy to engage in meaningful conversations and explore new ideas with enthusiasm.

Taurus: It's a day for balancing practicality with intellectual exploration. Use your grounded nature to communicate your thoughts clearly and explore new perspectives.

Gemini: The Moon in your sign amplifies your communication skills. Use this energy to connect with others, share your ideas, and explore new possibilities.

Cancer: Emotional reflection is important, but today also encourages intellectual exploration. Use this energy to connect with others and share your insights.

Leo: Leadership and creativity are emphasized today. Use your confidence to express your ideas and engage in stimulating conversations.

Virgo: Your analytical skills are sharp today. Use this energy to focus on problem-solving and refining your ideas.

Libra: Relationships feel intellectually stimulating today. Focus on engaging in conversations that broaden your perspective and deepen your connections.

Scorpio: Your emotional depth is strong today, but also take time to explore new ideas that challenge your thinking and push your boundaries.

Sagittarius: Adventure and learning go hand in hand today. Use your curiosity to explore new opportunities and engage in thought-provoking conversations.

Capricorn: It's a day for balancing discipline with intellectual exploration. Use this energy to refine your long-term goals and embrace new learning experiences.

Aquarius: Your creativity and innovative thinking shine today. Use this energy to explore new ideas and collaborate with others.

Pisces: It's a day for intellectual exploration and emotional reflection. Use this energy to connect with others in meaningful ways and share your insights.

For those born on December 30: Born under the Moon in Gemini, these individuals are curious, communicative, and eager to explore new ideas. In 2025, they'll thrive by engaging in conversations, learning new things, and using their sharp minds to connect with others and broaden their horizons.

Daily Insights: The Moon in Gemini continues to highlight communication and intellectual exploration, but as it transitions into Cancer later in the day, the focus shifts toward emotional reflection, nurturing relationships, and self-care. It's a day for balancing intellectual curiosity with emotional connection and personal reflection.

Aries: Start the day with lively conversations, but as the Moon enters Cancer, shift your focus to emotional reflection and nurturing your relationships.

Taurus: Use the morning for intellectual pursuits, but later, focus on creating emotional stability in your personal life and strengthening your relationships.

Gemini: Communication and curiosity are highlighted early in the day, but as the Moon moves into Cancer, shift your attention to deepening emotional connections with loved ones.

Cancer: The Moon enters your sign later today, enhancing your emotional intuition. Use this energy to focus on self-care and deepening your personal relationships.

Leo: Leadership and creativity guide you early in the day, but later, focus on emotional reflection and nurturing your personal connections.

Virgo: Productivity is high in the morning, but as the energy shifts, focus on emotional reflection and nurturing your personal well-being.

Libra: Relationships feel intellectually stimulating early in the day, but as the Moon enters Cancer, focus on creating emotional harmony and balance in your connections.

Scorpio: The day starts with curiosity and communication, but later, focus on emotional healing and strengthening your closest relationships.

Sagittarius: The morning is ideal for exploring new opportunities, but as the Moon enters Cancer, shift your focus to emotional reflection and personal growth.

Capricorn: Use the early part of the day for intellectual exploration, but as the energy shifts, focus on emotional well-being and nurturing your personal connections.

Aquarius: Creativity and communication are highlighted early in the day, but later, focus on emotional introspection and self-care.

Pisces: Emotional intuition is strong today. Use this energy to nurture your relationships and focus on personal healing and reflection.

For those born on December 31: Born under the transition from Gemini to Cancer, these individuals are both intellectually curious and emotionally intuitive. In 2025, they'll thrive by balancing intellectual exploration with nurturing their emotional well-being and focusing on meaningful personal connections.

Conclusion

As we close this journey through the stars, remember that astrology is not just a tool for predicting the future, but a guide to understanding yourself and the world around you. Each day, the universe offers us subtle clues and energetic shifts, encouraging us to grow, transform, and align more deeply with our true selves. The horoscopes you've read are not fixed destinies, but rather invitations to reflect, take action, and embrace the flow of life with intention and awareness.

In 2025, you will encounter moments of joy, challenge, and transformation. Through it all, the stars remind us that we are part of a much larger cosmic dance—a dance that asks us to honor both the light and the shadow within ourselves. Whether it's through the steady discipline of Saturn, the expansive opportunities of Jupiter, or the deep emotional insights of the Moon, each planetary influence provides a chance to learn, adapt, and become more in tune with who you are at your core.

Embrace the shifts, cherish the quiet moments, and seek balance in all that you do. Use the guidance of the planets to deepen your self-awareness, and let their wisdom empower you to make conscious decisions, both big and small. Astrology is a tool for introspection, a reminder that the answers you seek are already within you, waiting to be discovered.

As you navigate the days, weeks, and months ahead, trust that the universe is always supporting your growth, even when the path seems unclear. When challenges arise, remember that these are opportunities for learning and that with each turn of the zodiac wheel, you are given a fresh chance to realign with your purpose. Stay grounded in love, open to new experiences, and committed to your personal evolution.

Thank you for sharing this journey through the stars with us. We hope that 2025 brings you clarity, joy, and a deeper understanding of yourself and the world around you. Let the wisdom of the cosmos be your guide as you move forward with courage, compassion, and balance.

May this year be filled with growth, fulfillment, and endless opportunities for transformation. Trust in the process, stay open to the magic of the universe, and remember that every challenge you face is a step toward becoming the best version of yourself.

From all of us at **AstroLoom Publishing**, we wish you a successful, joyful, and truly cosmic 2025. We look forward to guiding you again next year. Until then, keep looking up, and let the stars light your way.

Made in the USA
Las Vegas, NV
24 December 2024

15332703R00319